Shakespeare and Contemporary Fiction

Shakespeare and Contemporary Fiction

Theorizing Foundling and Lyric Plots

Barbara L. Estrin

UNIVERSITY OF DELAWARE PRESS
Newark

University of Delaware Press
© 2012 by Barbara L. Estrin
All rights reserved
Printed in the United States of America on acid-free paper
Distributed by the University of Virginia Press

ISBN 978-1-64453-106-8 (paper)
ISBN 978-1-64453-107-5 (ebook)

British Library Cataloguing-in-Publication Information Available

Library of Congress Cataloging-in-Publication Data

Estrin, Barbara L., 1942–
　Shakespeare and contemporary fiction : theorizing foundling and lyric plots / Barbara L. Estrin.
　　p. cm.
　1. Fiction—History and criticism—Theory, etc. 2. Shakespeare, William, 1564–1616—Influence. I. Title.
　PN3331.E88 2012
　809.3—dc23
　2011034121

For Margot and Nadine Kelly

Contents

A Note on the Text	ix
Acknowledgments	xi
Beginnings	xiii
Preface: Defining and Replotting the Forms	xvii
Introduction: Drawing Aristocratic and Lyric Lines	1
Contemporary Pasts	**21**
1 Unraveling Narrative Order in Caryl Phillips's *The Nature of Blood*	23
2 The Irigarayan "Third Language" in Liz Jensen's *Ark Baby*	47
3 Trapped in the "Negative Gradient": Traumatic Dis-membering in W. G. Sebald's *Austerlitz*	65
4 "These Weeping Eyes, Those Seeing Tears": The Flow of Memory from *Fugitive Pieces* to Shakespeare	85
Shakespearean Presents	**105**
5 Turning Gender and Plot in *The Merchant of Venice*	107
6 "God Me Such Uses Send": Desdemona's Lyric Response in *Othello*	157
7 "I Am Heir to My Affection": Revising Family and Love in *The Winter's Tale*	193
Afterword: The Myths Redeployed	227
Index	249
About the Author	255

A Note on the Text

Unless otherwise indicated in the notes, all quotations from Shakespeare's works are from the *Norton Shakespeare*, 2nd ed., edited by Stephen Greenblatt, Walter Cohen, Jean E. Howard, and Katherine Eisaman (New York: Norton, 2008).

The following editions are cited for the four principal novels:

Ark Baby, Liz Jensen (London: Bloomsbury, 1998)

Austerlitz, W. G. Sebald (New York: Random House, 2001)

Fugitive Pieces, Anne Michaels (London: Bloomsbury, 1998)

The Nature of Blood, Caryl Phillips (London: Faber & Faber, 1997)

Acknowledgments

Ark Baby by Liz Jensen © 1998. Reprinted by kind permission of Liz Jensen and Bloomsbury PLC.

The Winter Vault by Anne Michaels © 2009. Cloth Edition 2009. Emblem edition 2010. Published by McClelland & Steward Ltd. Used with permission of the Wylie Agency LLC and the publisher and Bloomsbury PLC.

Fugitive Pieces by Anne Michaels © 1996. Trade paperback edition with flaps 1996. Emblem edition 2009. Published by McClelland & Stewart Ltd. Used with permission of the Wylie Agency LLC and the publisher and Bloomsbury PLC.

"So-and-So Reclining on Her Couch" from *The Collected Poems of Wallace Stevens* by Wallace Stevens, Copyright 1954 by Wallace Stevens and renewed 1982 by Holly Stevens. Used by permission of Alfred A. Knopf, a division of Random House, Inc., and Faber & Faber, Ltd.

The Nature of Blood by Caryl Phillips, © 1997 by Caryl Phillips. Used by permission of Alfred A. Knopf, a division of Random House, Inc.; published by Vintage Books. Reprinted by permission from Random House Group Ltd.

Austerlitz by W. G. Sebald, translated by Anthea Bell, translation copyright © 2001 by Anthea Bell. Used by permission of Random House, Inc., and Knopf Canada as well as Hamish Hamilton 2001, Penguin Books 2002. Copyright © the Estate of W. G. Sebald, 2001. Translation copyright © Anthea Bell, 2001. Reproduced by permission of Penguin Books Ltd.

Mona Hatoum
Measures of Distance
1988
Color video with sound/A Western Video Production, Vancouver
© the artist
Courtesy White Cube

William Merritt Chase
The Young Orphan
n.d.
oil on canvas
44 M 42 in. (unframed)
49 3/4 M 47 1/2 M 2 3/4 in. (framed)
National Academy Museum, New York

Excerpts from *Nothing Is Missing* courtesy of Mieke Bal
Cinema Suitcase, edited by Mieke Bal, Zen Marie and Gary Ward
Multiple screen video installation, 35 minutes, looped, 2006–ongoing
Photo of installation room by Astrid van Weyenberg
Photo of Ümmühan by Mieke Bal

Earlier versions (now considerably changed in each instance) of the following chapters were published as articles. I am grateful to the editors and publishers of the following periodicals and books for permission to quote from parts of those articles here: chapter 1, "'I had rather to adopt a child than get it': Mythical Lost Children in Caryl Phillips's *The Nature of Blood*," *Ariel* 34 (2003): 23–50; chapter 2, "Mutating Literary Form and Literalizing Scientific Theory in Liz Jensen's *Ark Baby*," *Critique* 47 (2005): 41–56; chapter 4, "Ending in the Middle: Revisioning Adoption in Binjamin Wilkomirski's *Fragments* and Anne Michaels's *Fugitive Pieces*," *Tulsa Studies in Women's Literature* 21, 2 (2002): 275–300; chapter 6, "Coming into the Word: Desdemona's Story," *Luce Irigaray and Premodern Culture: Thresholds of History*, edited by Elizabeth Harvey and Theresa Krier (New York: Routledge, 2004): 53–65; and chapter 7, "'Bettering' the Generic Domain of *The Winter's Tale*," *Exemplaria* 20, 3 (2008) 283–313 (www.maney.co.uk/journals.exm).

Beginnings

This book had several different names but the original title—"Orphan Envy"—came (before any of it was written) on a beach walk with my late husband, Mark W. Estrin. Quick witted and resourceful, he laughed with glee as he imagined its multiple possibilities. I wanted to link two plots that teased the relationship between art and nature: that of the foundling (where a child gone missing is raised by strangers and recovers at the end the birthright of its aristocratic destiny) and the lyric (where the poet loses out on love and, mourning his failure in verse, emerges as the self-created orphan of his virtual life). Challenging the mythological homogeneity in conventional interpretations of those plots, "Orphan Envy" brings to mind the innocence of that moment, the last day before I knew quite how sick Mark was—a day of sun and sand and free speculation. Though the book evolved differently, I clung to that title as if I could hold its formulating moment forever in my mind and as if it could bring back—like the rescued orphans and laureled poets—the humorous vitality, mutual understanding, and sustaining love of the more than thirty-eight extraordinary years we shared together.

That title was playful, reflecting Freud's more famous envy and toying with the homonym, *Orphan Annie*, part of the American vocabulary from its conception in James Whitcomb Riley's 1885 poem, and resulting in the perennially enchanting foundling of the musical—the plucky, smart, lovable child who retains her independence and finds a protector in the rich and powerful Daddy Warbucks. But the title also suggests what Amos Oz calls a "dark oedipal pleasure" revealed in the desire for the death of both parents, "leaving behind happy, light-footed orphans, as free as a flock of birds in the clear blue sky . . . [with] no one left to nag . . . [or] spoil life with all kinds of depressions, traumas, imperatives and ambitions. Just us. Alone in the world."[1] The simultaneous excitement and fear of the earliest stories inherent to our cultural memory of the exhilarating *abandonne* of abandonment is contained within the two central plots of this study.

I argue for a reemphasis, one that favors the in-between spaces and thus queries both the happy ending of the foundling plot (with the regained dynastic legacy of the orphaned child) and the unhappy beginning of the lyric (with its passion for an unyielding "other" through whom the poet finds an origin that parallels the glory of the foundling's legendary aristocracy). The insistence in each of those plots on one kind of family and one kind of beauty may explain why both appeared so frequently in the early modern period. Their identity politics coincided with the rise of the nation-state. Because the narratives are still flourishing in various emanations, they impact on the cultural unconscious behind the worldwide immigration crisis raging in Western Europe and in the United States, where nationalism seems once more in the ascendancy.

So the book changed from its seaside origin and is about the relationship between the discoveries of contemporary fiction and the uncovering of a Shakespeare who might in a curious prolepsis have envisioned what the novelists I study assume: that the stories we tell so innocently have social and political repercussions. Such a retrospective antecedent allows us, in turn, to envision a trajectory leading to alternative cultural paradigms. Though the book originated in the happy moment when the losses it thematizes seemed so far away from the reality of my own life that I could think of them in terms of an exhilaration that might be envied, its intent about the need to change plots central to our mythologies remains. But the title now more accurately reflects the different interpretations made possible early on by Shakespeare and contemporaneously by the novelists and filmmakers I study.

In reading differently, I have been encouraged by the poet Edwin Honig, my adviser at Brown, whose faith in the suppositions of the written word—"inklings"[2]—overcame what he later called the "inching[s]" (592) of hesitation about one's capacity to write: "You're rich, you beggar / You've got a clean page / To start with" (592). His recent death brings a great loss to my life. Enduring in friendship is Francis X. Murphy, my freshman English professor at Smith, who emphasized the opposite of Honig's expansiveness and who insisted on the pleasures of close—and tight—readings, a practice perhaps out of fashion now.

My daughter, Robin Estrin, and her husband, Seamus Kelly, have been consistently supportive of, and nurturing to, my life and work. Most of all, they have made a space for me in their lives and those of my grandchildren whose once-weekly granny nanny I have been for more than nine years now. From their infancy, as they awakened to the world and shared with me their sense of wonder and play, Margot and Nadine Kelly have been restorative, enjoying the fantasy of all those orphan stories I here declare need changing, though I tried, on occasion, to live up to my philosophy, favoring the adventures of Peter Pan, and his persistence in remaining lost, over the more conventional Snow White, whose marriage reclaims her royalty and morphs the dwarfs who raised her. Through Margot and Nadine, I understand why those stories are so powerful. Now in the midst of their childhood, as they themselves can read and write, they experience with me a delight in the sheer pleasure of words. I find with them a companionship and joy I never thought possible. Together with their parents, they have made the transitions of my life possible.

Throughout my career at Stonehill College, Chet Raymo, Robert J. Kruse, Elizabeth Pearson, and Wendy Peek have stimulated my work by believing in it. Provost and Vice President for Academic Affairs, Katie Conboy, is both a friend and an administrator (in this case not an oxymoron) whose presence in various executive capacities has made an enormous difference in the scholarly life of the campus. Unfailingly proactive, she used her good offices to help secure the licenses for publication. Because I was accustomed to working with writers out of the realm of copyright, the permissions stage of the project was particularly daunting. But two extraordinary artists—Mieke Bal and Mona Hatoum—were extremely generous. Bal, whose work seems every moment to grow in its timeliness, interrupted her busy schedule to send me photographs that would work in print, and Hatoum's careful editing of the "Afterword" and explanation of the process of her film bridged the "distance" her work so beautifully "measures."

My research benefited from the resources and quiet spaces of the Brown University Library in Providence and the British Library in London and by the resourcefulness of the Stonehill librarians, who always helped in ordering needed books and in answering questions.

I wish to thank Donad C. Mell and Karen G. Druliner of the University of Delaware Press for undertaking to send a manuscript that didn't fit into the usual slots to two anonymous readers whose encouragement, "gentle suggestions," and penetrating questions helped to put the book into its present—and, I hope, better—shape. For their guidance through the last stages, I am indebted to Brooke Bascietto, Liliana Koebke, and Patricia Stevenson at Rowman & Littlefield.

I am fortunate to have so many friends whose interest in my work has made it more meaningful. In particular, I thank my "adopted" sisters, Arlene Berrol, Sara Lee Silberman, and Barbara Sokoloff (and in memory Hannah Goldberg), for our almost daily conversations and once-weekly meetings, running through a range of topics close to our real lives but pertinent in differing ways to this study. Among those local friends to whom I am also grateful are Eva and Art Landy and Marilyn and Dietrich Rueschemeyer, as I am to those scattered about the United States—Anne Putzel, Sandy Rubin, Carol Nash, Doris and Len Fleischer, Leslie and Tom Freudenheim, Joseph

Plut, Jon Quitslund, Michael Stone-Richards, and Alexandra and Sheldon Weinbaum—and (in London) Peter Pullan, Merfyn Williams, Edward Brooks, Lyndon Van der Pump, and Matt Wolf.

Finally, this book would have remained forever an unrecovered orphan, lost in the middle ground, were it not for Berel Lang, who quite pointedly asked when I would find an end and thus challenged me to finish. That this late in my life I feel as if I am beginning again is in no small measure because I have been inspired by Berel, whose open and principled intelligence, capacity for imaginative creation, and unquenchable love of reading (and questioning) *everything*—newspapers, novels, philosophical texts, signs in the subways, anybody's scholarly articles—serve as models for the liveliness of the mind and body of life. My thanks to him do little to convey how much his presence in my world has meant.

NOTES

1. *A Tale of Love and Darkness*, translated by Nicholas deLange (New York: Harcourt Brace, 2004), 463–464.
2. *Time and Again: Poems, 1940–1997* (Philadelphia: Xlibris, 2000), 379.

Preface

Defining and Replotting the Forms

In one of the posters that helped bring the ultranationalist Swiss People's Party into a parliamentary majority in 2010, its designer, Alexander Segert, depicts three white sheep kicking a black one out of the crimson terrain of the national flag, back across and outside its borders. About its effectiveness in castigating foreigners, Segert boasts, "It looks simple but that's the art of it."[1]

The art of the simple is at the core of this study of the intersection between the foundling and Petrarchan plots in contemporary fiction and Shakespeare's plays. Culturally ingrained, the stories of both plots exert a significant influence on our political unconscious and, in that regard, there's a curious link between the sheep in Segert's poster and Shylock's use of the Laban story and its parti-colored flocks in *Merchant of Venice*, a speech that causes Antonio to demonize him as the "devil [who] cite[s] scripture" (1.3.94). As Zygmunt Bauman describes the continuity of xenophobia from early to late modern culture, "in civilized countries all across the world there are [a half a century after the Holocaust] still unwanted strangers in any society, and in any society there are some people who wish such strangers not to be there."[2] Signified by the exclusionary domain of the red Swiss flag in the poster, the animus against "foreign blood" is central to the dynamic of the two plots I study here: the story of the foundling involving an aristocratic child exposed or stolen in infancy, raised by substitute parents, usually of a lower class (but returned when the grown scion preserves a dynasty by marrying); and of the Petrarchan lyric, where the poet creates himself out of male parthenogenesis and substitutes artistic creativity for biological procreativity, thus becoming the self-generated orphan of his own life.

Both plots spill over into the popular culture of all times, that of the foundling stemming from biblical and classical tales, moving through Shakespearean comedies and romances, to the Orphan Annie of the comic strip, the lyric likewise transferring its losses from the operatic stratosphere to rock music, forming what Nancy Vickers chronicles as an "ongoing discourse of love"[3] that has its roots in the early modern Petrarch. Working from a dyad of fixed but self-reflective gender difference and an essentialist mandate of bloodline dynastic supremacy, the classic love poem and the foundling plot contribute to the feeling still so present today that immigrants or racial minorities in our midst constitute the same threat to our well-being that the Bavarians across the Alps posed to the nascent Italian state Petrarch valorized, when, in *Rime sparse* 128, he replaced the sometimes venomous Laura (the unattainable woman of the 365 other poems that comprise the model for subsequent Western lyrics) with the eradicable Teutonic barbarians across the border. About the inclusion of *patria mia* in the *Rime sparse*, Margaret Brose maintains "gendered binaries give rise to class and race hierarchies."[4] When the family and love stories mutate into hate speech, the foundling and Petrarchan plots feed into the reciprocal relationship between the arts and politics just as the poster advertising the new nationalism encourages a public attitude that is essentially exclusionary. As Jason deParle writes, "When scholars get to feeling expansive, they call today's migration networks a challenge to the order set by the 1648 Peace of Westphalia, which established the territorial sovereignty of the nation-state. Judging by the wall rising along the Mexican border, nation-states do not appear to be going away. Their people increasingly do."[5] Identifying the *cultural* walls that contribute to political gatekeeping in its early and late modern scenarios, I seek in *Shakespeare and Contemporary Fiction* to reveal how the stories that divide us might be (and might have been earlier than traditional criticism acknowledges) told differently.

I describe the connection between plot variations and gender revisionism first in the chapters on four contemporary writers whose work focuses on the intersections of the Petrarchan and foundling stories. In their use of both plots, Liz Jensen, Anne Michaels, Caryl Phillips, and W. G. Sebald demonstrate an understanding that mythical repercussions prove dangerous in the twentieth and twenty-first centuries even as they suggest how the heritage shaping their work—and to which they are themselves drawn—might open, in Luce Irigaray's terms, to "a new cultural elaboration."[6] Reading backward from the theoretical perspective offered in their novels enables us to read forward again with an alternative Shakespeare, one who frees us to ask other questions: At the time that the nation-state was beginning to coalesce, what does Shakespeare's frequent use of the foundling plot and his significant variations portend? How does his infusion of a reenvisioned lyric in *The*

Merchant of Venice, *Othello*, and *The Winter's Tale* change our reading of plays where the two plots coalesce in the same way that they do in the contemporary novels forming the basis of my late modern interpretations?

The foundling plot suggests a two-pronged promise. For the orphaned child, it offers Amos Oz's liberating "oedipal pleasure" in the desire for the death of all restrictive and guilt-giving grown-ups.[7] From the point of view of the expelling parent, it yields a temporary fix in the adoption, one that takes away all child-rearing difficulties, and a final compensation in the recovery, one that preserves a family line through the expected offspring of the by-then-marriageable heir. As they venture into the terrain of inexpressible cruelty and finally retreat into self-protective deniability—the desire to obliterate the child because of the difficulty of raising it solved by the initial exposure and the final erasure of such a murderous impulse in the redemptive happy ending—foundling stories simply cancel out the middle period of adoption. Conversely, for "wanna-be orphans," the reality they inhabit sustains the dream that aristocratic parents will replace the rather ordinary ones with whom they happen to be sharing a home. One day, they will discover that the life they have lived is a mistake.[8]

The principal story behind the poetic that forms the lyric complex is based on the god Apollo and his unappeasable love for the nymph Daphne who resisted his advances and ran away from him until, with the aid of her river god father, she was transformed into a laurel tree. Apollo was thereby stumped. Lamenting his impossible situation, Apollo made beautiful music out of his loss. The "impossible situation" gives life to lyric voice and, following in that tradition, Petrarch wrote the 366 poems of the *Rime sparse*, casting himself as Apollo and Laura as Daphne. In this role, the poet's existence depends on the open-endedness of the love pursuit: an unattainability that generates the production of more and more poetic lines. Who wouldn't want to be the inventor of a self constantly renewed by the power of his own resources? Who wouldn't say "no," if merely resisting inspires a language system that confers immortality?

Because the Petrarchan lyric depends on denial, the poet is liberated from the consequences of achieved love, just as the foundling is freed from intergenerational responsibility. Both orphan and poet are independent of obligatory ties—of marriage in the lyric, of family in the foundling plot—and in the sympathy they nevertheless derive from the very loss of romantic and parental support that constitutes their freedom. The liberation in both cases confers an aristocracy of suffering[9] that proves nourishing. The darker aspects of the plots break through their literary confines because both (maintaining the *status quo ante* of a perpetually same self, mirrored in Petrarchan narcissism and mired in the bloodline imperative of the foundling plot) are connected (in their insistence on one kind of family and one kind of beauty) to a nascent nationalism evident in the period when Shakespeare was writing his plays and that came into full fruition with the racist policies that proved so devastating in the middle of the twentieth century and are still being felt today. My focus is both on the appeal and repeal of the central plots as they come under the influence of the historical context in which they are used by writers as starting points for their work. But my hope, as well, is that the writer's understanding of, and engagement with, a changing cultural scenario will produce in the reader an imaginative willingness to let go of the presumably fixed "collective fantasies"[10] that shape us. Therefore, I contest "standpoint theory" (used by Marianne Novy in her seminal work, *Reading Adoption: Family and Difference in Fiction and Drama*[11]), which maintains that "people in marginal positions have a special opportunity to insight into their society." My premise throughout is that the stories are larger than personal ones and that we need to address issues of mythological homogeneity in terms that move beyond identity politics into the public arena where they exert the influence of their biases. I hope to encourage a collaborative activism in the reader that parallels that of the writer.

Throughout, I will refer to the intersecting stories of the foundling and love lyric as "plots" because their underlying assumptions work within the larger generic frames of drama and fiction as well as within those of tragedy and comedy. They might also be called, what Rosalie Colie identifies as, "small forms" that "interpenetrate"[12] the larger ones. It is the interpenetration that interests me here, particularly with regard to the Petrarchan plot—generally associated with the lyric—as it coincides with the foundling plot—generally associated with longer forms—as both fit into the frame of fiction and drama. The inclusion of the lyric dynamic in contemporary prose fiction emphasizes that "the ongoing discourse of love" ("Vital Signs," 157) is also an ongoing discourse of loss that links the Petrarchan to the foundling plot. For the purposes of this study, the usual elements of lyric (rhyme and meter) are subsumed by their narrative component. Shakespeare himself defined this interpenetration in the remarkable catalogue of genres Polonius enumerates when he praises the band of actors he has brought into the court to entertain (and so distract) Hamlet:

> The best actors in the world, either for tragedy, comedy, history, pastoral, pastoral-comical, historical-pastoral, tragical-historical, tragical-comical-historical-pastoral, scene individable, or poem unlimited. Seneca cannot be too heavy, nor Plautus too light. For the law of writ, and the liberty, these are the only men. (2.2.379–84)

When Polonius refers to genres, he speaks of them, in Alaistair Fowler's terms, "as domains of association . . . whereby meaning is communicated in ordinary speech."[13] In that sense, we refer to tragic and comic plays and novels as well as comic ones and further, as pastoral novels and plays as they evoke in us "a horizon of expectations"[14] before we read or view them. I follow those expectations with two tragic novels, *The Nature of Blood* and *Austerlitz*, and two comic ones, *Ark Baby* and *Fugitive Pieces*, and use them as theoretical lenses for reading backward to the tragedy of *Othello*, the comedy of *Merchant of Venice*, and the "tragical-comical-pastoral" of *The Winter's Tale*.

But, apart from categorizing genres as we ordinarily think of them, Polonius speaks of their dual capacity to invoke "law[s] of writ" and a "liberty." He thus theorizes Shakespeare's use of genres, in Rosalie Colie's terms, as "a set of interpretations or frames or fixes on the world" (*The Resources of Kind*, 8) and as "metastable [in that they] change over time and in conjunction with their context of systems" (*The Resources of Kind*, 30). But, even more remarkable, Polonius also produces a set of oxymorons that (while linking drama to poetry and anticipate the connection I make to poetic narratives within fiction) completely undoes the very systems he adumbrates. When he proclaims the actors capable of performing "scene individable or poem unlimited," he dissolves the spatial parameters of a play by extending into vague premises the visual landscape even as he eliminates its temporal markers by doing away with a sense of ending: an expansive vista paralleled by an indefinite timeline.[15] Inversely, Polonius first disregards the metrical structures that render the poem a poem, annulling Juliet's "sweet division" (*Romeo and Juliet*, 3.5.29), and then denies poetic boundaries altogether by similarly rendering conclusions indeterminate, interchanging sonnets with epics. Deforming the forms by giving them more Marvellian "world and time" than anyone would want, Polonius anticipates Peter Hitchcock's definition of postcolonial genre: "its generic distinction is to question genre, not just as a fulfillment of the law of genre but as a means to dissolve the very classifications that have produced it."[16] Thus we have Polonius as postcolonialist *avant la lettre*. Postcolonial theory and its backward glances and Polonius's looks ahead parallel the methodology of this study, which describes Shakespeare anticipating, and contemporary novelists restaging, the ancient plots that initiate the cohesive structure of their works. Polonius's bumbling[17] matches postcolonialist grumbling even as both point to the infinite possibility that genre offers to follow and to deviate from an expected course. Shakespeare's early anticipation and late modern belated reconstructions arouse both expectations and diversions to form a circle that follows "the . . . writ" and takes "libert[ies with the] law" of the "small forms" within the larger ones, thereby opening to a new cultural script.

About the continuity of genres (and their variations) across the centuries, Wey Chee Dimock writes that "the history of genres, like the history of media is above all a reproductive history, which suggests that it is a kinship network as well, exogenous to be sure, updated but resting always on some kind of fluid continuum."[18] Focusing on plots that reflect a continuum backward and forward, and that have as their subject issues of kinship networks and reproductive history, I emphasize networks whose kinship is *endogenous*, intrinsic to their very meaning. The insistence on endogeny (with its self-enclosed predilections) unites them since both the foundling and the Petrarchan plots have at their center not just "kind" as a system of literary classification having to do with form and content but also "kind" as a subdivision of parallel identities, having to do with genealogically inherited, or standardized constructed, systems of classifications, often referring to race or class distinctions.

Moving from the private to the political in the introduction, I emphasize the consequences of the old-new nationalism inherent to both the foundling and Petrarchan conventions because I regard the relationship between the arts and politics as reciprocal in the sense that Melita Schaum means when she refers to the fictive nature of both: an "engagement with the 'unreal' makes up a large part of all social, economic, religious, and political thinking."[19] I argue further that such a reciprocity also demands, as Schaum puts it, a redefinition of "the relationship between politics and art [so that] a clearer denominator emerges between the forces of cultural troping and the resistance or compliance of an individual trope" (8). Working primarily with contemporary fictional plots that produce "real life" results in our attitudes toward adoption and romantic love respectively, I read backward to indicate how, in his early modern work, Shakespeare had already redeployed the biblical and classical sources we have come to accept as givens.

Because the foundling and Petrarchan plots embody presumptions about racial, national, and class identity based on the preservation of a "pure" bloodline, they confirm, as Kwame Appiah maintains, that "culture talk is not so very far from the race talk that it would supplant in liberal discourse."[20] Appiah's point informs this book. The cultural nationalism, justified since 9/11, of the myths manifests itself in American and Western European deportation policies that, as Giorgio Agamben describes in *Homo Sacer: Sovereign Power and Bare Life*, regard refugees as "lives that [have] so lost the quality of legal good that their very existence no longer has value."[21] Of the current immigration crisis across Europe, Rafaela M. Dancygier maintains that "resource scarcity not ethnic difference is the key drive of immigrant conflict."[22] Her *economic* explanation goes a long way toward documenting the immigration wars that seem to be raging across Europe with such ferocity since the downturn of 2008, coming to a head with new laws that may bring about a U.S. constitutional crisis (particularly involving the Fourteenth Amendment and its guarantee of citizenship to anyone, even the child of illegal immigrants, born in the country). But my focus here is on the underlying *cultural* background of the current situation. Chronicling a recent ruling about recent harshly anti-immigration legal regimes, *New York Times*

Supreme Court writer Linda Greenhouse argues that "we have become so obsessed with rooting out those we've decided shouldn't be in this country that we're in danger of losing a moral center of gravity."[23]

The plot variations I cite in this book propose that telling the story differently, and even finding in the established stories openings we didn't see at first, might reveal another approach to policies that encourage the deportation of people of foreign descent, policies which (because of their hostility to those who don't fit a preconceived nationalistic frame) also reflect the biases of both the foundling and Petrarchan plots. When they bend the plots so that their fixed notions of social value are unhinged, the works in this study ask large questions based on assumptions that, as Zygmunt Bauman emphasizes, "the dark moments of the twentieth and twenty-first centuries are not aberrant episodes *in* modern history but are highly relevant integral parts *of* that history."[24] Is it possible to perform revisionist readings of ancient and contemporary art so that we can reconstruct the impact of its myths on the societal unconscious? Does interrogating the sources give us grounds to hope for another cultural script, one not governed by the presumably established formulae? My questions about the connections between the mind-sets that spill over from the mythical (carried forward in literary constellations) to the political (fleshed out in governmental policies) do not propose solutions to the very vexed problem of immigration, related to the class and racial prejudices and the masculinist hierarchical obsessions basic to the foundling and Petrarchan plots respectively. I merely indicate—in the "Introduction," the chapters on *The Nature of Blood*, *Ark Baby*, *Austerlitz*, and *Fugitive Pieces*, and the "Afterword"—the ways in which contemporary authors and filmmakers theorize ancient ties in terms of their twentieth- and twenty-first-century effects even as (in their plot revisions) they enable us to review Shakespeare's early modern and parallel radicalizing of the narrative formulae he, too, felt compelled to use.

The first chapter traces Caryl Phillips's self-described "disrupt[ion] of the form[s],"[25] as he turns backward to Shakespeare's Italy and, following historical and fictional parallels to *The Merchant of Venice* and *Othello*, catalogues "the recurrence of atrocity"[26] dictated in each instance by the bloodline mandate that plays itself out in both the love and foundling stories. With the "viable parabola" of his "moving and keeping a theme going,"[27] Phillips repeats but changes the formulae, circling backward in his intertwining stories to remind us of where we have culturally been so that we can discover how we might henceforth proceed in another direction. I begin with Phillips not only because his narrative inscribes two Shakespeare plays central to this study but also because, in both his fictional and critical work, he returns, imaginatively and historically, to sources that connect political emanations to cultural influences.

With a scientific parallel to the hierarchical superiority inherent to the foundling plot, Liz Jensen questions another genetic fixation, based on the assumptions of scientific thinking, specifically the Darwinian theory of "survival of the fittest," which casts the foundling plot's dynastic mandate of return in the opposite direction, toward a future whose final knowledge is dim. Chapter 2 moves into the twenty-first century to describe how, in *Ark Baby*, Jensen rewrites the definition of the bloodline procreative mandate even as she doubles the narcissistic mirroring inherent to creative generation in the Petrarchan ethos. Jensen's revisions produce what Irigaray refers to as the "the beginnings of a third language, a language that we still don't know, that is yet to be created."[28] But her linguistic experiments evolve out of the terms of the foundling and Petrarchan plots, a foray into science fiction that spins out of the dead end of a hypothesized postmillennial fertility crisis.

In its depiction of the effects of the Holocaust on the children of victims, the third chapter deals with a question central to *The Nature of Blood*: "How can [one] remember and move on?" (157). W. G. Sebald's *Austerlitz* details the stagnating effects—the inescapable romance—of the foundling and Petrarchan mythos as it demonstrates what happens when the central character cannot see beyond his cultural entrapment. In Sebald's foundling plot, the psychological impasse leaves his hero searching for parents lost in the Second World War and, in the love story, unable to return offered love.

In the novel that forms a bridge between the late and early modern sections of this study, Anne Michaels builds on the same set of assumptions influencing *Austerlitz*. She has a twofold aim in *Fugitive Pieces*: first, to recover memory, reemphasizing what her hero calls the "stabbing loss" (182) of the foundling plot's initial exposure even as she advocates adoption as an end in itself; and, second, to bypass the hierarchical structure in the lyric by altering the terms of the gender relations. That second change facilitates something overlooked in the recognition scene of the archetypal foundling plot. When she alters both plots, Michaels recharges the word "recognition" itself to include (rather than to erase) the brutality of the initiating event. Insisting that the reader can imaginatively experience both the loss and the rescue, she offers a contemporary telescope that enables us to come closer in our understanding of the generic subversions that Shakespeare enacts in *The Merchant of Venice, Othello*, and *The Winter's Tale*. While *Fugitive Pieces* signals the shift from contemporary fiction to Shakespeare, all four novels presuppose the need for a cultural sea change as they redefine the plots and so become theoretical models that pave the way for rethinking the Shakespeare we thought we knew and to assess the extent of his deformations.

It would seem to be no accident that, next to *Hamlet, Merchant of Venice* was the play most often produced in Weimar Germany, with the figure of Shylock exaggerated as the villain, experiencing, in a small prolepsis, the same lack of individuation Primo Levi describes when he catalogues his losses at Auschwitz as a member of a race destined for "demolition," robbed crucially even of the power of voice: "If [Shylock] speaks, they will not listen and if they listen they will not understand."[29] Following from Levi's sense of linguistic eradication—the very one that spurred the modifications of *The Nature of Blood*, *Austerlitz*, and *Fugitive Pieces* into being—I will also demonstrate (in the fifth chapter) how Shakespeare, in prospect, changes the language of the foundling plot; using an imponderable emotion (Antonio's opening sadness without cause) as a metonymy for the initiating mystery of the foundling plot ("how I caught it, found it, or came by it, / What stuff 'tis made of, whereof it is born" [1.1.3–4]), he raises questions about linguistic foundations in genetic terms. In the Petrarchan narrative, the play presents three gradually diminishing versions of the powerful lyric vocalist. Shakespeare also works by means of triadic groupings in the foundling plot—Antonio/Bassanio/Portia; Gobbo/Lancelot/the nameless Moor; Shylock/Jessica/Lorenzo. The lyric experiments of the play are subsumed by the foundling plot's reversions to an established order as, in Jonathan Goldberg's words, "the law of comedy"[30] discounts Shylock's originality in favor of the conformity represented by the triplicate Belmont marriages.

While Shylock's imaginative creations from the void defy Venetian conventions, Othello's (who also defines himself in terms of lyric amplification) are designed to secure him a fixed place in the Venetian social order that solidifies itself through the language of Petrarchan self-realization. But, as I will demonstrate in chapter 6, Desdemona gives the lyric a feminine voice when she retrieves Barbary's song in Act 4 and that evocation in turn creates an altogether different adoptive interlude, a small circle of a recovered memory that proffers a new reading of both the foundling and lyric plots. Countering Othello's reliance on Petrarchan ruptures (necessary to lyric construction and illustrated by Sonnet 95, the dynamics of which mirror the Cassio/Othello/Desdemona triad in the play and which I will analyze in the chapter), Desdemona recasts the lyric to make it the foundational source for a feminist interpretation of the foundling plot.

The Winter's Tale can be read (as it often has been) as *Othello* made good. Leontes recovers what Othello lost. But, in chapter 7, I argue that (unlike the Act 4 Desdemona) Hermione subscribes to the essentialism of the foundling plot, and comes back to Leontes at the end in terms of the masculinist constructions—the Petrarchan mirroring, the dynastic security—that he forfeited in the trial scene. With the remarkable lyric revisionism of the fourth act, Shakespeare "betters" the foundling and Petrarchan plots to challenge the primacy of inherited patriarchal bloodlines and the male-generated poetics they mandate. When he breaks down the fixed expectations of gender and plot in *The Winter's Tale*, Shakespeare projects forward, as Jensen, Michaels, Phillips, and Sebald read backward, to suggest an openness that might make a different cultural model possible.

In a brief "Afterword," I return to my opening argument that the cultural tropes of the foundling and lyric plots are connected to twenty-first-century political thinking by what Luce Irigaray terms a "fault line in the construction of history."[31] In that regard, I examine two contemporary video works as each explores difficulties experienced by asylum seekers who escape (mainly to Western Europe) untenable social and economic situations in countries around the world. In Mieke Bal's *Nothing Is Missing* and Mona Hatoum's *Measures of Distance*, mothers and daughters unite as "sisters together with nothing to hide from each other." Through that sisterhood of remembered and anticipated sexuality, augured by the Countess of Roussillon in Shakespeare's *All's Well That Ends Well* when she "adopts" Helena, they display a sense of shared passion even as they acknowledge a female desire repressed in Petrarchan conventionality. And, fleshing out the possibility that the middle section of the foundling plot presents a resolution that is gratifying in and of itself, they alter the connection between cultural and political constructs by changing the stories that would otherwise define them. With such backward-forward readings throughout, I participate in the "literary activism" that Rosi Braidotti encourages to evoke a "loyalty, not so much to what one is, or could be, as to what one will have been."[32]

NOTES

1. Michael Kimmelman, "When Fear Turns Graphic," http://www.nytimes.com/2010/01/17/arts/design/17abroad.html.
2. *Modernity and the Holocaust* (Ithaca, NY: Cornell University Press, 2000), 248.
3. "Vital Signs: Petrarch and Popular Culture," *Romanic Review* 77 (1988): 187.
4. "Petrarch's Beloved Body: 'Italia Mia,'" *Feminist Approaches to the Body in Medieval Literature*, edited by Linda Lomperis and Sarah Stanbury (Philadelphia: University of Pennsylvania Press, 1993), 10.
5. "A World Even More on the Move," *New York Times Week in Review*, June 27, 2010: 4.
6. *Between East and West: From Singularity to Community*, translated by Stephen Pluháček (New York: Columbia University Press, 2002), 139.
7. *A Tale of Love and Darkness*, translated by Nicholas deLange (New York: Harcourt Brace, 2004), 463–64.
8. Martha Satz ("Finding Oneself: Images of Adoption in Children's Literature," *Adoption and Culture* 1, 1 [2007]: 164) summarizes Jerry Griswold's analysis (*Audacious Kids: Coming of Age in America's Classic Children's Books* [New York: Oxford University Press, 1992]) to great effect on this feeling: "If one thinks about it, children's literature is replete with adoption plots, unhappy and happy ones alike, a phenomenon that Griswold [maintains is] a literalization of the common childhood fantasy of the family romance, whereby children imagine that 'those people' who live in their house and tell them what to do cannot possibly be their real parents. All children, according to this traditional psychoanalytic explanation, assume that they are adopted, that someday those who will understand them perfectly and appreciate their true merit will come and reclaim them. This common childhood fantasy is in turn linked to the developmental stage of separation anxiety: children's simultaneous desire to be independent and their fear of separation from their parents."
9. Zygmunt Bauman refers to "an aristocracy of victimhood" conferred on those who (by ancestry) were victims of the Holocaust. See *Modernity and the Holocaust*, 235–36.

10. Robert J. Lifton, "Commencement Address," Stonehill College, May 17, 2008.

11. *Reading Adoption: Family and Difference in Fiction and Drama* (Ann Arbor: University of Michigan Press, 2005), 27.

12. *The Resources of Kind: Genre Theory in the Renaissance*, edited by Barbara K. Lewalski (Berkeley: University of California Press, 1973), 32.

13. "The Formation of Genres in the Renaissance and After," *New Literary History* 34, 2 (2003): 190.

14. Hans Robert Jauss, *Toward an Aesthetic of Reception*, translated by Timothy Bahti (Minneapolis: University of Minnesota Press, 1982), 79.

15. Harold Jenkins refers to this phrase as "usually explained as a play which observes the unity of place, as distinct from *poem unlimited* which observes no unities." But Jenkins goes on to say that these meanings "are not obvious." *Hamlet*, edited by Harold Jenkins (London: Routledge, 1982), 259.

16. "The Genre of Postcoloniality," *New Literary History* 34, 2 (2003): 327.

17. In Nicholas Hytner's 2011 production of *Hamlet* at the Royal National Theatre, David Calder's Polonius appeared to be far more intelligent than he is conventionally portrayed, thus perhaps justifying my contention that the speech represents at least in part Shakespeare's own feelings about the possibility of "declassifying" (in Hitchcock's terms) the genres around which he structures his plays.

18. "Introduction: Genres as Fields of Knowledge," *PMLA* 122, 5 (2007): 1380.

19. "Lyric Resistance: Views of the Political in the Poetics of Wallace Stevens and H.D.," *Wallace Stevens Journal* 25, 1 (2001): 8.

20. *The Ethics of Identity* (Princeton, NJ: Princeton University Press, 2005), 136.

21. *Homo Sacer: Sovereign Power and Bare Life* (Stanford, CA: Stanford University Press, 1998), 81.

22. *Immigration and Conflict in Europe* (New York: Cambridge University Press, 2010), 292.

23. "Across the Border, over the Line," http://opinionator.blogs.nytimes.com/2010/04/08/across-the-border-over-the-line/?scp=2&sq=linda%20greenhouse&st=cse.

24. *Modernity and the Holocaust*, 223.

25. "Extravagant Strangers," *A New World Order: Essays* (New York: Random House, 2002), 288.

26. Andrew Armstrong, "BLOODY HISTORY! Exploring a Capacity for Revision, Restaging History in Wilson Harris's *Jonestown* and Caryl Phillips' *The Nature of Blood*," *Jouvert* 6, 3 (2002): 3.

27. Stephen Clingman, "Other Voices: An Interview with Caryl Phillips," *Salmagundi* 143 (2004): 128.

28. *Why Different: Interviews with Luce Irigaray*, edited by Luce Irigaray and Sylvère Lotringer (New York: Semiotext(e), 2000), 131.

29. *If This Is a Man*, translated by Stuart Woolf (London: Vintage Books, 1996), 32–33.

30. "Shakespearean Inscriptions: The Voicing of Power," *Shakespeare and the Question of Theory*, edited by Patricia Parker and Geoffrey Hartman (London: Methuen, 1985), 121.

31. *I Love to You*, translated by Alison Martin (New York: Routledge, 1996), 143.

32. "Afterword," *Luce Irigaray and Premodern Culture: Thresholds of History*, edited by Elizabeth Harvey and Theresa Krier (New York: Routledge, 2004), 168.

Introduction

Drawing Aristocratic and Lyric Lines

Luxuriating in perhaps only seeming melancholy, the girl in William Merritt Chase's *The Young Orphan, Study of a Young Girl at her Ease*, resembles "So-And-So Reclining on Her Couch" of Wallace Stevens's poetic sculpture:

> On her side, reclining on her elbow.
> This mechanism, this apparition,
> Suppose we call it Projection A.
>
> She floats in air at the level of
> The eye, completely anonymous,
> Born, as she was, at twenty-one,
>
> Without lineage or language, only
> The curving of her hip, as motionless gesture,
> Eyes dripping blue, so much to learn.
>
> If just above her head there hung,
> Suspended in air, the slightest crown
> Of Gothic prong and practick bright,
>
> The suspension, as in solid space,
> The suspending hand withdrawn, would be
> An invisible gesture. Let this be called
>
> Projection B. To get at the thing
> Without gestures is to get at it as
> Idea. She floats in the contention, the flux

> Between the thing as idea and
> The idea as thing. She is half who made her.
> This is the final Projection C
>
> The arrangement contain the desire of
> The artist. But one confides in what has no
> Concealed creator. One walks easily
>
> The unpainted shore, accepts the world
> As anything but sculpture. Good-bye
> Mrs. Pappadopoulos, and thanks.[1]

Both painting and poem provide entrée to the inter-relationship and appeal of the foundling and Petrarchan plots. Both also comment on traditional verbal and visual portraiture and explain how and why particular artists adjust—as I argue they occasionally do—standardized paradigms to suit differing cultural agendas. Like Whistler in his evocation of his mother, Chase presents "the principal motif of the female figure seated in a chair oriented to the left."[2] One hand holding an abandoned handkerchief, the foregrounded other is poised on the red chair as if, in another moment, she will move upward and away into the fullness of her own life. Judging from the indolence of her posture, she is in no hurry. Nor does she seem particularly afraid of what awaits her. The repeated circlings of eyes, lips, curls, and breasts correspond to the floating red blobs in the background, ghosts (perhaps) of a no-longer-needed maternal sustenance. Unlike Stevens's projection, "born . . . at twenty-one, / Without lineage or language / contain[ing] the desire of the artist," Chase's "girl" seems fully cognizant of where and who she is and that she "contains" the long-earlier desire of her biological progenitors: she is fully in command of her inheritance. Her expensively flocked and expansive "couch" is arguably part of the home she lived in. While Stevens portrays a fantasized abstraction, Chase paints an orphan who seems rooted in the heritage she now fully owns.

Stevens's lyric other constructed, as Thomas Greene phrases it, "out of the self's own language"[3] and the painting's essentialist assumptions about familial origins prompt questions that I will raise in the pages that follow. Without the wall card, would Chase's orphan be any different leaning back on her settee from Stevens's reclining "So-And-So"? The connection between narrative parentless orphans and lyric "lineage"-less personae comprises the dual focus of my analysis of the slippages between heritage as a dynastic mandate and selfhood as a function of imaginative construction.

Speculation has it that Chase might have taken for his model a randomly chosen young girl from the half-orphan house, located near his studio, an asylum caring for children who had only one parent and who were too great a

William Merritt Chase, *The Young Orphan*, n.d. Oil on canvas. (Courtesy of the National Academy Museum, New York)

burden financially and perhaps emotionally for a single guardian to raise.[4] But Chase's "young girl" doesn't look as if she's an impoverished waif and, when we view the painting, we base our assessment of her not on what might have been the nameless subject's biography but on what we know about orphans from myths. As one critic writes, the model was "making believe very much that she was an orphan," a comment that links Chase's image with the foundling plot,[5] where orphans recover their parents at the end, and Petrarchan poetics, where the poet creates the other who confirms his desire to express and so find his self as the orphan of his own life at the beginning. But Chase signs the painting in a way that is unique in his *oeuvre*, making all the more evident the linkage between his young girl and "So-And-So."

Placed to the upper left and above the feminine circlings, Chase's signature renders him a father to the narrative fiction of the scene he depicts. Starting from the direction we read (left to right), he seems to be authorizing (with his flamboyant insertion) a familiar plot even as he abandons his young girl when he finishes the painting. Because Chase collapses all intervening hardship, we see only his orphan's awakening to an independence guaranteed by an inheritance she never lost. Leaving the figure, he endows her with the best of all possible beginnings.

While the foundling plot provides artists with a form around which to structure their work, for readers it also promotes the fantasy that Chase's portrait conveys. Like Chase's model, we also somehow want to "make believe very much" that we're either fictional orphans, part of a larger story (concealing an eventually recovered aristocratic lineage), or the glamorous invention of a poetic genius who defies biological necessity (in the "arrangement / conceal[ing] the desire of the artist"). And like Bottom in *A Midsummer Night's Dream*, we want to play all the parts—poet talented enough to live by words alone, buttressed by "the laurel" of poetic fame, beloved idealized so much that she becomes part of a quest that frees her from entanglements as well. As privileged orphan Chase propels into being with his "signature," the "young girl" exists in what Stevens calls "the contention . . . Between / the thing as idea and the idea as thing"—or the "flux" between mythology and reality—an uncertain border that renders it difficult to distinguish one from the other because our feelings are so influenced by the story lines that govern our preconceived notions about procreative and creative conception.

With "So-And-So," Chase's orphan evokes both the static image of the woman as a reflection of the man (in the artistic mirroring of Petrarchan generation) and of the child as the culmination of a family line (in the continuity of the foundling plot's dynastic mandate). Curiously symbiotic mythologies, the foundling and Petrarchan plots reveal an identical sense of cultural purity, the lyric in its designation of one kind of beauty, the foundling plot in its endorsement of one kind of family. Thus, the plot that insists on physical inheritance and the poem that persists in imaginative invention are linked in their adherence to fantasized constructs that are embedded in our cultural unconscious. "So-And-So" takes her place in the long line of romantic pairs. As viewers of the painting, we assume that the telling point of the myth is the recovery of the aristocracy Chase's orphan appears never to have lost. She needs no one to adopt her and is ready to control the dynastic legacy that has always awaited her. Mythological orphans begin *again*, gaining back what Chase's young woman has handed to her on a silver platter that she never had to forfeit. Totally self-reliant, she is no longer burdened by the responsibility of caring for her parents. She comes endowed but not weighed down, centered but nonetheless feeling, in Robert Le Page's terms, "the vertigo you experience when you lose both your parents and you realize that they've been blocking your view of the horizon."[6] Chase's young girl is lush and her surroundings plush; the lavishness of the red settee indicates how full-blooded her life still is. There are no Dickensian Fagans lurking at her back. The subtitle, "At Her Ease," demonstrates how much she is on her own, self-possessed and revealing a sense of entitlement to all that she now commands. Nothing blocks her view.

If we didn't see the wall card, Chase's young girl would be the same as one of the many portraits Chase painted of wealthy Americans and models costumed as women of importance or talent, identified by their professions, like Stevens's "So-And-So," merely idealized but anonymous objects. Chase's title for this painting betrays an understanding of the foundling plot and its dynastic privileges. His subject is not Lizzie Borden (of the infamous joke), who killed both her parents and then pled mercy on the court because she was an orphan. With Chase, we jump right to the end, obviating the terrible losses at the conventional beginning. Here is Sleeping Beauty, slowly waking up to meet her presumed Prince Charming. The operative color of the painting is that of the myth in question: red and lusty, the blood of the girl's extravagant inheritance seeping out into all her surroundings. And it is blood, as genetic dynastic privilege, that is at the heart of the foundling plot. Chase's understanding of the story reflects a belief that red blood is sometimes blue. In the wall card's unwritten convention, Chase's girl is an aristocrat at the threshold of marriage. Without the wall card, she is the idealized other who, as mirror of the artist's self, appears unfettered by biological ties. Enmeshed in the foundling plot, Chase's "girl" will find a suitable marriage partner. As exemplar of the Petrarchan ideal, she will remain—with Stevens's "So-And-So"—eternally a projection. In either case, she reveals that Petrarchan idealization and the foundling plot have a similarly long-lived history. In both, the constructs that shape us are so embedded that we cannot separate out our genetic inheritance from our mythical inheritance. The foundling plot exists at the intersection of race talk and culture talk even as it often fuses class with race. It might therefore be thought of as a primal "kind," one that has as its subject questions of "kinds" as indigenous traits, just as the Petrarchan lyric proposes a standard of beauty that excludes those who don't match the "look" of what has traditionally been considered desirable. Both Petrarchan and foundling plots respectively presume that uniform constructed identities and dynastically inherited aristocracies are components of national heritage, an inference I will challenge when I deploy contemporary fiction as a theoretical lens to assess Shakespeare's revisions of the mythical archetypes.

At the time that the nation-state was beginning to coalesce, what do Shakespeare's frequent uses of the foundling plot and his significant variations portend? How does his infusion of a lyric generic subplot (which he also revises) in so many of his plays change our reading of the main plot? Can we make our way forward again from these interpretations to realize a different cultural paradigm, one more responsive to contemporary social exigencies? I seek, as Berel Lang suggests in his reading of Claude Lanzmann's *Shoah*, "to start out from the present and reach back to the past . . . [in such a way that] intensifies the reach of the past itself."[7] I assume further that "the reach of the past" in its intensification can be insidious. The retrospect of my study offers a theoretical lens that allows us to read forward again to establish alternative stories, ones that would enable us to mitigate the "reach" of a past that emerged so ominously in the twentieth and twenty-first centuries and which confirms that, as Zygmunt Bauman argues, those historical atrocities were "born and executed in the peak of human cultural achievement."[8] Because Chase's young girl represents the patrician bent of the foundling plot in its depiction of the orphaned state as a prelude to dynastic aristocracy, and because Stevens's "So-And-So" renders the abstraction of a desired other as a mirror of the self idealized, both projections coalesce around a sense of what Caryl Phillips calls "the mythology of homogeneity."[9]

I will preface my remarks about literary foundlings as I move briefly from the "making believe" of Chase's orphan to chronicle the social and political realities that stem from the imperatives of a bloodline mandate that has become part of our contemporary vision without our even being fully conscious of its effects. And I will also demonstrate how—in her idealized genealogy—the Petrarchan lineage-less woman mirrors a self who depends on binary divisions reflecting a constructed difference that nevertheless privileges a standardized model. Thus, both plots—the one in its insistence on the biological connection that extends to the preservation of a social dynasty, the second in its creation of an other curiously like the poet—coalesce in their emphasis on self-reflective identities and in their demonization of all others who don't "match" a preconceived mold.

DARKENING AND REDRAWING NATIONALISTIC LINES: CHRONICLING THE PAIN OF LOSS

Writing that a major difference between fictional accounts of foundlings and their reality in premodern societies is that "in fiction *someone always knows*" about the abandonment, John Boswell notes that secrecy increased in the early modern period.[10] Boswell concludes *The Kindness of Strangers: The Abandonment of Children in Western Europe from Late Antiquity to the Renaissance*, a historical study about how exposed children were saved in Europe and reared long before adoption itself was formalized as a legal procedure and long before children were institutionally housed in what we today call orphanages, with a disclosure that differentiates between the commonplace ancient and medieval rescue of abandoned children, largely undertaken individually and privately, and the later practice of governmental sequestration: "In Renaissance cities the infants disappeared quietly and efficiently through the revolving doors of state-run foundling homes, out of sight and mind, into social oblivion, or, more likely, death by disease" (433).

Boswell traces this new institutionalism to the disintegration of old structures, caused "in part by the Black Death, the Hundred Years War, the Babylonian Captivity, the Great Schism" and its contrast, an "explosion of humanist learning and culture, starting in the age of Dante, Giotto, Petrarch, Boccaccio and Chaucer. . . . Creativity must fill the void of collapse and impose new order on chaos" (426). In a study of modernist love poetry and its sources in the early modern period, I have argued that the old structures came tumbling down with a bang and that the univocal pre-Renaissance European culture fell apart in unexpected places.[11] The "explosion of learning" was accompanied by an increased awareness of the connection between individual and national heritage as well as cultural and genealogical inheritance. Basing his poems on self-reflective dyads, the great formulator of romantic (if unrequited) personal love, Francesco Petrarca, is also (and not unsurprisingly in Boswell's context) an early poet of nationalistic hate. In *Rime sparse* 128, he contrasts "Bavarian treachery" to "noble Latin Blood," "Teutonic Rage" to peaceful Italy, and "the green colored earth of the Italian fatherland" to the "scorched red earth" of a barbarian homeland.[12] The Bavarians and their genetically inferior characteristics are to the evocation of a nascent Italian nationalism what the poetic Laura and her resolutely adamant resistance are to the formation of Petrarchan identity: the necessary opposition. Like the insistence on the pure blondness of the beloved Laura, the fixation on the polluted blood of the foreigner demarcates the ideal from evil in genetically recognizable terms.

Because each creates a system dependent on a hierarchical gender structure and an essentialist mandate of bloodline dynastic supremacy, the Petrarchan and foundling plots respectively contribute to the cultural milieu that fed into the early modern rise of the nation-state and to the feeling still so present today that immigrants or racial minorities in our midst constitute the same threat to our well-being that the Bavarians across the Alps posed to the nascent Italian state Petrarch valorized. I will discuss the inter-relationship of the lyric invention of self and the foundling plot's insistence on familial inheritance as Shakespeare connects them in *Merchant of Venice*, *Othello*, and *The Winter's Tale*. In these three plays, Shakespeare does something remarkable with the constructed selves of the lyric and the biological exigencies of the foundling plot, focusing his attention on the crucial point in each: the marriage question. The recovery in the normalized foundling plot centers on an actual or promised wedding, the moment when the missing child returns to the familial fold with the partner who will secure the dynasty. In contrast, the Petrarchan lyric is based on the structural impossibility of marriage: the lady always says "no," thereby enabling the poet to find more "matter" for the sustenance of his poems.

Experimenting with lyric self-creation in *Merchant of Venice* and recasting the connection between what Toni Morrison calls "mother hunger—[Desdemona's desire] to be one and to have one"[13]—and a feminized lyric in *Othello*, Shakespeare revises both plots even further in the remarkable poetic ethos of *The Winter's Tale*. In these plays, Shakespeare experiments with conceptions of gender that challenge the reigning cultural fixations of his time, his re-visions a means also to question the growing nationalism chronicled in Boswell's historical study. Boswell argues that, in ancient and medieval times, exposed children were saved in much the same way that they were in fictional accounts: "'The kindness of strangers' seems to have been sufficient to rescue most abandoned children" (399). Ancient and medieval reality coincides with the happy—pastoral—moments of the myth. Boswell cites the establishment of orphanages or the professionalizing and nationalization of private practice at the conclusion of the middle ages as a death blow to the happy middle interim, emphasizing that "the strangers no longer had to be kind to pick up the children: now they were paid to rescue them" (433). That institutionalization was prodded by what Boswell calls "the increasing social significance of lineage and birth in the Middle Ages" (431). The restoration in the traditional myth resolves all anxiety about familial manifest destiny just at the time that national boundaries were beginning to coalesce as identifiable territories.

I will further suggest that Shakespeare's variations of the myth take into account the link between family and nation and I will use the two plays that specifically involve early modern proto-racial conceptions—*Othello* and *The Merchant of Venice*—to show how he alters the story. Finally, I will argue that *The Winter's Tale* shores up a wholly different concept of engenderment, one that renders the happy middle period, the very state that Boswell maintains vanished historically at the time that Shakespeare was writing, a viable alternative to the racial essentialism so crucial to the undiluted plot. Recouping, with the three plays of this study, a pre-Renaissance view of adoption, Shakespeare questions practices that promote only the importance of genealogical kind and that, with the disappearance of children behind the closed doors of orphanages, rendered the whole middle period, as Boswell writes, "an even greater mystery" (426). Restructuring the foundling plot to contest the bloodline obsession and the secrecy of the diaspora in these three plays, Shakespeare also breaks down the fixed gender binaries essential to Petrarchism to challenge the imperatives of lyric self-construction. Similarly, the four novels in this study offer theoretical models that enable us to see both the social necessity for reshaping the stories that script us and the cultural possibilities that such changes confer.

As I move backward in this study from contemporary fiction to Shakespeare, I keep in mind the effects of ancient mythology on current social behavior and the ways in which the stories we tell feed into the cultural and political institutions we perpetuate. Nowhere do we see the pernicious effects of the mentality fostered by (or reflected in) the foundling mythology than in the deportation policies that, especially since 9/11, are causing so much havoc in most Western societies, policies that treat asylum seekers within the country as threats to national security in the same way that Petrarch venomized those dangerous others across the Alps and in a foreign terrain.[14] I understand fully that reading the story differently cannot instantly bring about an end to the strident nationalism we see operating worldwide.[15] Nor do I propose concrete answers to the questions raised by the increased presence of immigrants and asylum seekers in the United States and Western Europe. But I do argue that an awareness of how we are influenced by the stories that make up the Western heritage demands that we emphasize moments in those myths that are frequently eclipsed.

The Boswellian "mysteries" of early modern orphanages were public solutions to private desperation, a keeping secret of individual parental poverty, shame, or self-interest. Contemporaneously, we witness another form of secrecy, similarly a state-imposed one, that operates to render nationalism even more exclusionary than in Shakespeare's day. The reality parallels sections of the foundling plot, reflecting the same notion of national "oneness" Petrarch identifies in *Rime sparse* 128. But in these brutal instances, the governing principle of the bloodline mandate at the end of the story circles round to spur the beginnings into being. Fleeing, rather than returning to, their homelands, asylum seekers view the diaspora as their only end. But instead of the expected mythological pastoral relief, they experience a disastrous middle period. Often housed in detention camps (the equivalent of orphanages in the worst of their cruelty), they are subsequently often sent—unwillingly and often unwittingly—back to the homelands they fled (a chiasmic version of the happy reunion in the typical plot). And, illustrating the curious connection between private love of "our own" and poetic denigrations of those "others" not like "our own," current public policy across Europe and in America covertly registers (as Petrarch did overtly) the gap between domestic "noble" blood and the "barbarian" blood that courses through the veins of national "aliens" who seek refuge on our shores.

On May 14, 2008, reporters Amy Goldstein and Diana Priest, writing in the *Washington Post*, identified "more than 250 cases in which the government has, without medical reason, given drugs meant to treat serious psychiatric disorders to people it has shipped out of the United States since 2003—

the year the Bush administration handed the job of deportation to the Department of Homeland Security's new Immigration and Customs Association, known as ICE."[16] In the twenty-first century, the return to the country of birth often amounts to a death sentence rather than a lifeline.[17] Whereas, in the myth, the middle interlude functions as a pastoral respite, in twenty-first-century reality, the detention camp exists as a totally hostile environment and the deportation to the homeland a further punishment rather than a triumphant return. Reporters Goldstein and Priest describe the advertisements used to recruit the medical escorts (who accompany deportees back to their homelands and who, en route or before, inject them with Haldol and Ativan in doses so massive that the asylum seekers remain disoriented for days). The ads depict the deportation as a holiday for the nurses licensed to inject the opiates: "Do you ever dream of escaping to exotic, exciting locations? . . . Want to get away from the office but are strapped for cash? Make your dreams come true by signing up as a Medical Escort for DIHS" ("Some Detainees Are Drugged for Deportation," A1). Such incentives render the specially hired government agents who participate in these transports ironic versions of the kind strangers who take in exposed children. Under the stewardship of the especially hired nurses, the pastoral retreat in exotic foreign lands so typical of fairy tales becomes a temporary respite not for the asylum seekers but for their guardians while their charges are shipped back to the very countries they sought to escape.

The reality of contemporary instances that allude to portions of the plot (exposure, adoption, return) distorts everything except for the fundamental underlying belief in dynastic supremacy, transmuted into national or racial purity. In August 2009, the Obama administration pledged to reform detention centers, but the policy of "remov[ing] immigration violators from the country" remains in place.[18] On October 5, 2009, homeland security secretary Janet Napolitano announced that "the Obama administration is looking to convert hotels and nursing homes into immigration detention centers and to build two model detention centers from scratch as it tries to transform the way the government holds people it is seeking to deport."[19] As reported on NPR by Daniel Zwerdling, Napolitano touted the program in terms of cost-effectiveness, not because the current system was "inhumane."[20] In 2007 the American Civil Liberties Union filed suit against the Don Hutto Residential Center (which the Obama administration closed in 2009), because it was holding families in detention and forcing some children under ten years of age to stay there as long as a year. According to the *New York Times*, "children told of being threatened by guards with separation from their parents, many of them asylum seekers from around the world."[21] While adult asylum seekers are labeled as "illegal aliens," as if they were somehow of another species, the children of asylum seekers (often held hostage to smoke out their parents) are, like Dickens orphans, also detained indefinitely in reception centers, not only in the United States, but all across Europe. The whole problem of immigration is compounded by the fact that, in the United States, the children of illegal immigrants born here are automatically granted citizenship. Julia Preston writes in the *New York Times* that "civil rights and advocacy groups protested that deportation policy divides families in that de facto deportations of immigrant children with American citizenship [meant that they were forced to return to live in their parents' home countries]. . . . Groups that advocate stricter enforcement say that illegal immigrants who have been deported have the choice of taking their American children with them or leaving them in the United States."[22] In short, those advocates promote policies that encourage politically motivated child abandonments.[23]

The relief organization, Save the Children, estimates that there are as many as one hundred thousand unaccompanied children living in Europe today.[24] In 2008 alone, three thousand Afghan teenagers sought asylum in Europe.[25] "In the UK, in the absence of government statistics, the campaigning umbrella group, 'No place for a child,' estimates that around 2,000 children are detained each year. In one case, a child was held for 268 days" ("They Are Children Too," 10). In March 2006, it was revealed that at least 400 children had spent three years in a Norwegian asylum reception center, of these 204 had their asylum claims refused ("They Are Children Too," 11). In Sweden, some asylum-seeking children facing deportation, have become "apathetic and withdrawn, often refusing to eat, drink, talk, walk, and care for themselves" ("They Are Children Too," 15), in marked contrast to the hearty foundlings of the myth who thrive in the middle period, and who acquire a strength that fortifies the thin blue blood of the aristocracy they inherited. Liz Fekete writes:

> [This] is a tale of two Europes. The first Europe consists of government created bureaucratic machines which reduce officials to automatons. In this Europe, the demands of states' Executives to speed up deportations can only be met if non-citizens are treated as a species apart, for example by removing children on no other grounds than their nationality, from the universal protection of the United Nations Convention on the Rights of the Child. In this Europe, officials seize children for deportation on their way to school and police officers terrorize them in their homes during dawn raids. In this Europe, officials see nothing wrong with putting children's health at risk either by incarcerating them in pre-deportation detention centres or by rendering their families homeless and destitute. In this Europe, it is even legitimate to extend this kind of heartlessness to lone children, even though the state is officially supposed to act as their parent and legal guardian. Thankfully, though, there is another Europe. In the second Europe are ordinary people, often acting in defiance of the law and with great courage, reminding governments what humanitarianism and social solidarity mean in practice. Drawing their inspiration from citizens' networks formed to protect Jews from deportation during the Nazi period, "native" parents are risking deportation by hiding "foreign" children. Unless the chil-

dren are rescued by defiant, courageous people, there are no alternatives: detention is merely a stop gap between snatching children and deportation. ("They Are Children Too," vi)

What we see operating here in the second Europe is the exception, just as it was during the Nazi period. There exists a "second United States" as well. Reporting in the *New York Times*, Nina Bernstein writes about a Reformed Church in Highland Park, New Jersey, whose members convinced the ICE to release Indonesian Christians from detention and to rescue congregants who were already deported. Working with ICE agents, church members vouched for the detainees and obtained their freedom, hiring lawyers to release those held hostage. "Amy Gottlieb, immigrant rights director for the American Friends Service Committee in New Jersey who has been dealing with the field office since 1996, called the collaboration an 'amazing moment.'"[26] But such examples of individual or small group rescues are rare and represent either an exception to, or an unusual accommodation of, national policies. Xenophobia, which prompts detention as a prelude to deportation, is the rule. Fekete's first Europe (with its indecent exposures, like post-9/11 America with its questionable asylum processes) is, as Boswell argues about early orphanages, a well-kept secret.

In the typical foundling plot, a return to the homeland is liberating and accompanies the desired happy ending. In Fekete's first Europe, the same sense of mythically endorsed nationality and blood governs all parts of the story, in the initial asylum seeking, in the presumed safe haven to which refugees escape, and in the detention and deportations which are an increasing sign of more sharply drawn national lines, despite the economic union of the common market. Unlike Chase's "orphan," asylum seekers are always nowhere "at [their] ease." Commonality is merely Eurocentric. In fact, the governing principle of the middle section—that the foreign terrain would be hospitable—precipitates the separation: for asylum seekers the diaspora is the aim. In keeping with the formula, Fekete's first Europe insists that only an essentialist and national concern matters. Sometimes that xenophobia breaks the bounds of secrecy. In Italy, where there are four million legal immigrants and even more illegal, mostly African, immigrants, allegedly Mafia-instigated riots broke out in the southern region of Calabria in January 2010. In an interview, the interior minister, Ernesto Maroni, called the situation in Rosarno, "the fruit of the wrong kind of tolerance." The day before, he had been quoted as saying the riots were "the fruit of 'too much tolerance.'"[27]

Using contemporary fictional examples as paradigms for a theoretical new look at Shakespeare, the revisionist reading of the plots that I offer in this book opens an alternative to the nationalistic thrust of dynastic preservation, a mandate which feeds into the bloodline fetishes, which, Fekete argues, are endemic to Western societies and that lead to the intolerance sanctioned by nationalistic political parties whose support is growing in Europe. Ending the story in the middle, where nationality is subsumed by universalism, augurs hope for a new way of thinking. As Edward Said writes, "better disparity and dislocation than reconciliation under duress of subject and object; better a lucid exile than a sloppy sentimental homecoming."[28] The four novels in this study—*The Nature of Blood*, *Ark Baby*, *Austerlitz*, and *Fugitive Pieces*—make a good case for changing the story in terms that Said advocates. With these novels as theoretical lenses for challenging received opinions about *The Merchant of Venice*, *Othello*, and *The Winter's Tale*, I suggest that Shakespeare might also have interrogated the mythical assumptions that frame so many of his plays. In this regard, he recast the middle interlude of the foundling plot as an end that challenged the bloodline mandate. Similarly, the gender revisions he enacts change the Petrarchan poetic to give the *inamorata* a voice silenced in the *Rime sparse* and its early and late modern exemplars, one that ensures that the other has what Luce Irigaray calls "an irreducible source of meaning."[29] In the chapters that follow, I will turn to contemporary examples and Shakespearean re-visions that unhinge the mandates of both the lyric's masculinist construction of the other and the foundling plot's insistence on the dynastic essentialist self to change the framework of expectation of the culturally imbibed fantasies we bring with us as we read a novel or see a play. An understanding of those fantasies does not constitute a solution to the problems they cause but, acknowledging the devastating effects of mythologies that foster them, the works in this study offer alternative paradigms through which we can read back—and then forward—again. While I use fictional revisions as theoretical models for opening the middle section of the foundling plot and for changing the gender dynamics of lyric origination, I also cite several literary and philosophical theorists whose work coincides with the ideas the novels generate.

FICTION AS THEORY, THEORY AND FICTION

In every childhood there is a door that closes, Marina had said. And: only real love waits while we journey through our grief. That is the real trustworthiness between people. In all the epics, in all the stories that have lasted through many lifetimes, it is always the same truth: love must wait for wounds to heal. It is this waiting we must do for each other, not with a sense of mercy, or in judgment, but as if forgiveness were a rendezvous. How many are willing to wait for another in this way? Very few.

We become ourselves when things are given to us or when they are taken away.[30]

In the preceding passage from Anne Michaels's novel, published in 2009 and which further explores some of the same questions *Fugitive Pieces* raises, German-born and Jewish Marina (who went to work in England before the war and learned, only after she married, that the parents she left behind perished at Fohrenwald) offers a philosophical awareness that parallels the work of the theorists I cite in the following chapters. Her terms include a universality that explains why, in their codification of familial and romantic loss, the foundling and Petrarchan plots encapsulate a separation anxiety recorded in "all the epics [and] all the stories": the closed door. Claiming that "we become ourselves when things are given to us and when they are taken away," she refers to an aspect of Winnicottian psychology at the heart of this study: the child comes to know itself when it learns that the mother's body is separate from it.[31] In the foundling plot, the door closes very early; in the lyric, it closes before the poem even begins. Marina uses a term for healing the pain of childhood loss associated with an adult sexual meeting—a "rendez-vous"—an appointment that is prearranged, that is somehow expected to be there at the start. The turning around in the French "rendez-vous" (render yourself to the other) speaks to mutual and lifelong giving back of what was initially taken away. That's the surprise here: it is only as adults who have "wait[ed] for the wounds to heal," that we bypass the dynastic mandate of return with the forward-looking expectation of the liaison. Michaels's Marina identifies an intragenerational healing for the pain of intergenerational loss, forgiveness granted not so much by the initially exposing source as by the later and consoling partner, a sustenance that includes the reciprocation of romantic love. At the end of *Fugitive Pieces*, a character, scarred by the familial inheritance of his parents' Holocaust experience, comes to understand the mutual necessity with regard to his wife: "I see that I must give what I most need" (294).

In the early and late modern works that I discuss in this book, the middle period of adoption as a creative enterprise is the focus and the absolutism of biological engenderment so important to the conventional foundling convention is redetermined by an ongoing process that also challenges the narcissism and isolation of Petrarchan invention. In proposing something like Marina's "rendezvous," Luce Irigaray, whose recent work bypasses her earlier identity politics and so enacts in theory the revisions I suggest the writers in this study perform in practice, argues for the "reciprocity between the engendered and the engendering":[32]

> An act that was originally apparently univocal becomes biunivocal. The mother seems to unilaterally engender the child but, as adults, man and woman have the responsibility of continuing to engender themselves reciprocally. (*The Way of Love*, 129)

Irigaray's "reciprocity" involves both a "capacity to stay in oneself" and allows for "a participation of the other in the provenance of the self" (*The Way of Love*, 128). Such a participation, she argues "is perhaps engendering" (*The Way of Love*, 128). Making room for the other in the self suggests an expansion similar to Polonius's "scene undivided" or "poem unlimited," creating a psychologically receptive inward dilation that parallels Polonius's external spatial and temporal stretching in terms that mirror the reenvisioned plots the writers in this study advocate. It entails an unending possibility for beginning again. In a similar move, Irigaray diverges from the "univocal" as singular in its proper meaning and rigid in its criteria to something slightly oxymoronic. "Biunivocal" does not mean merely a doubling but also a broadening of separate beings so that each flows into the other: the reciprocity works within a mutual, rather than an hierarchical, structure and that mutuality is undivided and unlimited, involving a disenfranchisement of the old meanings. Like Polonius's unwitting breakdown of genres even as he defines them, Irigaray's self-conscious acknowledgment of difference and insistence on connection evolves a regendering of gender, a going back that points to a way forward.

In the three principal works of this study, Shakespeare reinscribes nurturing, evolving from a self-sustaining ethos in *The Merchant of Venice*, a psychically remembered and communal mothering in *Othello*, and a romantic fostering in *The Winter's Tale*. Through the remarkable relationship of Florizel and Perdita in the play of his later period, Shakespeare casts the middle section of the long pastoral interlude as the site of a regendering that, in turn, alters the sexual dynamics of the lyric complex, re-visionings that, in Irigaray's terms, consider "the horizontal axis that joins the sexes to be [more important than] the vertical axis that links together the generations."[33] As I detail more fully in the chapter on *The Winter's Tale*, Irigaray's writings often depict such crossings but, in this particular phrase, there is a double cross that overturns the vertical line of dynastic continuity so important to the foundling plot and the mimetic identity crucial to Petrarchan self-replication. If the foundling plot begins with a rupture between parent and child that separates the self from its origin and the Petrarchan with a breach between self and the other that replicates the self in its inception, Irigaray's "expansion" makes possible a change in the "horizon itself" (*Between East and West*, 145), one that parallels the reformulations the writers in this study undertake. Irigaray's terms will be used throughout this study to represent the gender and plot revisions theorized retroactively by the novelists and proleptically enacted by Shakespeare.

Sujata Iyengar suggests that the connection between genre and race in the early modern period are inevitable and inextricable: "literary affiliations (the compulsion of narrative, the longing of lyric, the agendas of masques and the escape of romance) entangle with variable concepts of skin color and emergent racial distinctions."[34] She argues that "early modern representations of racial difference at once create and interrogate the assumptions about race, skin color and gender that we live today" (1). Writing about multiple genres, Iyengar identifies the methodology I will use here about *two* plots (or "subgenres" as Alaistair Fowler might call them[35]) largely because they are so very present in Shakespeare's plays and because they still prevail with significant variations in much of contemporary literature. The revisionist lenses suggested by my readings of *Austerlitz, Fugitive Pieces, The Nature of Blood*, and *Ark Baby* result in critical perspectives that might offer alternatives to the patriarchal, racial, and class supremacy propounded by the conventional formulae. The theories that derive from these interpretations parallel those of Alys Eve Weinbaum who argues that "by reading and interfering with purportedly perfectible translation processes . . . we will effectively rewrite and thus reshape the scripts by which we have until now been written, including those biologically determinist scripts that have consistently bound race to reproduction within the modern episteme."[36] One escape from what Weinbaum calls the "race reproduction bind" (5) is to unravel the old stories and read the generic strictures otherwise. The process is akin to the mandate Carol Thomas Neely issues about how to approach early modern literature from a feminist perspective: "to read over [male-authored] Renaissance texts from beginning to end as if for the first time . . . [and] to over-read, to read to excess the possibility of human (especially female) gendered subjectivity, identity, and agency, the possibility of woman's resistance or even subversion."[37] I take Weinbaum's argument that race is a construction and Neely's directive to regenerate our notions of identity by moving backward to the roots of the very construction that insists on reproducible genetic entities as I seek a substitute cultural past to the one that, in Weinbaum's terms, "scripts" us. Shifts in our reading of those "scripts" reveal the previously undetected seeds that never come to fruition in *Austerlitz* and *The Nature of Blood* and that flower in *Ark Baby* and *Fugitive Pieces* to offer, within the plots, the "alternative social and symbolic spaces" Rosi Braidotti advocates.[38]

If, through such repositioning, we find a different Shakespeare, we do so to chart a different historical antecedent. In this introductory chapter, I have briefly described the post-Holocaust effects of the link between ancient mythologies and current social policies, ones that indicate that the world we inhabit now cannot be viewed as altogether superior to the one that precipitated the cataclysmic events in the middle of the twentieth century. In its focus on the events leading to, and stemming from, the mechanisms of that history, Caryl Phillips's *The Nature of Blood* speaks to the connection between Shakespearean precedent and contemporary consequence, centering on the Holocaust but also moving beyond it to underscore how the bloodline imperatives of both the foundling and Petrarchan plots operate today. Perhaps more than any other contemporary writer, Phillips consistently places his work not only in the historical moment he unflinchingly chronicles but also in the cultural context he persistently challenges.

NOTES

1. *Collected Poems* (New York: Knopf, 1954), 295.
2. See Barbara Dayer Gallati and Bruce Weber in Ronald G. Pisano, *William Merritt Chase, Portraits in Oil, Volume 2*, completed by Carolyn K. Lane and D. Fredrick Baker (New Haven, CT: Yale University Press, 2006), 53–54. Gallati and Weber emphasize the similarities to Whistler's portrait of his mother, both with regard to the angle of the painting as well as to the handkerchief, but they also note the difference in mood suggested by the colors of the background.
3. "The Poetics of Discovery: A Reading of Donne's 'Elegy 19,'" *Yale Journal of Criticism* 2 (1989): 133
4. According to reports by UNICEF and Save the Children, "most of the children living in institutions around the world [today] have a surviving parent or close relative and they most commonly entered orphanages because of poverty." See Celia E. Dugger, "Aid Gives Alternative to African Orphanages: A New Approach to Aiding Orphans in Malawi," *New York Times*, December 6, 2009, A1. Around the world orphans face either a life of institutionalization and an opportunity at least for nutrition and education or care by surviving family members and a life of poverty. Recent work in Malawi has given extended families financial aid in helping to raise children orphaned particularly by the AIDS epidemic, at a cost that is much cheaper than keeping the same child in a state- or church-run orphanage.
5. Pisano notes that the work had many titles: *The Young Orphan, Study of a Young Girl, An Idle Moment, Repose*, and *At Her Ease*. In 1887, Chase returned to a simple *The Orphan*. And it was listed in Peat's 1949 Check List as *Study of a Young Girl*. See *William Merritt Chase*, 56.
6. *The Far Side of the Moon*, unpublished, quoted from the production at the American Repertory Theatre, Cambridge, MA, 2005.
7. Review of *Claude Lanzmann's Shoah: Key Essays*, edited by Stuart Liebman (New York: Oxford University Press, 2007), *Cineaste* 33, 4 (2008): 77.
8. *Modernity and the Holocaust* (Ithaca, NY: Cornell University Press, 2000), x.
9. "Extravagant Strangers," *A New World Order: Essays* (New York: Random House, 2002), 288.
10. *The Kindness of Strangers: The Abandonment of Children in Western Europe from Late Antiquity to the Renaissance* (New York: Pantheon, 1988), 8.
11. *The American Love Lyric after Auschwitz and Hiroshima* (New York: Palgrave, 2001).
12. "Rime sparse 128," *Petrarch's Lyric Poems*, translated and edited by Robert Durling (Cambridge, MA: Harvard University Press, 1976), 260.
13. *A Mercy* (New York: Knopf, 2008), 67.
14. Focusing on Caryl Phillips's *The Nature of Blood*, Ashley Dawson uses the novel (as I do here) to argue that "the exclusionary racial and cultural connotations of nascent definitions of European identity must be challenged." See "'To remember too much is indeed a form of madness': Caryl Phillips's *The Nature of Blood* and the Modalities of European Racism," *Postcolonial Studies* 7, 1 (2004): 85.
15. In Slovakia, one of the states that emerged after the breakup of the Soviet Union, legislation is ready to be passed that requires the reciting of the national anthem in schools and requires that schools display the national flags. According to the *New York Times*, "Last year the government passed a language law, which calls for public servants, from doctors to post office workers, to speak Slovak rather than Hungarian and other minority languages—or risk fines of up to $7,300. Hungarian speakers complain of being accosted on public trams or in hospitals, and yelled at to speak Slovak." Critics say the new laws are a manifestation of

"cultural insecurity" and reveal a distrust of ethnic minorities. See "National Identity Bill Divides Slovakia," *New York Times*, March 25, 2010, http://www.nytimes.com/2010/03/26/world/europe/26iht-slovakia.html?emc=eta1.

16. "Some Detainees Are Drugged for Deportation," *Washington Post*, May 14, 2008, A1.

17. In an article about how the Bush administration vetted immigration judges according to their conservative biases, Charles Savage concludes, "The authors of the study, called 'Refugee Roulette,' concluded that the facts of a case may be less important in determining whether someone is deported than which judge hears the case." See "Vetted Judges More Likely to Reject Asylum Bids," *New York Times*, August 24, 2009: A17.

18. Nina Bernstein, "U.S. to Reform Policy on Detention for Immigrants," *New York Times*, August 6, 2009, A1.

19. Nina Bernstein, "Ideas for Immigrant Detention Include Converting Hotels and Building Models," *New York Times*, http://www.nytimes.com/2009/10/06/us/politics/06detain.html?_r=1&emc=eta1.

20. Daniel Zwerdling and Michele Norris, "All Things Considered," National Public Radio, October 6, 2009.

21. Nina Bernstein, "U.S. to Reform Policy on Detention for Immigrants," *New York Times*, August 6, 2009, http://www.nytimes.com/2009/08/06/us/politics/06detain.html?emc=eta1.

22. "Study Sees More Young Citizens with Parents in the U.S. Illegally," *New York Times*, http://www.nytimes.com/2009/04/15/us/15immig.html?emc=eta1.

23. On February 25, 2010, Robert Mackey described in the *New York Times* a system that some refer to as foster care and others call slavery: "Some of the confusion might have been based on a Haitian tradition in which children from poor families in rural areas are often sent to live in cities with acquaintances or relatives. The Haitian Creole term for children who are sent to other families is 'restavek,' which is derived from the French words 'rester avec,' or 'stay with.' But critics of the restavek system say that it is closer to child slavery than any kind of foster care because many of the children are forced to engage in back-breaking work in return for their upkeep." The number of orphans in Haiti has increased exponentially since the terrible earthquake that occurred in early January 2010, heightening the country's devastation. See http://thelede.blogs.nytimes.com/2010/02/25/haitian-tradition-is-criticized-as-child-slavery/?emc=eta1. In many ways, the "restavek" tradition is age old, its roots in early modern wardship and apprenticeship, best illustrated by Lancelot in *The Merchant of Venice*. I discuss this situation in chapter 5.

24. See Liz Fekete, "They Are Children Too: A Study of Europe's Deportation Policies," *European Race Bulletin* 48–59 (2007): 35.

25. Caroline Brothers, "Afghan Youths Seek a New Life in Europe," *New York Times*, August 28, 2009: A3.

26. As quoted by Nina Bernstein, "Church Works with U.S. to Spare Detention," *New York Times*, http://www.nytimes.com/2009/12/13/nyregion/13indonesians.html?emc=eta1.

27. Rachel Donadio, "Race Riots Grip Italian Town, and Mafia Is Suspected," *New York Times*, January 11, 2010, http://www.nytimes.com/2010/01/11/world/europe/11italy.html?emc=eta1. On February 14, 2011, Rachel Donadio and Gaia Pianiani reported that in the days after the revolution three thousand Tunisian immigrants had come to the small island of Lampedusa by boat. Interior Minister Maroni offered to deploy armed forces *in Tunisia* to block the influx of what he called "an unprecedented biblical influx" from that island, again using the rhetoric of xenophobia on Italian television, as he jockeyed for more power for his anti-immigration Northern League party in the Berlusconi government. http://www.nytimes.com/2011/02/15/world/europe/15boats.html?emc=eta1.

28. "The Art of Displacement: Mona Hatoum's Logic of Irreconcilables," *Mona Hatoum: The Entire World as Foreign Land* (London: Tate Gallery Publishing, 2000), 17.

29. *I Love to You: Sketch of a Possible Felicity in History*, translated by Alison Martin (New York: Routledge, 1996), 133.

30. Anne Michaels, *The Winter Vault* (London: Bloomsbury, 2009), 93–94.

31. D. W. Winnicott, *Playing and Reality* (New York: Basic Books, 1975).

32. *The Way of Love*, translated by Heidi Bostic and Stephen Pluháček (New York: Continuum, 2002), 129.

Introduction 19

33. *Between East and West: From Singularity to Community*, translated by Stephen Pluháček (New York: Columbia University Press, 2002), 141.
34. *Shades of Difference: Mythologies of Skin Color in Early Modern England* (Philadelphia: University of Pennsylvania Press, 2004), 1.
35. "The Formation of Genres in the Renaissance and After," *New Literary History* 34, 2 (2003): 185–200.
36. *Wayward Reproductions: Genealogies of Race and Nation in Transatlantic Modern Thought* (Durham, NC: Duke University Press, 2004), 246.
37. "Constructing the Subject: Feminist Practices and New Renaissance Discourses," *ELR* 18 (1980): 5–18.
38. "Afterword," *Luce Irigaray and Premodern Culture: Thresholds of History*, edited by Elizabeth Harvey and Theresa Krier (New York: Routledge, 2004), 170.

Contemporary Pasts

Chapter One

Unraveling Narrative Order in Caryl Phillips's *The Nature of Blood*

Caryl Phillips's understanding that "in the face of overwhelming evidence the mythology of homogeneity not only exists, it endures"[1] plays itself out in the *Nature of Blood* as it proceeds first through local flashbacks delineating the Nazification of middle European countries after Hitler's *anschluss*, and tracing the slow decline in the fortunes of the heroine, Eva Stern, until her deportation to the death camps, from which she was the only one in her family who survived. Then it makes huge historical leaps backward to early modern Venice and two intertwining stories, one based on an actual recorded event in a plot that literalizes—and inverts—Shylock's demand for a "pound of flesh" in *Merchant of Venice* and the second one that rereads Shakespeare's Venetian tragedy, *Othello*. Literalizing the pernicious effects of the bloodline mandate and male-generated narcissism inherent respectively to the foundling and Petrarchan plots, Phillips links the two in the story of the vengeful murder of several Jews in the town of Portobuffole and by creating an Othello in *The Nature of Blood* who doubles for Shakespeare's Brabanzio, their collaborative behavior across the centuries presenting the dark underside of the parallel between parental and romantic engendering.

Phillips's connection to *Merchant of Venice* follows from two significant crises in Shakespeare's play: the demonization and dehumanization of Shylock by Antonio in 1.3.94 and by Graziano in 4.1.132, and then his total disappearance in Act 5. Casting forward in time from a historically documented event in fifteenth-century Venice—the burning and total evaporation of three Jews in revenge for the blood libel of a boy who only existed in fantasy—Phillips describes the extermination of millions of Jews in the gas chambers of the Second World War in the same words. The Jews in Portobuffole, a small town near Venice, and the Holocaust victims all vanished

23

into "white ash" (156, 178). Those disappearances lead us, in turn, to question what Shylock's absence from the circle of winners in Act 5 of *Merchant of Venice* might portend. Not even mentioned there, he seems never to have existed.

Phillips's connection to *Othello* likewise stems from two critical moments in the play: first, when Brabanzio, with his early modern callousness renounces, Desdemona, declaring, "I had rather to adopt a child than get it" (1.3.189), thereby annulling his only daughter even as he plays fast and loose with the dynastic mandate of the foundling plot; and second, when Othello vows that only Desdemona's absolute reflection of him secures his tenuous hold on the world: "and when I love thee not, / Chaos is come again" (*Othello*, 3.3.92–93). Brabanzio wipes away the past of his own life, and Othello that of the whole world as he pushes everything back to a time before time itself. When the art of his creation no longer mirrors him, he erases all creation. The very character whose marriage enrages Desdemona's father in the play abandons his own child and betrays his first wife when he leaves Africa to remake himself in the fifteenth-century Venice Phillips invents as a parallel to *Othello*. Thus, Shakespeare's Brabanzio and Phillips's Othello fuse in this novel that, centering on the Holocaust and drawing a mathematical line between late modern effect and early modern cause, displays the same belief in human disposability and anticipates the selective genetics inherent to the "genocidal mentality"[2] that inextricably binds the foundling and Petrarchan plots to their exponentially multiplied corollary in the twentieth century.

As elucidated by Shakespeare and challenged by Phillips's revisionism, the foundling plot becomes a vehicle for the imposition of a male order that renders gender as well as race key players in the drive for mastery and it does so as character after character betrays the women who seek the mutual engenderment Irigaray advocates. Like Theseus, who insists that it is the father's prerogative to "leave the figure [of his daughter] or disfigure it" (*A Midsummer Night's Dream*, 1.1.51), Shakespeare's Brabanzio and Phillips's Othello (along with their twentieth-century parallels in Phillips's novel, Gerry and Stephan) insist on the male generativity of the Petrarchan complex, a view that projects women as the creation of the men who at first pursue and then, in valuing the chase more than the achievement, let them slip heedlessly, needlessly, as they replace them with other causes or other women, a process that in turn parallels the abandonments of the foundling plot.

While the patriarchal characters in the play and novel gravitate toward the abusive side of the foundling plot, Phillips himself confirms his interest in the positive aspects of adoption in "*The Nature of Blood* and the Ghost of Anne Frank," an essay that attributes the origin of the 1997 novel to his initial confrontation with the Holocaust when, as a teenage émigré from St. Kitts who had lived in Leeds since infancy, he learned about the extent of its atrocities through a television series, *The World at War*. "Within the next few days," he writes, "I had written my first short story," a fiction also based on the ancient myth that governs Brabanzio's dismissal of Desdemona.[3] The early parable articulates a belief in redemption shattered by the multiple plots of *The Nature of Blood*. Phillips reminisces:

> The story concerned a young Dutch boy. His parents informed him that he had to wear a Star of David on his coat. This was now the law. But, of course, the boy was intensely upset to learn of this new decree, and saw no reason why he should obey. He was, after all, just the same as all the other boys. His parents tried to explain that it was not a mark to be ashamed of, and he should wear the star with pride. Reluctantly the young Dutch boy agreed. Soon after, while the boy and his parents were in the process of being transported to a camp in a cattle truck, the boy managed to prise open a small gap in the wall of the boxcar and leap from the speeding train. Unfortunately, he struck his head on a rock as he fell, and he knocked himself unconscious. He was bleeding heavily, and clearly he was in danger of hemorrhaging to death. Luckily a farmer, who was out working in his fields, happened to see the sun glinting where it caught his yellow Star of David. He found the boy, bandaged his head, and nursed him back to health. The boy survived.
> The Dutch boy was, of course, me. A fourteen year old black boy in working-class Yorkshire in the North of England. ("Blood," 2–3)

A "large poster of Anne Frank is above [his] desk" ("Blood," 7) as he writes *The Nature of Blood*, but the hero of Phillips's teenage fiction seems more like another girl of the same name. Phillips's Dutch boy is plucky. Able, like the comic strip character "Orphan Annie," to "leap" out of the boxcar of trouble, he gets lucky. The Dutch boy's Farmer-Warbucks acts as mother (nursing him back to health) and father (creating a pastoral retreat from the war). In Phillips's childhood fantasy, the oppressive yellow Star of David matches the "glint" of the sun and becomes the bright shining armor that leads the boy to his knight. The adoptive farmer circumvents all thoughts about biological ties and provides a resolution that makes for a happy ending. Art and nature coalesce in the image of a kindly substitute parent who shelters Phillips's boyhood hero from the "utter numbing shock" ("Blood," 3) of human cruelty.

The Nature of Blood contains many adoptions and fosterings that do not reflect the naïvely happy salvation his Jewish Dutch boy experienced. Some characters, like Phillips's teenaged hero, begin with the expectation of mythical rescue but, unlike the Dutch boy, are left languishing in dark variations of the ancient plot. The gulf between Phillips's early fantasy that racial hostilities can be overcome with a miraculous rescue and the foundling stories in *The Nature of Blood*, where the stereotypical adoptions culminate in recapitulations of loss, reflects his subsequent understanding of Europe's obsession with bloodlines and what Andrew Armstrong calls "the recurrence of atrocity."[4] At the core of Phillips's novel, which centers on Eva Stern and begins with her liberation from a concentration camp at the end of the Second World War, there are many examples of fosterings that approximate centuries-old mythical patterns. No heroic farmers grace *The Nature of Blood*. In fact, adoption itself is challenged as, time after time, the adopters either literally abuse the children they pick up or dash their expectations. Like the little boy in Phillips's story, the characters in *The Nature of Blood* start out hoping that they will find saviors such as the solicitous Dutch farmer. Instead, they end up confronting versions of Brabanzio as the plotlines become twisted in ways that endanger, rather than save, children.

In "Extravagant Strangers," Phillips writes that "every writer discovers that his or her main struggle is with this one word: form" (293). As he tells Stephen Clingman in an interview, "I knew I had to disrupt form."[5] Performing the permutations he theorizes, Phillips enacts his belief that "the writer who is by virtue of birth and upbringing both of and not of a society—and by extension its literature—will bend the shape of [the] traditional line of the literature to accommodate this positioning" (*A New World Order*, 293). Through the interwoven stories that make up the whole of *The Nature of Blood*, Phillips simultaneously integrates and changes the trajectory of the foundling plot or demonstrates how others (like Brabanzio) distort its premises even as—with the Othello story and its link to Eva—he illustrates the despair stemming from the cultural effects of the Petrarchan plot. Eliminating Iago with an Othello who incorporates his machinations, Phillips moves outside the parameters of Shakespeare's text and focuses on Othello's pre-Venetian life, rendering him a traitor who, having left a wife and child in Africa, strains "conveniently [to] forget [his] own family" (181): a "black Uncle Tom" (181), a "sad black man, first in a line of so-called achievers, too weak to yoke their past with their present" (182). The mythical happy endings fall apart as Phillips parallels his Othello both with Eva's Uncle Stephan, who left his wife and family in order to emigrate to Israel before the war, and with Eva's wife-intimidated would-be lover, Gerry, who forsook her in order to migrate back home after the war.[6] Both fail to offer the women in their lives the Irigarayan mutual engenderment that would bypass the effects of Petrarchan self-reflection.

Phillips's version of *Othello* posits a series of betrayals, having principally to do with the utter desolation of Eva. Like Desdemona, Eva is caught in the web of male self-actualizing fantasies. And, like Desdemona, Eva feels doubly forsaken, first by her biological parents who let her slip through their fingers, then by Gerry, one of the English liberators of her camp, who promises to marry her but returns to the wife and children he left at home when he enlisted for the war. As if to heighten the effect of the abandonments by her parents and by Gerry, Phillips interjects another story connected to the blood libel in *The Merchant of Venice*, one based on yet another phantasm: the adoption and subsequent keening over a presumed-to-be-orphaned child who never existed. In Phillips's other historical leap backward to Venetian environs (to 1480 and the town of Portobuffole), a boy is "discovered" and then goes missing. Everybody wants to adopt the nonexistent stranger ostensibly "sighted" by so many witnesses. Accused of the crime of killing "an innocent Christian boy named Sebastian New" (59), three Jews of Portobuffole are brought to trial and then burned at the stake. As the Christian citizens of the town begin to foster Sebastian New, he is shaped into someone worth fostering. The whole town falls in love with its fabrication.

Through its professed cannibalism of a child without a past, the Portobuffole story—and its reversion to still older anti-Semitic beliefs—anticipates the Holocaust and its attempt to render the Jews a race without a future. As Jean-Francois Lyotard writes:

> The sufferers in the gas chambers are victims of the double bind imposed by a representable law: to have seen a gas chamber work is to be dead, unable to speak of the wrong one has suffered. The victim is one who has suffered a "damage accompanied by the loss of the means to prove the damage."[7]

In the case of Sebastian New, the Jews allegedly ate the evidence. In the case of the Jews burned at Portobuffole, no one can "prove" that they existed either, since the evidence was burned. Phillips's narrator describes the disappearance: "The executioner threw the ash into the air and it dispersed immediately" (156). Twenty-two pages later, he skips five hundred years and speaks of the effects of Zyklon B in the gas chambers of the Second World War: "The ash is white and easily scattered" (178). Eva Stern muses about her own city: "In time, there would be no evidence that any of us lived here" (71). In *The Nature of Blood*, Phillips alternates between evidence and fantasy as he weaves Holocaust histories into family narratives and tells truths about documented events that are built on myths. Finally, Phillips superannuates fiction, giving Shakespeare's *Othello* a background that renders its African hero a child abandoner and a wife betrayer who—insinuating himself into Venetian society—views Desdemona (as Shakespeare's Othello does) only in terms that reflect him.

Influencing all the fictions are Ovidian stories that exist as ideals to be repeated in the future or as models against which present moments are judged. Like Petrarch fashioning Laura, Phillips's Othello and his avatars, Stephan and Gerry, invoke Pygmalion and Narcissus as they first idealize and then reject women, suggesting that they are "entirely disposable to those who profess to love [them]" (149). In both the Pygmalion and the Narcissus stories, the other is the self of the "I" who generates her. In that regard, the other is disposable since the "I" can go on creating indefinitely. In *The Nature of Blood*, Phillips follows the belief in interchangeable parts to its destructive conclusion in one version of the foundling plot and then picks up on his early hope for adoptive salvation in yet another subplot. Dispelling biological fatalism, his revisionist readings reconstruct narrative assumptions. Finally, in the last story of the book—that of Malka, the Ethiopian woman who turns away from Stephan—he bypasses the foundling and the Petrarchan plots, suggesting that the cultural traditions perpetuated in both may be in need of still other mutations, ones not yet realized in the established scripts of our literary inheritance. When Brabanzio changes the story in the hypothetical "next time" he projects, he chooses to end (as Phillips's *Othello* does) in the middle of the story, rendering the adopted child more amenable than its biological predecessor. In Brabanzio's subjunctive annulment, Desdemona can be replaced with any child who fits the socially constructed mold. In the instances of that cruelty, blood is irrelevant. But in *The Nature of Blood*, "the practice of using blood as a barometer of acceptability" ("Blood," 3) operates schizophrenically. On the one hand, it is at the bottom of the Nazi belief in the exclusionary superiority of race expressed in Himmler's injunction to be "honest, loyal, and comradely to members of our blood . . . and to nobody else."[8] On the other hand, following Brabanzio's doctrine of disposability, it is a contrivance for the imposition of the patriarchal order that renders gender rather than race the key player in the drive for mastery. With the Malka story, the genders are firmly transposed, as Malka, refusing her adoption in the Israeli foundling plot, also refutes her Petrarchan idealization by Stephan; her voice silences his and her questions emerge as the only ones worth answering.

In terms of the foundling plot, *The Nature of Blood* focuses on differing versions of the middle interlude of adoption: first, the patriarchal one that unites fathers and husbands, as it does in *Othello*. In Brabanzio's wish for a better future, he assumes that, through art, he can shape a child more readily in his image than he can through the nature of his bloodline. Phillips's Othello drops his African wife and biological child and fosters the Venetian Desdemona by making a marriage that cements his standing in the Venetian men's club. In the novel, the playboys of this variation of the foundling plot similarly pick up and then abandon women in order to fit themselves into images that adjust to changes in their own life situations. Gerry forgets Eva and returns to England; Uncle Stephan leaves a wife and child and acclimatizes himself to the Palestine of his dreams. These patriarchal variations are countered by mythical subplots influencing the women. The cast-off daughters and wives evoke the Ovidian stories of Ceres and Proserpine. Thus, while Gerry and Stephan follow Othello in their narcissistic versions of adoption, Eva clings to a different, more communal, idea of nurturing, one that suggests both a parental and societal determination to recover the missing child, very much like the stories that sustain Desdemona in the fourth act of *Othello*. Ceres never forgets the daughter she loves and is helped in her journey of recovery by a community of women who take on her loss. Bloodlines are restored through sympathetic interventions and a belief that the lost child should not be left alone against the elements.

Such communal adoptions are what Eva Stern hopes for as she struggles to continue her life after the war and they're what the women of Portobuffole offer Sebastian New as they take on his cause and relentlessly pursue the allegedly cannibalistic Jews. The mythic background in fact illustrates the slippery slope in the trope of the foundling story. What happens when the borders between fact and fiction are blurred both in the myth itself and in the way we assess identity? What are the effects of long-held mythological beliefs on real-life behavior? And what does the creation of reality in the compulsory essentialism of the myth have to do with the invention of reality in the Aryan elitism of the Holocaust and the subsequent denial of the genocide in the racist resurgence evidenced by the rise of neo-Nazi parties who would have us believe that the genocides of World War II never took place? As Stefania Ciocia argues, "No other episode in our past is so palpably surrounded by the fear that an improper artistic treatment of the historical facts might lead to an aestheticization of their abjection and inhumanity."[9] In light of Ciocia's hesitation about folding the Holocaust into the annals of fiction, we need to ask whether its offenses "require," as Lawrence Langer maintains, "a scroll of *in*human discourse to contain them, and [whether] we need a definition of the *in*human community to coexist with its more sociable partner . . . [before we can inscribe them] in historical or artistic narratives that will try to reduce to some semblance of order the spontaneous defilement implicit in such deeds."[10]

Langer's questions are important to raise about a work of fiction that seems to have such a deliberate pattern, a set of imagined actions and historical reactions, with measurable consequences. In weaving in and out of literary paradigms, establishing parallel antecedents and corresponding pairs—Eva Stern/Sebastian New; Gerry/Uncle Stephan; *The Merchant of Venice/Othello*; classical myths/twentieth-century repercussions—Phillips seems to be consciously "ordering" a pattern. But beyond the seeming order in *The Nature of Blood*, Phillips has a fundamental question about the normative plots on which his patterns are based. Isn't there something in the very narratives Langer claims should remain sequestered from the Holocaust and its atrocities that instead feeds into them? Can we address the concerns Ciocia raises by viewing Shakespeare and the myths that inspire him as cultural analogues for, rather than as pristine alternatives to, what went so terribly awry in the middle of the twentieth century? While the psychologist narrator of *The Nature of Blood* explains the psychic numbing of Holocaust survivors by asking how they can "remember and move on" (157), Phillips himself seems to be asking of our tendency to isolate recent cataclysmic events from anything that came before them: "How can we move on and *not* remember?" Attaching his Holocaust narrative both to actual historical events, and to accepted literary plots, Phillips reads backward and forward to offer, as Stephen Clingman so aptly puts it, "a crucial definition and alternative: of a *transnational* view of identity, inseparable from a transtemporal view of history."[11] How do all those old stories render the new ones inevitable? How are all our cultural scripts, as Kwame Appiah writes, "shopsoiled by history"?[12]

For Phillips, memory involves an understanding that our contemporary experience connects to our mythological past and that such an understanding requires us to read that history from the retrospect of its historical repercussions. In *The Nature of Blood*, he illustrates how language systems that override the alterity of sexual and genealogical perspective in favor of a seamless patriarchal prerogative make themselves felt in *Othello* and in the parallel stories of Gerry and Stephan. Though there seem to be divisions within those linguistic structures, they are in fact replications of an original construction whose early modern influence on Shakespeare's play collapses racial divisions into gender issues. In Phillips's view, that collapse had disastrous results in the middle of the twentieth century. The death of a few Jews in Portobuffole prefigures the death of millions in the Second World War and Desdemona augurs Eva. In Eva, Phillips creates a character who forces us to see that what we think of as unbelievable—the massiveness of the Holocaust murders—may in fact be ascribable in terms that our culture has been using all along.

The only character in *The Nature of Blood* who refuses to fit the mold and who resists the culture in its entirety is Malka. She doesn't appear until the very end of the novel in the incident that cemented Phillips's feeling that "the practice of using blood as a barometer of acceptability is very deeply ingrained in the European consciousness" ("Blood," 3). Bound by race to Othello and by gender to Desdemona, Malka turns the racial and national divisions of *Othello* against themselves by remaining defiantly outside the entire European *mythos* and its patriarchal biases. In contrast, Eva seems trapped by her belief in the tradition as she keeps searching for someone who—like Ceres—might protect her from the overwhelming social forces rendering her losses culturally inevitable. The mythical stories fueling her hope parallel her belief that, contrary to Petrarchan determinism, a lover (offering an Irigarayan mutual engenderment) might counter the parental abandonment she experienced in the camps.

MYTHICAL EXPECTATION: "WHY DID YOU NOT COME BACK FOR ME?"

Phillips presents two scenes between Eva and her mother that illustrate how her myth-inspired belief in parental sustenance enables her, briefly, to take control of her life. In the first, she appears as Perdita in *The Winter's Tale*, preparing for her future life; in the second, she begins as Hermione—retreating in order to preserve herself—and ends as Desdemona, claiming ownership of her death. At the opening of the novel, Eva still believes in the possibility of a saving community and a mother who will not give up on her missing daughter. When she imagines her mother alive again, she exhibits both the incredible faith of the foundling convention and its essential sense of loss:

> I was expecting [Mama] to return, for I never truly believed she had gone. And now she is back. I hold her hard and encourage her to tell her story once more.
> "But Mama," I ask, "why did you not come and look for me?"
> Mama looks sad now.
> "They told me that you were dead, and I believed them."
> I touch my Mama's face, her lips, her eyes, her nose. I stroke her wisps of hair. Mama is back with me. I can now begin to plan a future for both of us. (35–36)

In this reversal, Eva first plays mother to her mother, as "Mama" describes her escape into "another hut" and abandonment—"they left her for dead" (35)—by the very people who took her in. Eva's initial questions about the details of her mother's survival echo those of Hermione in *The Winter's Tale*: "Tell me mine own, / Where hast thou been preserved? Where lived? How found / Thy father's court" (5.3.124–25)? But when Eva switches roles again, she speaks as the lost child, questioning her mother's lack of faith. Her mother is not a Ceres willing to suspend all life until her daughter is found. Eva cannot move forward without an explanation of why her mother stopped looking for her. Planning the future depends on a presumption of maternal solicitude—a tenacity of love—in which her mother, like Hermione, "preserve[s herself] to see the issue" (5.3.127). Fortified by that imagined return, Eva invents a tableau out of the myth, recovering from her loss by dramatizing the recognition scene so crucial to the foundling plot.

In the second instance, Eva posits a past in which, like the hero of Phillips's early story about the Dutch boy, she attempts to flee with her mother from the pursuing Nazis and to resist for her mother their attempts to restrain her. In this recognition scene, Eva casts herself (once more) as guardian to her mother but, this time, both escape the misfortune they have already lived and experience the salvation promised in the foundling plot's resolution.

That future lies in the subterfuge Eva devises. Mother and daughter emerge—one to the other—the saving community. Like Hermione in *The Winter's Tale* and Ceres in Ovid, Eva uses the cover of disguise, playing dead in order to see the "issue" of an imagined rebirth. Hiding from the dogs hounding her family, Eva's one concern is to protect her mother:

> Eva offered her Mama a thumb to suck on and waited, and wondered if, lying here in the vast expanse of this platform, the soldiers might mistake them for a mound of abandoned garbage. . . . And then the creaking of the ladder as the soldiers mounted its rickety structure, and the triumphant shouting, and the laughter, and then she felt the warm thuds as the bullets found scraps of flesh in which to nest. (185)

In this fantasy, Eva turns the foundling plot recognition scene into the protective disguise of the middle interlude, using the figure of the recovered child and restored parent to confound her enemies. Coming later in the literal time sequence of the novel but reliving in imagined space a scenario that would have preempted all the suffering—the camp, the many betrayals—Eva actually survived, this dream follows the episode describing Gerry's abandonment after Eva confronts him in England. At the moment of her love rejection, Eva imagines herself shielding her mother from the parental and romantic disappointment she herself has lived through. In her protective cover, she mimics the very identity her betrayers force her to assume, and thus deprives them of the satisfaction of reducing her to nothingness. "Abandoned garbage," mother and daughter hide themselves as remnants of a past life simultaneously as, in the "mound" of an open grave site, they anticipate their revival in a new, and generationally fluid, relationship. Through that hibernation—mother sucking daughter's thumb, daughter encircling mother's body—they also appear pregnant with each other. Like creatures that play dead in order to stay alive, they deploy their dehumanization in the abandoned mound as a prehumanization, the stage before their entry into another life. Bonded together by mutualizing their plight, they feign their death as a signal for rebirth. As the bullets drive seminally through their bodies, the "scraps" of their flesh cohere to enable their metamorphic emergence from the "nest." Eva's imagined demise (which precedes her actual suicide) returns her to a belief in the possibility of a nurturing parent and a loved child. Restored in a mythical union, Eva and her mother protect and sustain each other.

The burial in the mound coincides with Eva's evolution from the worm of Gerry's serpentine appearance through the cocoon of her retreat until she emerges the "butterfly" (194, 197, 198) of her final metamorphosis. No longer bearing the imprint of male artistic vision, the imagined freedom of Eva's butterfly transfiguration is possible only through the suicidal choice she makes. The precipitating image linking romantic and parental betrayal corroborates a circular connection that Eva always felt. Earlier (when she finds the body of the married woman, Rosa, who shared the hiding apartment with her family and who took her own life because her husband was deported), Eva's reaction to the forsaken lover is the same as that for the foundling child—a one-word sentence: "Abandoned" (70). When Gerry leaves her, Eva silently begs, "I won't be able to survive being abandoned again. Not again" (195). Eva's final retaliation against all those who had disappointed her is to the one key that might bring her back into the world she now defiantly leaves, turning (in her revenge) the misunderstanding that led to her rejection into a refusal to make herself understood: language. She "abandoned words" (194, 197), her silence an indictment in the very terms— broken written and verbal promises—by which she was betrayed. In both the love plot and the foundling plot, the sense of separation anxiety persists, rendering the Nazis and their racial policies subsidiary in their pain to the genealogical and sexual wounds. In terms of the separation anxiety paramount to Eva (an anxiety that diminishes the impact of what she endured in the war), Phillips himself argues that "suffering is suffering is suffering."[13] To Eva, the personal feelings—not the political ones—repeat the abjection she experienced when she was released from the camps: "Now there seems to be just me and the night and the sky" (24). There is no protective barrier, no parent to shield her from the monumental indifference of the universe, no lover to protect her from the open expanse exposing her. Ironically, this overwhelming sense of vulnerability hits her just at the beginning of her relationship with Gerry, compounding the symbiosis between child abandonment and romantic betrayal. Both dashed expectations—the first, her realization that her mother will never come back for her; the second, her understanding that Gerry never intended to wait for her—are generated by a belief in the foundational mythology of return that Phillips challenges.

If there is a double version of Eva's foundling plot, so there is a double revision of the plot in the two Venetian flashbacks: those involving Sebastian New and *Othello*. The early modern stories illustrate, first, that mythical expectation can be annulled by fabricating the loss and that the life link in the myth can be actualized (as it is for Eva in the end and for Desdemona in the play) only through a death wish. In the Portobuffole subplot, Phillips tells us a story, presumably based on history, in which we experience the reverse effect. The recovery is impossible and the loss is invented. We are faced with the specter of a fabricated conclusion from a false start: *ekphrasis* without a visual antecedent. Instead of a mound of redoubled and doubling selves, we have the compounding of nothing, yielding nothing in the end. As he moves backward from the Holocaust foundling plot to the early modern event, Phillips makes clear that Sebastian New is a sign invented to displace other signs, the history of a people. His story—the invented picture of a child—turns real people into imagined ones, signs without an original. If Sebastian New is retroactively invented and subsequently vanquished, the Jews of Portobuffole, like their Holocaust counterparts, disappear totally; all resolve themselves as "white" ash. "Valueless," Eva muses toward the end (168). Women lose the signifying markers of gender: "Her full breasts, soon to disappear. An imaginary pebble near the nipple, distorting the length. Then the sack will shrink. Shorter. And then she will become a man. No breasts. Plumes of smoke" (169). As women fuse with men and so forfeit the maternal capacity to propagate the future, so all disappear. White ash and "plumes of smoke"—the Jews evaporate.

The invented foundling child who never was merges with the real child who disappears. Sebastian New is Eva now. He is nothing to begin with. She is nothing to end with. The legend opens with the expectation of return. The women await their husbands demobilized from a war sounding like the very one that Othello fought in the other racial story of the book. The year is 1480, the city Venice, a young beggar boy enters the town and asks directions to the Jew Servadio's home. Rumors build from the brief sighting of the boy until a village "story" takes shape:

> So, even as they looked for their men, the women also kept a sharp eye open for those they did not recognize. And then, on one evening, shortly before sunset, a young beggar boy entered the town, but sadly the women did not follow him closely.
>
> The blacksmith claimed he had been busily shoeing a horse at the time that he saw the young vagabond. . . . This "male" sighting of the boy became even more important when one considers that the innocent beggar child, who that day entered the small town of Portobuffole, was never seen again. (49)

> There was no doubt that the boy had entered the house of Servadio. . . . The image of the poor boy was clear, but the name was missing and then one old woman retrieved his name from the corner of her mind. His name was Sebastian. The Jews had killed a beggar boy named Sebastian, and the precise details of this monstrous crime were on everyone's lips. They had dared to make a sacrifice in the Christian town of Portobuffole. (59)

Out of these rumors, a child sighted and waiting to be named, comes the sacrifice of the Jews and a named adult, Servadio, waiting to become unnamed, identified only as a murderer. The alleged crime becomes a real crime. Burning for burning. Old Jew, Servadio, for young Christian, Sebastian New. The actual trial and execution take place in Venice, and the story of Othello's arrival there precedes by several pages the story of Servadio's annihilation. "Later, when the flames had abated, an executioner approached with a long-handled shovel. He put it between the smoking coals and when he pulled it out it was full of white ash. He threw it into the air and it dispersed immediately" (155–56). In between the discovery of the missing child who might never have been and the trial is the arrival in Venice of

Othello and that is followed by a return to the story of Margot's sister and her disappearance, which is followed again by a historical narrative describing in the same dispassionate voice as the Portobuffole story, the effects of Zyklon B, and its mass annihilation: "All bones will have disintegrated, but some small particles may remain. The ash is white and easily scattered" (178).

The novel begins and ends with the vision of Palestine peopled by the orphans of the war, already inhabited by the uncle of the central character, Eva Stern. Uncle Stephan emigrated to Palestine before the war, letting his wife and children drift to America, where they felt safe from their Jewishness. In the opening scene, an orphaned teenager—Moshe—asks Stephan a question about genealogical continuity, a natural question given his ruptured past:

> "Do you think I will find a wife?"
> I laughed now.
> "Moshe, you will be able to choose from hundreds of pretty women." (8)

Moshe's story unfolds into one of hope as Stephan promises that the boy will find a life for himself in Palestine, with a marital love that substitutes for the parental love forever lost. The narrator refers to an American postwar fantasy, that of the camp director, Mr. Bellow:

> Mr. Bellow took a special interest in these young people—the orphaned and the unattached, as he called them—both boys and girls who were too old to be placed with families, yet too young to be treated as adults. . . . *We must endeavor to treat them as though they were our own lost children.* He could have saved his words, for most had already been quietly recruited by armed emissaries from Palestine who regularly infiltrated the camp. The majority of the "orphaned and unattached" were now *Haganah* trainees, secretly preparing themselves for a life of military service in the underground army. (4–5)

In *The Nature of Blood*, one war leads to the next. Bellow's lost children shift their allegiances and find in the Haganah the family feeling they lost. The army becomes the revenge mechanism, the instrument that replaces biological ties with an attachment to the brotherhood of the underground, a communal adoption by a band of brothers, similar to the communal adoption Eva seeks in the search for something, anything, that might replace the mother who seems to have let her simply fall away. But she does not succeed.

Toward the end of the novel, Eva remembers a day in the park with her sister, whom she hopes to recover after the war. Here the childhood fantasy is lost even as image. Eva and her sister speculate about marriage in the same way as Moshe does, imagining themselves into familial normalcy. Margot's question was posed before the war, Moshe's after. Her retrospect in the memory sequence is tainted by what she lived through as her reality overtakes the childhood dream. There is no recoverable circle. The innocent past is effaced as memory. In the fictional "reality," Margot, the lost sister, is raped by the man her family entrusted to save her. In Eva's postwar fantasy, that unknown fact nevertheless dislodges her memory. The wished-for children bear silent witness to Nazi brutality:

> Margot and I sat together in the park and watched the small children playing on the grass with their parents. . . . Margot smiled. . . . How many babies do you want, Eva? I want to have three children. Three boys. Or three girls. Or four, maybe. . . . We sat together and watched as the mothers led their children away. And then, in the distance, as the final boat nudged up against the jetty, and the park became enveloped in darkness, I saw the man take away the older children and walk them to a large ditch, where one by one they were thrown into the fire. Having dispatched the last child, he walked back to where the infants were huddled with their mothers. One by one, he picked them up by the legs and smashed them against a brick wall. The pulped corpse of the infant was then pushed back into the mother's arms to prevent unnecessary littering. I saw Margot standing with three dead babies in her arms, the blood flowing freely from their crushed heads. They were boys. Dead boys. (192–93)

Eva's projected future now involves the inevitability of the severed dream. Childhood expectation is erased. The wartime blood-pulped corpse fills in for the imagined family. The dream child vanishes in the stream of not-lived life and the real child floats away in the bloodily wanton stream of smashed connections.

In *The Nature of Blood*, there is no normal future, no recovery for loss. The love plot merges with the foundling plot as Eva's initial temptation to withdraw from isolation fills her with separation anxiety for the sequestered existence in the camps. Befriended by Gerry, a member of the liberating English army, Eva is both hopelessly attracted by his attention to her and confronted by an inner sense of disbelief that she is in any way a woman at all, that she is nothing but a "skeleton facing men." The English man offers her an apple, the forbidden fruit looming here, as it does in *Fugitive Pieces* and *Austerlitz*, both as mythical signifier and actual nourishment:

> "Anything you need, you know that you have only to ask." He pulls an apple from his pocket. "I saved this for you."
> Gerry holds out his hand and I take the apple from him. Thank you.
> He fidgets slightly. I watch him as he sways first left, then right, and then on to the outside edge of his boots.
> "You can smile you know."
> He laughs as he says this. He doesn't know that, should I attempt to smile, my face would break clean in two. (23–24)

Gerry tempts and Eva/Eve accepts the apple, knowing that it sets a bind of obligation for her. Taking the apple compels her to begin a life she cannot trust. In his shifting, Gerry emerges serpentine, moving "first left, then right, and then onto the outside edge of his boots." Like a parent coaxing a child to mimic him, Gerry urges Eva to smile. But that demand leads only to a sense of fragmentation, a feeling that the helpful hand is hurtful. The serpentine extension becomes a whiplash, smashing Eva's face in two. The nurturing parent sinks downward into the snake in the garden, the long tail of terror that leaves Eva feeling utterly alone in a vast universe. There are no buffers for war orphans.

At the end of the novel, Eva is pulled to England in the belief that Gerry offers a sustaining hand, a parent who might help her find her lost sister, and a lover who might allow her to recover her womanhood again. The racially motivated evil of the camps is replaced by the personalized evil after the camps. The snakes slither away and Eva becomes what the Nazis wanted her to be: invisible, a wisp that will vanish. But, like Eve in the garden of Eden, she is betrayed by the snake who offered her the apple. When she finally reaches England, she discovers that Gerry already has a wife there, the woman who greets her at the door of his house. Finally, Gerry levels with her:

> "The wife. Well, I told her you were a bit crackers. I'm sorry, but I had to tell her something." Please, Gerry, do not do this to me. Do not be somebody else now that you are back home.... I watched him go.... Through the window, I saw people snaking along the evening street. (195)

For Eva, all of London flows into, and hooks onto, the reptilian Gerry. "Snaking along the evening street," everyone betrays her. When, in his parlance, Gerry "cracks a smile" (194), he proceeds to characterize her as "a bit crackers" and contributes to the breakdown that signals her death. Her initial feeling of splitting in two with the offered apple now becomes the catalyst of her final disappearance. Confined to a hospital after she falls apart, she imagines herself totally disappearing. Withholding speech, she is metamorphosed. The materiality of Gerry's worm in the cocoon of their earliest encounter precipitates her evanescence as she becomes an extension of his desire to make her disappear: "I scrutinize the doctor's face, but then I realize that he cannot see, on my shoulder, the butterfly that I have become" (197).

The doctor who treats her in the hospital uses her as a case study in his definition of psychic numbing:

> *Naturally, their suffering is deeply connected to memory. To move on is to forget. To forget is a crime. How can they both remember and move on?* (157)

The doctor's analysis is correct. How can Holocaust survivors proceed with normal lives after what they have experienced? But for Eva, who attempted to move on, the forward step pushes her back into the abyss of betrayal. Gerry's act of wishing her away fuses with the Nazi desire to eliminate her. Personal and political abandonment feel the same. The dream of Margot's dead babies comes just at this juncture, in the hospital, because it is there that Eva comes to understand that the life she anticipated as a young girl can never be realized. And, similarly, it is there that she becomes aware that the promise Gerry offered—the tempting apple itself—leads to her violent expulsion from the narrative. She didn't exist in the story. Like the Jews of Portobuffole, she is expendable, a butterfly at the vanishing point. It is the double deception that hurts. She is always outside until, finally, she is outside herself.

Phillips's invented story, that Othello already has a wife, that Othello "adopts" Desdemona and Venice and therefore is disposed to disposability, renders the failure of fidelity the source of disappearance: "My friend, the Yoruba have a saying: the river that does not know its own source will dry up" (182). Liquid life, associated with continuity as I will demonstrate in the chapter on *Fugitive Pieces*, congeals in *The Nature of Blood* as it reflects the unflinching mandates of the foundling and Petrarchan plots. Water evaporates into airy nothing—the butterfly, the ashes—or thickens into blood—the slimy inescapable inherited liquid. In the book's central story, Gerry betrays Eva by letting her slip, like water, between his fingers. Margot is similarly betrayed by the "hiding parent" who rapes her: "In the morning she awoke to discover her nightgown gathered about her waist, and her face bathed in the thin spokes of light that filtered around the edge of the curtains" (176). Light "bathes," merging with the flood waters, and washes over her individuality. Water floods out her personhood. Naked below the waist, Margot prepares for being put to waste, "naked among naked strangers" (176). Her italicized questions speak to her imminent sense of triple abandonment: "*Did you think of me that morning as I stumbled naked and shivering toward my death? Did you think of me?*" (176). Is Margot's question directed at her biological parents, her hiding parents, or her sister? What she feels is her sense of being nothing to all of them. In the end, she becomes nothing to anyone. She is turned to ash and "scattered." Phillips's description of Zyklon B follows this section. Chronicling historical events in the present tense and disintegration in the future perfect tense, the narrator suggests that the white ash is always about to be scattered, poised toward extinction. And citing the liquid element—the African river Othello traded in for the Venetian canal, Margot's drenched body, and Uncle Stephan's seaside epiphany at the close of the novel—Phillips connects water to evaporation and vaporization, the same disposability he finds in *The Merchant of Venice* and *Othello*.

Desdemona's story predicts what happens to Margot and Eva, their disintegration in the material world. But the novel closes, as it opens, with Uncle Stephan, who, like Phillips's Othello, is the betrayer of family, the man who walked out by choice. The narrator writes, "He was definitely leaving his wife and child and returning to Palestine" (213). Like Othello's, Stephan's decision to abandon his familial past so that he might live in another story is at the root of narrative disposability. While Othello becomes the other nation, Stephan chooses to become his own. But that choice, too, leaves him stranded and rootless. In the last section, Stephan, the white man, allies himself with Malka, the black woman, the Ethiopian Jew, in the second chiasmic inversion of Shakespeare. Like Desdemona in Othello's eyes ("monumental alabaster," 5.2.5), Malka, in Stephan's fantasy, "was carved like a statue" (211), an image of Petrarchan perfection: the statue Pygmalion carved. We find Malka thinking in Othello's images as an alien in an adopted culture. But whereas Othello voluntarily left Africa, Malka was pulled out of her homeland. While Othello assimilates into Venetian society, Malka defies colonization:

> *This Holy land did not deceive us. The people did. The man at the hostel, he said to us, "Welcome my black brothers and sisters. You are helping us to understand what we are doing here." Is this true? Are we helping you? I know what a stamp is. I can use a telephone. I, too, can turn night into day by simply pressing a switch. I wear shoes. I have seen a highway. But please. My people never killed themselves. Hunger, yes. Disease, yes. But never this problem. During Passover, we kill a lamb and sprinkle its red blood around the synagogue. But not here. You do not allow this. You say you rescued me. Gently plucked me from one century, helped me to cross two more, and then placed me in this time. Here. Now. But why? What are you trying to prove?* (209)

Adopting the Ethiopian Jews whom they infantilize, the Israelis turn them into Othellos, the sophisticated inviting in the primitive, but the reasons are ostensibly the reverse. And while the rhetoric is "you are helping us," the Israelis see the airlift as a way of bringing the "savage" Ethiopians into the contemporary world. That "plucking" from one century to the next becomes in fact an irrevocable betrayal, like Othello's of Desdemona, into a future that has already happened.

In this instance, transplanting place means transposing time. Malka and her family enter the twentieth century and acquire by that move all the accoutrements of a European present: "I know what a stamp is. I can use a telephone." But Malka is Othello with a difference. She refuses to acclimatize. She is also Desdemona with a difference. She recognizes that Western culture promulgates a death wish. When she resists all efforts to mold her, Malka subverts the expectations of her adopters, undoing a subplot Brabanzio might expect. And there is no happy ending. The European Israelis don't really accept her as their own. She and the other Ethiopian Jews fail the bloodline test that legitimates the child in the typical foundling plot. The specific news item inspiring Phillips's invention of Malka—the dumping of Ethiopian blood donated to Israeli hospitals during the summer of 1995 that reminded Phillips about "how appallingly circular history can be" ("Blood," 4)—is absent from *The Nature of Blood*. But Malka's ruminations nevertheless reflect on "the racism of Jews toward their own black people" ("Blood," 2).[14] Like the Bavarians over the Alps for Petrarch, the Ethiopians remain the polluted opposition to "noble [Jewish] blood."

The novel's inversions (Israelis rescuing Ethiopians, Ethiopians serving Israelis, suicide/sacrifice) keep pointing backward to the violations that simultaneously fuel the symbolic expectation and disappoint it. The plotline collapses in the same way that Stephan lets go: the children just slip through his fingers. Stephan embraces Palestine instead of his wife and children. The Sterns give Margot up to the saving parents. Gerry drops Eva and replaces her with Iris, the waitress in the tea shop. Acts of sacrifice and acts of selfishness merge and substitution displaces feeling itself. "Eventually Gerry accepted that his infatuation with the [tea shop] girl was leading him nowhere but it had served the function of removing Eva from the front of his mind" (179). The narrator comments about Othello, "You conveniently forget your own family, and thrust your wife and son to the back of your mind" (181). Only Malka remains the defiant alien, uncompromisingly herself.

In the concluding equivalent of the Othello story, with its reversal of race and generation, Stephan has an epiphany that comes too late. "And he understood that people are not made to live alone, neither when things are good nor when they are bad" (212). The final wooden bench by the sea in Israel transports his thoughts back to the bench in the European garden, where Margot and Eva are playing but where he cannot hold them. Like his wife and daughter, they fall out of his grasp. "Uncle Stephan watched as they skipped away and left him alone, on the bench, his arms outstretched, reaching across the years" (213). Finally, like Giacometti's statue, *Invisible Object*, and the French play on its name, "Mains tenant le Vide / Maintenant le Vide" ("Hands Holding the Void / Now the Void"),[15] Stephan, with his arms outstretched, offers nothing and contemplates the emptiness of his life from now on. In this tableau, as an inversion of Giacometti's black mother-lover, the white father-husband recognizes what he never gave and what, from now on, he will never be able to hold. The "statue" he imagined Malka to be freezes him and, Medusa-like, locks him in the void he made of his emotional life. Malka's story jams all the arteries of the foundling and Petrarchan plots and suggests that somehow the archetypal stories are in need of revision.

Early on in the novel's *Othello* story, we see how Phillips understands that the conventions of the plot were already skewed in Shakespeare's play. Phillips's Othello contemplates his wife and puts himself in the subject position of Desdemona's father:

> I now possess an object of beauty and danger, and I know that, henceforth, all men will look upon me with a combination of respect and scorn. I also know that never again will I be fully trusted by those of my own world, both male and female, but some of this I have already anticipated. For she who has now lain with me, and before her God declared herself to be of me, this will be her first taste of a bitterness to which she may never accustom herself. That she is entirely disposable to those who profess to love her will never have occurred to her. (148–49)

Othello's sense of entitlement—his "possession" of Desdemona—renders him a double-edged yet powerful object as well. "Men will look upon me with a combination of respect and scorn." Objectification has a domino effect. He becomes someone to fear and to hate, someone who, he himself affirms, has already betrayed a trust. When Othello looks at Desdemona, he first repeats Brabanzio's initial right of ownership ("She is now mine"). Then he becomes Desdemona's father ("[She] declared herself to be of me"). He has turned her into the Petrarchan other, born *of* him. Finally, he echoes Brabanzio's right of dismissal ("She is entirely disposable to those who profess to love her").

But the narrator interprets Othello's situation somewhat differently. He offers a double scenario. In the first hypothesis, Othello is an "Uncle Tom," too eager to accommodate to Venetian mores; in the second, he is already Venetian, part of the coalition that puts gender over race as the significant demarcator. In both scenarios, Othello abandons his African family: in the former to insinuate himself as "shadow" by playing into the rules of a new society; in the latter to behave identically as Venetians always do, collaborating (as a "figment") in the elaboration of the sexual and genealogical regulatory pattern. In the "shadow" play, Othello is the "wide receiver" who fails to hold the ball and who slips into a tertiary role in the male establishment, tracing the "moves" of its female minion:

> And so you shadow her every move, attend to her every whim, like the black uncle Tom that you are. Fighting the white man's war for him / Wide receiver in the Venetian army / the republic's grinning Satchmo hoisting his sword like a trumpet / You tuck your black skin away beneath their epauletted uniform, appropriate their words (*Rude am I in speech*), their manners, worry your nappy woolen head with anxiety about learning their ways, yet you conveniently forget your own family, and thrust your wife and son to the back of your noble mind.... You are lost, a sad black man, first in a long line of so-called achievers who are too weak to yoke their past with their present; too naïve to

insist on both; too foolish to realize that to supplant one with the other can only lead to catastrophe. . . . My friend, the Yoruba have a saying: the river that does not know its own source will dry up. (183)

Othello dismisses his past and abandons wife and child to a narrative from which he exempts himself. To attempt to cross the river is to double cross it, to fail to yoke the past to the present. Like his war, his love makes him the woman to Venetian men. He "appropriates their words" not by overtaking them but by accommodating himself to the Desdemona who gives birth to the Othello she marries. The "shadowing" process is threefold: first, as sleuth, Othello follows "[Desdemona's] every move"; then, as duplicative imitator, he mimics her; finally, he becomes her spawn, black negative of her white alabaster, nesting inside her monumental being. In terms of the replacement ethos of the book, Othello is "too foolish to realize that to supplant one with the other can only lead to catastrophe." Phillips's narrator overturns the Petrarchan plot, reversing the Desdemona whom his Othello declares "of" him into the Desdemona whom he "shadows." The narrator renders him a replica of her, as earlier she had reflected him. His assessment of Othello's duplication indicates that there is nothing solid behind the mirror, a *mise-en-abyme* of shadowed inventions.

If the happy ending of the traditional foundling plot depends on never forgetting (never letting one thing stand in for another, or the art of the finding family substitute for the nature of the biological family), then Othello, as the narrator describes him, is the precursor of both Uncle Tom, the betrayer of his race, and Uncle Stephan, the betrayer of his family. Othello fails because he relies too much on self-creation and ends up condemned as a "figment of a Venetian imagination" (183), the mirror mirrored as a signifier of Petrarchan emptiness. That puzzling epithet relates to the narrator's final indictment of Othello. Denying his origin in order to match his invention, Othello's accommodation itself is to an invention: an image created by defining the self in terms of another originally defined by the self. Like Stephan, who mimics the unyielding statue of his own design, Phillips's Othello has no existence other than as a spin-off of his own image making, just as Eva has no existence apart from the shadowy butterfly that prefigures her death.

For a brief moment, however, Eva comes to believe in the saving grace of adoption, living out (in her mind) an expanded version of the middle section of the plot that produces an intergenerational nurturing that allows her to mother her mother in the fantasy of the burial mound and then, in her expectations of Gerry, an intergender support that encourages her foolishly to believe in Gerry's empty promises. Of his own journey in writing *The Nature of Blood*, Phillips concludes that the "fragmented obsessional task . . . had enabled me to achieve a moment of temporary reconciliation with the young Dutch boy of my story of twenty-five years ago and to repay a small part of the personal debt I owed to the remarkable young girl in Amsterdam whose portrait sits framed above [his] desk" ("Blood," 7). Phillips thus uses the mythology with an understanding that he says derives from music, particularly Beethoven's Sixth Symphony. "I can whistle the whole symphony *now*. . . . I know every single moment, because it's about how you score emotion basically—how you move and keep a theme going. You keep going forward, but [you keep] reminding us where we've been; there's a viable parabola" (Clingman, "Other Voices," 130). In Eva's butterfly transformation and Phillips's memory of his early story, both leap—out of a cocoon, from a speeding railway car—in order "to remind [themselves]" of a past thought forever lost and a mythology thought forever elusive.

Such imagined recoveries revise the middle interlude of the foundling plot, not as an artistic invention of an immobilizing force but rather as a pastoral of the mind, peopled with noble Dutch farmers and saving earthen mounds. Both returns are fabulations, versions faintly connected to reality but doomed from the start because the plot itself depends on the authority of bloodlines, which, in turn, become part of the ideology that led to the midtwentieth-century horrors structuring Phillips's narrative. It is only in Phillips's creation of Malka, who refuses to be drawn into the fold, that we find another possibility, a reformulation of the form itself. The traditional ending of the foundling story recovers an essentially conservative foundation that depends on returning to the *status quo ante*. The typical ending of the Petrarchan plot depends on its remaining a quest with no end, one based on replication of an originative ideal. But Malka's resistance takes its shape as she asserts a subjectivity that interrogates the hierarchies of those normative forms. In emphasizing the fact that Eva finds herself only in death, Phillips demonstrates how her resistance is confined by the limits of Western culture: all the excitement of metamorphosis is reducible to a shadow; all the recoveries in the variants of the foundling plot reiterate an illusory past. But through Malka's insistence on remaining outside the circle, Phillips reveals the double bind implicit in his title where "blood" as "nature" also resists art as culture. There is no evading the bloodline connection except by subverting the expected intervention of art: "You say you rescued me. Gently plucked me from one century, helped me to cross two more and then placed me in this time. Here. Now. But why? What are you trying to prove?" Malka asks.

In the conventional foundling plot, the rescue is spatial and the intervening time usually moves backward, primitive country instead of sophisticated court. Here the so-called rescue is from the desert as the Ethiopians who "lived as farmers and weavers" (200) are transported and "herded" (200) like cattle until they "graz[ed] on concrete," the stony wall that yields no nurture. But Malka's defiant questions, like Eva's persistent silence, demand a set of alternatives to our cultural fixations. Desexualizing their relationship, she repudiates the Petrarchan statue Stephan molds even as, in a reversal of the scenario, she escapes the configurations of the foundling plot. Malka remains hostile to the mythologies of both narratives just as Eva, having failed to recover her mother and to achieve the love that might have sustained her, refuses to go on. Their defiance challenges the scenario that shapes them. Their recalcitrance demands other stories.

In *Ark Baby*, Liz Jensen similarly demonstrates an awareness of the devastating material consequences of the Western mythological heritage, identifying a scientific corollary for the genealogical stratification that worked itself out so relentlessly in the middle of the twentieth century. She takes the Petrarchan and foundling plots into another category—science fiction—as she points to an answer to the selective genetics of Darwinian theory simultaneously as she indicates an alternative to the linguistic hierarchies fostered by the mythical heritage she too challenges. While Phillips's timeline collapses from the mid-twentieth century to the early modern period, Jensen advances to the twenty-first century and then slides backward to the middle of the nineteenth century—with Charlotte Brontë and Charles Darwin—and even to a specific year relevant to both scientist and novelist: 1845. But, like Phillips, she questions the forms that shape and bind her nineteenth- and twenty-first-century protagonists to the determinism of ancient—biblical and classical—caste and class systems.

NOTES

1. "Extravagant Strangers," *A New World Order: Essays* (New York: Random House, 2002), 288.
2. Robert J. Lifton and Eric Markussen's term for the "cast of mind that created and maintains the threat of nuclear weapons" and that defines "the general nature of nuclear entrapment and then seeks insight from a major genocide that has already taken place." See *The Genocidal Mentality: Nazi Holocaust and Nuclear Threat* (New York: Basic, 1990), 1.
3. "Blood." Unpublished essay 1997, sent to me by Caryl Phillips, 2.
4. "BLOODY HISTORY! Exploring a Capacity for Revision, Restaging History in Wilson Harris's *Jonestown* and Caryl Phillips's *The Nature of Blood*," *Jouvert* 6, 3 (2002): 3.
5. "Other Voices: An Interview with Caryl Phillips," *Salmagundi* 143 (2004): 128.
6. Bénédicte Ledente reads the characters of Othello and Stephan much more positively: "Of the three consciousnesses explored in the novel, Stephan is the one who most successfully manages the labyrinth of his own existence." See "A Fictional and Cultural Labyrinth: Caryl Phillips's *The Nature of Blood*," *Ariel* 32, 1 (2001): 189.
7. *The Differend: Phrases in Dispute*, translated by G. Van den Abeele (Minneapolis: University of Minnesota Press, 1988), 5.
8. As quoted by Peter Haidu. Haidu explains, "Himmler's discourse is *unheimlich* because it reproduces, with all nuances and paradoxes in place, the discourses we know as the discourses of poetry, policy, of idealism and religion, of administration and bureaucracy." "The Dialectics of Unspeakability: Language, Silence and the Narratives of Desubjectification," *Probing the Limits of Representation: Nazism and the Final Solution*, edited by Saul Friedlander (Cambridge, MA: Harvard University Press, 1992), 292.
9. "'The Extravagant and Wheeling Stranger': The Othello Figure in Caryl Phillips's *The Nature of Blood*," *Confronto Letterario* 16 (1999): 15.

10. *Pre-empting the Holocaust* (New Haven, CT: Yale University Press, 1998), 122.
11. "Forms of History and Identity," *Salmagundi* 143 (2004): 162.
12. *The Ethics of Identity* (Princeton, NJ: Princeton University Press, 2005), ii.
13. Unpublished interview with Lars Eckstein, quoted by Bénédicte Ledente in "Caryl Phillips's *The Nature of Blood*," *Contemporary World Writers* (Manchester and New York: Manchester University Press, 2002), 167.
14. "According to the *International Herald Tribune*, it appeared that black Jews in Israel had been giving blood in the hope that it might be used to save somebody's life. However, the Israeli government, fearful of 'diseases' that might be contained in this blood, had instructed the medical teams to dump the 'black' blood. This 'secret' practice had now been exposed, and the black Jews were rioting and demanding that this racist practice be stopped. I could barely believe what I was reading. This, it turned out, was the story that would enable me to put the final piece of the narrative puzzle into place and finish my novel" ("Blood," 2).
15. Toni Stoos and Patrick Elliott, *Alberto Giacometti, 1901–66 Exhibit Catalogue for the Royal Academy of Art* (London: 1996), 154.

Chapter Two

The Irigarayan "Third Language" in Liz Jensen's *Ark Baby*

Though critically successful,[1] Liz Jensen's 1998 *Ark Baby* has been overlooked by scholars. But it plays an important role in what Caryl Phillips suggests is the current formal "reinvention" of traditional British fiction.[2] Reading backward from Jensen's questions about Darwinian hierarchical structures, which she enfolds within the foundling plot of her novel, we can find an anticipatory match for Tobias Phelps (her hero, genetically engineered by the novel's villain [Horace Trapp], who mated his mother with a monkey to solve the problem of the nineteenth-century end of the slave trade) in *Merchant of Venice*. There, Graziano portrays Shylock as a "currish spirit / Governed [by] a wolf" (4.1.133–34) who infused himself while the "currish Jew" (4.1.287) was still in the womb of his "unhallowed dam" (4.1.135). Further, if Shylock's alleged animal breeding suggests that he— along with all Jews—should be eliminated from civil society, Tobias has another Shakespearean counterpart destined to survive and serve, as Trapp intended with Phelps, for the purposes of personal enrichment. "Got by the devil himself / Upon [his] wicked dam" (1.2.322–23), Caliban is saved from his "vile race" (1.2.361) only by the self-proclaimed "good nature" (1.2.362) of Prospero, who enslaves him just as Trapp planned to use the unborn Tobias.

Jensen also reverses the direction of the Petrarchan chase and outlines a "biunivocal engendering" that resembles that of a very early Shakespeare play where a wife bypasses the Irigarayan "vertical axis" between generations by arguing defiantly that it is less important than the "horizontal axis that joins the sexes," as Adriana does in *The Comedy of Errors*, an example of what Shakespeare will flesh out in extended form in the relationship of

Perdita and Florizel in *The Winter's Tale*. Very much like the heroine does in *Ark Baby*, Adriana wrests from the Abbess (in fact, Antipholus's mother) the right to nurture her husband:

> I will attend my husband, be his nurse,
> Diet his sickness, for it is my office,
> And will have no attorney but myself.
> And therefore let me have him home with me. (5.1.98–102)

With her insistence, Adriana commands all the characters onstage so that the twins might find each other and, in the recognition scene, discover their biological roots. A similar scene is orchestrated by the heroine of *Ark Baby*, who facilitates a recovery of the hero's birth and a reconciliation with his adoptive parents. Thus, Jensen's forays into science fiction[3] reveal Shakespearean precedents for a cultural reformulation that challenges the expected paradigms of both the foundling and Petrarchan plots.

Setting the novel in two eras eight generations apart—1845 and 2005—Jensen pairs the scientific idea of evolution and its expectation for survival of the presumably fittest with the foundling plot and its formula for the salvation of the arguably weakest. The plot and the theory evidence the same trust in a hierarchical structure, the myth returning backward to a socially superior biological origin, the theory moving forward to a genetically improved biological destiny. Challenging the plot that she uses and questioning the optimistic distinctions generated by the concept of evolution, Jensen critiques a value system established at the height of British empire building. Thus, despite her credentials as British born and educated, Jensen can be considered among that group of writers whom Phillips calls "outsiders" ("Extravagant Strangers," 297). She counters the doubly positive end of theory and story even as she injects another mythical and scientific doubling—the biblical chapter of Noah's ark and the global extinction it thematizes with its more recent equivalent, the possibility of the end of all planetary life through weaponry or chemically induced sterility made all the more probable by the mechanics of late modern scientific cleverness, in turn a result of Darwinian belief in the words that Jensen interprets ironically: *survival* and *fittest*. The most successful doubling in the book is the one of the Irigarayan "exchange between two subjects" that opens to a "third language" simultaneously created in the principal love story of the book and then somehow negated as possibility by the harsh truths of twenty-first-century realities that signal the novel's opening and to which the novel returns at the end. Irigaray explains the necessity for such a linguistic reformulation in an interview with Brena Niorelli:

> For years I've been saying that a double subjectivity, a double truth, a double world exist. Doubling, which corresponds to a reality, implies a different way of speaking, a *dialogical* way which takes into consideration both man's way

and woman's way of speaking. Such a language doesn't conform to traditional Western logic, with its complement: poetry. It unfolds between two modes of speaking, two languages, man's and woman's. The exchange between two subjects creates a third language, a language that we still don't know, that is yet to be created.[4]

Irigaray's tripled doubling—of subjectivity, truth, and world—widens into the "dialogical way" of a discourse that expands because it involves both man's and woman's way of speaking. But the doubling she evokes also narrows with a dark undertow that threatens to collapse the enlarged vista and its actualization in a form of usable discourse. The secondary meaning of "doubling" suggests a shiftiness or sleight of hand that blocks the release Irigaray believes possible. The absent voice in what she advocates—the woman's—has yet to become part of the cultural legacy that is established in "logic, with its complement: poetry," because its inception requires a counterforce strong enough to challenge the linguistically ingrained, firmly fixed structures of its hold. The infusion demands, as Irigaray argues, an "exacting cultural effort" ("Introduction," *Why Different*, 10) on the part of women. For Irigaray the give and take of the hoped-for dialogic stagnates at present in all male giving and all male taking—a one-way street that cancels the evolution of a "different way of speaking." The female is still enclosed in itself; it has still to *unfold*, to open up to the possibility of the third language. "Unfold[ing]" suggests a latency, a hidden bud that has yet to flower into the release it might augur. In that regard, the heroine of *Ark Baby* finds the courage and the voice that loosens the mythological straitjackets—of the Petrarchan and foundling plots (part of the "traditional Western logic and ... poetry" Irigaray cites)—and so frees the hero. Though Jensen recognizes that something akin to the Irigarayan "third" language involves a utopian vista undone by the contemporary story with which the novel opens, she nevertheless evokes in the main plot of the book an "unfolding" that might bring such a language into being.

That redirection occurs in the *chronological* beginning of the novel where one of the heroes seems to have found a way out of the mythological trap, a pathway that appears through yet another allusion—the Jonah story—which Jensen uses to challenge the stratifications of both the foundling and Petrarchan plots as well as the biological hierarchies of Darwinism. The story of Jonah involves no distinctions. Signifying absolute forgiveness and "sparing," the myth demonstrates the possibility for unreserved, even undeserved, grace. Like the book of Jonah, *Ark Baby* has one unexplainable object in it: the gourd that appears at key points as a Winnicottian transitional object.[5] The dying mother in the novel's central story asks her adopted son, Tobias Phelps, to plant one on her grave so that she can take "the memory of [him] with [her] where [she] goes" (90). "I love that gourd," she croaked. "It is a freakish vegetable, without obvious purpose, but it has its place in our garden. God knew what he was doing when he made the gourd. . . . That gourd, in its oddity and freakishness, reminds me of you" (90). The gourd's "freakishness" undoes conventionalized Petrarchan standards embedded in the cultural constructs Jensen challenges. In the crucial love story of the novel, the one that defies both the emphasis on the genealogical aristocratic mandate of the foundling plot and the male-generated primacy of the Petrarchan poetic, Jensen offers yet another answer to Darwinian stratification, one concurring with Irigarayan ideas about the necessity for transformation of our social ordering in the third language she envisions. If Darwin theorizes a biological change, Irigaray counters with a constructed one: "The fixed base of a traditional society, the family, only survives because of mutations that reshape its norms and values" (*Between East and West*, 133). In *Ark Baby*, the critical "mutation" is possible because Violet—the hero's lover in the foundling plot—enacts the "exacting cultural effort" (*Why Different*, 10) and provides a glimpse into the "mutual engendering" that Irigaray proposes as a way of paving over "the fault line in the construction of history"[6] connected to Darwinian hierarchies, a fault line Phillips locates in the early modern period and which Jensen situates in the middle of the nineteenth century.

Like everything else in *Ark Baby*, the biblical myth of Jonah with its retrospective forgiveness sets in motion an opposite theory, one that proposes we cannot simply erase the past: it is woven too tightly into the fabric of the present simply to disappear. In *Ark Baby*, the juxtapositions play themselves out in the interconnected lives of the two narrators, Tobias Phelps, born in 1845, who does everything in his power to avoid learning about his biological ancestry, and Buck de Savile, reborn in 2005 as a self-created foundling who does not "give a monkey's about the future" (43). The narrators end up quite literally related through a series of unlikely occurrences revealing a very improbable mating (of a human with a monkey that produced Phelps) in the year 1845, the approximate time when Charlotte Brontë was writing *Jane Eyre*, the novel whose narrative voice Tobias Phelps continually mimics. Each of Jensen's intertwining stories returns to the same crucial year that determines all subsequent happenings in the novel: the moment when the Darwinian mutation occurs, not by chance, but by the deliberate plotting that results in the creation of Phelps.

Both narrators find their way back to an Irigarayan past in the year 1845: Phelps to an understanding of the true facts about his birth parents that he tried to avoid knowing; and de Savile to a recovery of the scientific paper about the origin of the whole species that he pursues assiduously. The article in question undermines the theory of evolution and offers an alternative to Darwin's idea of gradual progression. The author of that paper, Dr. Ivanhoe

Scrapie, maintains that his thesis is confirmed by Tobias Phelps's mere being. When they first meet, Scrapie explains his theory to Phelps, imploring him

> [to] imagine this as the answer to Darwin's time paradox: that man did not evolve slowly from a gorilla or chimpanzee. He appeared suddenly, like Adam and Eve in the Bible. Just one. A freak cross-breed. From two completely different—and perhaps incompatible—species. Two species that would perhaps otherwise not have *survived*! That would have *died out*! Two wrongs, therefore, Mr. Phelps, making a right! You are living proof that it's possible. (284)

If Phelps is the nineteenth-century "living proof" of the theory, de Savile is the twenty-first-century retriever of the theory and its "hitherto undreamed-of missing link" (290). Renaming Scrapie's unknown treatise after himself, de Savile twice asserts his importance. His doubling involves creative deception and procreative multiplication. First, he forges a scientific paper, based on Scrapie's insights, and then he spawns two sets of twins through his simultaneous fling with sisters, themselves twins, who happen to be Scrapie's great-grandchildren. With those acts, de Savile recuperates, regenerates, and perpetuates Scrapie's refinement of Darwin's "Theory of Evolution," claiming ownership both of a family and an intellectual property.

The novel shifts between the lives of the intertwined narrators: the earlier, Tobias Phelps, born in 1845, resembling Steven Spielberg's "E.T." in his charm and goodness; and his avatar, Buck de Savile, tied by paternity eight generations after Tobias to the same family tree. Having given up his former life, de Savile "emerged from the caterpillar that was Bobby Sullivan" (48) to become "the son of Elvis," who died the day he was born: "Like a phoenix, he was just waiting for me to come along, I reckon. Knowing he could hand over" (4). De Savile's self-defensive name changing along with his rehabilitation of Scrapie's theory as his own constitutes one of several wanted and unwanted births and rebirths in the book, each one following the centuries-old plot of the foundling. In de Savile's case, the aristocratic bent of the foundling plot manifests itself in the invention of a glamorous past. What lover of rock music would not want to be the son of Elvis?

But countering de Savile's annexation of a culturally superior ancestry is the central event that triggers the novel: a postmillennium fertility crisis. When the novel opens, no child has been born in the British Isles since the year 2000. Evolutionary progress is devoluted by what Robert Lowell, comparing the Nazi death camps to Darwinism's "irreversible liquidation,"[7] identifies as the toll of the concept of "survival of the fittest." In compensation for their losses, childless women adopt monkeys and treat them as human babies, dressing the females in pink with "the obligatory nappy beneath" (5). That "island" crisis is extended in the novel with the line from Donne's

"Meditation 17," which keeps recurring as a thematic element, like the gourd: "No man is an island, entire of itself! . . . Every man is a piece of the continent, a part of the main" (*Ark Baby*, 116, 117, 337).

Along with the question of natural extinction, *Ark Baby* offers another alternative to the formula, one that offsets the generic assumption of foundling plots: that the discovery of the biological parents—the reconciliation at the end—is what frames the happy ending. In its valorization of the middle interlude, Jensen's novel asks us to embrace the nurturing along with the originating parents. But the novel undertakes an Irigarayan double twist there as well, conferring on the biological antecedents a status based neither on intelligence nor wealth but on a higher ethical standard, one that fades out by the time the novel ends so that the twin granddaughters of Phelps—the intelligent, good man—turn out to be rather stupid and extremely venal inheritors of his seed. Thus, even in her reevaluation of evolution, Jensen asks us to think again both about the optimism of the scientific theory and the literary form. The foundling theme with its return to an earlier, higher social status countermands the theory of evolution and its expectation for improvement to a subsequently superior genetic constitution. In its forward thrust, the theory of "survival of the fittest" implies that the background can be outpaced by the foreground. Contrarily, the foundling plot proposes a retrograde perfection: the antecedents are always hierarchically better. Thus, Jensen thrice reinvents the form: first, by showing that the finding parents are critical to the hero's permanent sense of well-being and therefore cannot be effaced; second, by suggesting that the biological parents are genetically *inferior* to the adoptive parents, thereby seeming to support the theory of evolution; and third, subverting both the theory and the form, by offering a new definition of what constitutes superiority. But with each variation, Jensen asks still further questions.

The myth and the theory pull against each other. What if the recovered biological predecessors demand a totally other standard of proof? What if the Darwinian future points to a completely different idea of progression? Both these questions are rendered ironic by Tobias Phelps's archaic narrative style, his repeated invocation of the "dear reader," imitating Jane Eyre and her attempts to suture the audience into her biography. Jane Eyre's is a reversed-gender version of Phelps's story. Like Eyre, Phelps is totally unglamorous and, like Rochester, his lover is far from perfect. At the opposite extreme of the "quaint" voice of Phelps is the "hip talk" of de Savile, who, fusing the language of contemporary criminal aviation terror tactics with the ancient story of fictional abandoned children, undercuts the novel's "upbeat" impulse with the dark underside of nineteenth-century optimism: "My future was about to be hijacked by someone else's past" (5). The novel jettisons forward only to remind us continually of the necessary connection, a history we might perhaps prefer to deny.

TRADUCING ORIGINS, REDUCING DESTINIES

Unlike some foundling heroes who struggle against odds to find their biological parents, Tobias Phelps—sensing something is wrong—prefers to remain in the dark about his biological inheritance. At the central moment of the book, Phelps explains his adolescent reluctance:

> I was a fifteen-year-old who stared, and wondered, and made assumptions, and who signally failed to do the one thing he should have done, which would have possibly saved him so much grief. I did not insist on knowing.
> In short, I was a coward. And I was a coward because I feared the truth. And this, as you will see, dear reader, has been my story. A fear, a lack of courage, because of a further fear, that the thing itself, the truth, will be so unacceptable that—.
> "That what?" she asked me, years later, as we stared into our favourite rockpool.
> "That I will be rejected. And that you will not love me. That no one will."
> (176)

In one of the many flash forwards of *Ark Baby*, we learn that there is a beloved and that there is a future "us" for Tobias Phelps, the "she" who questioned "years later" and who formulaically does love the hero. Tobias and the curious "she" stare into a rock pool that yields the double image of the recovered and the soon-to-be-prolific pair. In that sense, his story fits into the usual foundling plot even as it reverses the Petrarchan emphasis on the romantic loss that facilitates the recovery of linguistic presence. Phelps is not rejected. Like Jane Eyre, he speaks to us, the "dear readers" of the nineteenth-century novel he lives, and to his beloved, the dear lover, whom he will find coterminously with the revelation of his origin. The fear Tobias voices that "no one will [love him]" is annulled by the usual marriage that reconciles the foundling to his past and that promises the genealogical continuity essential to the plot. But at the same time, the rock pool doubling rejects the Petrarchan image of the replicated single self. In listening to Tobias, Violet suggests something about what Irigaray calls "the creativity that difference produces, making it possible for each to be engendered naturally and spiritually by the other" (*I Love to You*, 146). The doubled reflection in the rock pool replaces the narcissistic attenuated self with the expanding image even as the mirrored pair will soon produce a child to continue the widening arc, forming an imagistic equivalent of the Irigarayan third language that Jensen evolves through Phelps and Violet but then retracts in her depiction of their offspring's evolutionary devolution.

The second narrator of the novel, Buck de Savile (a.k.a. Bobby Sullivan), lives in 2005, during the time of the "Fertility Crisis" (11) in England. De Savile's destiny, therefore, renders him a reverse foundling, taken out of his present by a historical event in the past that becomes his future. His loss is an inversion of Tobias Phelps's history. Phelps evades origins and is saved. De Savile relinquishes both his known and invented past and becomes a savior, the source of new life. Although Phelps is initially ignorant about his genealogy, de Savile fosters children who will fossilize his earlier identity. Each of the narrators is twice lost. Phelps's adoptive parent abandons him. De Savile chooses Elvis as his biological father but, in the end, he severs all connections with anything remotely ancestral. In this novel, the so-called recovery involves a different biological destiny: a radical change of the gene pool. The element that returns Tobias Phelps to his past eventuates into the fusionary device that changes Buck de Savile's generational future. Having discovered the so-called missing link in the Darwinian theory, de Savile ends up perpetuating the bond by fathering the eighth-generation twins, descendants of Tobias, whose father—a monkey—produced the child adopted in 1845 by the hitherto childless Phelps family. Impotent because of a childhood phobia, Pastor Phelps achieves his paternity only through adoption. De Savile proves so virile that he saves the entire English nation from childlessness with the offspring who, in their turn, will regenerate the island nation. "This is the future," intones the omnipresent and house-haunting voice of Scrapie's long-dead wife—the great-great-great-grandmother of the double set of twins with which de Savile's story ends. "Do your best to deserve it" (335).

Jensen's alterations of the foundling plot, her wreaking havoc with the typical recovery by redefining aristocracy, and her juggling of the middle interlude by rendering the finding parent a secondary abandoner simultaneously suggest that the formula and its assumptions (Why are the biological parents superior? Why are the founding parents forgotten?) can be redefined and that the basic thrust of generational continuity can be altered by another possibility: What if the optimistic ending, with a secure dynastic future made possible by the recovered past, were blocked? Her next hypothesis includes an equally frightening possibility: What if we survive? Meeting the challenge that the atomic bomb and DNA research impose, she questions: What if the future emerges as biologically impossible, not just genetically altered for the better by Darwinian expectation but also thrown back in some major way? And, further, what if we were forced to undergo a "period of mourning for what never was" (260)? A future based on an imagined past parallels the parabola of the foundling plot where the recovery annuls the life already believed to have been lived to affirm instead the possibility of a past never experienced, a déjà vu of what might have been. Each of the stories in *Ark Baby* imagines the end of the human chain and then each undoes the end, leaving us with the identical paradox: What is the advantage of continuity? Both central narrators originally face the same future. Phelps expects never to "produce an offspring of [his] own, after what Dr. Scrapie had said about the nature of the hybrid" (342); and the second story begins in 2005, in an

England with no human child born since the millennium, a country that finds itself in an "evolutionary cul-de-sac" (40), a euphemism for what is the dead end of an "Extinction crisis. People looking backward, rather than forward. Going a bit doo-lally over history" (128). Jensen uses the fertility problem to refer to the two other myths connected to her story—Noah and the endgame of inundation, and Jonah, with the threatened condemnation of Nineveh and temporary imprisonment in the belly of the whale. When his foster mother is dying, Tobias combines the two: "That night I dreamed I was aboard a vessel that was like a whale inside. I was Jonah but a son of Noah too. My job was to feed the caged beasts that surrounded me—tigers and hippopotami and the giant wingless birds—but I could not for I too was caged and manacled like a slave" (88).

In point of fact, Tobias's nightmare is his history. He was created as a slave, destined to be bound and manacled like the creatures in his dream ark. At the sociohistorical center of the novel is the crisis of 1845, the indisputable moral dead end of the slave trade and the need, therefore, for an alternative supply of cheap labor to keep the Western economy going. Mating Tobias's mother with a monkey to create what Prospero attempted to shape in Caliban, Trapp planned to produce a subspecies who could do the "dirty work" of slaves. Trapp lured Tobias's mother onto a boat he called *The Ark*, partly because he anticipated the political end of forced labor and partly because he lost out on a lucrative deal himself when his slave business failed in an accident at sea. Tobias's birth mother explains Trapp's plan:

> "He had this theory. After the scandal over his dead slaves and the campaign to have the trade abolished, he'd been hatching this plan to mate a human with a monkey, to get an offspring. To breed a new kind of slave, that's not completely human. 'A race of natural inferiors,' he calls it. If you're not strictly speaking a man, see," she said, "you haven't got no rights like men does."
> I gasped.
> "But why?" I asked.
> "Profit," murmured my new-found mother. "He was after making a profit. He'd seen the slave trade coming to an end. He reckoned the problem all along with the human slaves was that they'd end up with the same rights as other folk. The only way to ever get that kind of cheap labor again without a big hoo-ha was to create—"
> "I see," I said. (319)

The irony is that the middle interlude of the foundling plot also coincides with the historical reality of using children—through apprenticeship, wardship, workhouses—to run the economy, an irony that (as I suggest in chapter 5) plays itself out in the Lancelot story of *The Merchant of Venice*. Contrasted with Parson Phelps's sentimental notion that he was a rescuer of "a foundling babe whose own mother has attacked it and thrown it from the nest like a vicious herring gull" (23) and his resolution to be "the best father a boy ever had" (23) is Trapp's aim—to foster a child who could work like a workhorse. Grateful for the foundling creature he discovers, Parson Phelps not only vows to be a good father but also thanks God. Little Tobias Phelps had a happy childhood. "Like Jesus, and many other small boys whose parents dote on them, I grew up being told that I was 'a Gift from heaven'" (26).

The alternative to Jesus, the "gift from heaven," is another gift from heaven, Noah's rainbow. Having named his boat *The Ark* and fearing that "human slaves [would] end up with the same rights as other folk" (319), Trapp seeks to perpetuate the Noah story as he attempts to create a species to solidify the hierarchical structure that the biblical plot validates and make it work for him. Tobias Phelps buys into that myth, which his stepparent earnestly taught him, as we see from his description of a picture that hung in his room:

> And on the wall a picture I love: of Noah and his animals of the Ark. Noah stands on the deck, with his three sons and his nagging wife, and below him is spread the hierarchy of creatures, from mighty elephant down to humble ant. Looking down on them all from the top right-hand corner is the face of an elderly gent whose white beard dissolves into the grey storm-clouds of the Great Flood. Behind his head, a silver Heaven gleams. This is God, who has made us all. . . .
>
> Then I speak. "So according to this picture, man's place is between God and the animals." . . .
>
> "Why is a big question," says the Parson, smiling stiffly. "And it has a big answer. It's because we have souls, and the animals do not." (87)

The Noah story is doubly hierarchical. Against the fate of total annihilation lies the idea of the "clean and the unclean," an intraspecies caste system. Then, over and above that structure, is an interspecies stratification, with man at the helm. The foundling plot narrows the field with its happy ending based solely on a human social structure, caste and class determining the outcast. When, in creating Tobias, Trapp uses the Gentleman Monkey, he unexpectedly generates a new value system, one that cuts across both social and biological lines of demarcation. Describing Tobias's father, his mother, a contortionist from a traveling circus, tells him:

> [Trapp] hadn't bargained on my gentleman friend. . . . He loved life so much. . . . He was so funny, so clever, so innocent. So good-hearted. He was all instinct. I realised as soon as I saw him in the light of day that he wasn't a man. I never pretended he was. . . . He was more than a man. . . . [A]nd he was better than a man. . . . He laid down his life for us. . . . He wasn't called a gentleman for nothing. (319–20)

The Gentleman Monkey overturns the theory of genetic superiority twice—in himself and in his offspring Tobias. Rather than remaining "natural inferiors" (319), father and son each turn out to be morally "better than a man" (320). The outcome renders Tobias the opposite of centuries-old myths perpetuated against genetic outsiders like Tobias.

The cultural assumptions earlier mentioned about the disposable evil of Shylock and Caliban's usable inferiority both parallel Trapp's designs for the monkey-child he would breed as a slave. His name turns the ark that he builds into a "ship of fools," his "trap," a boat headed for death. Countering such genetic presumptions, Jensen creates in Tobias Phelps a character so lovable after a beginning so improbable that it is hard not to cheer him on. Embedding the biblical myth, *Ark Baby* illustrates how even its victims subscribe to its cultural inevitability.

Jensen's other reversal of the foundling plot involves a second loss that counters the tenacity of the saving parent. In most foundling stories, the middle-interlude saviors are wiped from the picture only when the biological parents are found. Like the seven dwarfs to Snow White, who remain steadfastly loyal until the prince takes her away, the saving parents become redundant and disappear. Not only does Tobias initially lose the biological parents he never knew but he is also painfully separated from his adoptive parents. Despite his efforts to be the good man, Parson Phelps succumbs to his faith in genetic stratification, rendering Darwinism an equivalent of Noah's story. Having learned of Tobias's father, Parson Phelps rejects his adopted son. Explaining why Phelps refuses to see Tobias, his physician, Dr. Baldicoot, answers, "I fear he still has no wish to see you. He has developed what I consider to be an unhealthy obsession with your origins" (209).

Tobias's dream, then, becomes a quest to recover his adoptive father: "I was suddenly filled with an immeasurable sadness, not only that my father might die, but that our relationship should be so soured by principles I could not understand" (208). In the sanatorium for pastors who had come unhinged because of Darwinism, Parson Phelps is admonished that "all children are gifts from heaven." Remaining adamant in his rejection of his adopted son, he replies to the clerical principal who had taken charge of his case, in terms reminiscent of Antonio's appellation of Shylock as the "devil [who] cite[s] scripture" (1.3.94), "Not this one. . . . He is from Hell!" (220). In response to his second abandonment, Tobias loses faith in his ability to find romantic love: "I would one day like a wife. . . . But I am prune-Face, Fartybockers. Hobble-de Hoy. The Bookworm. Only a blind woman would ever want me as a husband!" (207).

Twice bereft of parental love, Tobias thinks himself unlovable. Yet, despite his fears, he stages his own version of the traditional recognition scene. Confronting Scrapie, whom he believes could tell him the secret of his physiognomy, he takes his fate in his own hands:

> I'm pointing my revolver at him. My hand is shaking. Dr. Scrapie freezes.
> I can hear how thin and desperate my voice sounds. Like a tin whistle.
> I say, "You will do it, sir, or I shall blow your head off, and then my own!"
> Yes! a man at last! (271)

In most foundling fiction, the lost child learns of his biological heritage through a series of accidents or because the parent—like Ceres for Proserpine—keeps searching. Here, Tobias forces the issue, building on hints that he earlier could not face. But in finding his past, he comes to understand both that the contortionist abandoned him to save him and why Phelps went mad at the thought that the child that he saved might find his actual father. What he learns is that his biological mother and his finding father conspire to prevent him from discovering his ancestry:

> No wonder her visit had put the seal on my poor father's madness: shortly after the *Origin of Species* had rocked the Christian world, Parson Phelps had had his own, personal version of the crisis. I could imagine his distress on discovering that he had taken a half-monkey to his bosom all those years. He, who had so railed against the very idea of our origins being anything other than stated in the Bible! If you know of anything crueller than that, gentle reader, I would like to hear about it. (325–26)[8]

When Tobias meets his birth mother in the presence of his dead father, preserved through Scrapie's taxidermy and serving as a towel holder in Queen Victoria's bathroom, he demands proof of his origins. His mother provides the usual talismans, the equivalents of the birthmarks so central to the foundling convention:

> "How do I know you're not lying?" I asked her, weakly, in a sudden, last-minute attempt to make myself believe the whole thing was a falsehood....
> "You don't," she was saying. "I *might* be lying. Perhaps I wishes I was. But I bet you've a scar at the base of your spine. And a couple of strangely shaped feet stuffed into those fancy shoes of yours."
> I could not deny it.
> So here I was, at last, in the company of my two long-lost natural parents. Was that not something? I looked at my father. Despite being a towel-holder, he looked smart, I thought, in his ruffed shirt and his red pantaloons. There was nobility in the way he stood. And why not? He had after all died in an act of bravery, attempting to save the lives of a woman and her unborn child. (326)

If, in the nineteenth-century versions of the theme, wealth substitutes for royalty, here is another definition altogether, one based on a hierarchy neither of bloodline nor of achievement. Thus, the Gentleman Monkey "looked smart" and appeared noble not only in the attire signifying dignity but also in his desire to save "the lives of a woman and her unborn child" (326). Goodness of purpose determines genetic value.

Violet acknowledges that standard when she declares her love for Tobias. Warning him that he must escape with her quickly or risk becoming a specimen to prove Scrapie's theory, she hesitates:

> She did not answer my question immediately. Instead she looked me in the face and said slowly and delicately, "Mr. Phelps, I am—*aware*—of your true origins."
> Oh God. My heart plummeted to the floor. . . .
> "And?" I was quivering. "Do you—?"
> "Of course!" she cried. "I love you all the more!" (329)

That extraordinary passage—as Tobias waits for an answer and as Violet acknowledges the nobility she understands to come from behavior and not from biology—cements the happy ending of Jensen's foundling plot. Having ascertained his origin, Tobias has his selfhood confirmed by a redoubled sense of love.

SHORING UP THE FUTURE

The reaffirmation derives from the security of a Winnicottian holding space provided by Violet in a parallel spirit to the moment I mentioned earlier of Adriana in *The Comedy of Errors*.

In the bathroom of Queen Victoria, Violet enables the recognition with his father and asserts her right to nurture him. Tobias describes how he feels under the maternal spell of Violet, who "diet[s]" (*Comedy of Errors*, 5.1.99) him so well that he loses the tapeworm that had plagued him his whole life. It is Violet who enables the reconciliation, not to the biological parent but to the adoptive father, who, in the end, recovers his earlier love for his son and whose confession, "I was wrong," turns everything right for Tobias. As Violet, with her Irigarayan "biunivocal engendering," saves him and renders him a man by her love, she also restores him to his sense of innocence. In a remarkably lyrical passage, Tobias exudes nostalgia even for his adolescent pain:

> In my miasmic half-sleep, I see the beach again, and I see myself as a young child, clambering among the rocks on all fours, and climbing the little gnarled trees of Thunder Spit, and my parents begging me to stop. I see Parson Phelps guiding my hand as he teaches me to write with a goose-feather quill, and I see me and Tommy Boggs playing in the sand-dunes, burying each other among the spiky sand-grass. I see myself at fifteen, watching with Tommy as the

> Contortionist argues with my father in the graveyard, and her handing him a jar, and him returning with thunder in his face and stuffing money into her hand. . . . And in a ghastly caricature of consciousness that feels like half-dream, half-death, I pick along the shoreline of my past and I see my father, knitting in the Sanatorium. I see him knitting a scarf so long it could span the world. And I see Tommy in his forge, with his simple life and his bouncing babies, and the seashore, and the Thistle-Pulling contest. How memory changes things: I see it now touched by my own nostalgia, transformed from a scene of ritual humiliation into an idyllic rural tableau, the cheering, yelling faces of the Balls and the Cleggses and the Peat-Hoves awakening in me a cruel longing for home. . . .
>
> I awake to find myself in a bed, with her warm hand again on my brow. I open my eyes. She is clad in a huge red dress, with small beads that glitter in the light of the chandelier. . . .
>
> What a woman! Her hand on my brow reminds me of home. Sometimes, floating far above me, I see her face. She doesn't speak, or if she does, I have gone deaf. (288–89)

Safe in the haven of Violet, Tobias recovers a past he thought he had lost. In "miasmic half-sleep," he discovers not the earlier moments of ritual humiliation in the hinterlands of Thunder Spit but the traditional pastoral of the formulaic middle interlude: "an idyllic rural tableau." He writes that "memory changes things" but that is not it exactly: it is security that changes memory.

The words that Tobias uses to describe the return of his sense of safety, "the shoreline of [his] past," are Winnicottian; Violet's "hand on [his] brow" in the maternal gesture "reminds [him] of home." Jessica Benjamin describes Winnicott's holding space:

> Winnicott often quoted a line of poetry by Tagore, "on the seashore of endless worlds, / children play" that expressed what he thought about play in the transitional area. This image suggests something that both forms a boundary and opens up into endless possibility: it evokes a particular kind of holding similar to the first bodily holding by the mother.[9]

Winnicottian psychology assumes that a temporal reconstruction works retrospectively to invert spatial relationships, rendering knowledge cumulative. Depth as a function of inwardness is established secondarily to, and as a consequence of, permeability. Tobias's "miasmic half-sleep" enables him to enter a zone that remakes the Irigarayan past, one that marks a new beginning and "opens up to endless possibility." It is here that the "third language" might begin. The duplicity of Irigarayan doubling vanishes as it unfolds to the expansion acquired from a secure foundation. In this instance "the third language" is voiceless in a new way: "[Violet] doesn't speak, or if she does, I have gone deaf." Rather than being buried, it involves a mutual understanding that comes from a dialogic established by a "biunivocal engenderment": something already understood.

In *Playing and Reality*, Winnicott enacts the easy flow from a spatial to a temporal dimension as he describes his own gradually evolving interpretation of the Tagore lines that Benjamin cites, commencing with his adolescent initiation when the poem intrigued him, moving beyond Freud, to a sense of "unconscious symbolism" that actually involves a psychic exchange:

> As a student of unconscious symbolism, I *knew* (one always knows) that the "sea is the mother and onto the seashore the child is born." Babies come up out of the sea and are spewed out upon the land, like Jonah from the whale. So now the seashore was the mother's body, after the child is born and the mother and now-viable baby are getting to know each other. (*Playing and Reality*, 95–96, emphasis in original)

To arrive at the structural precondition that determines future flow, Winnicott redefines origins. As he describes his "growth" in understanding, Winnicott reconceives the mother, shifting her from a space that is all encompassing and all hers to a space that is shared and partly the child's. If the child is spewed from the mother "like Jonah from the whale," then the mother is overwhelming, a monster who engulfs the child. But the shore is not much better. In the isolation of its separation from the originary source, the shore is as frightening to the child as the whale. The child is overwhelmed by the massive mother *in utero* and subsequently resentful of her immense distance once he is cast onto land. Jonah inside the whale was dwarfed; Jonah spewed from the whale was lost. Only after he understands the gourd in the biblical text can he work out a transitional object as a God-given symbol of deific constancy. Still later, when the mother becomes the accessible seashore, rather than the remote and gigantic sea, the image changes again.

As seashore, the mother is partly herself and partly the child. She flows forward, like the wave, as he drifts backward, like the sand. In its dependence on the time of the tides and the alternating current of the waves, the seashore becomes the connecting link that accounts for temporality. Through such a belated understanding, the mother lapses into a landward slide, as the child finds her again in his seaward return. Each is separate, but contact is possible. The seashore becomes the territory that the child negotiates for himself, the place where the infant can return to his origins without drowning and can establish the connection between inner and outer reality. When Winnicott suggests that the seashore is both the mother's body *and* the child's body, he crosses over the divide to argue that the child can imbibe not just milk but also memory. The seashore is the child's territory too. The oxymoron works in both directions—the divisions coalesce, part sea-shore, part shore-sea. The happy ending of *Ark Baby* is celebrated with the same language. Even the geographical locale of the book negotiates between independence and security. Tobias describes Thunder Spit—"the herring-shaped peninsula" (338)—to his wife: "See, Violet, how it is in the shape of a fish?" I said. "Its tail nailed to the mainland, and its head training out to sea" (338). The fishy earth clings to land even as it edges out toward the ocean, just as Winnicott's Jonah goes both ways.

In half-sleep, Tobias awakens to a renewed sense of biblical faith. Later, he jokes with Violet, "If I am Adam . . . will you be my Eve?" (333). Thus, if Violet mothers him, he also fathers her, just as Eve burst forth whole from Adam's rib. Violet gives him both the seashore, the "beach again," with its benign childhood, and prepares him for the shore-sea of his confident new life. The constant reference to gourds in the book, both to their hybrid differences and to their inevitable eighth-generation recovery, explains the cycle of departure and return, reversal and renewal that forms the basis of the novel's play on tradition, as Tobias (switching genders with Jane Eyre) declares at the end, "Reader, I married her" (342), and as de Savile, who seems indifferent to the fertility crisis threatening England's survival at the beginning of the novel, changes his perspective.

Tobias recovers his mother in the mutual engenderment of Violet; de Savile discovers his humanity in his biological fatherhood. His "tears of joy" in seeing his children are matched by their contentedness:

> I felt tears of joy streaming down my face as I watched my offspring clinging tightly to their mothers with their perfect little hand-like feet. And, as they suckled, their four little tails, curled like question marks, twitched in happiness. (335)

The novel officially ends not with de Savile but with Tobias and Violet in the epilogue, anticipating the birth of their child who will lead, eventually, to de Savile's suckling babies. "[Lying] together on the big wrought-iron bed," they passively "await the evolution of events" (342). Big threatening ideas become natural chronological occurrences. Evolution, the theory, dwindles into evolution, the sequence. The ark Tobias pledges to describe to his expected daughter promises to be "a toy of wood and string," with "no cages and no captain." Land will be "on the horizon" (343), the rainbow and safety on the seashore guaranteed.

Reshaping the Noah story without a hierarchy while he awaits the birth of their child, Tobias feels excitement about his future: "boundless hope floods [his] heart" (343). As the hero of what emerges a traditional foundling plot, he is cheered by the thought of endless recurrence, the beating of his heart like the wave lapping against the shore of his future. But the noun of "hope" and the verb of "flood" also allude back to the original Noah story and to the fact that we cannot escape the genetic and class "bounds" that Phelps's new version—and its assured safety—challenges. The future that Tobias anticipates in his optimism results in the life to be lived by Buck de Savile's offspring. Rereaders, however, remember that, when he leaves behind the shady past of Bobby Sullivan and speeds his way to Thunder Spit in the car he bought from the profits of the veterinary practice he sold to start his new life, Buck de Savile, too, repeats the same words at the beginning and the end of the first chapter: "Boundless hope floods [his] heart" (4, 15). The original story of Noah's flood comes into the forefront and the inevitable human drift toward a caste system seems to prevail. When we circle round to the opening of the novel, Noah overtakes Jonah, leaving questionable the hopeful future augured by the birth of the quadrupled children at the novel's official end. Playing with various mutations in the foundling plot and proposing (in the Tobias-Violet love story) an alternative to Petrarchan self-reflection, Jensen opens up the possibility for an Irigarayan mutual engenderment even as, in the quadrupled offspring of de Savile's recoveries and plagiarized prose of his purloined manuscript, she reveals the difficulties of establishing the cultural transformation figured by, and enacted in, the "third language" of Tobias's double rescue.

W. G. Sebald's *Austerlitz* describes the effect of the cultural inevitability that Jensen bypasses in the third language she evokes as possibility and that Caryl Phillips identifies as the result of the bloodline imperative of the foundling plot and the pain for the woman in the male pleasure of Petrarchan pursuit. While Jensen moves forward to chronicle the twenty-first-century results of twentieth-century threats to the very existence of humanity, Sebald, like Phillips, reverts to the Holocaust he connects to a late modern racialized nationalism that Shakespeare also identifies as he metastasizes both the foundling and Petrarchan plots that fed into the rise of the nation-state in the early modern period. For Sebald, as for Shakespeare in *Hamlet* and in *Pericles*, those plots and their dynastic imperatives become burdens for the children fixated on making reparations in the Irigarayan vertical axis that links together the generations.

NOTES

1. *Ark Baby* was short-listed for the *Guardian*'s Fiction Prize in 1998.
2. "Extravagant Strangers," *A New World Order: Essays* (New York: Vintage, 2002), 293.
3. Jensen's latest novel, *The Rapture* (New York: Doubleday, 2009), continues in the science-fiction vein, only there Jensen sets her calamity in an unspecified future stemming from a deliberate and systematic denial of the effects of global warming.
4. "The Air of Those Who Love Each Other," *Why Different: A Culture of Two Subjects*, edited by Luce Irigaray and Sylvère Lotinger (New York: Semiotext(e), 2000), 129.
5. As the psychologist D. W. Winnicott describes it, the transitional object "stands for the breast" (*Playing and Reality* [New York: Basic Books, 1975], 3), for its nutritional love. But the object comes into play only after the infant is made to feel secure in the "holding" space

that Winnicott explains is "what the infant needs at the very beginning . . . a *live adaptation to the infant's needs*. The main thing is the physical holding, and this is the basis for the more complex aspects of holding, and of environmental provision in general. . . . With the care that it receives from its mother, each infant is able to have a personal existence, and so begins to build up what might be called *a continuity of being*" (*The Maturational Processes and the Facilitating Environment* [New York: International University Press, 1965], 5).

6. *I Love to You: Sketch of a Possible Felicity in History*, trans. Alison Martin (New York: Routledge, 1996), 143.

7. *The Dolphin* (New York: Farrar, Straus and Giroux, 1972), 125.

8. Martha Satz cites children's stories that speak of cross-species adoptions as metaphors for cross-racial adoption, citing such different stories as *Curious George* and *Babar*, animals raised by humans or different species. As the *ur* story, she refers to Hans Christian Andersen's "The Ugly Duckling," where the adoptive parent rejects—like Parson Phelps—the child she initially took in. As adult fiction, verging on sci-fi, Jensen's work comes close to the issues raised by these stories, particularly when they "speak[] of societal discomfort with transracial or transcultural familial relations through the figure of trans-species relations." See "Finding Oneself: Images of Adoption in Children's Fiction," *Adoption and Culture* 1, 1 (2007): 167.

9. "A Desire of One's Own: Psychoanalytic Feminism and Intersubjective Space," *Feminist Studies/Critical Studies*, edited by Teresa de Lauretis (Bloomington: Indiana University Press, 1986), 94.

Chapter Three

Trapped in the "Negative Gradient"

Traumatic Dis-membering in W. G. Sebald's Austerlitz

The title character in W. G. Sebald's *Austerlitz* is caught in the same Irigarayan "vertical axis" that compels Hamlet to make reparations for crimes committed by someone else against his father. Totally obsessed with finding his biological parents, Austerlitz has no life of his own. Sent to London in the *kindertransport*, and raised by a childless couple in Wales, he only discovers his true familial heritage as a young adult. From then on, his central focus becomes the recovery of parents who disappeared during the Second World War. For him, nothing else matters. Hamlet's response to the ghost is equally totalizing: "Yea, from the table of my memory / I'll wipe away all trivial fond records" (1.5.98–99) and "thy commandment all alone shall live / Within the book and volume of my brain" (1.5.102–103). Annulling his present and his past, Hamlet becomes his father. Everything is subsumed by the king's command—"remember" (1.5.91, 95, 97, 112)—echoed over and over again so that the bringing to mind becomes a form of bringing the self into the father.

Even as their plots record a triumph, Shakespeare's foundlings sometimes also feel responsible for embodying their parents. At the end of *Pericles*, for example, Shakespeare draws the lines of engenderment backward. Marina voices her need both to be contained by Thaisa and her wish to give back the nurture that sustained her in the womb:

> My heart
> Leaps to be gone into my mother's bosom. (5.3.44–45)[1]

Her words signify that she is altogether willing to exchange her life for that of her mother, to surrender her energetic source in order to revitalize her parent. The leaping to "be gone" expresses both a desire to *become* her mother's womb ("be[ing] gone" in the sense of providing the site of her mother's gestation) and to go missing ("be[ing] gone" in the sense of losing herself) in that same womb, transferring her lifeline through the umbilical cord she rewinds to her mother. Marina attempts to bring her mother into being at the very moment that she is ready to become a mother herself in her marriage to Lysimachus, who remains silent during the whole last scene. Having recovered her mother, Marina wants to give back to her the placental tissue that the growing embryo absorbs. It's as if the return at the end negates the individuated reality of the self Marina struggled so hard to retain throughout the play. In obviating the loss by pulling back to the before-before, Marina undoes the woman she has become, even the one who celebrated her birth moment at the beginning of the play. In transferring her heart to Thaisa, Marina confers on her mother the capacity for energetic life, removes her from the sequestered temple of Diana, and enables her to reclaim her child and proclaim her maternal possession: "Bless'd, and mine own" (5.3.47). Marina gives birth to her mother, her own life sacrificed to the dynastic mandate of the foundling plot.

Like Hamlet and Marina, Austerlitz consciously exempts himself from "the trivial fond records" of romantic and future events—because he is compelled, also like Hamlet and Marina, to render his parents' past his only present. That compulsion to make reparations for their loss subjects Austerlitz to "everlasting misery and never-ending anguish" (101) of his biological parents' lives. In *Austerlitz*, Sebald is determined to demonstrate how the structures of the foundling and Petrarchan plots paralyze. His hero remains the poor "lostling." While Hamlet knew the father he remembers and Marina finds the mother she infuses, Austerlitz cannot remember the parents he lost. Throughout the narrative, Austerlitz's only hope for personal salvation is based on the fictional expectation that he can recover the biological family so cruelly taken from him by the cataclysm in the middle of the twentieth century.

In response to an interview question about why he uses photographs in his work, Sebald answers in terms that render fiction not only unreliable as a measure of verifiable truth but also as inescapable as (like Hamlet's immersion in, and Marina's subscription to) a self-absorbing romance:

> [Photographs] have possibly two purposes in the text. The first and obvious notion is verification. We all tend to believe in pictures more than we do in letters. Once you bring up a photograph in proof of something, then people generally tend to accept that, well, this must have been so. . . .

The other function that I see is possibly that of arresting time. Fiction is an art form that moves in time, that is inclined toward the end, that works on to a negative gradient, and it is very, very difficult in that particular form in the narrative to arrest the passage of time. And, as we all know, that is what we like so much about certain forms of visual art—you stand in a museum and you look at one of those wonderful pictures somebody did in the sixteenth or eighteenth century and you're taken out of time, and that is in a sense a form of redemption, if you can release yourself from the passage of time. And the photographs can also do this—they act like barriers or weirs which stem the flow. I think that is something positive, slowing down the speed of reading, as it were.[2]

For Sebald, pictures allow us to escape the confines of literary formulae that are "inclined" too precipitously "toward an end." Still pictures—photographs in particular but also paintings—serve a dual function: First, they provide "proof," grounds for the legitimization that facilitates the reader's acceptance of what the narrative proposes as fact. Second, they distract from the fictional drive toward an end, arresting time, and releasing the reader as well as the writer from its passage. Slowing down the speed of reading becomes a means of forestalling the "negative gradient," an instance of fiction superannuated by life. As it alters the textual direction, even momentarily, the way a weir reroutes water, the image moves toward a diversionary space: its own. Photographs redeem us from the consuming drive toward the inexorable fictional "horizon of expectations"[3] that Sebald attempts to divert.

In both respects, Sebald's analysis counters the position of the title character in *Austerlitz*, despite the fact that he also photographs incessantly and uses these photos in his work. Describing his weekend activities, Austerlitz explains:

> Marie spent every second or third weekend . . . with her parents or wider family, who owned several estates in the wooded country. . . . At those times when she was not in Paris, which always cast me into an anxious mood, I regularly set off to explore the outlying districts of the city, to walk through the empty Sunday streets taking hundreds of *banlieu*-photographs, as I called them, pictures which in their very emptiness, I realized only later, reflected my orphaned frame of mind. (264–65)

While for Sebald, pictures enable entrance into another realm, for Austerlitz, photographs represent not an objective reality but an external mirror of his internal torment, "reflect[ing his] orphaned frame of mind." He can only see the culturally determined script that controls his thinking, disclosing his obsessive quest to make his reality part of the fictional plot he wishes—against all odds—to live. Austerlitz renders his situation as a presumably orphaned child—whose biological parents went missing during the war—not just a biographical fact but also the dominating aspect of his psychological self: he is caught in, and cannot deviate from, the formulaic position that the theoretical Sebald seeks to overcome as he portrays Austerlitz's cultural entrapment. The difference between Sebald's analysis of his use of photographs and his character's reflections about his compulsion to take and to study them illustrates the unresolved paradox of the novel. The element that grounds the photograph in reality—its function of stemming the rush of time—complicates Austerlitz's (directly opposite) desire for the forward flow of a fictional plot whose dynastic mandate insists on a verifiable heritage that he desperately seeks to authenticate. While Sebald theoretically enjoys the redemptive quality of paintings because they sometimes reverse (or at least slow down) the passage of time, taking him back to an earlier century—and placing him there, where things seemed happier—Austerlitz's sense of living outside of time (clockless and watchless, 101) leads him to believe that the present of the past and the past of the present are identical, that all time exists simultaneously. There is no escape.

Following the hypothesis that "past events have not yet occurred" (101), Austerlitz fails to distinguish between the mythological framework and the historical reality of his situation. The past that hasn't happened is the past that he wishes had never occurred: his abandonment. Part of the future perfect of a perfect future in the expected "inclination toward the end" of the formulaic foundling plot is the erasure of the initiating moment with the concluding "recognition." In fact, the conclusion involves a remission, rather than an acknowledgment, providing an alternative direction, one based on a recovered origin. Whereas for Sebald, the past can be "arrested," for Austerlitz the past that must be liberated is different from the past that he has hitherto experienced. Recovery involves an annulment of the lived life in favor of the discovery of an alternative history. In the foundling plot that governs Austerlitz's entire being, the exposure and the subsequent adoption vanish as the quest for the concluding recognition overrides everything else. Therefore, the "before-before" is the revised past of the desired future: a beginning that is, in the myth, already an end. Despite his own reservations, Sebald immerses his character in a structure that betrays, in Arthur Lubow's terms, "the author's unconventional mind creaking against the walls of [a] convention,"[4] one premised on a resurrection: the presumed dead come alive. For Sebald, photographs tell us what happened. For Austerlitz, they present a "might have been" that, in turn, leads into the subjunctive future. He wants to arrive at what might yet occur. At the end of the story, Sebald's character continues his nomadic existence, still waiting for his father to "reveal himself" (257) the way the missing, thought-dead-but-still-alive parent appears in the *scène à faire* of the archetypal foundling plot.

Austerlitz reverses the Petrarchan chase but remains mired in its "negative gradient" even as it evokes the elements of the foundling plot—the initial exposure, the middle adoption—as essentially unchangeable in their trauma.

We are left with the question his guardian raises on her deathbed: "What was it that so darkened our world?" (64). In the case of *Austerlitz*, that trauma is related to expectations whose cultural history goes back to ancient myths, particularly the Moses story that figures centrally in the novel. As Sebald writes in an early work, "How far back must one go / to find the beginning?"[5] Where does the horrific twentieth-century consequence find its origin? Describing his architectural work, Austerlitz answers that question specifically: "The whole history of the architecture and civilization of the bourgeois age, the subject of my research, pointed in the direction of the catastrophic events casting their shadow before them at the time" (140). With the phrase, "casting shadows before" (rather than behind), Austerlitz signifies his assumption that the height of civilization feeds into the depths of mid-twentieth-century devastation. On a personal level, Austerlitz's tendency to change forward strides into rear-ended falls is influenced by a plot that similarly transposes order. The dynastic imperative of the foundling plot insists on reversal. The end circles round to the beginning and then cancels out the precipitating event of the plot so that an earlier genesis reasserts itself. While Austerlitz's sense of historical reality turns him backward to a future populated by ruins, his "orphaned frame of mind" seeks only a prelude followed by a resurrection. He constructs a history of architecture where memory prophesizes destruction but he himself is committed to a fiction where memory promises redemption. Because the historical prophetic lens leads to annihilation and the fictional promised end never materializes, Austerlitz is trapped backward and forward in a "bleak prospect" (101).

I argue here that, for Sebald, the only way to bypass the particular entrapment of the "negative gradient" of the foundling plot is to subvert the form by demonstrating the extent of its generational and gender imperialism. In *Austerlitz*, we realize "that there was no transition, only this dividing line with ordinary life on one side and its unimaginable opposite on the other" (297). For Austerlitz "ordinary life" remains permanently elusive. Events pile up so that it is impossible to distinguish between perpetrator and victim, partly because the paradigm of a plot based on the fantasy of a recovered origin is disallowed by the impossibility of retrieving anything. The "unimaginable" atrocities of the war constitute the only reality. What lingers on in the end is what Austerlitz felt as a child: "the sense of rejection and annihilation that I had always suppressed" (228).

In many versions of the foundling plot, the reader becomes the memorializer and is sometimes addressed in the narrative, brought in by the hero, as witness but also seduced as the character shares his time and space and renders his experience compatible with the expectations, at once sympathetic and formulaic, inherent to the act of reading. When no one else is around to help, the reader steps in as surrogate parent. Like Jane Eyre, Tobias Phelps in *Ark Baby* has his "dear reader." Mindful of that presence, whose sympathy he enlists, he creates a formulaic adopter whose empathy takes him in and whom he will reward as he fulfills to completion the expected formula of the plot. Preeminently, Phelps acknowledges that, with his narrative, he creates the lifeline that keeps him afloat during the interim until he can somehow find himself so that, when he does, he can give the reader exactly the end desired and expected from the beginning: "Reader, I married her." With that declaration, Phelps dispels the frustrations of Petrarchan pursuit and the image of himself as genetically unworthy of Violet.

In *Austerlitz*, the narrator is the reader who breaks through "the walls of . . . confinement" (228) of the hero's plot so that the disjunction of abandonment is caught, like a disease. The narrator, too, is stranded in the search for an ancestry (not even his own) that cannot be resurrected. Like Austerlitz, he is lost in the middle and can find neither a beginning (because it is buried too deep) nor an end (because it cannot be extricated from that beginning). Sucked into and participating in the narrative, Austerlitz's "dear reader" merges with the "dear writer," trapped in his story and that of others that end in the black "chasm" he reads about at the end. There is no separation in the book, not even the dividing line of chapters. The last readers in the chain, those who actually hold the book in their hands, cannot always be certain whether it is the narrator telling his story or Austerlitz describing his own experience or, still further at the end, the story of another writer, Dan Jacobson, whose book the narrator carries with him from his first meeting with Austerlitz and which he never finishes. The compounding is thus a widening of the black hole into which "no ray of light could penetrate" (297). There is, in Dan Jacobson's words, "no transition" (297). The moment of loss remains the only significant event.

EVERY MOMENT IS ONE MOMENT: *AUSTERLITZ'S* STAGNATION

After thirty years of (sometimes lapsed) friendship, the witness (who is also the writer of the book we read) is given the key to Austerlitz's London house in Aldernay Street. There, he compiles the text we read from the accumulation of artifacts left behind. Hero and writer last meet in Paris, where Austerlitz remains at the story's end, searching for his biological father (in the foundling plot) and the woman whom he let slip through his fingers in the Petrarchan quest. From the very beginning, the writer is anointed by Austerlitz, "because he must find someone to whom he could relate [his] own story" (43). That very word, "relate," meaning simultaneously to narrate a history and to imbibe through empathy, casts itself forward to the end of the book, as we come to understand that there is no closure in the history of the Holocaust, that there stands only the void the narrator and Austerlitz share.[6] Sebald uses the critical word himself to describe the Brechtian distancing of his storytelling methodology as a "periscopic form of narrative [where] what [the writer] tells you is *related* at one remove or two or three."[7] But in *Austerlitz* itself, the separation is foreshortened and the double meaning of the word comes into play, the narrator unable to remove himself from the fictional frame that traps Sebald's hero. In one of his final gestures, the narrator takes "the book Austerlitz had given [him] on our first meeting out of [his] *rucksack*" (296). Because he has so pointedly commented on Austerlitz's bag and cited its connection to Wittgenstein (whose last work, *On Certainty*, resembles Austerlitz's sense that nothing can be said to be entirely real), the fact that he now carries a similar one indicates that he has absorbed Austerlitz's physical and psychological baggage and rendered it his own, closing the gap of the narrative methodology. Over the years, the rucksack had become, as it was for Austerlitz, a metonymy for the philosopher, "almost as dear [to Wittgenstein's sister] as himself" (40). The object signifies the narrator's inseparability from his subject and even with what he originally calls "the horror stricken expression" on the faces of both Wittgenstein and Austerlitz (40). Thus, we imagine the narrator assuming—with philosopher and hero—a lockjaw of the locked in: Edward Munch's depiction of the frozen face in *The Scream*.

By the end of the text, the narrator is so attached to his subject that the "relation" has made him a relative. Inheriting the keys to Austerlitz's London house, he also takes on Austerlitz's unfinished history, a story that remains in quest of an origin that refuses to yield a destiny. For Tobias Phelps of *Ark Baby*, the "dear reader" becomes the potential adopter who is freed at the end because Phelps himself is liberated from his fears. For Austerlitz and the narrator, the future of the past, all pasts, "lie[s] under a field of oats . . . into which no ray of light could penetrate" (297, 298) and the narrator is similarly absorbed into Austerlitz's inescapable quest.

Just before he leaves the narrator for the last time, Austerlitz explains his simultaneous expectancy and disappointment:

> I felt as if my father were just waiting, so to speak, for a good opportunity to reveal himself. I feel, almost physically, the current of time slowing down in the gravitational field of oblivion. It seems to me as if all the moments of our life occupy the same space, as if future events already existed and were only waiting for us to find our way to them at last, just as when we have accepted an invitation, we duly arrive in a certain house at a given time. Might it not be, that we have appointments to keep in the past, and in what has gone before and is for the most part extinguished, and we must go there in search of places and people who have some connection with us on the far side of time so to speak? (257–58)

Convinced that his preoccupation with the Holocaust had its roots in deep-seated mythological precedents, Sebald's title character only discovers his origins when he is about to enter the university. Obsessed from that moment with establishing his "connection . . . on the far side of time" (258), Austerlitz distances himself from everything near at hand. The nagging feeling that he had "appointments to keep" (258) with what went on before leads him to Theresienstadt in search of his birth mother's destiny and to Paris in the hope of ascertaining his biological father's whereabouts. But he remains, in the end, sucked into "the gravitational field of oblivion," stuck in the middle of his story. Bound by his "search" for a past he only vaguely recalls, he cannot move beyond his impasse to establish any new relationships. His stories become circular as he moves backward but, with those returns, he arrives always either too early or too late, forgotten as a living person. Invisible (like Eva in *The Nature of Blood*) because he casts himself as irretrievable, he is also unable to find what he is looking for because what he seeks is on the wrong side. The closer he gets to keeping the appointment in time, the further away the door that would let him inside moves away in space. The given house has no address. The *inexpressibility topoi* at the beginning and end of the passage—"so to speak"—underscores the insufficiency of language precisely to duplicate reality even as, in its assumption of an implicitly understood meaning, it proves to be another compression of Sebald's periscope. In this case, however, the reality can be understood only in relation to the whole panoply of a myth, one for which no solid state exists. The initial "so to speak" implies that the whole of the story Austerlitz tells is a cultural given that the narrator will understand without any elaboration and that the ending is destined to occur when the "right moment" for the *scène à faire* appears. In that realm, Austerlitz's father becomes the future through which he hopes to verify and rectify his past.

When Austerlitz speaks of his father's waiting for the right moment to reveal himself, he means partly that the foundling plot, as we understand it, lacks merely "a good opportunity" to play itself out. That feeling of imminence is conveyed in the "so to speak," an organizational structure that we all understand as our cultural heritage, what Amil Escher describes as a "situation where the effects of figurations themselves constitute the referent."[8] Austerlitz's allusion to his father's pregnant pause is clearly an effect of a mythological expectation. Like Eva in *The Nature of Blood*, he waits for a parent who has no "opportunity" even as he feels obliged to meet him on his own. Metaphor relies on an "as if" we can understand. But Austerlitz's "so to speak" assumes that an entire mythology is behind the "right moment" to which he refers. Contrastingly, the simile he uses to explain more precisely what he means—"as when we have accepted an invitation"—is based on a commonplace and specifically demarcated event, a few moments for the arrival and a few hours for the engagement, instead of on a lifelong plot. But because the first "so to speak" exists absolutely in the mythical realm and therefore cannot adhere itself to a commensurate substance, Austerlitz is pulled into the "field of oblivion" that governs his ability fully to define anything and that casts the second "so to speak" of the invitational simile (referring to a simple social obligation) into the same fictional realm as the grand scheme of the foundling plot. Within the insubstantial context of the larger fiction, the gravitational pull of a future conceived of as a past counters the precision commensurate to an appointment accepted but still not met. When Austerlitz attempts to concretize the experience, with the "appointment" in the second simile, he turns the story around and becomes his father waiting to reveal himself, casting his future as a past that has not yet occurred. It exists only as a cultural construct whose code cannot be unpacked and whose existence remains only a hypothesis.

The "far side of time" thus becomes the wrong side of time, partly because the only future Austerlitz wants is a past absorbed by the "gravitational pull of oblivion" that connects to an unrealizable mythology. The impersonal force of the gravitational pull gets internalized, as it is for Cleopatra when she proclaims the double edge of her forgetfulness: "O, my oblivion is a very Antony, / And I am all forgotten" (1.3.91–92). Cleopatra's inability to find the words for what she means to say, a psychological insufficiency in herself, situates her externally as what she speculates she has become internally: wiped out as an independent entity. She cannot express herself because she cannot impress herself as an individuated being. In defining herself as a "very Antony," she emerges as what she fears she is to him: "forgotten." No longer anything in herself, Cleopatra becomes her lover, inseparable from him and unable to find her own being just as her failing memory renders her unable to be remembered by others. Forgetful, she fears she is also "forgotten." While Cleopatra appends herself to Antony and finds her identity in his solidity, Austerlitz becomes even vaguer as he transfers his father into a mythological being and assigns motives to him that neither one can bring to pass. His "oblivion" is to a figment of his imagination; the concrete personified "very" of Cleopatra's Antony is reduced to the abstract vagueness of Austerlitz's "so to speak" as part of a story whose plot he attempts to resurrect. While Cleopatra slides into an Antony who exists, Austerlitz fuses with a father whose being he cannot verify as an absolute. The "far side of time" was never a place he has been, nor a place he can ever recover. Within the framework of the "so to speak," both expectations—his father waiting for the moment to arrive and his having a social obligation to meet—are impossible to realize.

The narrator uses the same catchphrase—"so to speak"—in the beginning when he describes the opposite, Austerlitz's extraordinary command of his material. The dexterity and scope of Austerlitz's precision—the facility with which he could articulate precisely an endless wellspring of knowledge—

acquires in the narrator's expression a vagueness that renders it commonplace, taken for granted. Like Austerlitz's explanation of his father's awaiting the opportunity to "reveal himself," the narrator's "so to speak" presumes that Austerlitz's historical metaphysics is a cultural legacy similar in its encyclopedic capacity to an already preconceived and universally accepted articulation. In the same way that Polonius's catalogue of genres both includes conventional meanings and deviates from within a universally held "horizon of expectations,"[9] the narrator describes Austerlitz's originality as it follows along—and departs from—standardized categories:

> From the first I was astonished by the way Austerlitz put his ideas together as he talked, forming perfectly balanced sentences out of whatever occurred to him, so to speak, and the way in which in his mind the passing on of knowledge seemed to become a gradual approach to a kind of historical metaphysic, bringing remembered events back to life. I shall never forget how he concluded his comments on the manufacture of the tall waiting-room mirrors by wondering, glancing up once more at their dimly shimmering surfaces as he left, *combien des ouvriers périrent, lors de la manufacture de tells miroirs, de malignes et funestes affections à la suite de l'inhalation de vapeurs de mercure et de cyanide.* (12–13)

The initial assessment of Austerlitz's verbal agility appears as a chiasm to Austerlitz's belated expectation of his father, the linking "so to speak" tying the architectural history to the fictional formula. "Whatever occurred to him" is rooted in fact at the story's beginning even as his father's waiting to reveal himself is fixed in fantasy at the story's end. Austerlitz's ability to conjure up historical events with such dexterity that they appeared as fictions that simply or haphazardly "occurred to him" lies at the other end of the spectrum of his acceptance of a literary formula (in his final expectation), as if it were about to materialize as literal reality. Austerlitz's image of his father is situated in a series of events that are about to happen. Conversely, Austerlitz's metaphysics is based on an accumulation of actions that have already taken place. The contemporary buildings emerge manifest memories of their original and intermediary pasts. Austerlitz thereby reveals the same obsession with "oblivion" and its gravitational pull.

The currently standing railway stations become synonymous anterooms to the formerly operating gas chambers, the gas chambers producing the same effect as the originally built railroad stations. Backward and forward, the solid buildings testify to human erasures, monuments to the annihilations their very efficacy facilitated. The "historical metaphysic" of Austerlitz's narrative is that all stories feed into one story. While the implicit erasures in the camps at the end of the railroad line duplicate the explicit "perishing" of the workers at the beginning, the image of his father projects a sequence of chapters in the life of a man impossible to transform into a substantial being.

Austerlitz's reference in the same context to "the family likeness of all buildings" (33) categorizes architectural edifices, like Pygmalion's statues, as clones of an originating ideal that, in Austerlitz's metaphysic, repeats his dynastic obsession: people are interchangeable with buildings. His architectural quest merges with his parental search. As rereaders, we realize that the story of Austerlitz's life *work* becomes the story of his life—and it does so as the images are compounded: stacked up one upon the other like the mass graves with which the novel ends. The named become the nameless. In his study of railway stations—the principal métier of his architectural research—Austerlitz is conscious of the price in human life, of the subtle way in which the history of the incline of Western civilization is the same as that of its decline. The inhalation of mercury or cyanide took away the life of the builders in the same way as the gas chambers did for the twentieth-century victims who left from those stations to the concentration camps that killed them. By breathing, one died. The history of the railroad stations remains static. The future of cyanide merges with its past just as, in *The Nature of Blood*, the "white ash" (156, 178) of Portobuffole merges with the scattered remains of the death camps. In this regard the Holocaust is not, in Berel Lang's terms, a "novum, a breach or a turning point in moral history"; rather, it is an expansion of an original cultural ambition, what Lang calls a "continuum."[10] Austerlitz's personal articulation becomes his cultural expectation.

Austerlitz's European architectural studies first fuse with and then dwindle in their scope to the quest to find his own history, a search that leads him always backward toward the chasm that the narrator is left with in the end. Trapped in the myth from which he cannot extricate himself, his initial verbal dexterity becomes (in the parallel "so to speak") another sign of culturally caused oblivion. Thus the signal for metaphor, "so to speak," merges with the metaphor itself as the "gravitational pull of oblivion" sucks up the very power of speech. The narrator at the beginning is caught—like Austerlitz at the end—with a sense of imprecision. His "so to speak" about Austerlitz's linguistic capacity sutures into the "so to speak" of Austerlitz's fantasy at the end when the periscope collapses. Trapped in the myth from which he cannot extricate himself, his initial articulation becomes, in the parallel "so to speak," another sign of culturally caused annihilation. When the study of railroad stations fuses with the study of trains leading to the camps, the lost child loses the ability to record his situation, to signify his loss. The symptom of narrative efficiency becomes the sign of narrative ineffability and the disease is infectious. In the context of this convergence, the amasser of information about railroad stations burns his papers.

In the middle of the narrative, Austerlitz tells his friend how he has inadvertently forfeited the signifying marker of his humanity. The very precision the narrator praises at the opening dissolves as Austerlitz becomes more and more to feel his psychological isolation:

> The very thing that may usually convey a sense of purposeful intelligence—the exposition of an idea by means of certain stylistic facility—now seemed to me nothing but an entirely arbitrary or deluded enterprise. I could see no connections anymore, the sentences resolved themselves into a series of separate words, the words into random sets of letters, the letters into disjointed signs, and those signs into a blue-gray trail gleaming silver here and there, excreted and left behind by some crawling creature and the sight of it increasingly filled me with feelings of horror and shame. (124)

For Austerlitz, the evanescence that comes from feeling disconnected descends into a sense of excrescence—the remains of something elusive and ugly. Describing his gradual loss of speech in terms of a concomitant visual abstraction, Austerlitz transforms his increasingly dissolute sounds into decreasingly apparent sights until he emerges in what he sees in the mirror of the "gleaming silver," which condemns, and punishes, him for *something he did not do*. Sentences lapse into "disjointed signs" that, in turn, reduce him (like the serpent in Eden) to a "crawling creature," simultaneously spineless (like a helpless, not-yet-erect baby) and prelinguistic, horrifying even to himself. In yet another turnaround, he emerges a replica of his linguistic formlessness, a visual duplication of his verbal imprecision. Like the silver mirrors of the train stations, the remaindered "sliver" portends an inevitable erasure: a "gleam" reflecting only a lingering memory of a body. Reduced to the state of psychic infantilism, Austerlitz's lack of sustained nurture renders him unsustainable, indistinguishable from the self that shames him.

In the course of *Austerlitz*, the hero discovers that his presumed parents, a Welsh minister and his wife, had taken him from the Liverpool station in London, where he was deposited as part of the *kindertransport* that sent Jewish children who would otherwise have perished to England. Of his foster parents, Austerlitz recalls, "They were slowly being killed by the chill in their hearts" (62). For Austerlitz, the vista of the past is obscured as "things themselves" break apart, like icebergs splitting from a solid glacier, as menacing in their lack of specificity as the chill killing his foster parents. The linguistic waters are filled with danger so that "finally even the nouns were enveloped in an impenetrable fog" (124). The opaque language is the product of an indefinable self. Austerlitz's emotional emptiness produces a sense of verbal disjunction and the linguistic failure compounds his loss of humanity until he calls himself an excrescence, the detritus of something indecipherable to himself, indescribable to others; he no longer possesses the means even to express his alienation. Austerlitz cannot recall anything stable. Throughout the narrative, he repeats his *anomie*: "I had never really been alive or was only now being born, almost on the eve of my own death" (137). "I had always felt that I had no place in reality" (185). "At some time in the past, I thought, I must have made a mistake, and am now living the wrong life" (212) or "the vague sense that [I] did not belong in this city . . . or indeed anywhere else in the world" (254). Describing the derailment of the foundling experience, Austerlitz feels simultaneously off track and responsible for mistaken moves.

Always asserting that a graspable reality eludes him, Austerlitz nevertheless spends the better part of his life searching for a verifiable past that might stabilize him. In that quest, he discovers two women who nurtured him: Vera—the family friend of his biological parents who, as a child, allowed him to feel "safe as I knew myself to be in the care of my solicitous guardian" (157)—and Marie de Verneuil—an aristocratic lover who, when he had one of his many bouts of illness, came day after day to the hospital to help him recover. In this self-characterization, Austerlitz crosses the psychological boundary between acceptable and unacceptable behavior and the physical boundary between reality and the abstract. His body is sucked into the "impenetrable fog" of his failing linguistic acumen. The detachment of his childhood carries over into adulthood, simultaneously leaving him unable to form romantic ties and desperate to repair the rift. He cannot move forward because he has no past. His monstrous loss, in turn, makes him feel inhuman. Austerlitz declines, as he dissolves from an appalling creature to a noxious vapor. He suffers in the immobility of Lyotardan "immemorial: that which can neither be remembered (represented to consciousness) nor forgotten (consigned to oblivion)."[11] Indicating that there are no specific facts to enumerate and that (even without them) a vague sense of the need to recover something, anything, prevails, the Lyotardan phrase defines Austerlitz's quest for the parents who simultaneously exist in his mind but cannot be represented as real. The more Austerlitz seeks his past, the more he aligns himself with the unrecoverable state of his family, becoming, like them, irredeemable. Austerlitz's fixation with the memory of his parents is buried so deep that he fails to find a language commensurate to it even as he cannot expel it from his mind. He is consigned to the "gravitational pull" of Lyotardan "oblivion," absorbed into what happened to his parents.

When the history of his personal lack of connection overtakes his studies, he describes first an imbalance:

> Like a tightrope artist who has forgotten how to put one foot in front of the other, all I felt was the swaying of the precarious structure on which I stood, stricken with terror at the realization that the ends of the balancing pole gleaming far out on the edges of my field of vision were no longer my guiding lights, as before, but malignant enticements to me to cast myself into the depths. . . . I already felt in my head the dreadful torpor that heralds disintegration of the personality, I sensed that in truth I had neither memory nor the power of thought, that all my life had been a constant process of obliteration, a turning away from myself and the world. (122–23)

A tightrope artist who cannot remember even how to walk, let alone traverse a narrow and shaky path, Austerlitz also fails to reach the poles that might steady him. "Guiding lights" emerge as mirages, casting him even further into the depths. Moreover, the supposedly helpful poles are malignant, designed to make him fall. If, with his appointments to keep in the past, Austerlitz finds himself lost in time, reaching for something that he always misses, here he experiences a spatial disintegration that leads him to distrust the very markers that structured his lifework and that would have allowed him to resurrect his ancestors. The ends of the balancing poles become for him absent presences: unavailing. A toddler who cannot find supporting hands, he founders. Turned down by the absence of bodily support, he despairs and turns away from "[himself] and the world."

If there are no dependable spatial markers, so for Austerlitz there are no verifiable temporal parameters:

> If Newton really thought that time was a river like the Thames, then where is its source and into what sea does it finally flow? Every river, as we know, must have banks on both sides, so where, seen in those terms are the banks of time? What would be this river's qualities, qualities perhaps corresponding to those of water, which is fluid, rather heavy and translucent? In what way do objects immersed in time differ from those left untouched by it? Why do we show the hours of light and darkness in the same circle? Why does time stand eternally still and motionless in one place and rush headlong by in another? Could we not claim . . . that time itself has been nonconcurrent over the centuries and the millennia? It is not so long ago, after all, that it began spreading out over everything. And is not human life in many parts of the earth governed to this day less by time than by the weather, and thus by an unquantifiable dimension which disregards linear regularity, does not progress constantly forward but moves in eddies, is marked by episodes of congestion and irruption, recurs in ever-changing form, and evolves in no one knows what direction? (100–101)

Austerlitz's distrust of time is expressed in terms of his dynastic obsession: its supposed river prompts his question about "where is its source and into what sea does it finally flow?" As he loses his physical balance—with the poles of the tightrope walker— so he forfeits his psychological equilibrium and is left dangling without banks at the shore, his question about time reflecting an anxiety about his origin and destiny. Much has been written about this passage. Amir Eschel calls it a "poetics of suspension."[12] Jens Brockmeir explains that Austerlitz's vertigo can be seen as "a mode of simultaneously coexisting moments and episodes from very different periods of clock and calendar time, moments that include present experiences and memories from the past, yet also from the future" (349).[13] Austerlitz's suspension in time is different from Sebald's theoretical weir. While Sebald finds in the image from the past a still point of arrest, Austerlitz feels himself totally adrift. The dislocation caused by Austerlitz's spatial loss merges with the compression resulting from his temporal disjunction: the future he cannot reach is inseparable from the past he cannot remember. There exists no predictable flow, only "ever-changing" form. As he tells the narrator, "it all arouses in me a sense of disjunction, of having no ground beneath my feet" (109). There are no guiding poles that might serve as helping hands that would allow him to thrive on his own. He remains a crawling infant, indistinguishable from the spineless serpent. Left to his own resources, he condemns himself as guilty of his own suffering. With no recoverable source, he "evolves in no one knows what direction." Austerlitz is lost in time and space.

Sensing himself out of control, Austerlitz sees truth only in the weather, itself subject to unpredictability and capriciousness. In Austerlitz's view, "time has been nonconcurrent," somewhere else both physically and psychologically, leaving no room for clear demarcation or identification, and hence far from where he ever was or ever could expect to be. Never a stream he could navigate, time's flow remains always oppositional, moving against, rather than with (or for), him. If time's banks are nonexistent, if its form is ever changing, then there are no stable parameters, no bastions of support that would allow him, as parents might, a sense of secure origin.

One thread running through the book is that of an ancient river myth (yet another foundling plot), which at first terrifies him: "I can only still see myself, said Austerlitz, muttering intently and spelling out the story of Moses again and again from the large-print children's edition of the Bible. . . . I have only to turn a couple of pages of that book said Austerlitz, to remember how anxious I felt at the time when I read the tale of the daughter of Levi, who made an ark of the bulrushes and daubed it with slime and with pitch, placed the child in the ark and laid it among the reeds by the side of the water" (55). Paralleling his image of the bankless river in Austerlitz's Newton story, the murky reeds in his Moses parable are equally perilous. As a model for the *kindertransport*, the baby Moses episode is Austerlitz's experience before he knows it. The unease the allegory provokes is one of many early premonitions of a past he cannot recall, a sense of what he has yet to learn about his life. The slimy vessel that saved Moses is aligned in the inaccessible recesses of his mind with the soot of the *kindertransport* train. But the ark daubed with slime and pitch is not the whole of the story. What he leaves out—the Hebrew mother's desire to save her child when the only option is death, the Egyptian princess's compassion—is as significant as what he remembers. But for Austerlitz, the initiating event is troublesome and only the diaspora itself—the story in the wilderness—was what he "particularly liked," meaning as well what he particularly *was* like, forever leading a nomadic existence. In his allusions to the Moses story, Austerlitz navigates from baby Moses saved to adult Moses stranded. Over and over again, he refers to the flight from Egypt until, finally, Turner landscapes and Rembrandt depictions of that flight replicate for him the valleys in Wales and of the time with his foster parents. Images of the Jews wandering become images of his own endless voyages. He can never reach the promised land of his originating heritage.

When he chronicles a memory told to him by his childhood guardian, another moment of the Moses story applies not to his situation but to that of his victimizers. Recapitulating Vera's summary of a German film that his father had seen in Munich cinema, he cites his father's conclusion: "[The film] confirmed his suspicion that, out of the humiliation from which the Germans had never recovered, they were now developing an image of themselves as a people chosen to evangelize the world . . . a bird's eye view showed a city of white tents extending to the horizon, from which as day broke the Germans emerged singly, in couples, or in small groups, forming a silent procession and pressing ever closer together as they all went in the same direction, following, so it seemed, some higher bidding, on their way to the Promised land at last after long years in the wilderness" (169).

The description of the Nazis feeling themselves as "chosen" (175), appropriating their victims' text, in Vera's recounting of his father's analysis, returns us to Austerlitz's self-characterization at the beginning when he learns of his given name: "All that school year I felt that I had been chosen and, although, as I also knew, such a belief in no way matched my uncertain status, I have held fast to it almost my whole life" (72–73). Thus, the application of the Moses parable by his father to the Nazis is yet another link to Austerlitz's belief that he is also somehow responsible for what happened to his parents. As he does with the slithering creature registering his inarticulation, Austerlitz merges himself with the guilty perpetrators of his separation anxiety. After he learns his real name, Austerlitz explains where he remains throughout his life:

> It is still possible to be outside time, a state of affairs which until recently was almost as common in backward and forgotten areas of our own country as it used to be in the undiscovered continents overseas. The dead are outside time, the dying and all the sick at home or in hospitals, and they are not the only ones, for a certain degree of personal misfortune is enough to cut us off from the past and the future. . . . I have always resisted the power of time out of some internal compulsion which I myself have never understood, keeping myself apart from so-called current events in the hope, as I now think, said Austerlitz, that time will not pass away, has not passed away, that I can turn back and go behind it, and there I shall find everything as it once was, or more precisely, I shall find that all the moments of time have co-existed simultaneously, in which case none of what history tells us would be true, past events have not yet occurred but are waiting to do so at the moment when we think of them, although that, of course opens up the bleak prospect of everlasting misery and neverending anguish. (101)

The circularity of Austerlitz's state—the fact that, at the end of the story, he feels that he has appointments to keep in the past—comes round to the beginning, where he fails to differentiate between those who are already dead and those who are sick and dying. There are no degrees of separation. Past events have not "yet occurred" and he has an appointment to keep with them. As he is in the river of time and struggling to hold on to the balancing poles, Austerlitz feels that "a certain degree of personal misfortune is enough to cut us off from past and future." Always and ever, Austerlitz is out of synch temporally and out of place physically. Subject to "everlasting misery and neverending anguish" of the centrally determining moment of his parents' lives, he remains the poor lostling.

Recalling a childhood story about the seasons that Vera (the family friend who was his guardian) read him, he demonstrates that his obsession with memory predates even his exposure:

> I never tired of the winter pictures in particular, scenes showing hares, deer, and partridges transfixed with astonishment as they stared at the ground covered with newly fallen snow and every time we reached the page which described the snow falling through the branches of the trees, soon to shroud the entire forest floor, I would look up at her and ask, "But if it's all white, how do squirrels know where they've buried the hoard. . . . How indeed do the squirrels know, what we do not know ourselves, how do we remember and what is it that we find in the end?" (204)

Unlike the squirrel, Austerlitz cannot scratch out the kernel of himself. He remains in the end trying to recover what he could not change: the initially painful parental tragedy that led to his abandonment and the subsequent inability to accept the alternative life/love support that Marie offered him. In terms of the foundling plot, Austerlitz is trapped by the belief that he is compelled to recover parents he cannot remember.

In terms of the love story, he understands his isolation. Austerlitz describes his final rejection of Marie, whom at the end of the narrative he seeks in the same quest as that for his father. With regard to his dynastic source, he is unrecognizable as himself. With regard to the Petrarchan plot, he is already transformed into an object that leaves his pursuer unable to find gratification in a form that might satisfy her. Turning both stories backward, he is simultaneously the child seeking his lost parent and the resistant lover, like Laura, unwilling to yield to Petrarch:

> The silent facades of the buildings knew something ominous about me, how I had always believed I must be alone, and in spite of my longing for her I now felt it more than ever before. But it isn't true, said Marie, it isn't true that we need absence and loneliness. It isn't true. It's only in your mind. You are afraid of I don't know what. You have always been rather remote, of course, I could tell that, but now it's as if you stood on a threshold and you dared not step over

> it. That evening in Marienbad, said Austerlitz, I could not admit to myself how right everything Marie said was, but today I know why I felt obliged to turn away when anyone came too close to me, I know that I thought this turning away made me safe, and that at the same time I saw myself transformed into a frightful and hideous creature, a man beyond the pale. (216)

Austerlitz recognizes the horrible, the ineffable, behind his "turning away," his becoming the sought after in the Petrarchan complex, even as he is the seeker in the foundling plot. Like Laura he resists but, like Petrarch, his creative enterprise derives from the feeling of emptiness (the absence and loneliness Marie identifies) that inspires his search and that compels him to go on searching for his present in a past he can never recover. Thus, in both the foundling and in the love plots, he reverses the order: child chasing the parent in the one, beloved running away in the other. On a quest for what he cannot find, he renders himself unrecoverable. He remains "beyond the pale," unable to distinguish himself from his victimizer, as Hamlet-like, he feels himself "sicklied o'er with the pale cast of thought" (3.1.87) attempting to make reparations for something he never did.

In that respect, he seems trapped like the animals the narrator observes at the opening in the Antwerp Noctorama. Condemned to an artificial dusk, they are also "beyond the pale," their external situation matched in its gloom with Austerlitz's later expressed feelings about himself. The narrator observes a raccoon whose repetitive motions—like those of Austerlitz—futilely strive "over and over again" to overcome the "transformation" of its diaspora:

> As it sat beside a little stream with a serious expression on its face, washing the same piece of apple over and over again, as if it hoped that all this washing, which went far beyond any reasonable thoroughness, would help it to escape the unreal world in which it had arrived, so to speak, through no fault of its own. (4)

The cultural marker turns the raccoon into Lady Macbeth, vainly struggling (like Austerlitz in his journeys) with all that washing, to erase the guilt of his temporal and spatial expulsion from the Eden of his early life into the unreal world of his present. The narrator's "so to speak" at the very opening, like Austerlitz's "so to speak" at the end, evokes the whole of a mythology, holding the innocent raccoon, like the helpless lost child, accountable for a state reached "through no fault of its own."

The fall of man—and the apple story—is evoked in the tiny "piece" with which the raccoon attempts to return to its former state. Like Austerlitz feeling the burden of recovering his father and therefore alluding to a myth that is part of the cultural unconscious, the narrator himself replays a central passage of Western mythology, with the fruit of Genesis 2, as an inescapable romance that similarly holds the victim responsible for his own victimization. In *Fugitive Pieces*, an apple story figures centrally in the life of the second narrator, but Anne Michaels revises both the foundling and Petrarchan plots so that their mythological hold can be bent to accommodate the very cultural revision that Shakespeare performs in *The Winter's Tale*. With its emphasis on "washing clean" the wound that neither the raccoon nor Hamlet, nor the narrator, nor Austerlitz can assuage, her novel forms the bridge that leads us backward to the Shakespearean progression I chronicle in the second section of the book.

NOTES

1. *Pericles*, edited by Suzanne Gossett, The Arden Shakespeare 3rd series (London: Methuen, 2004), 401.
2. Interview with Eleanor Wachtel, "Ghost Hunter," *The Emergence of Memory: Conversations with W. G. Sebald*, edited by Lynn Sharon Schwartz (New York: Seven Stories Press, 2007), 41–42.
3. Hans Robert Jauss, *Toward an Aesthetic of Reception*, translated by Timothy Bahti (Minneapolis: University of Minnesota Press, 1982), 79.
4. "Crossing Boundaries," *The Emergence of Memory: Conversations with W. G. Sebald*, 169.
5. *After Nature*, translated by Michael Hamburger (New York: Random House, 2002), 133.
6. As Judith Ryan writes, "The narrator and Austerlitz become reflections of each other, bound together like the positive and negative images of photographs that also 'haunt' this text. We are to understand that the search is a double search for identity: that of Austerlitz and that of the narrator." See "Fulgurations: Sebald and Surrealism," *Germanic Review* 82, 3 (2007): 242.
7. As quoted in Michael Silverblatt, "A Poem of an Invisible Subject," *The Emergence of Memory, Conversations with W. G. Sebald*, 83.
8. "The Poetics of Suspension in W. G. Sebald's 'Austerlitz,'" *New German Critique* 88 (Winter 2003): 73. Eschel refers to Austerlitz's continual obsession with "clocks, diaries and ruins" but it is also possible to consider plots as an effect of figuration.
9. Jauss, *Toward an Aesthetic of Reception*, 79.
10. See discussion in *Philosophical Witnessing: The Holocaust as Presence* (Waltham, MA: Brandeis University Press, 2008), 17–32.
11. *Discours, figure* (Paris: Klincksiek, 1971), 378. The translation is from Bill Readings, *Introducing Lyotard* (London: Routledge, 1991), 26.
12. "The Poetics of Suspension in W. G. Sebald's 'Austerlitz,'" 74.
13. "Austerlitz's Memory," *Partial Answers* 6, 2 (2008): 349.

Chapter Four

"These Weeping Eyes, Those Seeing Tears"

The Flow of Memory from Fugitive Pieces *to Shakespeare*

While Sebald's Austerlitz endlessly "journeys through [his] grief," as Marina in Anne Michaels's *The Winter Vault* proclaims necessary, he fails to achieve "the rendez-vous" Marina also deems essential.[1] He cannot keep his "appointment with the past" because he is on the wrong "side of [a] time" (258) that, as for Hamlet, is always "out of joint" (1.5.189). Like Hamlet, and like the metonymic raccoon who tries "with all that washing" to escape "the world . . . in which [he] had arrived through no fault of his own" (4), he can "set [nothing] right" (*Hamlet*, 1.5.190).

But at the end of *The Winter Vault*, the central character learns how she might bring about the reconciliation she needs: "She knew now how careful she had to be. Not to erase, but to wash away" (336). Erasure is an annulment; "washing away" cleanses the wound without denying the pain of loss. In *Fugitive Pieces*, Jacob Beer benefits from such a comfort, one very like the one Marvell extols in "Eyes and Tears."[2] His lover, Michaela, "sees" his grief and reflects that understanding through the watery healing of her "tears":

> The light and heat of her tears enter my bones.
> The joy of being recognized and the stabbing loss: recognized for the first time.
> (182)

Without invalidating "the stabbing loss," Michaela's tears enable the twice acknowledged recognition, a bringing back to mind that involves a beginning again, a primal "first" that precipitates a rebirth through what Irigaray identifies as "a movement towards the other subject rather than the construction of this latter by the action of the 'I.'"[3] Penetrating from the outside, the tears emerge as an inner source of life, circumventing sacrifice (of the sort Marina makes in *Pericles*) and providing instead a recovery of self by both the lover and beloved through the Irigarayan horizontal axis.

In *Othello*, a similar watery permeability occurs in the willow song that fortifies Desdemona. As I demonstrate in the chapter on that play, Shakespeare gives to Desdemona a moment of recovered memory that enables her, in Act 4, to face Othello with all the courage of Shakespeare's comic heroines. In the "willow song" of the boudoir scene, she recalls a maternal nurturing very similar to the one Eva longs for in *The Nature of Blood*; the song enables her to attempt an Irigarayan "mutual engenderment" that might free her from the bind of Othello's hold and allow her to replace his narcissism with her love. Because her mother's maid, Barbary, and her song will "not go from [her] mind" (4.3.29), Desdemona (at this juncture in the play) is the opposite of Hamlet, who has devoted his mind totally to recovering his father. It's as if the "murmur[ing] streams" (4.3.42) of the song—and all the strength it encompasses (of women supporting each other, of the commiseration of pastoralized nature with human frailty)—are an enlarged person who refuses to abandon her even as, by its containment, it voices her pain:

> The fresh streams ran by her and murmured her moans,
>   Sing willow, willow, willow.
> Her salt tears fell from her and softened the stones. (4.3.42–44)

Through Barbary's song, Desdemona envisions a future that sustains her and that also reconceptualizes the middle period of the foundling plot. The maid and (vicariously as she sings) Desdemona secure an adoptive interlude based on a reciprocation of feeling, one that encompasses a sympathetic nature, as the streams "murmur her moans" and the tears "soften the stones" to form a holding space created by the very fluidity Othello distrusts.

But it is in *The Winter's Tale*, where Shakespeare makes *Othello* right again, that we find exactly the recognition Michaels so emphatically theorizes. At a crucial moment in the play (as I will detail in the last of the Shakespearean chapters) Florizel renounces the "vertical axis" that is so important to the foundling plot:

> From my succession wipe me, father! I
> Am heir to my affection. (4.4.468–69)

When Hamlet vows to "wipe [away] from the table of [his] memory" (1.5.98) all thoughts but those of his father, he "succeeds" his parent, becoming him just as Austerlitz, in devoting himself fully to the dynastic mandate, ceases to have any life of his own. In Hamlet's context, "wipe away" means to obliterate the self. Removing himself from all "pressures" past, Hamlet trivializes his own feelings and submits to his father's "command[ing]" presence. In contrast, Florizel's "wip[ing]" allows him to find himself and to command his father. His defiance comes after a remarkable lyric sequence, one where Florizel and Perdita re-create their lives in an interchange that culminates in Florizel's description of Perdita as "a wave o' the sea" that "move[s] still, still so" (4.1.141–42). That wish for a reliable constancy, an adaptable fluidity, strengthens Florizel's confidence and overflows the boundaries of his fated position. As it does in *The Winter Vault*, "wipe" in this context signifies a washing clean that gives Florizel the determination to substitute the mutual pull—the give and take—of "affection" for the push—the command and obey—of "succession." In toppling "succession" from its meaning of prospering through inheritance to his intention of enjoying through love, Florizel reverses the order, superannuating dynasty with the "affection" of his willed alliance with Perdita. Paralleling the liquid permeability of *The Winter Vault* and the life-giving tears of *Fugitive Pieces*, Florizel's redefinition links Shakespeare's prospect to Michaels's retrospect, rendering her work the bridging novel in this study.[4] Traversing the centuries and "interpenetrat[ing]" the larger forms of fiction and drama, both early and late modern writers use the Petrarchan and foundling plots they inherit even as they free themselves from the strict adherence to the "law of writ" of the forms whose cultural consequences they question as they invoke the watery consolation of "these weeping eyes, those seeing tears."

Fugitive Pieces builds on the same set of assumptions that governs *Austerlitz*. "Every recorded event is a brick of potential or precedent, thrown into the future. Eventually the idea will hit someone in the back of the head. That is the duplicity of history: an idea recorded will become an idea resurrected" (161).[5] In both novels, recorded events are not just historical documents. They are also cultural texts ranging from architecture in *Austerlitz*, to poetry and music in *Fugitive Pieces*. Both *Austerlitz* and *Fugitive Pieces* insist that the "recorded event," the artifact itself as revered in Western society, is part of the cause, the potential brick that will smash someone in the back of the head and will rear its nasty head again *in the name of civilization*. In terms of her relationship to old texts, Michaels has a twofold aim: to recover memory by bending the foundling myth so that the precipitating event is acknowledged and to change the sexual balance (in the Petrarchan ethos) by altering the terms of the love story as well. The principal difference between *Austerlitz* and *Fugitive Pieces* is that, near the end of Michaels's novel, the central character of the second part of the book finally discovers "the elation of ordinary sorrow" (292) because his "unhappiness is [his] own" (292), unconnected to the familial history that makes him feel (like Hamlet and Marina) compelled to make reparations for his parents' suffering.

If, like Phelps in *Ark Baby*, Austerlitz has a "dear reader" who becomes him and so provides the "relation" he craves, in *Fugitive Pieces* such a lifeline gets complicated, as character after character actively assumes the role of "dear reader" of another character's experience. At the end, *rereading* within the novel itself becomes the method for changing, rather than for fulfilling, the narrative structure. In that regard, the rereader, the central character in the novel's second story, demonstrates how Michaels's emendations to the Petrarchan and foundling stories give us what that reader, a child of Holocaust survivors who functions also as a narrator, calls the "miraculous circuit" (294) that redirects the formulae. Principally Michaels also refuses to cover up or gloss over the originating event. By redefining the nature of engenderment, she changes the end of the story even as she acknowledges the brutality of the initial exposure annulled, along with the subsequent adoption, in the traditional plot. In the rewitnessing Michaels performs, the wound is opened up again so that a genuine healing can occur and that opening is part of what Marina means when she insists on "journey[ing] through." In the typical plot, the "grief" and the "journey" are put aside as the concluding events overshadow the precipitating ones. Thus, Ben's "circuit" in *Fugitive Pieces* involves a reality Austerlitz seeks to deny as he hopes to recover his missing father. Austerlitz's "inclin[ation] toward the [fictional] end" Sebald questions keeps him from acknowledging the reality Sebald deems essential. Obsessing over the vertical generational axis, he remains incapable of returning romantic love.

As it does in *Austerlitz*, Genesis 2, with its burden of guilt passed on to progeny for crimes they did not commit, looms menacingly. In *Fugitive Pieces*, an apple story dominates the life of the second narrator, Ben, the Canadian-born child of survivors, who turns his biological father into the psychological equivalent of a Nazi tormenter and then fantasizes that he is his father, and hence the SS guard who brutalizes both of them. Ben is caught in a quandary similar to the one that torments Austerlitz. There are four links between Austerlitz and Ben: (1) the loss of a family narrative (Austerlitz has stepparents who cannot bring themselves to tell their foster child the story of his life, and Ben has biological parents who similarly fail to talk about his history; in this case, they never tell him about two siblings who perished in the war before he was born); (2) a sense of inherited victimization from—and a responsibility for—familial suffering; (3) an inability to return offered love, rendering Ben, like Austerlitz with Marie, the unavailing object of his wife's Petrarchan quest; and (4) an obsession with the connection between uncertain biography and unpredictable weather. Thus, like Austerlitz, Ben feels mostly the whimsy of sudden meteorological upheavals, not the steady progression forward of time. And, like Austerlitz, he concentrates on the arbitrariness of chance, viewing the oxymoronic "random precision of malevolence" (224) as the norm.

Though Austerlitz does not explicitly connect his assessment of the weather and its episodes of congestion and irruption to the Holocaust, Ben does. He cannot separate his fascination with the weather from the merciless shock of the war, "the sinister black funnel slithering across the landscape whining with the sound of a thousand trains" (224). He describes a tornado and its haphazard volatility, inevitably linked to the "capricious[ness]" of Nazi aggression:

> As a boy, twisters transfixed me with their bizarre violence, the random precision of their malevolence. Half an apartment is destroyed, yet an inch away from the vanished wall, the table remains set for dinner. A chequebook is snatched from a pocket. A man opens his front door and is carried two hundred feet from the treetops, landing unharmed. A crate of eggs flies five hundred feet and is set down again, not a shell cracked. All the objects that are transported safely from one place to another in an instant, descending on ascending currents: a jar of pickles travels twenty-five miles, a mirror, dogs and cats, the blankets ripped from a bed leaving the surprised sleepers untouched. Whole rivers lifted—leaving the riverbed dry—and then set down again. A woman carried sixty feet then deposited in a field next to a phonograph record (unscratched) of "Stormy Weather."
> Then there are the whims that are not merciful: children thrown from windows, beards torn from faces, decapitations. The family quietly eating supper when the door bursts open with a roar. The tornado prowls the street, it seems to stroll leisurely, selecting its victims, capricious, the sinister black funnel slithering across the landscape, whining with the sound of a thousand trains.
> Sometimes I read to my mother while she made dinner. I read to her about the effects of a Texas tornado, gathering up personal possessions until in the desert it had collected mounds of apples, onions, jewelry, eyeglasses, clothing—"the camp." Enough smashed glass to cover seventeen football fields—"Kristallnacht." I read to her about lightning—"the sign the Ess Ess, Ben on their collars." (224–25)

In his reading, Ben moves backward to Kristallnacht and then forward to himself. But like Austerlitz, he aligns himself with the victimizers. Only for Ben, the SS is also a homonym with the "Ess Ess," derived from his father's victimization, which, in turn, assigns to Ben the Nazi insignia he wears on his collar. The apples in the tornado mound evoke an earlier apple incident with his father:

> My father found the apple in the garbage. It was rotten and I'd thrown it out—I was eight or nine. He fished it from the bin, sought me in my room, grabbed me tight by the shoulder; and pushed the apple to my face.

"What is this? What is it?"
"An apple—" (213–14)
Even my father's humour was silent. He drew things for me, cartoons, caricatures. Appliances with human faces. His drawings offered the glimpse: how he saw.
"Is an apple food?"
"Yes."
"And you throw away food? You—my son—you throw away food?"
"It's rotten—"
"Eat it. . . . Eat it!"
"Pa, it's rotten—I won't—"
He pushed it into my teeth until I opened my jaw. Struggling, sobbing, I ate. Its brown taste, oversweetness, tears. Years later, living on my own, if I threw out leftovers or left food on my plate in a restaurant, I was haunted by pathetic cartoon scraps in my sleep. (218)

Here, the Oedipus myth is superimposed as the parental authority becomes the SS with his "Eat it . . . . Eat it!" In his refusal, the resistant child emerges the killer of the father. And the guilt doesn't leave him. Grown up, he turns the childhood "glimpse" of "how [his father] saw" into his own vision. The nightmare cartoon scraps retrace his father's drawings. Like the bits of food he rejects, the fragmented experience keeps impinging on his consciousness. He is bound to the story. Years later, throwing out scraps of leftover food, he sees not his own suffering but his father's: the pieces of apple become the shrapnel shards of bullets. The edible turns into iron; the cartoons are killing machines. The child's lack of desire for the apple betrays the father, as Eve's excess of desire renders her disloyal to Adam. In Ben's version of the apple story, the child becomes his father—"how he saw"—and then perpetuates the father's nightmare: "cartoon scraps haunt [his] sleep." He is pursued by mechanized trains of food, tortured by images that convert slips of paper into the same deadly material as the original (and mythological) poisoned fruit.

But in *Fugitive Pieces*, the habit of animating dead memories saves as well as stifles, becomes the savior as well as the tormentor of children. As Ben holds on to the cartoon scraps that haunt him, so (in the primary story) Jakob Beer keeps his lost sister Bella alive inside him: "But Bella clung. We were Russian dolls. I inside Athos, Bella inside me" (14). Jakob is pregnant with his sister, feeding her memory from the placenta of her wished-for recovery. But Michaels also manages to separate out the strands of interlocked histories, to make distinctions so that, finally, Jakob understands that he must no longer remain stagnant: "To remain with the dead is to abandon them" (170). That insight answers the question central to *The Nature of Blood*: "How can [one] remember and move on?" (157).[6] The oxymoron in Jakob's realization (remaining/abandoning) illustrates the foundling plot's essentialist bias: its loyalty to a past that may—outside the fiction—be impossible to recover and a physical stagnation that fails to acknowledge a present with any psychological meaning. Jakob imagines his missing sister spurring him on to the life he has, since her loss, lived: "All the years I felt Bella entreating me filled with her loneliness, I was mistaken. I have misunderstood her signals. Like other ghosts, she whispers, not for me to join her but so that, when I'm close enough, she can push me back into the world" (170). Unpacking his earlier Russian doll images (his mother [8] and sister [12] both inside him), the new signal recasts the story and pulls Jakob out of the trap of what Austerlitz calls the "orphaned frame of mind" (265). Such an acceptance assumes that love is not (as the formulaic foundling plot insists) biological even as it presumes that clinging to an elusive other (as the Petrarchan mythos stipulates) is fundamentally a death wish. And in another twist on what nurturing might mean, Jakob's savior, Athos, carries him: "On the island of Zakynthos, Athos, scientist, scholar, middling master of languages—performed his most astounding feat. From out of his trousers he plucked the seven year old refugee, Jakob Beer" (14). The running thread of adoption binds the pieces of the story together. Michaels fuses generations as well as genders as she reinvents the plot. Athos, the Greek archeologist, gives birth to Jakob, the narrator of the first part of the book, and Jakob sustains Naomi, wife of Ben, the apple victim in the second part. In turn, she then stands as luminous wife-mother for Ben, who is the narrator of the concluding section.

This bringing to life of the dead is partly inspirational—making visible the invisible—and partly restitutional—offering reparation for the loss. In each story, lost children are the central narrative crux. The end is foretold at the beginning of the novel: "No one is born just once. If you're lucky, you'll emerge again in someone's arms; or unlucky, wake when the long tail of terror brushes the inside of your skull" (5). Michaels's revisions actually get to the heart of the foundling plot and its simultaneous insistence on authenticity and dependence on fantasy. In the mythical formula, the first rescue— the emergence again in someone's arms—is conventionally seen as a temporary period of healing, a pause until the moment of recovery when the child finds its actual parents. Biology is subverted as the "emerge[nce] again" of adoption becomes an end in itself. Burying himself nightly after he ran from the home where his family was attacked, Jakob awakes one morning and is rescued by Athos, who, hiding the child under his coat at the border crossings, carries him to Greece. That was lucky. The alternative is the total effacement of subjective history, as the long tail of terror wipes from the table of memory, at the inside of "your skull," all personal feelings.

In *Fugitive Pieces*, opposing psychological positions are worked out: the lucky version where a Winnicottian holding space, like the one in which the Violet of *Ark Baby* enfolds Phelps, is preserved; the unlucky version, where the serpent in the apple story precipitates a claustrophobic cycle of projection and introspection that prevails. What is the long tail of terror but the snake, the eraser of all connections? Emerging again in "someone's arms" means being allowed, as Ben realizes at the end, to feel "the elation of ordinary sorrow" (292), a normalization Austerlitz never attains. When the tail of terror brushes the "inside of your skull," it annuls the individuated events of the child's life, making it feel as if the only history that matters is that of the family tragedy. The fugitive, the one who flees into safety, keeps the personal past from being evanescent, fragmented, and torn to bits.

Fugitive Pieces elaborates two kinds of parental influence: the first (the one that afflicts Ben so terribly) is the parents' desire to pass on their experience to their son and so to extend "the long tail of terror" forward through the generations, a parallel to the *Hamlet* ghost's insistence that Hamlet "remember" his father's victimization and Austerlitz's determination to make reparations for his father's death. Ben feels entombed by a family burial mound: "history only goes into remission, while it continues to grow in you until you're silted up and can't move" (243). Paralyzed by what happened to his parents, Ben expresses his sense of exposure as the initial event of a foundling plot. He is "forsaken even by those who claim to love you most" (243). That is the long tail of terror, "brushing" away selfhood at the inside of the skull. The second kind of parenting is supportive. It involves differing adoptions: the literal taking in of the lost child, as Athos switches genders to parent Jakob, and (secondarily) the feeling of sympathy for the loss itself as, switching generations, Jakob's second wife, Michaela, absorbs and makes reparations for his loss. *Fugitive Pieces* suggests that feeling *for* the other is a way of *becoming* the other. Such a becoming crosses gender and bloodlines in the Athos adoption and equates the sexual to the maternal instinct in Michaela's empathy. Changing the form, Michaels intertwines peripheral hints in the original myths and expands them so that the adopter and the adoptee take on each other's causes. When Athos dies, Jakob discovers a hidden cache, stuffed with letters of inquiry: "In the ... drawer ... is a thick folder, containing faint blue carbons and newspaper cuttings: Athos's search for my sister, Bella" (117). In *Fugitive Pieces*, others (not involved by biology in the central story) come to feel the loss. In Michaels's reworking, the missing pieces, precisely the element effaced and belittled in the traditional foundling plot, are foregrounded. In the traditional story, recovery is all. In *Fugitive Pieces*, *imagining* the loss is all. Adoption is the second birth that substitutes for mythical recovery.

In his work, Athos struggles to overcome the Nazi impulse to render the world Aryan by rewriting history. Privately, he rescued Jakob. Professionally he attempted to return the past to its rightful owners:

> *Bearing false Witness* plagued Athos. It was his conscience; his record of how the Nazis abused archaeology to fabricate the past. In 1939, Biskupin was already a famous site, already nicknamed the "Polish Pompeii." But Biskupin

was proof of an advanced culture that wasn't German; Himmler ordered its obliteration. It wasn't enough to own the future. The job of Himmler's ss-Ahnenerbe—the Bureau of Ancestral Inheritance—was to conquer history. The policy of territorial expansion—lebensraum—devoured time as well as space. (104)

Athos's life as a writer and his life as foster parent coincide. In his profession, he restores the geological past and so preserves "space" from the after-effects of Nazi expansionism; he resurrects the "Polish Pompeii." Intellectually, he adopts the Jewish cause; emotionally, he adopts a Jewish child, restoring Jakob and likewise redeeming "time" from the Nazi attempt to "conquer history" and eliminate the past and future Jew. When Athos dies, Jakob finishes his work, traveling back to Poland to continue Athos's research as an archeologist. Jakob completes the book that exposes the Nazi falsified digs "to prove that Greek civilization started in . . . neolithic Germany" (104) and, in that backward turning, he adopts his adopter: "Athos was an expert in buried and abandoned places. His cosmology became mine. I grew into it naturally. In this way, our tasks became the same" (49). Regarding the mutual give and take, Jakob writes, "Athos believed we saved each other" (51). And still later, he learns to appreciate "what [he] felt: not that I owed Athos everything but that I loved him" (60).

In the recovery section there is a sense of shared burden: "Athos said: 'We must carry each other. If we don't have this, what are we[?]'" (14). Michaels offers several versions of her revisionist foundling plot, sometimes outside any of the stories as a child mothers the woman who adopts her, and sometimes centrally, as a lover mothers the man she marries and a wife mothers her husband. The tangential story again reverses the Russian doll mechanism. A Greek woman—not essential to the Jakob or Ben plot—finds an abandoned child on the road and protects her. The child in turn nurtures her finder and brings her to a self she never knew she had:

> *Zdena felt Bettina's little finger through the thin cloth on different places on her body; it was like the game of connect-the-dots. Zdena took shape.*
> *The little girl sat on her lap and listened to stories. Zdena felt her forty-year-old breasts and belly go warm against the weight of the child. The grief we carry, anybody's grief, Zdena thought, is exactly the weight of a sleeping child.* (158)

As in the Jakob-Athos story, the circle of recovery—the finding of self—works two ways: Zdena mothers the child and—in connecting the dots—the child mothers the mother, just as, when he buries himself nightly to hide from the Nazis, Jakob "knew suddenly [that his] mother was inside him" (8) and, later, Athos carries Jakob inside him.

Chapter 4
THE MIRACULOUS CIRCUIT

In the Jakob story, a love plot revolves around another adoptive principle, bending the form of both. When the Petrarchan chase is closed up—and the love story is mutualized—the foundling plot, too, is tilted so that the Irigarayan horizontal axis dominates, forming a circle of recovered innocence:

> Michaela's hands above her head; I stroke the fragile place on the back of her smooth, soft upper arms. She is sobbing. She has heard everything—her heart an ear, her skin an ear. Michaela is crying for Bella.
> The light and heat of her tears enter my bones.
> The joy of being recognized and the stabbing loss: recognized for the first time. (182)

Michaela's sobbing for Jakob's grief overcomes the pain of his loss: its simultaneous excess in terms of the scale of the violence and loss of access in terms of the generational severance. Jacob's double use of the word "recognize" is itself crucial here. The typical "recognition scene" of the foundling plot "corrects" the child's history: the moment when the biological parent reclaims it. In that respect, it is almost a nonrecognition scene as, when the ruptured family line is restored, the initial abandonment is forgotten and the adoption ignored. Everything is one thing once the dynastic mandate is fulfilled. Here *"for* the first time"—with its joy—occurs only after a "recognition" *of* the first time—with its pain.

The "recognition" works doubly, acknowledging the past (denied by the convention) and changing the future (predetermined by the plot). First Michaela listens. All the parts of her body become porous as she shares Jakob's pain. Then she returns the grief she has absorbed to him, an act that allows Jacob to acknowledge where he is *now* in his joy and how he felt *then* in his pain. In recapitulating the loss, the tears also wash it away, allowing a new platform for debarkation "for the first time." How does this doubling happen? In *Austerlitz*, the Petrarchan chase is reversed as Marie pursues a hero who is incapable of returning her love. In *Fugitive Pieces*, such a pursuit grants a second birth. Michaela both loves and mothers Jakob. As Irigaray puts it, "man is engendered not created"[7] and her use of the word "engendering"—which is gender neutral, applying parenting to both sexes—describes the mutuality of this scene. At the same time, in terms of Petrarchan tropes, there is a gender reversal that forms yet another circle of mutuality. In the Apollonian light and heat of the stab, Michaela inseminates Jakob with a masculine strength, fortifying him even as (with the feminine moisture of her tears) she nurtures him, making way for this new, totally other, beginning. Hands above her head, she enfolds him with the comfort of her holding space. The tears provide a different sense of creation—a reciprocal rather than a univocal one, precisely what Irigaray advocates when she speaks of the mutuality made possible when the horizontal axis of romantic love replaces the vertical lines of the dynastic imperative. The recognition scene in this revisionist foundling plot involves both accepting the original feeling of abandonment and moving forward in time. Nothing is forgotten but everything is transformed into a new script, that of intragenerational nurturing.

The liquid tears in *Fugitive Pieces* heal even, as in their empathetic expressiveness, they share, rather than ignore, the pain. As Bettina's fingers do in the Zdena story, the stream of Michaela's weeping connects the dots in Jakob's shattered self, rendering him whole. The Petrarchan image of marble softening rain ("a little water by always trying, finally wear[s] away marble and solid rock"[8]) becomes, when the pain is borne by someone who never actually experienced it, simultaneously the bone piercing and the softening liquid, a stabbing penetration that reactivates the initial loss and regenerates the wounded body and mind. In the same way that the liquid tears melt away suffering in the Jakob section, so their mercy spreads its effect, as a twice-rescued Jakob overflows with words that shower on a subsequently blooming Naomi in the Ben section: "I saw [her] open like a flower" (230). Empathy enables further growth, sustenance spreading—like rain—across different spaces. Michaela mothers Jakob, and Jakob fosters Naomi. Michaela also changes the love story, creating Jakob not (as the Petrarchan poet might) out of absence in the image of herself but out of fullness and comfort. The mutuality of rehabilitation in the love plot enables the psychological evolution of rebirth: "Every cell in my body has been replaced, suffused with peace" (182).

If Michaela gives Jakob back his life by allowing him to feel the whole of his past in the comfort of the present, Ben (in the second story) stands outside the encirclements and resists his wife's enclosures, becoming (as Austerlitz was to Marie) the unavailable object of the Petrarchan quest, another instance where the generational burden of guilt obviates the possibility for reciprocal love. At two crucial points in the narrative (which I present in reverse chronological order) Ben uses scientific hereditary terms, describing the "molecular past" he will transmit to a hypothetical child and then (after he discovers a photograph of his dead brother and sister) the DNA of a family story from which he was excluded. The orphan of his own life, Ben feels unable to father a child. In the first instance, he can see nothing but the past of the life he has lived. In the second, he exposes the DNA of a history he never actually was allowed to know, a narrative from which he was cast away. Explaining why he doesn't want children of his own, Ben recounts his argument with his wife:

> Naomi says a child doesn't have to inherit fear. But who can separate fear from the body? My parents' past is mine molecularly. Naomi thinks she can stop the soldier who spat in my father's mouth from spitting into mine, through my father's blood. I want to believe she can rinse the fear from my mouth. But I imagine Naomi has a child and I can't stop the writing on its forehead from growing as the child grows. It's not the sight of the number that scares me, even as it bursts across the skin. It's that somehow my watching causes it to happen. (280)

Ben continues to feel not only the effects of his parents' suffering but also as if he is the source of its initial and subsequent repercussions. His "watching" spreads, rather than blocks, the pain, because Ben supposes that his fear is inseparable from the transmission of it. A child would bear the mark on his forehead that he himself imagined he wore, so that Ben would become to the future generation what his father was to him: the cause of an inherited guilt. His keeping "watch" to prevent will instead cause the numbers to (re)burst through the skin: the outside will emerge in the future what is inside him now. If Michaela's tears penetrate from the outside and heal, Ben's fears explode from the inside and traverse generations, ballasting a child not yet conceived with the rage it might inherit. In his backward turning, Ben remains the Nazi he was in the nightmares of the opening. His hypothetical son, with "SS" similarly on his collar, would be to him what he was to his father. That's the molecular inheritance, the biological imperative in its worst emanation. Contrastingly, Naomi believes in the adoptive principle. Fear is not genetic. Grounded by his father's exclusion of any history but his, Ben is afraid of his own vigilance in passing on the mind-deadening tail of the snaky terror. For the liquid rain gently nurturing in the Jakob story, Ben experiences instead the contempt of another liquid—spit. Ben's awareness—his watching—is not a protective barrier against an inscribed history but a premonition of its inevitable continuation. He cannot escape his molecular past. It remains the only story he knows and the only future he can envision. In such a history, Ben becomes his father. The vigilance that might protect the future child instead damages it.

But revealed after his parents' death is the buried secret that they lost two children in the camps. So there are two histories: the one Ben lived, in which he clones his father, each victimizing the other, and then a narrative in which he functions as a foster child, dissevered by his parents' refusal to connect him to his siblings. Though he is a biological heir, he is also banished from the family story: "Naomi explained something else I'd never known. My parents prayed that the birth of their third child would go unnoticed. They hoped that if they did not name me, the angel of death might pass by. Ben, not from Benjamin, but merely 'ben'—the Hebrew word for son" (253). Missing in the abbreviated name is its fully fleshed out mythical heritage. As "merely Ben," he is someone who happens into the family haphazardly, like a child left on the doorstep. Without the biblical suffix, he has no derivation, neither "of" nor "from" his family, in the way that Benjamin was Jacob's last—and perhaps most treasured—son in Genesis 35. There, he is the child of Rachel's suffering (Benoni, as she called him), and then he is renamed by his father (Benjamin, the progeny of Jacob's right—and stronger—side). In the biblical legend, the family history (both sides of it) is preserved. In Ben's narrative, the family history is effaced, "wip[ed] away" (in a chiasm to Hamlet's selfhood) from the family narrative.

As the last child of his parents, the Ben of *Fugitive Pieces* is denied the security of the connective link inherent to biblical naming. In the face of irreparable loss, the biological child feels adopted, a substitute for what the parents couldn't protect, a child fostered instead of the "real" children. Accidentally coming upon a photograph hidden away in his father's drawer after both parents had died, Ben discovers his dead brother and sister: "We think of photographs as the captured past. But some photographs are like DNA. In them you can read your whole future" (251–52). Ben can never be himself. In the story of his lived life, he becomes both his father and his father's victimizer. In the story of the lost narrative, he is merely a replacement for a brother and sister he never knew or could know. In both stories he is deprived of self, imprisoned by his "molecular" past, cloistered by a DNA future he cannot escape. Functioning the way images do in Austerlitz, the picture of the children who didn't survive the war, whose lives were unknown to him, becomes the inevitable print of his parents' concerted effort to keep him from his own history. Since he never knew it, he is denied the right to mourn. Ben begins by noting his feeling that something was missing, something that leaves the family exposed: "There was no energy of a narrative in my family. Not even the fervour of elegy. Instead our words drifted away, as if our home were open to the elements and we were forever whispering into a strong wind" (204).

If water preserves life in the Jakob story, wind dries up memory in the Ben story. The family house is forever subject to the whims of weather. The "watch" of preservation bears witness instead to the inevitability of disintegration. His family lived in a foundling plot where the missing children were not even mentioned. When he learns of their existence and death, Ben feels like a replacement without an antecedent: a foundling manqué. As biological child in one story, he is responsible for his parents' suffering: the "S.S. on his collar." But in the second story, he doesn't even play a part. When Ben discovers the photograph of his dead siblings, the lack of narrative is clear. The photograph fulfills Sebald's sense of historical accuracy, "arresting time." While for Sebald that sense of objective reality counters the fictional "negative gradient," for Ben it erases his history, making him feel excluded suddenly because only the dead children seem to have meaning. His story—and that of the life he has hitherto led—is totally separate from that of his family, even though (within those parameters) he is made to feel responsible for what happened to his parents. While Jakob grieves for Bella, Ben never knew he had siblings to mourn. He ends up feeling the castaway of his own life. Exposed in the retrospect of adulthood, he is deprived of a recognition that might have freed him of guilt. But if Ben remains forever feeling that his parents didn't *allow* him into the story (perhaps in the way that Austerlitz's foster parents kept his inheritance a secret), he does discover, at the end, what he might still achieve, a knowledge that comes from "re-memory," an insight he missed on his first viewing.

When he begins to feel that "at last [his] unhappiness is [his] own" (292), he removes himself both from the guilt of the biological mandate and from the narrative of the foundling plot from which he was excluded. Returning to Naomi after his voyage to Greece to find Jakob's papers, he sees that he can indeed "journey through [his] grief" (*The Winter Vault*, 93) in another way, by "[giving] what [he] most need[s]" (294). Apart from the story he thought was his biography and from the family narrative of his "orphaned life," there is another story: the one Naomi believes he can enter. Ben envisions how such a rebirth is possible, something his father had (as Jakob did through Michaela) because of his wife. Belatedly, he sees that engenderment is mutual; forgiveness involves an elimination of the Petrarchan quest and a rendering of the self to the other:

> The plane descends in a wide arc.
> Once, I saw my father sitting in the snow-blue kitchen. I was six years old. I came downstairs in the middle of the night. There had been a storm while I slept. The kitchen glowed with new drifts piled against the windows; blue as the inside of a crevasse. My father was sitting at the table, eating. I was transfixed by his face. This was the first time I had seen food make my father cry.
> But now, from thousands of feet in the air, I see something else. My mother stands behind my father and his head leans against her. As he eats, she strokes his hair. Like a miraculous circuit, each draws strength from the other.
> I see that I must give what I most need. (294)

In the empathetic vision, Ben discovers that all organs are permeable enough to absorb grief. As Jakob writes, "[the] heart an ear, [the] skin an ear" (182). The shifting of bodily parts in Beer's homage to Michaela—a fusion that seems somehow as magical as "Bottom's Dream" in *A Midsummer Night's Dream* "the eye of man hath not heard, the ear of man hath not seen" (4.1.205)—effaces generational difference and merges wife with mother. Healing the wounds, tears of sympathy surface as the life force of blood. The novel concludes with circles enclosing circles, as Ben comes to understand the sustenance his mother gave his father, that Naomi had already given him, and that he, now restored, might be able to give back.

When Michaels changes the foundling plot and renders the adoptive parent (Athos) virtually the repairer of a family line and then portrays the wife (Naomi, Michaela, Ben's mother to his father) as the supportive mother, she makes a case for the middle ground and centralizes, rather than marginalizes, the adoptive interlude. In *Fugitive Pieces*, identification occurs as the conventional genders and generations of the Petrarchan and foundling plots respectively are themselves challenged. If the Petrarchan ethos begins with the poet giving birth both to himself and to the woman who mirrors that desire, regeneration in *Fugitive Pieces* emphasizes a nurturing, rather than a reflective, creativity. Like Athos, men give birth to children, children foster their parents, wives mother their husbands, and husbands, in turn, mother their wives.

Finally, there are two additional alterations to the usual conventions that define Michaels's variations: the first stresses the fact that alimentary nurture—the most primitive bond between parent and child—supersedes familial barriers; the second, the fact that language itself bypasses the signature of a culture. In each of the food stories, family secrets are shared. Jakob watches Michaela bake a pie: "She smiles and tells me that her mother used to roll the pastry this way. Unknowingly, her hands carry my memories. I remember my mother teaching Bella in the kitchen. . . . I remember my mother urging Bella not to reveal the secret ingredients of her honey cake—the envy of Mrs. Alperstein—not ever, except to her own daughter, God willing" (192–93). And, in the Ben story, "How my mother must have pressed Naomi's hand, held on to her, conspired with her. Naomi emerging from the kitchen, smiling with a recipe for honey cake" (247–48). The formula for nurture—the recipe—is smuggled past the barriers of kinship, kinship violated ever so slightly. Sustenance, rather than heritage, links one family to another: sweet honey for rotten apples.

But it is with the self-conscious border crossings of language that Michaels's characters deliberately bridge differences. Even in their professions, Athos, Jakob, and Ben seem obsessed with the event and its sign. For his doctoral thesis, Ben chooses "the real life objective correlative—weather and biography" (211), a topic that fleshes out a connection he had already made as a child when he described a tornado in terms of the SS. The three central characters journey from Eastern Europe (Poland for Jakob and Athos, Russia for Ben) to Greece and eventually to Canada. Language (with its erasures and foreclosures saved by translations and adaptations) parallels the characters' lives. New vocabularies first sever geographical and historical ties and, in translations and poetry, make them possible in unexpected configurations. When Michaels's characters digress into language theory, they simultaneously split with the past and uncover histories that bypass normative imperatives:

During the occupation graffiti required swiftness and courage. Graffitos who were caught were executed by the Germans on sight. A single letter was exhilarating, it was spit in the eye of the oppressors. A single letter was a matter of life and death.

. . . In Athens, there was Palamas and the graffitos, whose heroism was language. I already knew the power of language to destroy, to omit, to obliterate. But poetry, the power of language to restore: this was what both Athos and Kostos were trying to teach me. (78–79)

And, later, when I began to write down the events of my childhood in a language foreign to their happening, it was a revelation. English could protect me; an alphabet without memory. (101)

Translation is a kind of transubstantiation; one poem becomes another. You can choose your philosophy of translation just as you choose how to live: the free adaptation that sacrifices detail to meaning, the strict crib that sacrifices meaning to exactitude. The poet moves from life to language, the translator moves from language to life; both, like the immigrant, try to identify the invisible, what's between the lines, the mysterious implications. (109)

I thought of writing poems in this way, in code, every letter askew, so that loss would wreck the language, become the language.

If one could isolate that space, that damaged chromosome in words, in an image, then perhaps one could restore order by naming. Otherwise history is only a tangle of wires. (111)

In *Fugitive Pieces*, writing enables a confrontation with loss and the recovery of broken connections. Jakob identifies Athos's intervention: "There were the few, like, Athos who chose to do good at great personal risk: those who never confused objects and humans, who knew the difference between naming and the named" (167). The "named" in the past tense becomes the biological trap of the culturally distilled and stifling "tangle of wires" (111) that makes up history as we know it. As an ongoing and transformative act, the participial "naming" involves a loosening of identities to suit the particularities of alternative destinies.

While the formulaic foundling plot depends on wiping out the loss and pretending it never happened, Michaels's version of the story depends on naming the loss and acknowledging, through the name, its material consequence. Longing to uproot history, Jakob sees English as his protector: "an alphabet without memory" (101). Yet, in his profession as translator, he settles on a metaphor that nevertheless reveals his situation and recovers his past. Translation, he writes, is "like the immigrant" (109), someone who moves between places but who struggles to identify the bond between where he has been and what he is. Recognizing the middle interlude between the lines, the immigrant neither returns to the beginning nor hearkens too easily toward the end. He comes close but remains in the indeterminate zone where authentication is replaced by an approximation that is good enough. Jakob explains that the immigrant strives to identify the invisible, "what's between the lines" (109), anticipating how Michaela (181–82) crosses the boundary to uncover "the mysterious implications," the penetration facilitating the movement of "language to life." Wordless, tears evoke a language of their own, the liquid that becomes, as in *The Winter Vault*, *Othello*, and *The Winter's Tale*, the energetic lifeblood of renewal, permeating the "invisible" to "wash" (*The Winter Vault*) it clean and replace every cell in the body to "suffuse it with peace" (182). Such a replacement is not a forgetting; it involves a reconfiguration of the forms, which Desdemona does in *Othello* when she vows that she will "by bad mend" (4.3.103). Mending rather than ending the formula and settling for the middle ground, Michaels changes the story and challenges the imperative that we continue to be "constructed by the construction"[9] of mythical authenticity.

Fugitive Pieces ends with the discovery of a "miraculous circuit" (294), an invented link that redirects both the Petrarchan and foundling plots. Part fabulous in the "miracle," part mechanical in the "circuit," the novel offers alternative readings both of the mythologies that determine the form and the named who are formulaically bound by it. In her variations, Michaels eliminates the racist and nationalistic blood ties of the essentialist family and renders the adoptive interlude as an end in itself, even as (in the circuit) she bends the Petrarchan lines into a ring of mutual engenderment. Such a telling difference points the culture toward a new mythology and a different telling, one that might, in the future, make *all* the difference.

Speaking of *Fugitive Pieces* in London in 2009, Michaels argued that "it's not the writer and it's not Athos who pulls [Jakob] out of the mud, it's the reader."[10] With that statement, she transforms the reader into a participant very like the chronicler in *Austerlitz*, who, defying Sebald's periscopic methodology, makes Austerlitz's quest, symbolized by the metonymic rucksack, his own. Through the adoptive fostering she advocates, Michaels's radical modification enables us to feel the losses the way Michaela does, experiencing them imaginatively without glossing over anything. The recovery acknowledges the whole of the picture. For Sebald, the "negative gradient" of the plot and Austerlitz's unending desire to fit into its frame block the reader from crossing the "dividing line" to bring Austerlitz "up from the depths" (297). The final vision in *Fugitive Pieces* comes from the other direction as, returning to Naomi in the plane and "thousands of feet in the air" (294), Ben looks down, remembering his father's tears but seeing in the wider frame of second sight his mother's empathetic holding; with that second sight, he learns that he "must give what [he] most need[s]" (294). He thus transforms the narrative line into the ring of the "miraculous circuit" where man and woman can be realigned each "draw[ing] strength from the other" (294). Such a vision is possible because Michaels's telescopic lens closes the gap between father and son in the foundling plot and the pursuing self with the sought-after other in the Petrarchan quest even as it draws the reader into the saving circle.

From the vantage point of late modern retrospect, all four novels in this study challenge the bloodline inheritance of the dynastic mandate. By questioning (in *The Nature of Blood* and *Austerlitz*) the male usurpation of female generativity inherent to the Petrarchan mind-set or by changing its mimetic tendency for a mutual nurturing (in *Ark Baby* and *Fugitive Pieces*), they rewrite the lyric dynamic. In *The Winter's Tale*, Shakespeare performs Anne Michaels's double revision—first, of Petrarchism (with the Irigarayan horizontal axis of Florizel and Perdita's engenderment a parallel for the Jakob-Michaela story) and, second, with the elimination of the need for intergenerational support (with Florizel's dismissal of familial "succession" when he announces "I / Am heir to my affection" [4.4.468–69]), an early modern expression of Ben's release from parental obligation in his declaration that "at last my unhappiness is my own" (292). Florizel's silence at the end of Act 5, like Shylock's absence from Belmont, speaks to Shakespeare's ambivalence about the bloodline inheritance and lyric expectations Michaels recasts in the "miraculous circuit" (294) Ben discovers. In *Othello*, Shakespeare similarly regenders the lyric with Desdemona's remarkable expressiveness in Act 4. The willow song (4.3.25–57) depicts a feminine community that transforms the adoptive interlude with a newly remembered, albeit short-lived, maternal space.

In the chapters on contemporary writers I emphasize that Phillips, Jensen, Sebald, and Michaels follow the "law[s] of writ" and take a "liberty" with the foundling and Petrarchan plots to create a dynamic that enables us to see how ancient biblical and classical mythologies are enclosed within the larger generic framework of fiction. In the next chapters, I will describe how those same plots function within the dramatic forms—tragic and comic, and "tragical-comical-historical-pastoral"—proleptically as Shakespeare, during the period of the rise of the nation-state, anticipates the disastrous consequences of the bloodline mandate inherent to both plots and as he diverts the script into something totally different. Particularly in *The Merchant of Venice*, and *Othello*, he connects an early modern racism to the imperatives of those plots, and in *The Winter's Tale*, he matches the subversions *Fugitive Pieces* enacts. Thus, I work two ways to demonstrate that theoretically informed contemporary writing enables us to reenvision the Shakespeare we thought we knew and that the perspective offered by such a newly viewed Shakespeare can, in turn, transform our present-day prospects. Linked by the "small forms" of the Petrarchan and foundling plots, the backward turning of fiction leads us to the forward movement of drama as Shakespeare anticipates what contemporary fiction writers similarly acknowledge when they restage the stories: the standard plots that prove tempting as a "a set of interpretations or frames or fixes on the world"[11] also adversely influence, in their sociocultural repercussions, the very life that inspires them. In *Merchant of Venice*, we see just how the interpenetration of the lyric and foundling plots undermines the "miraculous circuit" (294) Michaels advocates here, as the Belmont winners triumph over Shylock's energetic presence in the Pinteresque menace of the concluding comedy.

NOTES

1. *The Winter Vault* (London: Bloomsbury, 2009), 93.
2. "Eyes and Tears," *The Poems and Letters of Andrew Marvell*, edited by H. H. Margoliouth, revised by Pierre Legouis and E. E. Duncan Jones (Oxford: Clarendon Press, 1971), 88.
3. Alison Martin uses this phrase to explain Irigaray's conception and insistence on "to" in *I Love to You: Sketch of a Possible Felicity in History*, translated by Alison Martin (New York: Routledge, 1996), 102.
4. The instances of healing water in *Fugitive Pieces* counter the deadly waters (exemplified by the dried-up Yoruba in the Othello story, the slimy behavior of Gerry's slippages with Eva, and the "bathing" light cast on the naked Margot) in *The Nature of Blood*. The transformation illustrates how Michaels bends the Petrarchan and foundling plots that stultify in Phillips's work.
5. Writing that *Fugitive Pieces* illustrates the "complexity of bringing feminism with its attention to gender and sexual politics into the field of Holocaust studies, with its attention to trauma and racialized politics" ("Empathic Identification in Anne Michaels's *Fugitive Pieces*: Masculinity and Poetry after Auschwitz," *Signs* 28, 1 [2002]: 273), Susan Gubar cites this passage when she praises Michaels's "deployment of lyrical fiction." She argues further that "poetry's opacity and figural density write what cannot be written so as to excavate, preserve, or at least, evoke the transmitted and untransmitted memories of those obliterated or incapacitated by the Shoah" (273). Maintaining that Michaels redeploys other genres, specifically elegy and pastoral, Donna Coffey ("Blood and Soil in Anne Michaels's *Fugitive Pieces*: The Pastoral in Holocaust Literature," *Modern Fiction Studies* 53, 1 [2007]: 48), referring to an earlier version of this chapter (published in *Tulsa Studies in Women's Literature* 21, 2 [2002]: 275–300), writes that I am "a little too glib in celebrating the role of adoption." See "Blood and Soil in Anne Michaels's *Fugitive Pieces*: The Pastoral in Holocaust Literature." Like Gubar, Coffey notes that Michaels fails to give the elegiac consolation based on the continuing cycles of life and that she changes her use of pastoral to demonstrate that "within the wasteland, acts of empathy and compassion enable the transmission of memory." Coffey demonstrates how Michaels rewrites genres to make them answer the immense loss incurred by the Shoah. But my celebration of adoption has to do with Michaels's dual aim of mourning the losses both Gubar and Coffey find necessary and emphasizing that the very culture we revere might have contributed to the mind-set that fed into the trauma.

On remembering and genre, Meredith Crislington writes of the radical reenvisioning of *Fugitive Pieces* in its relationship to traditional forms of commemorative art. As a "counter-discourse, counter-memory challenges the dominant discourses of history and myth." Refer to "The City as a Site of Counter-memory in Anne Michaels's *Fugitive Pieces* and Michael Ondaatje's *In the Skin of a Lion*," *Essays on Canadian Writing* 81 (2004): 131. With allusions to James Young's "counter-monuments," Crislington demonstrates how the city of Toronto becomes for Athos and Jakob the site of contested memory that leads backward to history and forward to a different kind of commemoration.

6. Méira Cook ("At the Membrane of Language and Silence: Metaphor and Memory in *Fugitive Pieces*," *Canadian Literature* 164 [2000]: 12–33) presents the problem I identify here when she writes about Michaels's use of metaphor and metonymy in *Fugitive Pieces*:

Michaels's project in *Fugitive Pieces* might be perceived as an attempt to metaphorize history, memory, and narrative precisely in order to challenge the literal, to articulate catastrophe in language that is densely allusive. Yet Michaels's lush poetic discourse jars uneasily with the horrors she is narrating and so contributes to our discomfort as readers at the same time that it provides a way of thinking about metaphor and metonymy as figurative devices that alternatively reveal and conceal the materiality of the event. (16)

Cook argues that Michaels's poetic metaphors refute Theodor Adorno's claim that "after Auschwitz it is barbaric to write a poem," maintaining that Michaels "restore[s] to language what Adorno once mourned as necessarily lost forever" (29). While Cook views poetry as a means of overcoming the sad facts of history, I maintain that literary conventions sometimes contribute to the devastation they are expected to contrast.

7. *I Love to You: Sketch of a Possible Felicity in History*, 36.

8. Francesco Petrarcha, *Rime sparse* 265, in *Petrarch's Lyric Poems: The Rime Sparse and Other Lyrics*, translated and edited by Robert M. Durling (Cambridge, MA: Harvard University Press, 1976), 434.

9. Witold Gombrowicz, *Ferdydurke*, translated by Danuta Borchardt and introduction by Susan Sontag (New Haven, CT, and London: Yale University Press, 2000), 72.

10. Keynote address for the Orange Prize Committee, July 6, 2009, Royal Festival Hall, London.

11. *The Resources of Kind: Genre Theory in the Renaissance*, edited by Barbara K. Lewalski (Berkeley: University of California Press, 1973), 8.

Shakespearean Presents

Chapter Five

Turning Gender and Plot in *The Merchant of Venice*

Reading backward from Harold Pinter's *No Man's Land*, we can find a curiously similar play on "turn" in *The Merchant of Venice*, one involving Lancelot's position in the foundling plot and the other Portia's answer to her helplessness in the Petrarchan plot. Anticipating a Pinteresque menace, *Merchant*, like *No Man's Land*, "turns . . . ill-gotten [financial] gains" into ill-begotten psychological losses. In *No Man's Land*, there is no way out, the "turns" paralleling, in their spatial "confusions," the linguistic misdirections of *The Merchant of Venice*:

> A car drew up. He asked me the way to Bolsover street. I told him Bolsover street was in the middle of an intricate one-way system. It was a one-way system easy enough to get into. The only trouble was that, once in, you couldn't get out. I told him his best bet, if he really wanted to get to Bolsover street, was to take the first left, first right, second right, third on the left, keep his eye open for a hardware shop, go right round the square, keeping to the inside lane, take the second Mews on the right and then stop. . . . All he's got to do is to reverse into the underground car park, change gear, go straight on, and he'll find himself in Bolsover street with no trouble at all. I did warn him, though, that he'll still be faced with the problem, having found Bolsover street, of losing it. I told him I knew one or two people who'd been wandering up and down Bolsover street for years. They'd wasted their bloody youth there. The people who live there, their faces are grey, they're in a state of despair, but nobody pays any attention, You see. All people are worried about is their illgotten gains.[1]

Gobbo: Master young man, I pray you, which is the way to Master Jew's?

> *Lancelot*: This is my true-begotten father. . . . I will try confusions with
> him. . . . Turn up on your right hand at the next turning, but at the next turning
> of all on your left, marry at the very next turning, turn of no hand but turn
> down indirectly to the Jew's house. (2.2.27–30, 33–36)[2]

> *Nerissa*: Why, shall we turn to men? (3.4.79)

Directions to Pinter's Bolsover Street and to Shylock's house in *Merchant of Venice* end in the same "one-way system"—the circumstance Lancelot identifies for his father as he elides "confusions"—the fact that he's already not spatially where he is expected to be (with "conclusions") and the fact that he inverts the order temporally: he will be the begetter of his father at an indeterminate time (2.2.28). Having found his son, Gobbo will feel, in Pinter's terms, as if he's "losing it." The link between Bolsover Street as a "state of despair" and Lancelot's dead end—the "Jew's house"—shifts backward twice, first to Lancelot's animus toward his father and then to Antonio's situation at the opening of *The Merchant of Venice*. In its "turn[ing] of no hand," *Merchant* challenges the impetus of the normalized foundling plot where all hands point to a recovered beginning, one that disallows the independence of Shylock's self-creation in Act 1 and that renders Antonio as uncertain about his capabilities at the end as he was in his opening speech.

There are endless "turnings" in the play, most notably characterized by Antonio, the merchant of the title, who slides in and out of parallels and chiasms to Lancelot, Bassanio, and Shylock, each turn representing a direction that becomes an indirection, confirmation of what Bassanio calls "such confusion in [his] powers" (3.2.177). Only in the end, after multiple positional exchanges with Shylock in Act 4, does Antonio find himself safe—but dependent on the good graces of Portia—sheltered among all the other winners in Belmont, part of the enclosed ring so important to the foundling plot. Expressing his desire to remain dangling in the middle, Lancelot represents one alternative to the formula, choosing to switch masters rather than to move forward and become child to his father or to acknowledge his paternity of the Moor's child. Similarly excluded from the concluding recognition, Shylock begins by declaring his independence from the ordinary genealogical concerns of the foundling plot. In that respect, he signals a turn sequestered from its conventional dynastic imperatives, declaring his being in terms of self-creation, his "breeding" a component of lyric construction, a "turn" comprising the second of Shakespeare's experiments in *Merchant of Venice*. The two essential challengers to the foundling plot—Lancelot and Shylock—are exempt from the recoveries at the end: the clown because he prefers to remain (in apprenticeship) where he is, and Shylock, first, because he declares himself in terms of Petrarchan independence and, second, because having had his lyric voice silenced in the trial of Act 4, he is deprived of linguistic and physical presence in Belmont, cast away just when everyone else is found.[3]

Apart from the time and space "turns" in *Merchant* is the one that Nerissa fears when Portia reveals her plan to "*turn* two mincing steps / Into a manly stride" (3.4.67–68)—the two-for-one deal that changes gender and mythical underpinnings. Connected to the sexual switching Portia embraces and Nerissa fears is another meaning of "turn," centering on the plots of the play; in its rhetorical meaning during the sixteenth century, "turn" signified a mode of speaking. Posing a challenge (an antistrophe) to the foundling plot (with its temporary adoption and final insistence on biological heredity), Shakespeare deploys the lyric (with its births from nowhere and unmitigated persistence as artistic invention) as a counter to the familial abandonments and societal adoptions that structure the essentially comic conclusion.[4] The lyric's creative enterprise and its steadfast evasion of marriage offers an alternative to the dynastic exigencies of the foundling plot. Its presence in the play is delimited—first in the banishment of Shylock and, second, in Portia's stepping out of the role as desired and distant other in Bassanio's wooing sequences when, in Act 3, she convert(s) herself to Bassanio and with her ring consecrates herself to—and so adopts—him. Shakespeare ultimately wears down the lyric (where the poet invents the woman and the woman refuses, thereby giving the poet more reason to continue his invention) and stifles it with the end run (the "turn of no hand") imperatives of the foundling plot, which emphasizes the bloodline as biology over the "hand-line" as poeticizing. Hands down, the lyric loses.

By pitting the two plots against each other in *Merchant*, Shakespeare demonstrates how much independence is given up for the sake of the traditional closure of comedy, exemplified when Graziano vows to "keep . . . safe" (5.1.306) Nerissa's ring, his lewd gesture a sign of the deterministic structure of the comic mandate. In terms of gender, there are two related turnings: the man-for-woman exchange in the foundling plot, as Portia plays the man who enables the dynastic recoveries in Act 5, and the man-for-woman exchange in the lyric as Portia and Shylock trade places.[5] The more Portia steps out of her role as the lyric desired other, to convert herself into the "adoptive" nurturer of Bassanio and therefore of Antonio, the more she slides into the patriarchal mode of comedy that situates the happy ending with the lovers' reunion and the implicit postplay fulfillment of Graziano's earlier wager for the "first boy" (3.2.213).[6] The more Shylock takes Portia's place as woman in the lyric, the more he loses the control he reveals in the Laban speech.[7] There, he combines male creative enterprise with female reproductive capacity and emerges the self-generator who has no need for anyone.

The Petrarchan switchings follow my questions about the cultural influence of the foundling theme. In its fixation on "blood inheritance," *The Merchant of Venice* upholds the genetic bias of the usual plot. But Shakespeare's inclusion of a lyric substrata—with its gender turnarounds—forces us to question the triumph of the concluding Belmont revelations and returns. In its insistence on self-creation, the lyric counters the dynastic mandate of the foundling plot and so offers an alternative origin and an altogether different destiny. When he writes the lyric out, obviating its linguistic emphasis on foreplay as opposed to the foundling theme's promulgation of replay (in the enacted restoration of an earlier genealogy) and afterplay (in the expected progeny), Shakespeare leaves us feeling that something vital is lost at the end, even when, in the Belmont gloating, everything seems to be found. Shylock—the challenger of the foundling plot's emphasis on biologically inherited beginnings—and Lancelot—the resister to the mandated dynastic endings—are both absent at the end, deprived of the voice they evidenced so brilliantly early on. Using a tripartite structure in each instance, Shakespeare crosses plots and genders to double cross and so undercut the comic conclusion.

Merchant presents three (gradually diminishing) versions of the powerful lyric vocalizer (all of which have their sources in Petrarch): First, Bassanio is in total control of Portia (3.2.24–36) in an almost-sonnet sequence where Portia's Laura plays Daphne to Bassanio's Petrarch as Apollo. Then, in the casket-choosing speech, Portia becomes the woman occasionally present in the *Rime sparse*: a Laura-Medusa who turns everyone who looks at her to stone (3.2.73–114). Finally, once Bassanio chooses the right casket, Portia appears (briefly, until her "conversion") as the artist controlling him (3.2.115–30); in that sequence she plays a rare, yet important, part of the lyric complex—a Laura who responds to Petrarch by demonstrating her own powers, as she does in *Rime sparse* 23 when she declares, "I'non forse chi tu credi (I am not perhaps who you think I am),"[8] referring to an impenetrable self. It is precisely such a Laura-Portia who (in his imaginings) so undermines Bassanio's confidence that he feels himself "a wild of nothing" (3.2.182)—out of control in terms of formal linguistic structure and empty of power in terms of self-sustaining energy: in short a woman and an unruly one at that.

Reversing the sequence that temporarily unmans Bassanio, Shylock—in relation to Antonio—begins where Portia ends in Bassanio's final depiction, as the shaper of his destiny with the Laban speech of 1.3.67–92, passes briefly into the avenging Medusa in the "hath not a Jew eyes" speech (3.1.45–62), and finally is cast (in Act 4) as the resistant Daphne defined by the Venetians, the most well-known Laura that Petrarch devises. In the last change, he emerges totally—as Laura is to Petrarch in most of the *Rime sparse*—an entity created by a narrative that renders him powerless, circumscribed by a language structure that confines him to Venetian terms. Unlike the Belmont winners, who seem, through various transformations, to get back at the end everything missing in the foundling plot at the beginning, Shylock is bereft both of his lyric inventiveness and of the dynastic enterprise he had hoped to perpetuate. Lorenzo simply inherits what Shylock does not wish to bequeath.

Portia's role as coveted and threatening woman in the lyric (revealed in Bassanio's three speeches about her in Act 3) is thus transferred to Shylock who, in his initial confrontation with Antonio, presents himself as the agent of an independent generativity. Setting himself apart from the concerns of everyone else in the play, the Shylock of the Laban speech pronounces his physical and psychological originality, growing his fiscal empire with such enthusiastic pleasure that "the curse never fell upon our nation till now—I never felt it till now" (3.1.72).[9] Until he loses Jessica, he finds himself totally independent of the genetic, racialized heritage ascribed to him by his Venetian enemies. In a play where biological origin is of such importance, the performativity of self-generation (essential to lyric imaginings) poses a threat to all levels of society. Antonio is enraged at the Shylock of the Laban speech just as Bassanio is terrified of the Portia (taking over the male part in his imagination) whom he wins once he's chosen the right casket. When Portia steps back into the foundling plot in her conversion, her lyric role is transferred to Shylock, whose diminishing linguistic control provides one means of describing his situation in the play.[10] Once Shylock is remanded to the scripted woman in the lyric, he is robbed of the "means" (4.1. 372)—both the financial foundation and the creative enterprise—that energized him.[11] Alone, he experiences Lancelot's "turn of no hand" as a turn of no end, abandoned (as he is) and left in a place very like Pinter's "no man's land. Which never moves, which never changes, which never grows older, but which remains forever, icy and silent" (*No Man's Land*, 153). Paul Stevens describes Shylock's Pinteresque desolation: "Shylock is deprived of individual agency—he has no choice—and, just as important, he is deprived of his difference—he loses his Jewishness, his own way of being in the world."[12]

In my reading, Shakespeare also presents triadic groupings in the foundling plot—Antonio/Bassanio/Portia; Gobbo/Lancelot/the nameless Moor; Shylock/Jessica/Lorenzo. The deadlock in each figures in the absence of a different stage of the convention. Initially, Antonio cannot find an origin for his estranged self; Lancelot, seeking only to exchange one middle period for another, misplaces conclusions as directional confusions; and Shylock—who has a sure beginning, one that he invents for himself—loses out on the dynastic continuity of his invented self because of Jessica's betrayal and Portia's taking from him the imaginative and literal "means whereby [he] live[s]" (4.1.372). Each of the stories shadows a complicated mythical origin: Lancelot/Gobbo/the Moor—Esau and Isaac; Antonio/Bassanio/Portia—Medea-Jason; Shylock/Jessica/Lorenzo—Jacob and Laban. And each of the sources indirectly involves a history of trickery, an attempt by subterfuge (in yet another meaning of "turn") to change the course of events in one's favor. Jacob initially deceives Isaac when he pretends to be the hairy Esau but nevertheless becomes the father of a great nation. Medea beguiles her father only to restore Jason's father. Jacob manipulates Laban, even though he was at first ill used by his father-in-law. All the mythical antecedents underscore aspects of concern to the foundling plot: the Esau-Isaac one with the question of inheritance rights, the Medea-Jason one confounding (by ending it) the generational future, the Jacob-Laban one over issues of marriage dowry.

In *Merchant*, the triumphal moments of the myths are pushed to the foreground. Lancelot teases Gobbo about a hairiness like Esau's in the recognition scene with his father (2.1.32–107). Portia is twice seen as the helpful golden Medea in the sequence where Bassanio persuades Antonio to back him in his suit (1.2.161–76) and at the moment when Graziano announces Bassanio's winning the prize (3.2.240). Shylock connects himself to Jacob in the Laban reference when he speaks of his seminal mercantile methodology in 1.3.65–90. But behind all those success stories lurk the Ovidian and biblical shadows: the specter of Medea, who murders her children, overlooked but not unremembered in the final "keeping safe" (for male use) of the female ring in the Pinteresque menace of Graziano's last line (5.1.306). Contrastingly, the end of the Jacob story (where Joseph pardons and helps the brothers who wronged him) is notably *absent* after the trial. Shylock remains unforgiven, a response in kind to his refusal of mercy. My contention throughout this chapter is that Shakespeare and his audiences reserve in the back of their minds the whole of the mythical underpinnings (the conclusion of the Medea story and the happy reunion of the Joseph section in the Genesis plot) even if only parts of the story are invoked by specific mention in the play. The Belmont triumph is thus darkened and Shylock's losses are compounded in the context of the Ovidian and biblical allusions.

Over and above the mythical and biblical constraints (unfulfilled as destiny in the case of Portia-Medea, withdrawn as promise in the case of Shylock-Jacob) are two intertwined concerns—the linguistic ones connected to literary formulae and the sexual reversals which occur as a result of the gender slippages. Women turn to men (Portia/Bellario) and the Moor (as I will explain in the next section) is characterized as a man playing a woman played by a man, an unnecessary Shakespearean joke as s/he never is seen in the play. Alan Sinfield speaks of Lancelot as part of the "traffic in boys" endemic to the play and emphasizes that Shylock has already passed him on to Bassanio before Gobbo even offers his dish of pigeons.[13] But it's more complicated than that because Lancelot himself is an instigator of a traffic he commands in the Gobbo scenario and later denies when he claims not to have known that the Moor was even a woman (in this case, as the Elizabethan audience clearly understood, played by a boy). If, as Sinfield argues, same-sex passion was downplayed in the end "because women may bear children and [because] relations between women and men affected the regulation of lineage, alliance and property,"[14] then a real challenge to the impetus of the foundling plot's continuity is Lancelot, who (in terms of filial and paternal responsibility) refuses to play the generational game, delaying his return to his father and denying all responsibility for fathering the Moor's child. Shylock, too, charts his own territory, presenting himself as the powerful Jacob, interfering with generativity and wafting his wand (as Medea, restoring her father-in-law, wields a similarly grafted branch), but is finally seen as the female victim in the last acts when the Venetians convert him to the resistant Laura of the Petrarchan poetic dyad.[15] Antonio changes places several times in the play, lost at the opening as a man without words (until he finds them when he supports Bassanio), and desperate in Act 4 (until Portia saves him) as the "tainted wether of the flock" (4.1.113). Bassanio likewise (when he woos Portia) is full of conventional male-generated love talk and (at the moment he wins Portia) finds himself unable to articulate anything. Those shifts in verbal power follow the gender switches as Shylock and Portia change generic places, she moving out of the lyric and serving the patriarchal claims of the foundling plot, he changing places within the lyric form, slipping from creative inventor of his own dynamic to the feminized object of everyone else's conscription of his powers.[16]

Shakespeare returns ends to beginnings in other plays where the characters get back an innocence lost in the course of the action, plays where he also underscores the difference between comic and lyric expectations. In *Much Ado about Nothing*, for example, the concluding act makes possible a recovery of the beginning as Claudio exults, "Sweet Hero, now thy image doth appear / In the rare semblance that I lov'd it first" (5.1.235–36). Conversely, in *Merchant*, the images fall apart as Shylock deliberately cuts himself off from the generativity of the Jacob story when he "finds" (out about) Jessica—"I would my daughter were dead at my foot, and the jewels in her ear" (3.1.74–75)—and then is denied even the possibility for reconciliation (as, for example, even Lear achieves with the Cordelia he renounced) when he becomes a nonentity, not even spoken of in Act 5. Benedick tries to write a sonnet to Beatrice in *Much Ado* but fails because he can "find out no rhyme to 'lady' but 'baby'" (5.2.32–33), so absorbed is he in the comic confines— and sexual procreativity—of comedy rather than the vocabulary afforded by the form-giving creation *ex nihilo* of the lyric.

In *Merchant*, what Jonathan Goldberg calls the "law of comedy"[17] similarly takes over as Portia "adopts" both Bassanio and Antonio and makes reparations for their mutual losses. But the lyric, with all its verbally shaping powers, is given unusual place in this play. Bassanio appears as Petrarch to Portia's Laura before he chooses the right casket, and then (momentarily when he wins her) becomes frightened of his own creation. Finally, Portia plays into the patriarchal role when, in the trial scene, she takes on the male voice and cause. Sliding into her place in the last act and condemning everyone outside the ring as part of the "naughty world" barred from the effects of her "good deed," she upholds the Venetian code.[18] She kills the energy spawned by the lyric in the same way that Medea kills off her children. If, as I am suggesting, the foundling plot betrays a desire, in the opening exposure, to be rid of the child and its burden, then excluding the self-created child, the different Shylock, is a way of ridding the state of an imagination not in synch with the genetic mandate fulfilled at the end. Shylock is thus part of the "naughty world" (5.1.90) Portia admonishes when she returns to Belmont, "naughty" a word appropriate to the idyllic Belmont but not quite adequate to the harsh realities of Act 4.

The problem in Venice is the same as that of Bolsolver Street; nearly everyone seems unable to escape the confines of a path from which one "can't get out." Portia's future lies locked in a casket; Gobbo's son is presumably inside a house he has already left behind; Lancelot's child is hidden within the Moor, a darkness he simultaneously cannot fathom and refuses to acknowledge. Bassanio also seems unable to discern his own sense of self—at the very moment he should most enjoy it—when he opens the casket and discovers what he has won; Jessica, at first escaping the familial bind ("and if my fortune be not crossed / I have a father, you a daughter lost," 2.5.54–55), is inextricably tied into the Belmont narrative, also "kept safe" (5.1.306) in the marriage and love games that confine her spirit. All are somehow "curbed" (Portia's term, 1.2.21) by the feeling that they are psychologically in danger of never getting out. The one character who defines himself as free from the outset is Shylock and he is at liberty only until Jessica takes from him the insignia that identifies him as an independent agent, securing his belief that he can, like Jacob, establish by his own means the present of his potency and the future of his progeny, the physical flesh seen as indistinguishable from the semiotic system that he makes "breed" so "fast" (1.3.92) both quickly and permanently. The pattern in the play is thus circular, as the rings of Venetian power keep shifting homoerotic ties and literary plots until, at the end, they are confined within the patriarchal frame of the comic "turn."

While critics and directors have tended to read the Bassanio-Antonio relationship as part of a homosocial undercurrent,[19] they have failed sufficiently to note that the power struggle between Antonio and Shylock has a sexual component, as each becomes (in "turn") the source of the other's "turn" into the feminine object of male control.[20] However, once Antonio moves into the winner's circle, he exits the lyric (where he is pitted against Shylock) and finds a place of safe harbor, energized as parent (in the end both to Bassanio and Portia), and financed (with his recovered ships) and presumably engineered by Portia's behind-the-scenes backing. In the context of the foundling plot where he finds a place (and from which Shylock is exempt), there is yet another foil to Antonio: Lancelot, who appears to have everything Antonio (at the opening of the play) lacks. If the Shylock-Antonio sparring is sexual, and the Bassanio-Antonio pairing is parental, the Lancelot-Antonio split centers on verbal dexterity—Antonio feels unable to find words and Lancelot is too clever by half.[21] But both Antonio's linguistic blather and Lancelot's witty rejoinders are voiced in the context of the foundling convention: Antonio expressing his feeling of malaise by questioning its birth in him; Lancelot attempting to bypass the conventional recognition scene with his father even as, in his self-defensive accusations against the Moor, he abandons his child before it is even born. Lancelot knows the end and the beginning but prefers to "try confusions" (2.2.30), islanding his present from his past and future. As he demonstrates in the opening speech of the play, Antonio doesn't know where he is or how he got there. Empty of linguistic energy, his mental space is defused. Certain of his physical bearings, Lancelot attempts to transform his temporal place and to substitute his verbal agility for his familial connectivity. Antonio and Lancelot seem to have opposite feelings about the "turning of no hand"; Antonio neither knows his beginning nor envisions an end, and therefore wastes exhaustedly in the middle, while Lancelot, certain of his origin and destiny, wishes desperately to extend the diaspora that renders Antonio so uneasy. Thus Antonio and Lancelot are sequestered in the middle of the foundling plot, with Antonio having no knowledge of how he arrived and Lancelot only wanting to stay there.

Before I turn in my analysis to the three stages of the lyric, exhibited first by the Bassanio-Portia sparring and then by the Antonio-Shylock dueling, I explore Lancelot's power in terms of his resistance to, and Antonio's loss as he expresses it in terms of the initiation of, the foundling plot. Shakespeare's original "take" on the theme in this pairing counters his inventive use of the Petrarchan tradition where he substitutes lyric openness for dynastic closure.

THE FIRST "TURN": LANCELOT, THE CHILD WHO KNOWS TOO MUCH, AND ANTONIO, THE MAN WHO DOES NOT KNOW HIMSELF

In the recognition scene between the blind Gobbo and the young Lancelot that occurs in Act 2, the typical ending of the foundling plot—the restoration of child and parent—is promised but deferred. Like wardship for the upper classes, apprenticeship is a form of adoption, auguring the final return of the improved child to his family.[22] Lancelot's parody is a triple inversion of the usual thematic situation; he knows the father who is literally in the dark; he controls his destiny, choosing to use his wit to avoid assuming his obligation to return partly because he enjoys the status by approximation of his lateral move from Shylock's to Bassanio's house and the prolongation of the middle interlude it confers. Postponing a recognition he is reluctant to fulfill, Lancelot "tries confusions," testing the child's support of the parent in the expected conclusion of the foundling plot:

> O heavens, this is my true-begotten father who being more than sand-blind—high-gravel blind—knows me not. I will try confusions with him. (2.2.27–29)

Lancelot jumps to the end of the story as, in speaking of his father, he calls himself the "true beget[er]" of his parent, acknowledging that he will eventually become father to his father, anticipating but nonetheless dreading the filial obligation to support the parent concomitant to the concluding recognition in the convention.[23] "Try[ing the] conclusion," he ends in a middle he wishes to, and does, change. His experiment—in trying—is not just an adjudication of his position as future protector of his father. In yet another meaning of "try," his game is meant to subject his father to the affliction or trial of the delaying tactics he imposes. Putting the present before the past parallels the backward turning of Lancelot's misdirection: an inverse of Polonius's "indirections [to] find directions out" (*Hamlet*, 2.1.65) since Lancelot already knows the answer to the questions his father raises, providing an example of what Patricia Parker calls "*hysteron protoron*—putting the cart before the horse."[24] Only in this case, it's a cart without a horse. The "turn of no hand" belies the "measure" (as a "hand" gauges a horse's height) of Lancelot's fully grown self.

In the next lines, Lancelot accentuates the spatial topsy-turvy that parallels the temporal reversals (and retractions) in the interplay of generations, first with his father and then with the Moor:

> Turn up on your right hand at the next turning, but at the next turning of all on your left, marry at the very next turning, turn of no hand but turn down indirectly to the Jew's house. (2.2.34–37)

In *Merchant*, where conversions are inescapable and returns of monies and of children are impossible, Lancelot's directional twisting—the turn of no hand—shadows the destabilizing tendency at the heart of the play. Lancelot's teasing is gratuitously cruel. Each advance he proffers is a detraction (from right hand to left hand, to the "turn of no hand"), a process that gradually leaves his father stranded in a "no *hand* land." Since the measure of the blind Gobbo's sure footing resides in his fingers rather than his toes, the "turn of no hand" renders the father helpless, deprived of the prosthetic eye that would extend his hand by word of mouth. Handless, he is doubly eyeless.

Gobbo is therefore twice deprived: what he assumes is a sure temporal placement has been displaced by a later sequence; what he regards as a certain destination is spatially unattainable, replaced by yet another location. There is no point, either as physical assurance or as psychological confidence. The Jew's house already is no house for Lancelot. As he tells his father, the nurturing of the adoptive interlude is nil: "I am famished [in Shylock's] service" (2.2.94).

What Lancelot wants is neither a new beginning nor another end but another chance, another turn before the inevitable return when he will be expected to restore his father. Thus he equivocates, temporarily undoing Gobbo's expectations. While Lancelot anticipates his eventual support of his father—the obligation to be (as Gobbo assumes) his "staff"—he begins by speaking of himself in an aside as the instrument for bludgeoning, rather than sustaining, his father.

> Do I look like a cudgel or a hovel-post, a staff or a prop? (2.2.59–60)

> Nay, indeed, if you had your eyes you might fail of the knowing me. It is a wise father that knows his own child. Well, old man, I will tell you news of your son—[*Kneeling*] Give me your blessing. Truth will turn to light, murder cannot be hid long—a man's son may, but in the end truth will out. (2.2.65–70)

The birth that is about to take place here is linguistically preceded by a murder, a deed done in the darkness of nonrecognition, as the man outgrows the child he was. Lancelot is not Gobbo's "boy." In the interlude, he has become the bearded man who stands before Gobbo and who reclaims the time he lost. Like Jacob, pretending to be the hairy Esau, Lancelot equivocates and, like Isaac, Gobbo does not know his own child. But the horseplay—the hairy beast, the hairy man—anticipates, in its beguilement of expectations, Lancelot's later interchange about the Moor.

At first, Lancelot hoodwinks his father about his retrospective role as son. Later, he denies his part as prospective parent of the Moor's child. Feeling the back of Lancelot's head, Gobbo declares that Lancelot "hast got more hair on [his] chin, then Dobbin my fill-horse has on his tail" (2.2.84–85). Lancelot's answer (that the horse's tail grows backward) parallels his quibble about taking the Moor from behind. Deceiving his father here, in the next act he claims the Moor played false with him. But as he confuses temporal and spatial backwardness in his revelations to his father, he also turns around the issue of his issue with the Moor, placing the responsibility of paternity on the Moor's irresponsible (unreasonable) behavior with him. Why does Lancelot babble about violence in the early scene? In speculating about bludgeoning his father is he also commenting on the parental desire to "kill the kid"—the impulse that kick-starts so many foundling plots? Is he perhaps, still further, saying that even giving a child over to apprenticeship feels, to the sent-away child, like death? Moreover, does annulling the past into which he was born continue into perpetuity the cycle of abandonment by foreshadowing the denial of his own paternity later? Is the eventual—but postponed—reunion with his father undone by his refusal of responsibility in the next act of the play? Lancelot's defense against Lorenzo's accusation that the Moor is with child "by you" ends in the middle: "Murder will[s] out." He undermines all that the Moor is:

> It is much that the Moor should be more than reason; but if she is less than an honest woman, she is indeed more than I took her for. (3.5.34–36)

If the Moor is more (pregnant), she is also something other—and far more complex—than what Lancelot expected in "taking" her. That is, if the Moor is "more than reason," she is more than the gendered expectation for thinking, or "reasonableness." To have an excess of reason is to be out of reason—that is, unreasonable: what a man expects a woman to be. On the other hand, if she displays more than the reasonableness of a woman, then she is the man he "took [her] for" (3.5.36) and she cannot be "with child" (3.5.33). The whole question of agency is figured here. The Moor is less than a man since the woman is nothing—lacks the thing that would make her a man. If she were more than "reason," she would have been the man that Lancelot assumed s/he was. Identified only by race as the Moor, the gender question is subsumed.

Lancelot's doubling on "take" pits his comprehension (and therefore the Moor's culpability in disguise, yet another shadow of the Jacob-Esau story) against his aggression (and therefore his own agency in overpowering her). What *did* he "take" her for? If she is more than a she—more than the empty female—then Lancelot took her from behind, as earlier he claims his father takes him (perceives his growth) from behind when he spins the tale of Dobbin's tail to explain that the son is more than the father takes him for and less than his father expects him to be. Remaindered in the middle—halfway between the boy that was and the "child" he will one day be—Lancelot (in relationship to Gobbo) remains in a Pinteresque Bolsover Street. Time murders the son he was. But Lancelot "wills out," murdering his child by renouncing it before it even comes into being. Wishing to remain in the middle of the foundling plot of his own life, he becomes the abandoning parent in the foundling plot of his future child's life. The Moor is not there to be potentially uncovered for what she is. Thus, Lancelot postpones his future-future as sustaining father to his father, choosing to procrastinate in the dead end of Bolsover Street and simply moving from one middle period of apprenticeship to another in a circle that will keep him from fulfilling the generational expectations his father has.

The forward-backward climbing and sliding from much to more to less to more inverts Lancelot's own play from "cudgel [to] hovel-post, [to] staff, [to] prop" (2.2.59–60) as Lancelot pulls himself temporally ahead toward his father and then backslides away from the Moor, retracting from his original perception of her—taking as understanding—to his subsequent usurpation of her—taking as overcoming. For the foreseeable future, Lancelot will remain (as stay) in the middle ground, unwilling even to acknowledge his own sexuality. There is also no sign that Lancelot will move into the expected dynastic generativity of the plot that he outlines when he returns to a more culturally normalized chronology:

> I am Lancelot, your boy that was, your son that is, your child that shall be. (2.2.74–75)

If this is a classical recognition scene, then what Lancelot promises is the end that comes round to the beginning: he will be the prop he at first denies. The gender reversals in this promise render Lancelot the child, a term mostly used in early modern times to describe a daughter. Playing about the woman both here with regard to Lancelot's own future relationship to his father and later with regard to the Moor's gender unhinges the security of the recognition. There is no son that is because Lancelot's present inclination, his first reactive impulse to the presence of his father in the fourfold response to Gobbo's assumption, is to be a "cudgel"—to deny himself as supportive of the Moor and restorative of his father. The child that will be is less than his father takes him for.

That gender reversal inverts what will happen in the Bassanio/Portia/Antonio triad where Portia's immediate response to Bassanio is to be nurturing mother and regenerative source who fulfills Bassanio's initial promise to Antonio to return past and future debts. Only behind that story is the Medea-Jason one, which (as Lancelot anticipates in refusing even to acknowledge the reproductive capacity of the Moor) ends in child murder. Lancelot's jabbering about a "murder" that cannot be "hid long" brings to the foreground the bloodletting that is at the heart of the Medea story, the failure at the very end of children to sustain their parents. Like Medea, Lancelot cuts off his genealogy. *The Merchant of Venice* dances around the Medea story (that ends in child murder) and the Jacob story (that ends, with Joseph, in brother forgiving brother). But in using those stories as background, Shakespeare comes close to the edge: the dark end of the Jason reference is not fulfilled, nor is the happy end of the Jacob-Joseph story. But Lancelot crosses the border into the Medea story both when he refuses to acknowledge the Moor's child as his and when he challenges his father's use of him as sustaining son in the question, directed at the audience's gaze, rather than to his father, who cannot see. Even phrasing the question in visual terms is a swipe at Gobbo: "Do I *look* like a cudgel, or a hovel-post, or a staff or a prop?" he asks, gradually moving into an accommodation of his father but not before he acknowledges his impulse to do in the parent just as, in refusing to acknowledge the Moor's child, he (Medea-like) cuts off the expected progeny. A staff can be used to bludgeon a man to death, just as a hovel-post and prop can be used to sustain a house and family. The blind Gobbo—totally confused— agrees to extend the middle period by transferring the apprenticeship with his dish of pigeons to Bassanio, forming another link to Antonio, who finds himself by fathering Bassanio.[25] Refusing to acknowledge his child, Lancelot curtails the dynastic end of the foundling plot. Contrastingly, when we first see him, Antonio doesn't know where to begin.

Unmoored, the Antonio of the play's first lines cannot even find the words to identify his loss to himself. Like Austerlitz, Antonio feels that "the very thing that may usually convey a sense of purposeful intelligence—the exposition of an idea by means of certain stylistic facility . . . seemed to me nothing but an entirely arbitrary or deluded enterprise" (*Austerlitz*, 124). Antonio's sense of abandonment leads to a feeling of personal culpability from which there is no escape. While Lancelot is totally in control, Antonio is lost in Bolsover Street. The most significant thing about the obscure origin of his sadness is that it leaves him without a feeling of purpose in the terms (business and romance) for which he has a vocabulary. The circularity of his emptiness, drained by the cause that shapes him, deprives him of the very tools that would enable him to feel as if he's leading any sort of life at all. He gets one as surrogate parent to Bassanio at the end of the first scene, as his sexual longing (so pronounced in recent productions) is subsumed by his sense of parental cause, just as Portia later describes her conjugal relation to Bassanio in terms of her need to engender him. In the opening speech, Antonio is both the child he found, unable to discern his lineage, and the parent who, having been burdened by that child, similarly is in the dark about its origin:

> In sooth, I know not why I am so sad.
> It wearies me, you say it wearies you,
> But how I caught it, found it, or came by it,
> What stuff 'tis made of, whereof it is born,
> I am to learn;
> And such a want-wit sadness makes of me,
> That I have much ado to know myself. (1.1.1–7)

Experiencing his position both as finding parent and exposed child and using the language of reproduction to describe his psychological isolation, Antonio has lost himself because of what he has found. As Lancelot is quick to answer, Antonio is slow to voice, unable to account for himself in the foundling plot, unable to articulate himself as someone with a "purposeful intelligence" (*Austerlitz*, 124). The lyric speaker knows exactly why he is sad. In fact, his lack is solidified by his expression of it, as the other becomes in its unassailability the source of his subjectivity. From the very outset of the play, the metaphors stage an introduction to the two plots: the waywardness of the foundling defined by the loss, the lyric absence expressed by the very inexpressibility of that loss. Antonio is weighed down by a feeling that simultaneously absorbs, and eludes, him. Declaring himself an emotional orphan, suffering as a victim of a sadness without cause, he identifies his intellectual bankruptcy as a loss he cannot express. In his evocation of the "stuff" that shapes him, Antonio moves chronologically backward, characterizing his *anomie* as something he has caught, like a contagious disease invading his body, and discovered, like a child he adopted and, finally, as something out there, alien to him, an external force that worms its way into his sense of self. He can neither ascertain its source (in that respect, it's like a foundling left off at his doorstep) nor release himself from the quest (in that respect, it's like a parent he must seek). Sadness becomes his sole occupation, filling him (the way an army invades a city) and emptying him (the way an army siphons off the city's resources). Antonio's act of catching (or seizing something) becomes the snare by which he is trapped. His *modus operandi* is fixated on a quest for the origin of a self that feels foreign in its accessibility and unobtainable as destiny. The more he moves toward his future (still to learn), the less able he is to account for any meaningful past accomplishment. Feeling himself the child of a parent who cannot sustain him, he also portrays himself as the father of a child who gives him no gratification in return. Antonio describes a malignancy that overtakes his organic self, rendering his biological certainty (the stuff of his physical being) hostage to his psychological position (feeling neither here nor there). He begins, therefore, as rootless, unhinged from his past and searching for a present that is absent and a future that offers him no return.

At the end of the scene, he assumes a firmer presence by appending himself to Bassanio and adopting Bassanio's romantic and financial needs—the very two causes Antonio earlier dismissed when answering Solanio and Salario about his sadness:

> Then do but say to me what I should do
> That in your knowledge may by me be done,
> And I am pressed unto it. (1.1.158–60)

"Pressed" into being by Bassanio, who in that sense fathers him, he attaches himself to a still older story, one that reveals a good deal about both Bassanio and Antonio.

"THE GREATEST GOD IS MYSELF": THE MEDEA CONNECTION TO PORTIA AND SHYLOCK

If, as Graziano confirms, Bassanio and Antonio are Jasons, then Portia becomes not only the desired object but also Medea, the sorceress who enables them to win and to keep the prize. The pattern Antonio establishes at the beginning in the link between finding (as active instigation) and catching (as passive victimization) is completed in the Portia analogy, which is confirmed as he assumes Bassanio-Jason's "quest" in the extended analogy of 1.168–74. Shaped by the son, just as Gobbo is begotten by Lancelot, Antonio takes on his task. While his opening sadness is exclusively his own, his presence by the end of the first scene is attached to Bassanio's desire, so that Antonio becomes an extension of Bassanio, not the other way around. The knowledge he lacks at the opening is replaced by the information—the logical sequence of tasks—Bassanio will give him. Eating the child, he becomes him. It's no accident that the story preceding that of Medea in Ovid is that of Tereus, the father who, in coveting his wife's sister, consumes the child who would have become his destiny. Medea and Procne are thus alike, destroying the father by killing the sons. Antonio—who opens confused by what he found—is victimized by the son he adopts. The story of Philomela/Procne begins with an unfaithful husband; the story of Jason and Medea, as it is told in Ovid, ends in unfaithfulness, for which the father is deprived of the seed. Framed by those child murders is the story of Medea's helpfulness to Jason, first in the winning of the fleece and, second, in the restoration of the father, just as, in *Merchant*, Portia gives herself to Bassanio by converting all her gold to him and then restores Antonio, infusing him with life.

But if, in finding Bassanio as his son, Antonio parallels Gobbo in the foundling plot, the second "turning" in the play is the exchange of roles between Portia and Shylock when they shift places in the lyric dyad. Medea forms the link between the two. Initially (like Portia), she gives herself over to Jason without a second thought and (as Portia does Antonio) saves her father-in-law. Wielding a magic wand very like the one Medea uses to rejuvenate Aeson, Shylock generates himself even as—like her—he cuts off his future progeny when, hearing for a second time of her betrayal, he declares, "Would [Jessica] were hearsed at my foot, and the ducats in her coffin" (3.1.378). If Lancelot and Antonio are linguistic foils for each other, so Shylock and Portia play parallel roles, linked to Medea. Portia appears as Medea in Bassanio's comparison and, later, in her willingness to succor Bassanio's surrogate father. In that regard the Ovidian parallel sutures into the foundling plot and its adoptions. In "peel[ing]" (1.3.77) his wand, and in his grafting, Shylock resembles the self-creative Medea, the one who, forsaking kith and kin, finds an invented, rather than an inherited, identity.

If one of the issues in *Merchant* is bloodletting, Medea is the bloodletter par excellence, restoring Jason's father by slitting his throat, replacing his blood, and, in the end, robbing her children (and thus Aeson and Jason) of the family line she earlier restored. "And in her own deare children's blood had bathed her wicked knife / Not like a mother but a beast bereaving them of life."[26] The Ovidian designation of Medea's bestiality will later be applied to Shylock in the trial scene, when, accusing him of being the son of a demon father and an "unhallowed dam," Graziano calls him "wolfish, bloody, starved, and ravenous" (4.1.137).[27] As the Ovidian story progresses, Medea is transformed from the blushing maiden to the powerful witch; the exponential increase of her power matches the meteoric rise of her love. Once having met Jason, she emerges the maker of her own being, proclaiming her self-sufficiency and her independence from her family:

> And shall I then leave brother, sister, father, kith and kin?
> And household Gods, native soyle, and all that is therein?
> And saile I know not whither with a straunger? Yea; why not?
> The greatest God is in myself: the things I do forsake
> Are trifling in comparison of those that I shall take. (7.70–72, 78–79)

The second time Medea sees Jason, she is transfixed by him:

> So farre she was beside hir self, she thought it should not bee
> The face of any worldly wight the which she then did see,
> She was not able to turne hir eyes away.
> But when he tooke hir by the hand and speaking gan to pray
> Hir softly for to succor him, and promisde faithfully
> To take hir to his wedded wife, she falling by and by
> A weeping, said: Sir what I do I see apparantly
> Not want of knowledge of the truth but love shall me deceive
> You shall be saved by my meanes. (7.125–33)

Not only does Medea save Jason, not only does she return him to his father whom she revives, but she also uses the same weapon she will wield against her sons, "letting his blood" as she will later spill that of her own children:

> Such other kinde of namelesse things bestead hir purpose through
> For lengthening of the old man's life, she tooke a withered bough
> Cut lately from an Olyf tree, and jumbling al together
> Did raise the bottome to the brim; and as she stirred hither
> And thither with the withered sticke, behold it waxed green
> Anon the leaves came budding out (7.361–66)

> Which when Medea did behold, with naked knife she goes
> And cuttes the old man's throate: and letting all his old bloud go
> Supplies it with the boyled juice, the which when Aeson tho

> Had at his mouth or at his wounde receyved in, his heare
> As well of head as beard, from gray to coleblacke turned were.
> His leane, pale, hore, and withered corse grew fulsome, faire and fresh:
> His furrowed wrinckles were fulfilled with yong and lustie flesh.
> His limmes waxt frolicke, baine and lithe: at which he wondring much,
> Remembered that at fortie yeares he was the same or such.
> And as from dull unwieldsome age to youth he backward drew:
> Even so a lively youthful spright did in his heart renew. (7.370–81)

Medea saves Jason's father by grafting—taking "a withered bough / cut lately from an Olyf tree. . . . and stir[ring] the withered stick / . . . [until] it waxed greene." The magic wand becomes the means by which she restores Aeson, even as (at the end of the story) she cuts off the progeny that would preserve the lineage.

If Medea ends the dynastic mandate that links her to the foundling plot, she hovers behind the lyric sequences as well. With its grafting, Shylock-Jacob's wand in Act 1, parallels Medea's. Like Medea, Portia gives herself totally to Jason-Bassanio. And, like Medea, Portia is more than willing to take on all of Bassanio's burdens. But as the Laura of the Petrarchan complex, she empowers Bassanio by seeming to be not yet won—by being too remote to save him with all her Medea-like "meanes." The closer Bassanio gets to winning her, the more the lyric Portia frightens him. And the closer Shylock gets to helping Antonio with the bond in Act 1, the more Antonio must demonize him. I will chronicle the lyric sequences (first) in terms of Portia's increasing power in them, and (then) in relation to Shylock's decreasing authority in them. The Medea connection to Shylock begins as he wafts the wand that, like her restorative of Aeson, depends on altering the course of nature. It ends with the threatened bloodletting and, in the Venetian view, his Medea-like bestiality. The Medea connection to Portia returns to its positive aspects as (once converted) she restores both Bassanio and Antonio. It is only in her gradually shifting roles in the lyric complex that she comes close to the witch of the Graeco-Roman legend. If Portia is equated with the Medea of the golden fleece before Bassanio wins her, in the poetic sequences she lurks as threatening demon behind those moments where Bassanio loses his self-confidence.

THE THREE STAGES OF PORTIA'S LYRIC DANGER

Heather Hirschfeld maintains that there is a sense in which the Venetians both want and do not want Shylock to convert[28] and that ambivalence, I argue, has a parallel in Bassanio's relation with Portia, furthering the links between Medea, Portia, and Shylock. "The Venetians' compulsion to convert

Shylock—to change him so that he doesn't change is a way to enjoy their symptom" ("'We all expect a gentle answer,'" 77). In its psychological effect, the symptomatic enjoyment equals the pleasure of the Petrarchan woman's denial: the more she resists, the more the poet finds his sense of self. The conversion that is an issue in the religious plot is paralleled in the same way as Hirschfeld argues by the ambivalent desires of the Petrarchan plot.[29] Only when she is seen to resist is Portia really enjoyed by Bassanio and by extension therefore by Antonio. The longer she delays him, the stronger is his sense of self. I will argue that Bassanio's successful achievement of Portia in the casket scene precedes his greatest self-doubt, just as Antonio's winning of Shylock's financial backing at the end of Act 1 provokes the identical sense of inferiority, one that he masks by abruptly ending the conversation, calling Shylock the "devil [who] cite[s] scripture" (1.3.94). In the later parallel scene, Bassanio (who earlier praised Portia's "sunny locks" [1.1.169]) calls them a "golden mesh t'entrap the hearts of men" (in 3.2.122). When Portia "converts" herself to Bassanio, she drops out of the lyric complex. No longer playing the "symptom" of the lyric, she becomes the cure in the foundling plot.

In the lyric plot, Bassanio prefers to keep Portia at a distance, afraid he'll catch the vulnerability he attributes to her. The sonnet sequence of 3.2.24–38 reveals that Bassanio is what Antonio failed to be at the opening, the Apollonian shaper of his own desire, the very capacity he forfeits when he imagines the Portia he wins (in 3.2.114–29). In both speeches, Bassanio refers to instruments of semiotic male phallic form—rack (3.2.25) and bar (3.2.118)—as descriptions of female torture instruments.[30] The two speeches record his decline from all-powerful linguistic master to the impotent artist whose art utterly fails him. In rendering Portia the object of his (failed) suit, he is the "greatest God," retrieving from her denial what Jason acquired from Medea's commitment. Winning her, he loses the very control he earlier had. In both speeches, Bassanio conflates visual images with Petrarchan poetic practices. The physical site of his situation merges with the verbal description of it, as he shifts: in the first speech, from the rack of public torture to the poetic forum for private pain; in the last, from animator of Portia's being to dismembered Jonah, suspended somewhere inside Portia's menacing whale of a mouth (3.2.118–19). In between, Bassanio introduces a third woman who also appears in the *Rime sparse*: Laura-Medusa. It is the specter of this Laura that petrifies him and causes him to reject both the gold and silver caskets, in favor of the "meagre" lead. The problem is that the Portia whose image he sees once he opens the casket resembles the Portia he rejects before he chooses: both Lauras have frightening golden locks—the first crisped snaky ones (3.2.92), the second entrapping spidery ones (3.2.122).

Despite her eagerness to say yes and her impulse oxymoronically to "peise"[31] the time until Bassanio chooses, the Portia of the first speech is the equivalent of Daphne, the woman at the center of the lyric quest. Her physical inaccessibility inspires Bassanio's ability to transform her sexual denials into poetic material. Like the typical Petrarchan lover, Bassanio is most himself *before* he knows he has won Portia: the further away the prize, the more he can control it. While Portia speaks in the hyperbole of civil suit and public declamation, Bassanio turns inward. She calls treason a crime against the state in power; he paints treason as a crime against the self in love. She can anticipate only the ease of release—"confess and live"; he envisions instead the self-enclosed echo chamber of unending linguistic expression— "confess and complain." For Bassanio, talk results in life deferred, his confession retaining the poetic circle of male-generated fantasy. Love for him seems all talk, a lay "formulary" or semiotic system that turns women into words.

In the role of Petrarchan sufferer, Bassanio initiates a virtual sonnet duet, much like the interchange that signals the end of Romeo's Petrarchism in *Romeo and Juliet*. But while Romeo finds deliverance through Juliet's lips, Portia's verbal encouragement sets Bassanio right back on the Petrarchan torture instrument:

> *Bass*: Let me choose,
> For as I am, I live upon the rack.
> *Por*: Upon the rack Bassanio? Then confess
> What treason there is mingled with your love.
> *Bass*: None but that ugly treason of mistrust
> Which makes me fear th'enjoying of my love.
> There may as well be amity and life
> 'Tween snow and fire as treason and my love.
> *Por*: Ay, but I fear you speak upon the rack,
> Where men enforced do speak anything.
> *Bass*: Promise me life and I'll confess the truth.
> *Por*: Well then, confess and live.
> *Bass*: "Confess and love"
> Had been the very sum of my confession.
> O happy torment, when my torturer
> Doth teach me answers for deliverance! (3.2.24–38)

Portia immediately recognizes that what Bassanio describes as a locus of uncertainty actually provides a forum for male voice; the "rack" serves as a platform from which "*men* . . . speak anything." From Bassanio's vantage point, Portia herself emerges—like the Laura-Daphne of the Petrarchan lyric—a torturer. And when the "torturer / doth teach . . . answers for deliverance," that freedom is a linguistic maneuver that returns Bassanio to the safe confines of Petrarchan form. The torment is happy precisely because it leads to the oxymoronic situation that feeds the Petrarchan signifier. Like Petrarch, who builds Laura's rejection into the laurel of poetic fame, Bassanio converts his psychic uncertainty into a vehicle of poetic confidence. In the sonnet's conventional extremes—"snow and fire," "happy torment," and "confess and love"—the self-canceling oxymoron completes the woman-canceling form. Both sustain the triumphant laurelizer. In the doubleness of Bassanio's configuration, Portia's denial produces the rack that defines Bassanio's self. Through the semiotic state of Portia's "deliverance," Bassanio is actually freed from the fleshly woman he claims he needs. For Bassanio, the rack of poetic form structures a framework that allows him to consolidate his maleness. He comes into being through the sublimating experience of the poem. Fearing "th'enjoying of [his] love," he prefers the imagined to the real woman.

In the casket-choosing speech, he does his best to pick the woman with the least flesh. As he narrows down his choices, Bassanio opts for the same absence he coveted in the initial sonnet. The safe woman is the single-dimensional "meager" other whose presence Bassanio can control through his semiotic image.[32] When Bassanio rejects the Medusan gold and its mirroring double—silver—he seems directly to echo the Petrarch of *Rime sparse* 197, who similarly refers to Laura's hair as curling snare, her shadow as impaling magnet, and her gaze as ultimate silencer of his voice:

> The heavenly breeze that breathes in that green laurel, where love smote Apollo in the side and on my neck placed a sweet yoke so that I restore my liberty only late,
>
> has the power over me that Medusa had over the old Moorish giant, when she turned him to flint; nor can I shake loose that lovely knot by which the sun is surpassed, not to say amber or gold:
>
> I mean the blond locks and the curling snare that so softly bind tight my soul, which I arm with humility and nothing else.
>
> Her very shadow turns my heart to ice and tinges my face with white fear, but her eyes have the power to turn it to marble. (*Petrarch's Lyric Poems*, 434)

Petrarch's Laura-Medusa acts on him. The blackness of her shadow turns his face ashen even as the hint of death in her shade freezes his heart.[33] She systematically reduces, humbles, and pales him until she molds him into the marble stone of her shaping design. In *Rime sparse* 197, Petrarch is the old Moorish giant, not the cleverly manipulative Perseus or even the slightly erring one of 366. Here, he's not just stone; he's the marble statue Medusa makes of him, retaliating—with her distillation—for the artistic object Petrarch made of Laura.

While Petrarch cites the Medusa as distant "power" whose danger he gradually embraces, Bassanio sets out to disempower Portia by rejecting the golden snare that pulls Petrarch in. His Medusa is the double-edged demon she is to Freud: she stiffens him into erection even as she threatens him with castration.[34] Pulling out all his maleness, the Bassanio who fears petrification uses his Medusa (as Freud also suggests) against her own person. While Petrarch views Medusa as the single-minded and one-dimensional designer of his fate, Bassanio doubles her. First, he feminizes the caskets. Then he turns them into men-eating women who must be eschewed. He isn't therefore choosing a substance that can enrich him. He's opting for an other he can embellish. His desire is for a mistress he can linguistically master, one whose being is fleshed out by him. Bassanio enumerates three traps for the one Medusa. Her multiple layers are triply deceiving: golden curls yield a death's head; the guiled shore hides the dangerous sea; the beauteous scarf covers a dark Indian. In rendering the devils female, Bassanio reveals the connection between his racial and gender bias. The "Indian beauty" and the death's head are equally demonic; the seemingly safe shore islands the treacherous (and also feminine) sea. The snake has a skin and, when it sheds it, it reveals another snake:

> Those crisped, snaky, golden locks
> Which make such wanton gambols with the wind
> Upon supposed fairness, often known
> To be the dowry of a second head,
> The skull that bred them in the sepulchre.
> Thus ornament is but the guiled shore
> To a most dangerous sea, the beauteous scarf
> Veiling an Indian beauty; in a word,
> The seeming truth which cunning times put on
> To entrap the wisest. Therefore, thou gaudy gold,
> Hard food for Midas, I will none of thee.
> Nor none of thee thou pale and common drudge
> 'Tween man and man. But thou, thou meagre lead
> Which rather threaten'st then dost promise aught,
> Thy paleness moves me more than eloquence. (3.2.92–106)

What Bassanio fears in the golden casket is the death's head; what he fears in the veil is the foreign head; what he fears in the silver is the mirrored head. In their anamorphic blurs, the sea, the scarf, and the mirror obscure the demarcation between self and other upon which Bassanio constructs his confidence. Having introjected Portia, Bassanio projects her out again as the dangerous other to the self. Bassanio's double-pronged Medusa, who, in the myths, "looks very much like Athena,"[35] has ties to Portia. Tobin Siebers writes of the mythic origins of Medusa's mirrorings:

Turning Gender and Plot in The Merchant of Venice   129

The queen of the city and the queen of hell share a history of rivalry, which is dramatically stressed by the fact that the birth of Athena presents the mirror image of Medusa's death. After either Hephaestus or Prometheus opens Zeus's head with an axe, Athena, fully armed, springs from the wound. Medusa dies from the sword blow of Perseus, and from her head spring Pegasus and Chrysaor. These two scenes, by virtue of their similarity, again present the violent competition between goddess and monster.[36]

In describing how dangerous Medusa-Athena-Portia is, Bassanio reveals another hazard of Medusa's trap. His fear is of becoming her, of being feminized through the complex mirrorings that the very necessity of resistance brings into focus. Bassanio here resembles Antonio, who (later on) will also engage in yet another turnaround into Shylock. Adopted son and adopting parent both fear the danger of feminization. Here Portia is the potential source of Bassanio's turning. Later Shylock (who also becomes Medusa) will turn on the Venetians and capitalize on their similar fear of becoming what they see. If the beginning of the myth ties Athena, Medusa, and Portia, the last moments of it tie Bassanio to Perseus and then—in the end—to Medusa. With the Medusa on his shield, Perseus-Bassanio would then become Medusa who is already Athena-Portia. Wearing the image of the enemy, he is what he seeks. If the other is source, then the self is eventually eliminated. And if Portia is Athena and if Athena is Medusa, then ultimately Perseus-Bassanio—wearing the Gorgon's reflection to defeat her—mirrors Medusa and is thereby subject to Athena and hence to Portia. The snaky locks, the Indian veil, and the wavering mirror render Bassanio indeterminate. What Bassanio rejects is what he projects in the self: the multiple and self-duplicating layers. Horrified of "entrapment" in both the web and the myth, Bassanio seeks to avoid its dangers altogether: "I will none of thee."

At the center of the Medusan circle is Portia who, in the golden light of her image, threatens to turn him into a reflection of her. All those layers—crisped curls, guiled shore, and veiled beauty—are diaphanous to the viewer who reads anamorphically. Shift slightly and the picture changes. In the mirror is the Medusa whom Bassanio must become if he conquers the glittering Portia. Bassanio's apotropaic revenge is to do to Portia what—in the anamorphic image—she threatens to do to him: he reduces her to a wavy specter of a demonic self—his. Since Portia-Medusa threatens to turn him to stone and Portia-Athena to feminize him, the casket-woman he chooses must be the "meager" and single-layered other whose "lack" he can infuse with his own predetermined idea of a woman. The lead casket allows him to remain, as he was, Petrarch-Apollo to the empty Laura-Daphne. It is still the poet who speaks. Equating visual pallor with linguistic silence, Bassanio returns to his subject position in the initial sonnet. The woman yields to his shaping powers. Turning the caskets into women, Bassanio chooses the "other" who will give him what he most desires: his own capacity to shape her.

With the portrait-of-the-winning-casket speech, Bassanio moves chronologically backward and spatially inward. There, he begins in male triumph—artist creating woman—and ends in male disgrace—woman decreating man. The woman in the portrait deals a fatal blow to the artist's other-usurping self. She undoes the artist's art. The portrait is "unfurnished" (3.2.126) and leaves Bassanio defenseless. Central to the portrait speech are the circular reprisals of "stealing." Bassanio loses the formulating gaze through which men "fix" women. The portrait remains as incomplete artifact, a constant reminder of Bassanio's inadequacy. In its "unfurnished" state, it signifies the vulnerability of the artistic system that originally determined Portia's image. To her creator, she has ceased to be because he cannot see her. Depriving him of access to a representational matrix he can control, she exceeds his boundaries. But to her imaginer, she is still dangerous because he cannot write her out. Denying him closure, she remains outside the realm of his intentionality.

At the beginning of the speech, Bassanio revels in his triumphant vision. Speaking from the subject position of the artist commissioned by Portia's father, he conflates biological insemination with artistic creation in the same way that Theseus does in *Midsummer Night's Dream* when he claims that, since fathers "figure" their daughters forth into life, they hold the right to "disfigure" them into death (*Midsummer Night's Dream*, 1.1.47–51). When he first describes the portrait's eyes, Bassanio also establishes the seminal control of his gaze:

> What demi-god
> Hath come so near creation? Move these eyes?
> Or whether, riding on the balls of mine,
> Seem they in motion? (3.2.114–18)

Bassanio doubles his power. As male viewer, he first impales Portia in a specifically sexual image, tying her movement to his outward motions and inward emotions. Portia's gaze is derived from him, as she reflects his vision and his ideas. Her eyes are contained by the ring of his "balls," his phallic lines determining the pattern of her dependency. She "rides"; he thrusts. As "demi-god" by extension, his eyes animate the portrait's being in the same way as, in Genesis 2, God breathed life into man. Bassanio's assessment of creativity involves an exclusionary collaboration, expanding the demigod artist (who came "so near creation") into a whole god: him. Completing the portrait merely by looking at it, he rounds out the patriarchal coterie of male painter and male audience. In describing the casket scene, Rebecca Gatward, who directed a production of *Merchant* at the London Globe Theatre in 2007, argues that Bassanio "falls in love with her instantly, ironically not by looking at her but at her portrait."[37] Interestingly, the "portrait" in Gatward's production is portrayed as a tiny statuette, which Bassanio holds and fondles, rendering the scene a miniature of the final moment of *The Winter's Tale* with its *statuas moving*. But unlike Leontes, who grows more confident as he approaches Hermione, Bassanio—at the moment Portia appears in the flesh—falls into a state of abject terror. As he speculates about the woman's voice, he unwinds the circles spinning on the axis of his centrifugal eyes and ends up caught in Portia's web:

> Here are severed lips
> Parted with sugar breath. So sweet a bar
> Should sunder such sweet friends. (3.2.118–20)

When Bassanio defines Portia here, the rack of the sonnet has turned into a "sweet bar," an obstacle that places him within the imagined Portia's hold and that leads to his dissolution. Evoking the portals of Portia's speaking power, Bassanio is almost immediately consumed by what he imagines. It is unclear whether the severed lips are separated from each other (as Catherine Belsey suggests[38]) or whether the "sweet friends" sundered are the male comrades—of painter and audience—who (as morsels to the portrait's reigning monarchy) are devoured by her. Oxymoronic imprisoners, the "sweet bars" appear as the tantalizing entrance to a source whose power Bassanio can neither fathom nor control. Does Portia collapse the male signifier with her words, separating the alliance between viewer and artist, or does she split herself in order to stimulate and consolidate her originative and creative primacy? As sugar breath, her musical "bars" sweeten the lips they sunder and thereby feed Portia's self-sustaining strength. Friend to herself, she needs no one else.

In the "severed lips," Bassanio sees the exponential increase implied by the auditory homonym "several" even as his fractured self anticipates what Luce Irigaray calls the "non-suture" of the woman's lips.[39] The imagined voice suggests "a different economy, more than anything else, one that upsets the linearity of a project, undermines the goal-object of a desire, diffuses the polarization toward a single pleasure, disconnects fidelity to a single discourse" (29–30). As the multiplying chords of music sundering friends, the portrait's "sweet bars" are, in fact, doubly oxymoronic. Both musical phrases and separating devices, the flowing sound "bites" emerge visual obstacles. Sugar coated and dangerous, the musical bars siren men into prison; the visual bars cut them off. They affect such a dissolution because they "bar" men from the title of originator and instead generate the multiplication of sign systems. The picture's imagined breath shatters the semiotic union the male alliance of artist and audience commands. Finally, as chords of music, the painted Portia's imaginary bars split Bassanio from the double self he sees in her eyes.

When Bassanio describes Portia as the creator of a language in which he becomes her symbol, he begins to fear that he might be a figment of woman's originating imagination, as he was once the product of her physiological body. Her "breath" infantilizes him and therefore makes it impossible to divine men as fathers of language. Her imagined "sweet words" reduce men into diminutive sugar babies, spawns of a regulating mother figure. Finally, the portrait that began as an extension of unchallenged male single-mindedness instead becomes an image of female duplicity and maternal multiplicity. The lips of the mouth holding him suggest the lips of the vulva beginning him. Women's words mold men in their symbolic likenesses as their bodies render them helpless infants. Women are the source of language and sustenance. Men are reduced to semiotic and physical indeterminacy. At this point, Bassanio falls victim to the portrait's centrifugal power and finds himself enmeshed "faster than gnats in cobwebs" (3.2.122), confined by the complexities of the female womb. Turning a second time to her eyes, he finds his infantilization corroborated still further. In this visual reference, he and the painter are not yet born; they are, instead, subject to the enormity of female generative powers:

> But her eyes—
> How could he see to do them? Having made one,
> Methinks it should have power to steal both his
> And leave itself unfurnished: yet look how far
> The substance of my praise doth wrong this shadow
> In underprizing it, so far this shadow
> Doth limp behind the substance. (3.2.123–129)

This is no Galatea who will fulfill in life what her maker desired; this art undoes the maker by joining, as one-eyed monster, the power of creation with the power of destruction. "Unfurnished," the painting is both demolished and not yet conceived, half undone and half begun, split at the root. Do the portrait's eyes rob the artist of his visual capacity and therefore render it the dazzling source of his subjugation? Or, in remaining "unfurnished," do they leave everything open and therefore vulnerable to a revision that challenges the representative matrix through which Bassanio determines his selfhood? The portrait preempts Bassanio's words and undoes his gaze, its presence a sign of his lack of significatory mastery, its absence designating his physical incapacitation. When Bassanio acknowledges the painting's power to "steal," he grants it an independent life and transposes his appropriations of the woman in the Petrarchan process to its supererogation of him in female generativity.

It is precisely in the moment of undecidability—half demolished, half finished—that the portrait reaches its zenith of power, tripling Bassanio's fears. Peter Berek notes the unease created by Shylock as a "plausible representation of the idea that identity is not stable."[40] In its "unfurnish[ing]" that is precisely how Portia's portrait functions. First, it steals the artist's eyes, taking from him what Bassanio earlier described as the origin ("riding on the balls of [his eyes]," 3.2.115) of its life. Second, in leaving itself "unfurnished," as defenseless in its early modern sense, it renders the whole semiotic system vulnerable to attack from something it can neither define nor locate. Third, as incomplete, it also deprives the artist of closure. Not quite itself, it threatens to render the artist not quite himself. In moving backward chronologically—to the time before the portrait was finished—Bassanio transports himself psychologically to the state before he was completely or fully himself—not yet born, totally engulfed by the female procreational pool. Is he Actaeon at the water's edge awaiting Diana's revenge for having seen her? Will he be torn to bits for his having scattered her parts in the fragmenting details of Petrarchan praise? Over and above all these threats in the art is the most harrowing thought of all: the imagined woman is merely a shadow of the real woman. The object of male creation "limps behind" and is outpaced by the woman Bassanio sought to subject. It is he who is blinded, he who staggers.

Portia ends up where Bassanio begins. She is the demigod as one-eyed Cyclops who will complete the "unfurnished" image he only half sees. With Bassanio's increasing morbidity, his prize falls apart. As shadow, the statue is a phantom copy of Portia's defining presence. And since the phantom envelopes the scattered signs—eyes and heart—of Bassanio's visual and energetic self, Bassanio's lyric strength is eviscerated. He is haunted by the ghost of his imagining self. If the model is "unfurnished" and the original underprized, then the woman remains an impenetrable mystery. She "bars" Bassanio from the secret of her power and reduces him into inconsequential immobility. As incomplete portrait, the "unfurnished" image stands at the intersection of discourse, in a place that threatens all stability. "Unfurnished"—scattered to pieces like the tower of Babel—it remains partly the end of male signification, partly the beginning of a new power complex. With such a Laura, it is easy to see how Bassanio might demonize all women and how an imagined construct can feel like a material danger. Bassanio's triumph in the marriage scenario leaves him unmanned in the lyric dynamic. Like Antonio's causeless depression at the opening, Bassanio's emptiness here seems to elude meaning. Bassanio feels himself "bereft . . . of all words" (3.2.175). Portia's "substance" (3.2.129) converts him to "a wild of nothing" (3.2.182). At this moment, Bassanio becomes what Antonio was at the opening: unable to retain a formulative self. One of the many turns of the play is the fusion of adopted father with adoptive son. The Portia of the portrait uncovers Bassanio's instability, as he regresses to an infant, totally at her mercy. Like Antonio at the opening, Bassanio is a want-wit, feeling only "such confusion in [his] powers" (3.2.177).

Yet when the actual Portia bows to him, she renders herself an object of his "account" (3.2.155), a "figure" in his mercantile and signifying economy. With that surrender, she also prefigures the resumption of Venetian hierarchies. Turning herself over to Bassanio, Portia resets the selves unraveled in the portrait, agrees to his defining presence, and accedes to his dominion over her goods and imagination: "this same myself [am] yours." Catering to Bassanio's patriarchal supremacy with the ring she offers, Portia substitutes the language of social commerce for that of poetical metamorphosis:

> Myself and what is mine, to you and yours
> Is now converted. (3.2.166–67)

Thus Portia gives Bassanio back to himself even as she shrinks into a smaller version of him. Converted, she returns signifier and self, changing her currency into his. As commodified gold, the marriage ring represents restraint.[41] It is the "sign" of a relegitimized patriarchal discourse. Portia is the empty vessel ("yours") Bassanio will fill with the mastery of his now solidified patriarchal order. He possesses her and all that is hers.

Converting her physical and financial property to Bassanio, Portia gives up her resistance. In the trial scene, she demands a similar conversion of Shylock. As Kim Hall writes, "Reading Portia as the heroic subversive female particularly proves problematic when we place her actions in relation to other categories of difference. While her 'witty' remarks about her suitors display a verbal acumen and forwardness typical of the unruly woman, her subversiveness is severely limited for her strongest verbal abilities are only bent toward supporting a status quo which mandates the repulsion of alien outsiders."[42] Taking her place, Shylock must adhere to the signifying mastery of Christian discourse, the same mastery Portia ratifies when she "signs" herself as Bassanio's possession (in 3.2.151–74) and endorses when she defeats Shylock to rescue Antonio in Act 4. If Bassanio turns Portia into the various Lauras he identifies in Act 3, so Antonio plays Petrarch to Shylock's gradually differentiated Lauras. The transference of Petrarchan imagery from Portia to Shylock "shifts the focus of cultural anxiety from the body of the woman onto the body of the racial other."[43] But in casting Shylock as the woman of the lyric, the Venetians retain the image of a feminine threat. Bassanio calmed his anxiety by turning Portia to a Laura-Daphne he could use to solidify his sense of self. Portia pacifies him even more when she steps out of the Petrarchan economy and into the comedic circle of the ring. Thus, the Antonio/Portia/Bassanio triad returns to the foundling plot as Portia becomes nurturing mother to her earlier Petrarchan lover. Unlike Antonio, who feels only, like his adopted son, the "confusion of [his] powers" (3.2.177), Shylock announces his lyric consolidation at the outset. In Act 4, Antonio annuls Shylock's power by reducing him to the one-dimensional other he can vilify in order to confirm his linguistic, economic, and social dominance. But

Turning Gender and Plot in The Merchant of Venice   135

the semiotics of sexual and religious patterning are the same. If Shylock replaces Portia, Antonio stands in for Bassanio. And if the Petrarchan Portia undoes Bassanio's manhood, so the lyrical Shylock threatens Antonio's.

THE THREE STAGES OF SHYLOCK'S LYRIC DEMISE: FIGURING AND DISFIGURING POWER

Shylock begins (where Portia's "counterfeit" ends) as the multidimensional and therefore linguistically threatening other. What frightens Bassanio about Portia in the casket speech is that her very "sweet[ness]" (3.2.119, 120) becomes a weapon capable of "sunder[ing]" (3.2.120) the established coterie of male signification. In the Laban speech, Shylock similarly offers a whole new semiotic system. Despite its offer of help, it terrifies Antonio. When he asserts his creative agency in his initial confrontation with Antonio (1.3.65–92), Shylock evades conventional forms and redefines expected practices, insisting on the secrecy of his energetic resources: "I cannot tell" (1.3.91). In his second emanation, in the "revenge" speech of 3.1.45–61, he mirrors the Medusa who so frightened Bassanio. As the retaliative woman, raped by an impaling culture, he answers the Venetians in kind. Finally, in Act 4, Shylock defines himself in the same way as the Venetians demonize him: as the denying Daphne in the Petrarchan complex. Refusing to yield his self, he becomes the resistant other they objectify and then dismiss. His downfall in the play follows in reverse order Portia's ascending power in Bassanio's three versions of the lyric. She begins as passive Daphne, turns into the retaliative Medusa, and emerges (in Bassanio's appellations) as the uncontrollable confounder of his mental and verbal power.

 In that first confrontation with Antonio, Shylock declares his independence from the attachments that consolidate Antonio's sense of self at the end of the first scene. As Portia alarms Bassanio in the casket victory, so Shylock frightens Antonio when he offers him what he wants. Where Antonio needs the other, Shylock is self-sufficient. Antonio begins the play as a "want-wit" (1.1.6), announcing his lack of another in terms of an absence of a formulative self. In contrast, Shylock has layers of richness, and long historical ties, which he simultaneously reveals and conceals, as he tantalizingly peels his magical wand in the Laban speech.[44] Playing the literalist, Antonio interrupts Shylock's disquisition before it begins, questioning Jacob's relevance and undercutting the allegory (in 1.3.70): "And what of him? did he take interest?" Afterward, again (in 1.3.90), he literalizes Shylock's figure of speech with his "is your gold and silver ewes and rams?" Shylock's answer to the second question is the self-satisfied return to a generating primacy that establishes his exclusive terminology: "I cannot tell, I make it breed as fast" (1.3.91).[45] Turning the division of Antonio's belittling remark into the multiplication of his vision, Shylock retains the originality of his inventiveness. Antonio's disinterest is Shylock's interest, his story a counter to Antonio's boredom. In the dual meaning of "interest," Shylock anticipates Antonio's, at first libidinal and then financial, bankruptcy. He multiplies sexually and monetarily, identifying his linguistic system in terms that undo Venetian hierarchies, creating imagined selves that multiply in terms of self-generating images. He eschews the biological origins so central to the foundling plot and, embodying the lyric mentality, invents himself as parent capable of producing exactly the offspring he wants. Contrastingly, when Jessica rebels, she fails to subscribe to what he here defines as a pleasure in his amplification, a creation *ex nihilo*. Escaping his house, she appears totally unaware of the creativity in Shylock's enterprise, speaking only in terms of the foundling plot's abandonment: "I have a father, you a daughter lost" (2.5.55). Orphaning herself, she exhibits no interest in the "interest" her father claims to "make" (1.3.91).

In his answer to Antonio's question about "tak[ing] interest," Shylock establishes his identity and questions Antonio's *modus operandi*. The connection behind what is expendable or replaceable (the ram) and spendable or multipliable (gold) heightens the mystery behind Shylock's story, a mystery that Antonio both belittles in his literalization and covets in his "interest." While Antonio fixates on taking, Shylock concentrates on making, shifting the focus from the literal toward the indirect and from the immediate toward the intervening. Shylock's redefinition of the word "take" in his sparring with Antonio reverts interest back to imaginative kindling. Antonio's derivative "take" becomes Shylock's self-generative *undertaking*—"mark what Jacob did." What Jacob *did* involves Shylock. Interest as medium of exchange and spur to excitement is the augmentation—the creation of a phallic excess—Antonio seeks and disclaims. His opening boredom continues here, his insistence afterward on magic yet another example of his expectation that creativity demands a helpmeet who might fill his want-wit.

As self-sufficient, Shylock inserts into nature what Antonio wants from him. His indirect taking of interest is a self-justified intervention. Flaunting the phallic wand, Shylock holds to his masculinity even as (in making them his), he awakens the ewe's generativity:

> *Shylock*: When Jacob grazed his uncle Laban's sheep—
> This Jacob from our holy Abram was,
> As his wise mother wrought on his behalf,
> The third possessor; ay, he was the third—
> *Antonio*: And what of him? did he take interest?
> *Shylock*: No, not take interest, not, as you would say,
> Directly int'rest. Mark what Jacob did:
> When Laban and himself were compromised

> That all the eanlings which were streaked and pied
> Should fall as Jacob's hire, the ewes, being rank,
> In end of autumn turned to the rams,
> And when the work of generation was
> Between these wooly breeders in the act,
> The skilful shepherd peeled me certain wands,
> And in the doing of the deed of kind
> He stuck them up before the fulsome ewes
> Who, then conceiving, did in eaning time
> Fall parti-coloured lambs; and those were Jacob's.
> This was a way to thrive, and he was blest:
> And thrift is blessing if men steal it not. (1.3.65–86)

According to Shylock, Jacob did not take interest—he made it, turning the instrument of generation into the magic wand that Shylock reflexively "peeled me." Inserting himself with the "peeled" and the "me" into the sexual situation, Shylock insists on the relationship between nature's regeneration (the sheep at mating time) and his divinely inspired intervention (the wand as Medea's caduceus). To the listening Antonio and to the audience, Shylock's wand, like Medea's grafted stick, suggests a black magic, a devilish capacity. Hovering between the business of mating and reproduction in his procreative wand and the business of representation as desire with his creative wand, Shylock incorporates female reproductivity and female unruliness, conflating his handiwork with nature's and appending the secret fecundity in the biblical passage to himself. Using "peel[ing]" as a revelation of personal power instead of as a pillaging of others, Shylock demonstrates how he works with what he was "given" to invent a whole new breed. As he directs female desire, Shylock—magically in the "peeled me"—turns it first toward himself and then pulls it inward. Thus, he both attracts female libido and adds female generativity to himself.

In peeling the wand, Shylock is also pulling it out and making it disappear, alternating between revealing and burying the sources of his sexual and linguistic power. His secret productivity is Medea's creative magic; his blatant maleness is Jacob's (surrogate) penile intervention. In this scene, Shylock places himself at the center of the story by (1) becoming the ram to his own ewes, using the wand to get the results that he wants, and (2) presenting the ewe to his own ram, reproducing the eanlings he needs. His gold is both ewes and rams, his energy capable of reproducing (breeding) itself. While Antonio cowers as "want-wit," Shylock's wit generates "want" and the excitement of libidinal energy. His ewes are "rank" and "fulsome," oversexed and panting for the erotic hand of the skillful shepherd whose "wand" directs the course of future eanlings. Shylock-Jacob's intervention, his "peel[ing] certain wands," is at once assured and secret. In the hands of the skillful shepherd, the aphrodisiacs subject the ewes to his direction as (insinuating himself yet again) he projects the sexuality he needs. In the biblical story, Jacob's spotted lambs leap almost algebraically into wealth—"cattle and maidservants and men servants and camels and asses" (Genesis 31:41)—as Jacob's mysterious investment goes beyond kind into kingdoms of chattel. His initial wand results in subsequent dominion, a wealth immediately coveted by Laban's jealous sons in Genesis 31–32.

Shylock's allusions to Genesis 31 set him up as the holder of a desirable secret (the certain wand) and the purveyor of a desirable end (the multiplying flock), his conversion of *genus* partly concealing his inseminating genius, his invasion of gender, partly exposing his transformational power. According to Shylock, Jacob merely takes from Laban what was his, his thrift (the setting aside) not stealing but a way of thriving (growing what was already there). Defining interest finally as thrift, Shylock suggests that it is simultaneously a retention and a multiplication of self. As an extension of Shylock's hand, the wand simply lengthens and redirects the hand of God. While Antonio declares that the biblical Jacob's "success," as Heather Hirschfeld notes, "is a result of blessedness,"[46] Shylock turns that blessing into the inspiration for his own parallel resourcefulness. Shylock's "work of generation" is an imitation that gets the results he wants. But Shylock's conflation of feminine reproductivity and masculine inscription turns procreative energy into creative impetus; he thereby increases and multiplies his own vision. The female sheep desire his maleness because they have been converted into versions of his self. The wand is Shylock's pen, his insertion an inscription into the story, his "hand" the wand that writes the story in the first place. The sheep are "rank," sexually desirous of what he offers and economically offering what he desires. They march "in rank," subservient to the commanding direction of his instrumental force.

Shylock insists on creative autonomy, the course of telling his story expressing the will to control language, the course of swelling his interest emerging a desire to propagate his self-image. For Shylock, the "breeding" of merchandizing is inventive and productive, its incorporations self-inspirational and self-multiplying. In the Laban speech, Shylock creates all the others he needs, even as he links his telling of the story to the penning of the sheep. Directing them to their trap, Shylock casts artistic representation as sexual insemination. The ewes are eager for his wand; it functions as instrument of male allure and locus of female excitement. As manipulator of the ewes, Shylock determines their maternity, writing them into the "script" he hoards. Responding instantly to the seductive sight he "peel[s]," the "wooly breeders" obey his self-aggrandizing demands. His story becomes their destiny as his "interest" arouses their libido. For Shylock, creative enterprise is both sexy and semiotic. His wand is the master-signifier that, first, cuts a hole in the reigning discourse by directing the ewes to his wand and then redirects the discourse by producing—and perpetuating into the future—the "eanlings" he needs. The w/hole is his, as the ewes "ring" themselves around his originating wand. His penile supremacy licenses his signifier. In turn, his female generativity materializes his linguistic replication. He controls the wayward ewes as he shapes the discourse, the "ring" of his corralling flocks as central to his mastery as the "ring" of marriage is in the Bassanio-Portia plot.

With the pun on wounding and feeding (graze) that opens the Laban speech, Shylock foreshadows the equation between alimentary and sexual privilege, exposure and secrecy, witness and witnessed that defines his Medusan victimization in Act 3. In Act 1, Shylock is determiner of the scene, beginning in a specific time that involves the specific place of his plan: "When Jacob graz'd his uncle Laban's sheep" (1.3.66). The original feeding of "graze" prefigures the subsequent wounding of graze. But the sheep corralling also directs the visual space, rendering Antonio the audience, as Bassanio will be to the artist in the casket portrait scene. Diverting Antonio's eye to the vista that centers on him, Shylock directs the sight lines to his centralizing vision. Shylock reveals and conceals, his "grazing" both a revelation of power as visual determinant and a privileging of it as verbal secret. In his "I cannot tell, I make it breed as fast" (1.3.91), Shylock equates his artistic strategies with the sexual reproduction he controls. His wand "tells," in multiplying figures, what his lips won't reveal in prescriptive words. Shylock's temporal sweeping back to history—like the grandiose visual line he directs—makes the "when" a "where." Splitting himself between Jacob and Antonio, Shylock is first the historical overlooker (reading the text) and then the active participant (being the text). In a grand Petrarchan gesture, Shylock rewrites the world in his image. The sheep multiply his vision as, following his "fall[s]" (1.3.82), they rise to his will and corroborate his sight lines. His self-replicating world rings around the wand of his mastery. But as Shylock changes places, so does Antonio, who replaces him as reader. Interpreting the biblical original, Shylock offers himself as text. Imposing a complicated reading of the biblical Jacob-Laban original, Shylock's insistence on leading Antonio to the site ("Mark what Jacob did") transfers the discourse from the confining terms of Antonio's labels (or markings) to the previously undefined terms of Shylock's dilation, or remarkings. His "mark," a command to see and to copy, conceals the source of his magic even as it calls attention to his resignifying powers. Shylock's command to make note of history— "Mark what Jacob did" (1.3.71)—is actually a command to subscribe to his reinvention of a myth.[47] Shylock bids for a different originary story and that is the threat Antonio recognizes in connecting him to the devil.

When he answers Antonio with a command to "mark," Shylock renders Antonio witness and recorder of the semiotic revolution he evolves. Commanding him to see the moment of exchange in which the master-signifier is opened up and revealed as renegotiable, he asks Antonio both to imagine a missing link in the old story and to acknowledge how, in peeling his wand, Shylock fills it up with his new one and turns the resultant black hole into a linguistic economy of his own. In the portrait speech, Bassanio finds only an abyssal void—"the wild of nothing" (3.2.182)—hollowed out by the unfurnishing image. Shylock presents something else. He *replaces* the master-signifier with his libidinal construct. Commanding Antonio to "mark what Jacob did," he asks him to record a new world order: his. Antonio dwindles into the scribe to Shylock's self-replicating poet. Shylock invites Antonio to observe the reframing of narrative so that entire sets of assumptions about gender and race—thrift (hoarding) and multiplying (thriving)—are opened up in a way that is magical (with the wand) and decreative (with the peeled). To peel is both to move toward the center and to empty it out. In the replicative image of his multiplying vision is the self-inventive Shylock. There is nothing beneath the label but a hole that Shylock enters with his wand. Playing with semen and semiotics at the very moment that a new breed is possible, he shatters the reigning discourse the way Bassanio fears the portrait of Portia does: by making it impossible to fathom the process of creation. He renders it a sexually desirable mystery. The portrait-Portia unmans its creator. Shylock is the re-creator, deconstructing maleness at its origin and directing femaleness to his centralizing self. In the nourishing womb fed by his "thrift," Shylock "breeds" the quickened life of a redefining discourse held "fast" by its parallels to the "deed of kind" (1.3.79).[48] Obscuring sexual demarcators, Shylock threatens to realign semiotic ones. In the Laban speech, Shylock identifies the center of lyric danger: its autogeneration mimics sexual regeneration and thereby threatens the very linguistic binaries it ought to establish. While Shylock renders himself the Medean "god in [him]self," creating his own ancestry and his own progeny, Antonio calls him the "devil [who] cite[s] scripture" (1.3.94). With that remark, Antonio begins the process of demonization that reaches its height in Act 4. When Shylock offers an alternative to the reigning discourse, Antonio's response is to name him the vampire of the master-signifier—the evil force who siphons off the good god of language and faith. The castigation of Shylock begins in Act 1, not as a result of his threat to extract a "pound of flesh," but in reaction to his promise to inseminate a new language.

The reconfiguration, however, inaugurates the wooing sequence, the invitation to dine an attempt to break down the barriers of resistance, definitions that Shylock himself imposes in Act 1, expressing the Petrarchan lady's sexual reluctance in terms of dietary scruples. In Act 1, he defines his selfhood before he even speaks to Antonio: he will share what he chooses to impart; he will privilege what he cannot give:

I will buy with you, sell with you, talk with you, walk with you and so following, but I will not eat with you, drink with you, nor pray with you. (1.3.30–33)

Clearly separating his formulative self from the intercourse of commerce, Shylock's provisos sanctify the two sources of his energy as physical and spiritual sustenance: eating and praying. His muse is private. What he absorbs remains a secret from the world. He "grazes" separately from the Venetians. Wary of their desire to "convert" him, he calls their dinner invitation a violation of his privacy. As unreasonable parent, he refuses to share his nutritive riches with them: "I will not eat with you." As author of a discourse sacred only to himself and as guardian of a language whose sources he will not divulge, Shylock will not "pray" with the Venetians.

Having nevertheless succumbed to their alimentary seduction in Act 2, Shylock vows, in 3.1.46, to "feed on them," the grazing and breeding of the Laban speech turned into the public revenge of the mirrored's mirroring. If Shylock's *wounding* graze in Act 1 renders him Jacob to Laban's sheep, his *wounded* graze in Act 3 renders him Medusa to Antonio's violation. That reversal, in turn, inspires Shylock's revenge. Antonio will be for Shylock what Shylock was for Antonio, the bait swallowed and cast out into the reflecting sea:

> To bait fish withal. If it will feed nothing else, it will feed my revenge. He hath disgraced me, and hindered me half a million; laughed at my losses, mocked at my gains, scorned my nation, thwarted my bargains, cooled my friends, heated mine enemies, and what's his reason?—I am a Jew. Hath not a Jew eyes? Hath not a Jew hands, organs, dimensions senses, affections, passions; fed with the same food, hurt with the same weapons, subject to the same diseases, healed by the same means, warmed and cooled by the same winter and summer as a Christian is? If you prick us do we not bleed? If you tickle us do we not laugh? If you poison us do we not die? And if you wrong us shall we not revenge? If we are like you in the rest, we will resemble you in that. If a Jew wrong a Christian, what is his humility? Revenge. If a Christian wrong a Jew, what should his sufferance be by Christian example? Why, revenge. The villainy you teach me I will execute, and it shall go hard but I will better the instruction. (3.1.45–61)

Reducing his active initiative in the Laban speech—determined by the equation between the specular objectification of the sheep in the configuration based on the eye's gazing, and sexual intercourse with the ewes in the regeneration of the wand's grazing—to the humiliations of Venetian representation in the revenge speech, Shylock describes himself as, first, the violated and then the avenging Medusa. The psychological wounds here are designated sequentially as oral, visual, and then genital "grazes." If the Laban speech turned figurative into material "interest," the revenge speech begins with a verbal wound that escalates into a physical victimization. Everything in it is the result of Antonio's "word." In the Laban speech, Shylock determines the scene. In the revenge speech, he is predetermined, his reduction circumscribed by his representation as a figure in the controlling Venetian discourse. Shylock's rage in the first third of the speech is pitted against Antonio's presumptive name-calling. His fury has little to do with the immediate cause of his misery (Jessica's pilfering, and Antonio's dissolution, of his wealth) and more to do with the lingering injustices of a reputation wronged. The Christian sins are libelous, "hindering" (48), and "thwarting" (50), impediments that referred (in the sixteenth century) to slander. "Mock[ing]," "scorn[ing]," "cool[ing]," and "heat[ing]" were denigrations that injured Shylock's name and that rendered him the object of Antonio's reconfiguration, his visual "look" confined to Antonio's word that the master-discourse defines him as devil.

Reacting to Antonio's representation, Shylock remakes himself in Antonio's image. His assertion in the second third of the speech that he is Antonio's double forces him into the bind that confines him first as Eve to Antonio's Adam. If, as Patricia Parker maintains, the sequence of Genesis 2 gives "man the hierarchical superiority of his coming before" the woman,[49] here Antonio is the man whose woman—Shylock—comes second. When he gives himself "hands, organs, senses, affections, passions" (3.1.52–53), Shylock assembles his feminine and secondary body from Antonio's. The androgynous Shylock of the Laban speech is here reduced to the single-dimensioned woman who assembles her parts as an afterimage of man. David Katz suggests that "an actor interpreting the role of Shylock could have pointed to his own genitals when reciting that most famous line, turning Shylock's heartfelt plea into a moment of high comedy."[50] But Katz's historicized woman is just a bleeding—and abject—victim. As I define her, she is a Medusa, turning her victimizer to stone.

In the last section of the speech, Shylock confirms his Medusan "look," emerging, in his reactive gestures, as the diminished vessel for male excess—a ventriloquist's puppet whose orgasmic movement depends on Antonio-Pluto's masculinist initiative. The spasms from tickling, the smart of pricking, the sickness of poison complete his objectification and rape. Left with an orifice for pricking and one for poisoning, Shylock is force-fed by Antonio's insinuation. His openings convert him—mouth and vulva—into what a ewe was to Jacob's wand: an empty container for the male graze. As corporeal Jew, Shylock codifies his victimization, his female body here countering Antonio's invasive masculinity. Fish caught in the Christian hook, he is trapped in his image. Defending his humanity, Shylock describes the violations that spur his rage. Pricked, tickled, and poisoned, he is skewered. He reacts like an injured animal to the prodding, poking, and prying of

Antonio's tool. His "Jewish" revenge is an imitation of a Christian initiative, a belated second coming back from the death of Antonio's representation. Caught, the baiting Shylock will cut off the Christian worm.

In rendering himself Antonio's feminized mirror, Shylock equates his Medusa to Antonio's Athena and vows to become his tormenter. As the violated victim, he enacts Medusa's revenge on her violators, merging Christians with Pluto and therefore turning all men to stone. If Perseus, wearing the mirror, becomes Medusa, and if Medusa already is her victimizer, then the "villainy" and its executioner merge. In the final moments of the speech, Shylock, the victim, vows to become—as Medusa did—the victimizer: "I will resemble you in that." If he already parallels the Christians in his "dimensions," then the next step is to follow them in their actions. Like a robot gone awry, his simulacrum moves. But the resemblance in act stems from his prior victimization in language. In this speech, Antonio is returned to his position as the signifying master. Within the semiotic system he reclaims, he casts Shylock as (what Portia was in Bassanio's initial sonnet description) the denying Daphne of the Petrarchan complex.

Setting himself up in the Laban speech as an independent authority who contains in himself the mystery of natural magic, Shylock ends up, in the revenge speech, as the Medusa who must take back, through terror, the energetic secret that was hers. Later, in Act 3, Shylock defines himself as nay-saying lady to the Christian pleas for mercy. There, he retreats from the retaliating Laura-Medusa to the unavailing Laura-Daphne, refusing even to hear the words of the Petrarchan Christians:

> I'll have my bond. I will not hear thee speak.
> I'll have my bond, and therefore speak no more.
> I'll not be made a soft and dull-eyed fool,
> To shake the head, relent, and sigh, and yield
> To Christian intercessors: follow not.
> I'll have no speaking. (3.3.12–16)

Shylock thrice cuts off discourse, and in so doing contrasts himself to those women who, encouraging their suitors, exchange permissive sigh for imploring complaint. He is the adamant Laura who won't be made (as Portia was) the "soft and dull-ey'd fool" of comedy. Defining what he won't do, Shylock equates the bartering in commercial exchange with the progression of courtship, which begins with "yes" (shaking the head), proceeds through the opening of relenting, moves through the "sighs" of pleasure, and ends by yielding, at once the exhibition of self that marks the woman's sexual surrender and the biological reproduction of self that characterizes the woman's procreative passivity as sustainer of the male signifying economy. Accusing the Christians of violence, Shylock's insistence on silence ("I'll have no speaking") establishes him both as the "meager" woman of the lyric complex and its resistant other.[51]

In Act 4, Shylock's position as recalcitrant woman in the lyric is confirmed over and over again. First, the Duke argues that Shylock is "uncapable of pity, void and empty / From any dram of mercy" (4.1.5). Like the Laura-Daphne who refuses Petrarch-Apollo's advances, Shylock is "monstrous," indifferent, unavailable, and merciless. Alluding to the Venetian code of racial hierarchies, the Duke voices the hope that Shylock will be softer than those others—still lower in the pecking order, with "brassy bosoms and rough hearts of flint" (4.1.30)—the Turks and Tartars. Bassanio adds that such a hope is futile since Shylock is an "unfeeling man" (4.1.61). From heartless *man*, Shylock descends to heartrending *wolf* in Venice's final estimation of him. In resigning himself to his fate, Antonio portrays Shylock as the embodiment of Petrarchan *impossibilia*. Like Shylock, who refuses to listen, Antonio, finally, refuses to speak: "Make no more offers, use no further means" (4.1.81). In canceling the discourse, he pits himself as reluctant Petrarch to the very Laura that Shylock played at the end of Act 3. If Shylock will have no more speaking, Antonio will no longer "question with the Jew." Thus Antonio and Shylock play off (and turn into) each other as Shylock becomes the hard-hearted adamant and Antonio the Petrarchan victim of that resistance:

> I pray you think you question with the Jew.
> You may as well go stand upon the beach
> And bid the main flood bate his usual height;
> You may as well use question with the wolf
> Why he hath made the ewe bleat for the lamb:
> You may as well forbid the mountain pines
> To wag their high tops and make no noise
> When they are fretten with the gusts of heaven,
> You may as well do anything most hard
> As seek to soften that—than which what's harder?—
> His Jewish heart. (4.1.70–80)

Turning the amorphous "harsh heart and wild cruel desire" of *Rime sparse* 265 (*Petrarch's Lyric Poems*, 434) into specifically bestial fierce tigers, Antonio's warnings echo the animal imagery of the play: the wolfen (Shylock) "ma[king] the ewe bleat for the lamb," and the maternal (Antonio) fearing for the generation stopped, the antifamilial violations of rape doubled in the image of incest. The ewe calls to her child for a help she cannot give. Mothers are motherless.

Ending in an inexpressibility *topoi* that resonates against Portia's "gentle rain" (itself a variation into comedy of the Petrarchan *impossibilia* of rain softened marble in *Rime sparse* 265), Antonio defines Shylock's "Jewish" heart as that of the unyielding woman. Unable to find any other word but "Jewish" to characterize Shylock's resistance, he sounds like Lear in his rage against his hard-hearted daughters: "I will do such things . . . what they are, yet I know not" (*Lear*, 2.2.446–47). Antonio's inability to formulate suggests that he has become, once more, the inarticulate want-wit of the opening: "You may as well do anything most hard / As seek to soften that—than which what's harder?— / His Jewish heart" (4.1.79). Like the defeated Petrarch of 366, Antonio pits himself—the "stone dripping vain moisture" (111–12)—against the "enstoning" Shylock. Reduced to childish blabbering, the "ewe bleat[ing] for the lamb . . . the mountain pines [wagging] their high tops," Antonio can no longer "question." Having emerged rock to Shylock's Medusa, Antonio is himself petrified. In his own defense, he can say "but little" (4.1.260). Antonio defines himself as gelded:

> I am a tainted wether of the flock,
> Meetst for death. The weakest kind of fruit
> Drops earliest to the ground. (4.1.114–16)

In his own analogy, Antonio has become the weak sheep Jacob left behind for Laban. As wether, he has been unmanned by Shylock's castrating woman whose shield of silence holds the mirror up to Antonio. Recognizing himself as damaged, a male unable to inseminate, a female unable to give birth, Antonio underscores his impotence. Victimized by the hard-hearted Medusan other crying for revenge, he remains (like the Petrarch of 197) immobilized by his own devices. He has turned the projection against himself, rendering the Shylock he invented the source of his unmanning. In stressing his victimization, Antonio takes his cue from Shylock, reversing the process of the "revenge" speech. He is the ultimate victim, the passive sheep, the weakest fruit, who cannot be saved. Shylock's stoniness has turned Antonio to stone, just as Laura-Medusa rendered Petrarch impotent in *Rime sparse* 197. Blaming his inability to yield on Shylock's unyieldingness, Antonio is what he was at the beginning: wanting. The "taking" of an earlier interest has become (in this approximation) the "tainting" of a transmitted disease, the mirror now mirrored.

In casting Shylock as the Petrarchan woman and Antonio as frustrated poet, Shakespeare emphasizes the danger of the lyric, isolating these two, even as he explores its terror, reducing these two to one, the reflecting merchants—like Narcissus and his watery double—attenuated in identity. Antonio and Shylock trade places in the trial scene, as Antonio shifts from a poet depressed about his art ("make no more offers," 4.1.81) to an emasculated object defined by yet another poet: "I am the tainted wether of the flock" (4.1.114). In the end, Shylock "go[es] from hence" (4.1.391), signed and ratified, his ducats now the Duke's, and the play's triumphs now are Portia's, who, in the doubled self of Bellario and wife, bends the strands of the state into the self-enclosing ring of comedic marriage. The Shylock who refuses to be framed is left outside the circle. That the poetic ethos involves something that resembles the "work of generation" but isn't it, that elaborates itself in a different *genus* (Shylock's self-breeding interest), is at the heart of what Shakespeare defines as lyric excitement. When Shylock leaves, Antonio (until Portia revives him) is "dumb" (5.1.279), expelled with Shylock from the verbal economy of the lyric. Without Shylock to spur him on, Antonio is the old man left, now that Bassanio is safely wedded, at the mercy of the young. As the excluded woman, Shylock is exempt altogether. Since the lyric is cast out, he has no narrative place. Bound by the enclosures of Venice—a city islanded—Shylock is put to sea; having refused the codes of enclosure, he ends up with the repressed, outside of the discursive frame. Shylock has no lyric voice, no comic place. He remains wandering up and down Venice's Bolsover Street.

LYRIC LOSSES AND FOUNDLING RECOVERIES

The only way to repress Shylock's subversive gestures is to cancel the lyric form he energizes. Identifying the lyric as a journey into the unconscious that, evolving out of nothingness, produces likenesses that threaten rather than sustain the other, the Shakespeare of *Merchant* remains in the islanded seclusion of a safer plot. In writing lyric energy out of the play, he charts its appropriations and annihilations, opting for the comic certainties of procreating couples over the borrowed representations of stolen couplets. But if the lyric is scrutinized out of existence, the comedy—despite what critics say about the harmonies of Act 5[52]—also seems to be wanting. Connecting the material to the spiritual marriages by arguing that "rings are utopian money," Michael Ferber speaks about a circle of exchange that weds the values of Belmont to those of Venice: "The ring that Portia gives to Bassanio and Bassanio gives to Balthazar, Portia finally gives to Antonio to give again to his friend. It is as if they are all married to each other and all the richer for the one ring."[53] Against so much Venetian happiness, one is tempted to say, with Hamlet, "We will have no mo marriage" (*Hamlet*, 3.1.149). That's what Shylock seems to echo, as he refutes comic persuasion with his ban on all petitioners ("I'll have no speaking," 3.3.17), and what Antonio reflects when he begs his fellow Venetians to "make no more offers" (4.1.81). In the end, the lyric indicts the comedy by its absence.

Michael Ragussis argues that "Shylock's failure to reappear, his manifest absence from the stage during Act 5, makes of the converted Jew something between a ghost and a pure hypothesis. After conversion, the Jew has neither eyes, hands, organs, dimensions, senses. . . . He is the dark absence that quietly, invisibly, haunts the last act of the comedy."[54] In Trevor Nunn's 1999 National Theatre production of the play, Shylock's absence is marked by Jessica, who, alone on the stage and humming a Yiddish lyric she had earlier sung with him, seems somehow drawn to her absent father.[55] In Jonathan Miller's 1985 production, Laurence Olivier's Shylock marks his absence by mouthing the Kaddish, mourning thereby his own missing person.[56] By adding words and even languages Shakespeare never intended for the play, both directorial gestures acknowledge the elimination of Shylock's linguistic presence in Shakespeare's text, challenging the legalism[57] of *Merchant*'s fourth act. Deprived of a forum, Shylock cannot bear witness.

With the suspension of the Petrarchan lyric, Shylock has no culturally available linguistic platform. His plot—his mode of being—is superseded by the comedy that has no use for his kind.[58] By excluding Shylock from the circle of winners, the Belmont coterie effectively curtails lyric defiance: to society, implied by Shylock's unyieldingness; to maleness, figured in Laura-Medusa's imitative revenge; to art, suggested by Shylock's revision of linguistic signification. A play that begins with an expression of self-loss, seen in terms of the questions of the foundling plot—"what stuff t'is made of, whereof it is born" (1.1.4)—ends in a consolidation that, while it "keeps [the formula] safe," returning everyone in the central triad to the conventional recovery, forfeits an imaginative freedom so often found in the reinventions of the middle interlude. As Lancelot chooses to remain stranded in service, anticipating his eventual return as child to his father but also refusing to acknowledge his own paternity of the Moor's child, so Shylock, deprived of the "means" by which he lives, is retrospectively denied the language system he so energetically defined for himself. Like Antonio at the beginning and Bassanio with Portia, Shylock at the end finds his powers "confus[ed]" (as Bassanio said of himself in 3.2.177), the "means" (4.1.372) of articulation having been taken from him.

In *Merchant*, Shakespeare concludes in a world void of lyric mystery, with an order held together by the pinion of a self-replicating society. But at key moments in the play, the lyric gets the best lines. In the Laban speech, Shylock displays a creative power, positing a matrix of "thrift" that "breeds" and multiplies its resources to reconfigure the "deed of kind" (1.3.79) and thereby to suggest a narrative redefinition. Shylock's "fast" breeding (1.3.90) is frightening to Antonio both because it represents a sudden overturn of everything and the fixed—seemingly unshakable—center of a new thing, the multiplication threatening to take over word and world. In the semiotic definition, Shylock opens up the discourse to a fundamental revision. In the autogeneration of the speech, he materializes that economy. He threatens Antonio's stability in the same way that the Portia-portrait "unfurnishes" Bassanio's: by replacing the Venetian symbolic order with a new configuration.

When Shakespeare writes the lyric out of the play, he renders the curtain that falls at the end a signifier of an iron-bound comic ascendancy. It is Shylock's absence that calls attention to the missing alternative offered by the lyric. As Paul Stevens writes, "Shylock is robbed of his 'cultural memory,'"[59] experiencing, in a small prolepsis, the same lack of individuation Primo Levi describes when he catalogues his losses at Auschwitz: "Then for the first time we became aware that our language lacks words to express this offence, the demolition of a man. In a moment, with almost prophetic intuition, the reality is revealed to us: we had reached the bottom. It is not possible to sink lower than this; no human condition is more miserable than this, nor could it conceivably be so. Nothing belongs to us any more; they have taken away our clothes, our shoes, even our hair; if we speak, they will not listen to us, and if they listen, they will not understand."[60] Without the lyric voice he energized, Shylock is written out. Nothing belongs to him anymore. Nameless in Act 5, he no longer exists. He is irretrievably lost, allowed no foundling recovery. The order of comedy fell into place as soon as Portia offered Bassanio her ring as symbol of her self-denial and it remains in place as Graziano secures Nerissa's ring as symbol of his libidinal possession.[61] The breakdown of order associated with Portia's unfurnishing in the casket speech and Shylock's imaginative generativity in the Laban speech has been corrected. The foundling plot comes to fulfillment as the maternal Portia mysteriously finds Antonio's lost ships and gives him exactly what Shylock is denied: "life and living" (5.1.286). Left without means, Shylock cannot be sewn into the circle of recovery.

In *As You Like It*, Rosalind's manipulative solutions are downplayed. Hymen enters as a *deus ex machina* to repair all the breaches. But in *Merchant of Venice*, Portia explains away all the "turns" as she proudly reveals that she "was the doctor, / Nerissa . . . her clerk" (5.1.268–69) and that she has "even but now re*turned*" (5.1.272) to Belmont. The mysteries have been found out and Graziano will make sure that, in future, all openings are "kept safe"—the women locked in, the Jew locked out. There will be no more "turns." In its obvious and lewd gesture, Graziano's fingered ring (an inversion of Shylock's peeling several wands) keeps the winner's circle closed. Something is lost in this play. With Lancelot dangling in the middle and Shylock unseamed at the end, the foundling restorations in Belmont leave us wanting more than we get.

NOTES

1. Harold Pinter, *Complete Works* (New York: Grove Press, 1975), 4:120.

Turning Gender and Plot in The Merchant of Venice   149

2. See Janet Adelman's connection of the crucial and many-times-used word "turn" to the issue of conversion in the play: "'Turn' [Latin *vertere*] is of course at the root of *conversion* and the obsessive repetition here would seem to confirm that conversion is indeed on Shakespeare's mind as he encodes Lancelot's 'conversion' in this encounter between father and son." *Blood Relations* (Chicago: University of Chicago Press, 2008), 65.

3. Lowell Gallagher writes of the absence of both father and son in Act 5 ("Waiting for Gobbo," *Spiritual Shakespeares*, edited by Ewan Fernie [London: Routledge, 2005, 73–93]). Of Lancelot's absence, he comments, "The absence is easy to overlook, for several reasons. The Gobbos belong to the periphery of the play's social world, and what we know of the story of their lives dissolves into white noise when pitched against the dominant key of the premarital banter in the final act" (73). And of Shylock's absence, he notes, "Shylock is mastered by the Venetian court: he is brought into a determinate civic identity whose prerequisite is religious conversion" (80).

4. On other generic shifts in the play, see Elizabeth Spiller, "From Imagination to Miscegenation: Race and Romance in Shakespeare's *The Merchant of Venice*," *Renaissance Drama* 29 (1998): 137–64. Spiller maintains that there is a connection between romance—"a genre organized by genealogy"—and *The Merchant of Venice*, which enacts the shift (in the early modern period) "as a moment of transition from an understanding of race as genealogy to one of physical appearance to reflect on the changing relationship between the genre of romance and the racial representation it allows" (138). Spiller's work on genre relates closely to mine and, in the respect she elaborates, I would say that the foundling plot is a subgenre to the romance she describes. While Spiller stipulates that romance operates to preserve a genealogy, I suggest that the plot of *The Merchant of Venice* is subverted by Shakespeare's use of the lyric which challenges the marriage imperative of romance. Kenneth Gross (*Shakespeare Is Shylock* [Chicago: University of Chicago Press, 2006]) refers to the lyric when he writes that "Shakespeare's sonnets seem to belong to the mid 1590's (the dating is a murky matter), roughly contemporary with *The Merchant of Venice*, written around 1596. This may account for the play's peculiar crossing of concerns with the sonnets, its way of echoing their paradoxical, self-enfolding, and self-canceling pictures of desire, their jamming up together of the language of possession and dispossession, praise and slander" (22).

5. Writing about the emasculation of circumcision, Janet Adelman argues, "The same set of fantasies is always available to turn any Jew into a kind of woman." See *Blood Relations*, 101.

6. Portia's "conversion" to comic power values undercuts her subversion of those values even if such powers are "inverted with a difference," as Lisa Jardine and Karen Newman so convincingly argue. Lisa Jardine, "Cultural Confusion and Shakespeare's Learned Heroines: These Old Paradoxes," *Shakespeare Quarterly* 38 (1987): 1–18; Karen Newman, "Portia's Ring: Unruly Women and the Structures of Exchange in *The Merchant of Venice*," *Shakespeare Quarterly* 38 (1987): 19–33. Expelled with Shylock are the questions about marriage, maleness and form that are consistently posed by the multiple dimensions of a Petrarchism multiply understood. In the end, the comic confederacy prevails over the Petrarchan "other" as Venice—made one with Belmont—casts the lyric out of the winner's circle. What interests me here is not to provide an all-encompassing solution to the question of critical methodology but to see how genre thinking and its necessarily hierarchical structures (of invention and closure) can be understood in this play by equating racial categories with gender binaries. Portia replaces Shylock in the main plot and a "Jew" works as well as a "woman" in the lyric dyad. When Shakespeare closes out the lyric in the end, he also closes off the possibility for redefinition that Shylock offers in the Laban speech of 1.3.66–85, where he reworks the form by regendering the dyad and multiplying its energy.

7. John Drakakis ("Historical Difference and Venetian Patriarchy," *The Merchant of Venice: Contemporary Critical Essays*, edited by Martin Coyle [New York: St. Martin's Press, 1998], 181–213) maintains that the feminization of Shylock in the play has a good deal to do with the feminization of usury. Quoting Philip Caesar's *A General Discourse against the Damnable Sect of Usurie* (1578), he argues that it is "conceived as a form of self-deception analogous to an unruliness associated with the figure of the Biblical Eve" (190). On the issue of

gender and Jessica's ambiguous conversion as a function of her status as a racialized Jew, see also Mary Jannell Metzger, "'Now by My Hood, a Gentle and No Jew': Jessica, *The Merchant of Venice* and the Discourse of Early Modern English Identity," *PMLA* 113, 1 (1998): 52–63.

8. *Petrarch's Lyric Poems*, edited and translated by Robert Durling (Cambridge, MA: Harvard University Press, 1976), 85. Future references are cited in the text.

9. Kenneth Gross similarly suggests that for Shylock "the history of Jewish suffering becomes truly palpable to him only in its being translated both by the loss of his gold and his daughter and by the pain of trying to undo the loss; these contingent, private afflictions for Shylock point more truly to the sources of the curse. It is an apprehension by which he cuts himself off from Jewish history as much as he aligns himself with it." *Shakespeare Is Shylock*, 24.

10. Referring to Heliodorus's *Ethiopian Romance* and Pierre Boaistuau's *Histoires prodigieuses*, Elizabeth Spiller suggests that "these stories—themselves clearly the product of various forms of imaginative excess—allow readers to indulge in speculations about new races produced not through physical mixture but through the perhaps more troubling power of the imagination." See "From Imagination to Miscegenation," 143. Spiller maintains that Shylock's use of the Laban story enacts a similar kind of imaginative reproductive system, one that challenges the Venetian idea of intergenerational relations.

11. Recent critical investigations into early modern conceptions of the body conclude that there is a connection between racial and gender perceptions. About the question of race in *Merchant of Venice*, Martin Japtok and Winfried Schleiner write that "while 'race' was not yet fully formed, racism was." See "Genetics and Race in *The Merchant of Venice*," *Literature and Medicine* 18, 2 (1990): 171. Such research further emphasizes how racial *and* sexual anxiety were projected onto the Jewish body. David D. Katz maintains that the Jewish threat worked two ways: oversexed Jewish men assaulted good Christian women, or undersexed Jewish men were, in fact, actually women. Pushed into an indeterminate gender zone, "male Jews were rendered even more slippery and untrustworthy in theoretical conception than they were in real life. . . . The [element] of effeminacy was unruly, unstable, uncontrolled. An effeminate man was an *Untermensch*, almost by definition. . . . As was so often the case in early modern England and Europe, the Jew simply did not fit into any clearly definable category. There was simply no room for him." See "Shylock's Gender: Jewish Male Menstruation in Early Modern England," *Review of English Studies* 50 (1999): 459.

While literary historians agree that Shylock reflects a deep-seated anti-Jewish bias endemic to the English culture that had expelled most Jews during the reign of Edward II, I will argue that the bias is built into the structure of *Merchant* and is most noticeable when Shakespeare fuses Shylock—the patent threat to Venetian commerce—with Portia—the latent threat to Venetian manhood. The feminized Shylock simply takes Portia's place in the Petrarchan dyad. When Shylock is cast as the troubling woman in the lyric, he corroborates the image of the slippery and effeminate Jew Katz identifies. As the gender and racial binaries converge, so the hate speech in the comic genre of the play springs from the identical mechanism as its lyric love talk. On the issue of Shylock as touchstone for historical anti-Semitism, see Michael Ragussis, who calls *Merchant* "the ur-text" for the construction of Jewish identity and asks whether Shylock is the figure through which "we learn to *hate* real Jews." *Figures of Conversion: "The Jewish Question" & English National Identity* (Durham: Duke University Press, 1994), 11, 62. See also Anthony Julius, who argues, "The shift from hostility to Shylock to hostility to Jews in general is achieved by the play." *T. S. Eliot, Anti-Semitism and Literary Form* (Cambridge: Cambridge University Press, 1995), 79.

D. Cohen writes of the effect of such representations on Jews themselves. In *The Politics of Shakespeare* (New York/London: Macmillan, 1993), 37, he maintains that, for Jew-haters, Shylock will always be a villain: "Towering over all Jewish giants of wickedness and giants of Jewish wickedness is the lonely figure of Shylock. His words will continue to be used, as they have been, to demonstrate Shakespeare's prescient awareness of the twisted Jewish psyche." Describing his own self-consciousness when *Merchant* was taught as a prescribed text in his Pretoria, South Africa, English class, Cohen explains, "My most vivid memory of that experience was the acute embarrassment I felt at the constant, deafening repetition of the word *Jew*. Having to read it aloud myself only exacerbated the shame since it seemed to me that it was almost always used as a term of opprobrium" (23). Cohen finds that the word "Jew" and related words like "Jewess" and "Hebrew" are used 114 times in the play (24). Interestingly enough, critics, too, often call Shylock "Jew" without putting the word in quotation marks. And reading their commentaries—through the lens critics such as Cohen provide—makes one feel that racial patterning and its habits of terminology are embedded more deeply in our culture than we would like to admit. An example of the way in which the term "Jew" and its anti-Semitic overtones slide into popular culture is its use as a verb in Michael Jackson's "Scream": "Jew me, sue me, everybody do me / kick me, kike me, don't you black or white me." See John Pareles, "Michael Jackson Is Angry, Understand?" *New York Times*, June 18, 1995. Here the verb "Jew" is used precisely as "prick . . . tickle . . . poison . . . [and] wrong" are used in the revenge speech, as a means for justifying revenge. And the implication is that the "scream" is a battle cry to rewrite the binaries from "black or white" to "kike or Christian." After the hubbub in the press, Jackson announced he would change the lyrics. But the "Jew" as the "kicker" will not be erased from the minds of those who choose to see him as the oppressor in exactly the same way as Shylock will always represent the villain of the play for those who choose to call him "Jew."

In some ways, *Merchant* can be viewed as an acid test for *critical* political correctness as well. Its critics are quick to indict other critics for failing to "invent an adequate method of inquiry" ("The Two Antonios and Same-Sex Love," *English Literary Renaissance* 22 [1992]: 221), which would include aspects of the play left out of their agendas. James Shapiro comments about those who share his methodology: "Though the new historicists have rediscovered virtually every marginalized other that passed through early modern England—including witches, hermaphrodites, Moors, cross-dressers, Turks, sodomites, criminals, prophets, Eskimos and vagabonds—they have steered carefully around the other of Others in the Renaissance, the Jews." *Shakespeare and the Jews*, 86. Feminist critics tend to exclude Shylock from their analyses. Karen Newman doesn't apologize; Catherine Belsey does. Newman writes that she has "chosen deliberately to leave Shylock out of [her] reading of *The Merchant of Venice* in order not to disturb readings of the play that center their interpretive gestures on *the Jew*" (italics mine, but they could have been Cohen's). See "Portia's Ring: Unruly Women and Structures of Exchange in *The Merchant of Venice*," *Shakespeare Quarterly* 38 (1987): 19. Belsey is more concerned about censoring herself. "It is surely perverse in a volume on Politics and Shakespeare to talk about *The Merchant of Venice* without discussing Shylock, who has quite properly come for twentieth-century criticism, particularly since the Second World War, to represent the crucial issue of this puzzling play. The history of anti-Semitism in our epoch demands that this question be accorded full attention. If I say nothing about it, that is not because I regard it as less than central, but only because I have nothing of value to add to the existing debate" ("Love in Venice," *Shakespeare Survey* 44 [1992]: 41).

Critics who deal with questions of race fail to include Portia in their conclusions; see Girard, "To Entrap the Wisest," and D. M. Cohen, cited above. Gender critics claim that both fail adequately to deal with Antonio in terms of homoerotic desire; see Joseph Pequigney, "The Two Antonios and Same-Sex Love in *Twelfth Night* and *The Merchant of Venice*," *English Literary Renaissance* 22 (1992): 201–22. A notable exception to the tendency to isolate gender and race is Lynda E. Boose's brief commentary in "The Getting of a Lawful Race," in *Women, "Race," and Writing in the Early Modern Period*, edited by Margot Hendricks and Patricia Parker (New York: Routledge, 1994), 38–42 and Kim F. Hall, "Guess Who's Coming to Dinner? Colonization and Miscegenation in *The Merchant of Venice*," *Renaissance Drama* 23 (1992): 87–111. Among those who wish to "rescue" Shakespeare's play from charges that Shakespeare is unfriendly to Jews is Martin Yaffee, who argues that, in comparison to Marlowe's Barabas, Shylock is sympathetic. "Far from simply succumbing to putative Elizabethan stereotypes concerning Jews, Shakespeare understands both Shylock's piety and his departure from it." *Shylock and the Jewish Question* (Baltimore: Johns Hopkins University Press, 1997), 5–6.

12. "Heterogenizing Imagination: Globalization, *The Merchant of Venice*, and the Work of Literary Criticism," *New Literary History* 36 (2005): 431.

13. "How to Read *The Merchant of Venice* without Being Heterosexist," *New Casebooks: The Merchant of Venice*, edited by Martin Coyle (New York: St. Martin's, 1998), 170, 171.

14. "How to Read *The Merchant of Venice*," 170.
15. Janet Adelman writes of Shylock's feminization: "By the end bereft of both lineage and livelihood—both losses predicted by the 'stones' that Jessica takes from him—Shylock is . . . marked as the castrated and feminized Jew, reabsorbing into himself the taint that he had threatened to reveal in Antonio." *Blood Relations*, 129.
16. On the similarities between Shylock and Portia, see Marianne Novy, *Love's Argument: Gender Relations in Shakespeare* (Chapel Hill: University of North Carolina Press, 1984), 63–82.
17. "Shakespearean Inscriptions: The Voicing of Power," *Shakespeare and the Question of Theory*, edited by Patricia Parker and Geoffrey Hartman (London: Methuen, 1985), 121.
18. Noting the doubling of cultural values in *Merchant*, David Lucking ("Standing for Sacrifice: The Casket and Trial Scenes in *The Merchant of Venice*," *University of Toronto Quarterly* 58 [1989]: 360) identifies a "curiously specular relation between the domains of Venice and Belmont [that] establishes itself through a dense network of verbal and situational echoes. . . . Each world draws upon language appropriate to the other for what appear to be purely figurative purposes, a process that might be described as one of metaphoric transposition between realms." While Lucking details the "transposition" between the polarized sites of Venice and Belmont, I describe a similar "transposition" between the seemingly opposite worlds of comedy and the lyric to argue that Shakespeare unhinges the fixed assumptions of two genres in *Merchant*.
19. On homosexuality in the Antonio-Bassanio ties, see W. H. Auden, "Brothers and Others," *The Dyer's Hand and Other Essays* (New York: Random House, 1962), 218–37; Keith Geary, "The Nature of Portia's Victory: Turning to Men in *The Merchant of Venice*," *Shakespeare Survey* 37 (1984): 55–68; Lawrence W. Hyman, "The Rival Lovers in *The Merchant of Venice*," *Shakespeare Quarterly* 21 (1970): 109–16; Coppélia Kahn, "The Cuckoo's Note: Male Friendship and Cuckoldry in *The Merchant of Venice*," *Shakespeare's Rough Magic*, edited by Peter Erickson and Coppélia Kahn (Newark: University of Delaware Press, 1985), 104–12; Thomas W. MacCary, *Friends and Lovers: The Phenomenology of Desire in Shakespearean Comedy* (New York: Columbia University Press, 1985), 160–70; Joseph Pequigney, "The Two Antonios and Same-Sex Love in *Twelfth Night* and *The Merchant of Venice*," *English Literary Renaissance* 22 (1992): 201–21; and Leonard Tennenhouse, "The Counterfeit Order of *The Merchant of Venice*," *Representing Shakespeare: New Psychoanalytic Essays*, eds. Coppélia Kahn and Murray M. Schwartz (Baltimore: Johns Hopkins University Press, 1980), 54–69.
20. Seymour Kleinberg writes about Antonio's struggle with Shylock:

> He hates himself in Shylock: the homosexual self that Antonio has come to identify symbolically as the Jew. It is the earliest portrait of the homophobic homosexual. The basis for that identification between Antonio and Shylock is complex. They are both merchants of Venice, both lend money, both are involved with Bassanio, and both indirectly and painfully become involved with Belmont. Most of all, they have in common that they are heretics. Shakespeare equates the sodomite and the Jew symbolically and psychologically, as they were already equated under Elizabethan law, which allotted the common fate of witches, heretics, and sodomites.

"*The Merchant of Venice*: The Homosexual as Anti-Semite in Nascent Capitalism," *Literary Visions of Homosexuality*, edited by Stuart Kellogg (New York: Haworth Press, 1983), 120–21.
21. Lorna Hutson views Lancelot's verbosity as a parody and Lancelot as "graceless. . . . (Gobbo means hunchback). . . . Believing himself to have achieved [service in Bassanio's household] through his eloquence, Lancelot crows with delighted irony 'I cannot get a service, no! I have ne'er a tongue in my head.' . . . The propitiousness of timely speech and a decorous manner, parodied in Lancelot's suit, is seriously expressed in the allegory of successful self-mediation (the mediation of the self through clothes, manners, facial expression and forms of speech) that is the drama of Bassanio's and Graziano's relationship and of their expedition to Belmont." See *The Usurer's Daughter: Male Friendship and Fiction of Women in Sixteenth Century England* (London: Routledge, 1997), 230. Hutson contrasts Bassanio's effectiveness

Turning Gender and Plot in The Merchant of Venice   153

with Gobbo's, whereas I view Gobbo's quick-wittedness in the context of his own self-preserving presentation in contrast to Antonio, who seems incapable of finding a self he wishes to preserve until he steps into Bassanio's cause, a step that ultimately endangers the self he found through that cause.

22. Of the cycle of wardship, Patricia Fumerton writes, "Child-giving also sums up the complex manner in which many Elizabethan gifts and ornaments circulated both horizontally between social equals and hierarchically between patron and client. Born in unformed animality, we may thus say, children were trifles whose circulation 'finished' them in a way an artwork is finished. Through circulation, the child underwent a translation from mere trifle to polished ornament—from being peripheral, detached and primitive to being central, connected, and cultivated" (*Cultural Aesthetics, Renaissance Literature and the Practice of Social Ornament* [Chicago: University of Chicago Press, 1991], 44).

23. Of Lancelot's reversal here, Suzanne Penuel argues, "In an aside, he calls Old Gobbo his 'true-begotten father' (II.ii.26)—the puzzling address not only denies bastardy, but also shows his desire to reverse biological processes and take control of his reproductive roots." See "Castrating the Creditor in *The Merchant of Venice*," *Studies in English Literature* 44, 2 (2004): 265. Connecting usury (as a fiscal obligation) and parenting (as a psychological debt), Penuel maintains that one can see the "ease of the slide from resentment of the father to hatred of the usurer." See "Castrating the Creditor in *The Merchant of Venice*," 260. "Obligations to parents and creditors in *Merchant* are similar enough that the emotions produced by a relationship with the first feed into the emotions felt of the second" (258). Penuel also sees that "family dynamic" is present in the Antonio-Bassanio relationship: "Genitals that are used for another person can function not just in an exchange of sexual pleasure but also in the production of another, in the conception of a child" (260).

24. Patricia Parker elaborates comic versions of the disorder I name here, cataloguing (among others) the "generational" reversals of *The Winter's Tale*, where the shepherd's son declares, "I was a gentleman born before my father" (5.2.139–40). Referring to such turnarounds in *Lear*, she cites the fool who "taunts his master for making his daughters his 'mothers,'" in a scene that explicitly allies such generational and gender reversal with a familiar proverbial instance of *hysteron protoron*—putting the cart before the horse" (1.4.172–74, 223–24). See *Shakespeare from the Margins: Language, Culture, Context* (Chicago: University of Chicago Press, 1996), 22.

25. Lowell Gallagher elaborates on the cycle of gift giving, framing it in theoretical terms, in "Waiting for Gobbo," 73–93.

26. *Ovid's Metamorphoses, the Arthur Golding Translation of 1567*, edited by John Fredrick Nims (Philadelphia: Paul Dry, 2000), 138. Future references are cited by book and line numbers in the text.

27. Of the connection between bestiality and sodomy, Seymour Kleinberg ("*The Merchant of Venice*: The Homosexual as Anti-Semite in Nascent Capitalism," 121) writes, "Shylock, the Jewish dog, already a heretic, is also symbol for the sodomite; conversely, Antonio the sodomite with his heretical desires is linked to the other alien in Venice, the not quite human Jew."

28. "'We all expect a gentle answer, Jew': *The Merchant of Venice* and the Psychotheology of Conversion," *English Literary History* 73 (2006): 63. Janet Adelman also writes of the Venetian ambivalence about conversion: "Already too different and too much the same, Jews were a contradiction that conversion—particularly state-enforced conversion—turned into a crisis. And insofar as *Merchant* worries the contradiction between Jessica's conversion and her blood, it responds in its own way to the pressures that were, elsewhere in the sixteenth century, forcing a protoracialized definition of Jewish difference." See the discussion in *Blood Relations*, 79 and following. Challenging Adelman, M. Lindsay Kaplan ("Jessica's Mother: Medieval Constructions of Jewish Race and Gender in *The Merchant of Venice*," *Shakespeare Quarterly* 58, 1 [2007]: 18) describes the difference between the conversion of Jewish women and Jewish men, even as (like Hirschfield and Adelman) she speaks to a certain ambivalence: "If racial assumptions about Jewish men pose obstacles to their successful conversion, gender assumptions about female inferiority generally and subordination to men in reproductive matters provide a model for a Jewish woman's incorporation into Christian culture via a Christian husband or devotion to Jesus, if she chose to enter a religious order."

29. In differentiating between the conversion of women seen as merely passive vessels for the shape of paternal seed, Kaplan also writes that "the female convert has, in effect, no racial identity to pass on to her child" (18). Jessica's playful resistance to Lorenzo's poeticizing in Act 5 poses no serious threat. Shylock's absence in Act 5 may suggest that his "conversion," unlike that of Portia to Bassanio and Jessica to Lorenzo, is itself suspect. It's easier just to exclude the vehicle of his resistance and banish the lyric as the form of his *impossibilia*.

30. On the connection between the impaling Petrarchan mistress and the torturing prison interrogator, see Scott Wilson, "Racked on the Tyrant's Bed: The Politics of Pleasure and Pain and the Elizabethan Sonnet Sequences," *Textual Practice* 3 (1989): 234–49.

31. On the hint of lead in "peise," see Albert Wertheim, "The Treatment of Shylock and Thematic Integrity of *Merchant of Venice*," *Shakespeare Studies* 6 (1970): 81. On whether Portia coaches Bassanio, see Harry Berger Jr., "Marriage and Mercifixion in *The Merchant of Venice*: The Casket Scene Revisited," *Shakespeare Quarterly* 32, 2 (1981): 155–62. Finally, David Lucking summarizes the argument for Portia's intervention, ultimately concluding that Bassanio changes in Belmont and is "at least morally equipped to make the correct choice." See "Standing for Sacrifice: The Casket and Trial Scenes in *The Merchant of Venice*," 367.

32. Marjorie Garber phrases Bassanio's choice in Freudian terms. "If one looks at it structurally rather than narratively, it is a man's choice among three caskets—and since (this is Freud) caskets, as symbolic containers, are emblematic of women, what we really have here is a *man's choice between three women*. In other words, behind Shakespeare's uneasy comedy lies Shakespeare's most profound tragedy: the choice of *King Lear*, a man choosing among three daughters." *Shakespeare and Modern Culture* (New York: Pantheon, 2008), 149.

33. William J. Kennedy writes of the importance of this sonnet for Renaissance poetry. Refer to *Authorizing Petrarch* (Ithaca, NY: Cornell University Press, 1994), 202–3.

34. As Freud writes, "The erect male organ also has an apotropaic effect. To display the penis (or any of its surrogates) is to say: 'I am not afraid of you. I defy you. . . . I have a penis.' Here then is another way of intimidating the evil spirit." *The Standard Edition of the Complete Psychological Works of Sigmund Freud*, translated by James Strachey (London: Hogarth, 1973), 18:274.

35. Roberto Calasso, *The Marriage of Cadmus and Harmony*, translated by Tim Parks (London: Jonathan Cape, 1993), 228.

36. *The Mirror of Medusa* (Berkeley: University of California Press, 1983), 14.

37. "Rebecca Gatward Talks to Heather Neill about Directing," "*The Merchant of Venice*, Production Playbill," Shakespeare's Globe Theatre, 2007, 15.

38. "Love in Venice," 44.

39. *This Sex Which Is Not One*, translated by Catherine Porter (Ithaca, NY: Cornell University Press, 1985), 216.

40. "The Jew as Renaissance Man," *Renaissance Quarterly* 51 (1998): 129.

41. On the thematic importance of the ring exchange, see Anne Parten, "Re-establishing Sexual Order: The Ring Episode in *The Merchant of Venice*," *Women's Studies* 9, 2 (1982): 150–51.

42. "Guess Who's Coming to Dinner? Colonization and Miscegenation in *The Merchant of Venice*," 104.

43. "An English Lass amid the Moors: Gender, Race, Sexuality, and National Identity in Heywood's *The Fair Maid of the West*," *Women, "Race," and Writing in the Early Modern Period*, edited by Margot Hendricks and Patricia Parker (New York: Routledge, 1994), 102.

44. Christy Desmet writes that, for Shylock, "the text of Genesis is not a storehouse of types to be matched with Christian anti-types in typological method, but a family history—his history." See "Poetry, Proof, and Pedigree in *The Merchant of Venice*," *Cithara* 46 (2006): 42.

45. Marc Shell notes that the play involves "the similarity between natural sexual generation and monetary generation" (*Money, Language and Thought: Literary and Philosophical Economies from the Medieval to the Modern Era* [Berkeley: University of California Press, 1982], 48), but I argue that, through Shylock, Shakespeare distinguishes between the processes of nature and the production of art even as he demonstrates (in the Laban speech) how art mimics nature. On the Laban speech as a short-lived triumph for usury, see Lars Engle ("'Thrift Is Blessing': Exchange and Explanation in *The Merchant of Venice*," *Shakespeare Quarterly* 37

[1986]: 32), who writes, "Shylock loses control of the Laban story as he introduces it. He becomes Laban, his daughter and idols stolen, or Esau, bereft of blessing and compelled to witness a younger people thrive." Of the Laban speech as a hint of "overt sexuality used to disturb Antonio's containing presence," see John Picker, "Shylock and the Struggle for Closure," *Judaism* 43 (1994): 177.

46. "'We all expect a gentle answer, Jew,'" 61.

47. Of Shylock's use of the Laban story, Stanley Stewart writes, "On closer examination, the analogy that Shylock perceives between the Old Testament story and his contestation with Antonio is faulty to the core. He claims to hate Antonio 'for [because] he is a Christian.' But Bassanio is a Christian, and there is no evidence that Shylock wishes him any special harm. Indeed, he seems unbothered by the fact that the young man will benefit from the 'merry bond,' with or without Portia's ersatz divine intervention in the judicial proceeding. It seems to me that, like Iago, Shylock is a hater in search of a rational motive." See "Shylock and Jacob the Patriarch," *Cithara* 46 (2006): 32–33.

48. Supplementing both the theories of René Girard, about misplaced signifiers, and of Marc Shell, about puns without origins, Lynn Enterline writes of Shylock's "unnatural breeding" that "this seeming autogeneration of signs without reference . . . to what they were supposed to have stood for in the world specifically puts the origin of value into question. For doing so, usury becomes a story of money's unnatural origin, of its perverse mothering." With Antonio, Enterline reads Shylock as a threat to the prevailing narrative of state. *The Tears of Narcissus: Melancholia and Masculinity in Early Modern Writing* (Palo Alto, CA: Stanford University Press, 1995), 238. I argue that Shylock describes artistic regeneration, a realigning of the material that already exists into a new form: in this case, his. The Jacob of Shylock's story merely makes more of what he was given, "mends" rather than "changes" nature, as Polixenes puts it in *The Winter's Tale* (4.4.89–96).

49. *Literary Fat Ladies* (London: Methuen, 1987), 179–80.

50. "Shylock's Gender," 461.

51. Kenneth Gross notes that Shylock is "throughout the play a great refuser of answers." *Shakespeare Is Shylock*, 56.

52. See especially Lawrence Danson, *The Harmonies of Merchant of Venice* (New Haven, CT: Yale University Press, 1978). Marc Shell writes of the limitations of the concluding comedy: "The Jewish moneylender behind the scenes of the last act of the courtly world is not easily forgotten. The aristocratic court of the comedian Portia cannot long exist without a day of reckoning in the court of tragedy" (*Money, Language and Thought*, 83). Arguing that the letter announcing the recuperation of Antonio's fortune in Act 5 "comes from nowhere and from no one's hand," Howard Marchiettello reasons that its mystery destabilizes the sense of comic closure. "Our confidence in the letter is actually our profound and desperate faith in it." See "[Dis]embodied Letters and *The Merchant of Venice*: Writing, Editing, History," *English Literary History* 62 (1995): 249. For other measured responses to the concluding comedy, see Janet Adelman, "Male Bonding in Shakespeare's Comedies," and Coppélia Kahn, "The Cuckoo's Note: Male Friendship and Cuckoldry in *The Merchant of Venice*," both in *Shakespeare's Rough Magic*, 73–103 and 104–12, respectively.

53. "The Ideology of *The Merchant of Venice*," *English Literary Renaissance* 20 (1990): 448. On Portia's including Antonio in the ring, see also Joseph Pequigney, "The Two Antonios and Same-Sex Love in *Twelfth Night* and *The Merchant of Venice*," 218.

54. *Figures of Conversion: The Jewish Question and English National Identity*, 79.

55. Of Jessica's alienation at the end, Mary Jannell Metzger writes, "The Jessica of Act 5 *may* be read not as an alternative and fully integrated Jew but as a homeless figure that suggests the dangers of consummating relationships across such [racialized] differences. In this reading, she becomes an emblem of postcoital regret, ruing not her rebellion against patriarchal authority but the terms of her new commitment to it and the meager possibilities for unalienated pleasure they provide." "'Now by My Hood, a Gentle and No Jew': Jessica, *The Merchant of Venice*, and the discourse of Early Modern English Identity," 59. Janet Adelman refers to protoracism in the play and the mixed feelings about the potential for conversion, arguing that Jessica cannot fully change her blood and that the impossibility of her true conversion "ground[s] Jewish difference in the apparently immutable and visible category of race rather

than the mutable and invisible category of religion." See *Blood Relations*, 91. Contesting Adelman's insistence on male blood imprinting but also agreeing that the question of conversion underscores an unease about the purity of the rising English nation, M. Lindsay Kaplan maintains, "*The Merchant of Venice* employs a double strategy to signal the efficacy of Jessica's conversion: by representing her as a subordinate female who remains inferior despite her elevation as a Christian, and by invoking Aristotelian views of maternal passivity in the formation of her husband's children that circumvent questions of Jewish race.... Jessica serves to solve the 'problem' of converting racially Jewish men as represented by Shylock.... In contrast to her father, who troubles Christian difference and superiority, Jessica will not threaten or challenge the Christian community. Jessica's mother, her antecedent in medieval constructions of Jews, provides the solution to early modern England's problem of imagining a successful conversion of the Jews." See "Jessica's Mother: Medieval Constructions of Jewish Race and Gender in *The Merchant of Venice*," 30.

56. Of this addition, Michael Shapiro writes, "It is not clear whether we are hearing Shylock mourning a daughter who is now dead to him, or whether someone else is mourning Shylock's death, but either way, the mournful sounds move even those unfamiliar with the liturgical chant to register the pain of the man with the feral teeth, lower-class gestures, and funny accent." "*The Merchant of Venice* after the Holocaust, or Shakespearean Romantic Comedy Meets Auschwitz," *Cithara* 46, 1 (2006): 12.

57. For a reading that contests the very basis of *Merchant*'s legalism, see Regina M. Schwartz, "The Price of Justice and Love in *Merchant of Venice*," *Triquarterly* 129 (2006): 225–49.

58. Kenneth Gross comments (*Shakespeare Is Shylock*, 104) on the "lack of a tragic matrix or surround in the text of the play itself. The absence of any final vehicle for Shylock's rage makes it harder to measure or mourn Shylock's defeat, or to build a sense of future on that loss. The one thing we are left to pursue is the idea of conversion, something that acknowledges and turns against itself the troubling, occluded inner life we have seen in Shylock."

59. "Heterogenizing Imagination: Globalization, *The Merchant of Venice*, and the Work of Literary Criticism," 437.

60. *If This Is a Man*, translated by Stuart Woolf (London: Vintage, 1996), 32–33.

61. On the ring sequence as a "joke which even extreme age has not made respectable," see Anne Parten, "Re-establishing Sexual Order," 144–45. In a more optimistic reading of what she admits is a bawdy pun, Joan Ozark Holmer asks, "In this instance, how is mutually chosen sexual fidelity in marriage an act of subordination?" See *The Merchant of Venice: Choice, Hazard and Consequence* (New York: Palgrave, 1995), 271–72.

Chapter Six

"God Me Such Uses Send"

Desdemona's Lyric Response in Othello

Philip Roth's definition of "fictional amplification [as] . . . evolving uncertainly out of nothing" might be used to define Othello's lyric self-invention in Shakespeare's play. Roth duplicates in late modern terms the early modern process of Othello's verbal expansiveness, similarly dependent on the resources of a psychologically necessary absence:

> But isn't one's pain quotient shocking enough without fictional amplification, without giving things an intensity that is ephemeral in life and sometimes even unseen? Not for some. For some very, very few that amplification, evolving uncertainly out of nothing, constitutes their only assurance, and the unlived, the surmise, fully drawn in print on paper is the life whose meaning comes to matter most.[1]

In *The Merchant of Venice*, Shylock also multiplies an imaginary original so that it emerges a practical means for living. "Ampli[fying]" the little he has, he converts it into the financial "means by which [he] lives" (4.1.372), an "assurance" the Belmont winners deny him in the end. In *Othello*, by contrast, "the unlived" Roth defines is for the hero the "life whose meaning comes to matter most." Shylock's creations from the void defy Venetian conventions; Othello's are fully within the cultural terms of the aristocracy to which he aspires. It is through those expansions (what Maurizio Calbi calls "the excess of . . . linear representation"[2]) that he hopes to insinuate himself into—and remain permanently fixed as a member of—the masculinist Venetian social order that defines itself in terms of Petrarchan self-reflection.

But in the later acts of the play, Desdemona gives the lyric a feminine voice as she retrieves Barbary's song from her memory and that evocation in turn creates an altogether different adoptive interlude, a small circle of foundling recovery that changes the formulaic plot in yet another way, one that is rendered impossible with the tragic unfolding of Act 5 but offers, however briefly, a new way of reading both the foundling and lyric plots. The many turnings of *The Merchant of Venice* lead either to the enclosures of Belmont or to the one-way system that leaves Lancelot reveling in the self-imposed quarantine of the middle interlude and Shylock deprived of the lyric creativity that energizes him. That life is taken from him, first by the Venetians whose slander renders him the "devil [who] cite[s] Scripture" (1.3.94) and also early on by Jessica, who—ignorant of what matters to him—from the very beginning declares "though I am a daughter to [my father's] blood, / I am not to his manners" (2.3.17–18). Her acknowledgment of an essentialist heredity reveals her indifference to the "matter" comprising Shylock's "manners." His "means" (4.1.372) mean nothing to her.

The Belmont victories fail to produce a recovery of the imaginative "amplification" signaled by Shylock's creative breeding. We are left in the last scene with a reiterated notion of patriarchal safety (figured in the very financial and love terms of Antonio's initially limited vocabulary). That repetition is secured by Antonio's mercantile (5.1.284) and Graziano's sexual (5.1.299–305) interest, the "com[ing] to road" (5.1.287) of an anchorage that has been previously fixed. Shylock's daring creation is a process in the act. His response to Antonio's question about his profession describes a moment that exists in mythical and contemporary territory simultaneously. For Shylock, the past is present and points toward the future. "Fictional amplification" is the fully lived life, his casting backward into the Jacob story, a stretching forward into usable multiplication. "Fast . . . breed[ing]" (1.3.92) for him presumes that the "amplification" of his "intensity" yields a continuing confidence dependent on "increase," the very movement that (I will later argue) so frightens Othello. In fact, Shylock depends on change. Commanding Antonio to "mark what Jacob did" (1.3.72), he asserts that his retelling involves a currency that carries an old text into a new world order. Shylock bends the story to his uses and then defines usury as a form of "mak[ing]" (1.3.92), weaving the materials into a text that can expand indefinitely. His command to Antonio, in the "mark[ing]" (1.3.72), presumes a present verification, a future acceleration, and a linguistic record of his process. In *The Merchant of Venice*, Shakespeare's lyric experiments evolve into multiple imaginative opportunities that signal a future opposite to the foundling plot's recuperation of a genetically determined *status quo ante*.

While Shylock's invention counters the prevailing social contract, Othello's, in Shakespeare's Venetian tragedy, where lyric "amplification" also is the source of identity, duplicates it. As Caryl Phillips puts it, "[Othello] relies upon the Venetian system."³ And while Shylock's process proclaims a fluidity that includes growth, Othello's demands a rigidity, a solidifying of the order to which he so desperately aspires. For Othello, "after" must remain the same as "before." When Desdemona moves out of the static frame Othello creates for her, she leaves him deprived of the vocabulary that fits the mold of what he expects her to be and, like Graziano's ring for Nerissa, is meant to keep her confined. What frightens him is Desdemona's excess, as I will demonstrate when I analyze the postmarital dialogue of their Cyprus reunion. Confronting her real and available body in Acts 2 and 3, Othello ultimately renders her as monstrous as the Medusa Bassanio feared. Even before Iago completes his machinations, Othello's sense of self is intricately connected to Petrarchan absence and to his conviction that his love life is totally implicated in the exciting but dangerous continuation of his military life. They emerge parallel, the "content" in love he proclaims in 2.1.96 identical in its impact to the "content" in warfare he loses when he comes to believe (in 3.3.351) that Desdemona no longer is what he created her to be. His professional "occupation"—with all its pomp—is lost without his "occupation"—with all its self-reflection—of Desdemona's body. Containing her amorously and retaining himself militarily pose similar pleasures and challenges. Othello appears in the play as a self-invented man, "amplifying" himself and consequently Desdemona with a design that sets him on a course rendering the near-death experiences he chronicles (in 1.3.127–71) fictions that lead inevitably to a tragic end. If Shylock offers the life of the lyric, signaling in his inventiveness a new and independent terminology, Othello precipitates its conceptual death and that death is compounded by the distorted bodies he produces in the course of the play, his notion of "breeding" creating either a fictionally lived past or a grotesque future expectation, one he cannot bear to see enacted. Shylock's invention is insistently self-contained, his generation in the Laban speech dependent on an imaginative parthenogenesis that is self-inclusive. Contrastingly, Othello's involves a doubling, the mirror he produces in the creation of the Desdemona he first desires and then distrusts as he comes to believe in her failure to remain constant in her reflection of him.

Othello's imaginative construction is also different from Shylock's because its terms echo the master-discourse of Venice with its fabled set pieces of heroism fuelled by what Mark Rose calls Othello's "romanticizing imagination,"⁴ and because it depends entirely on remaining, in Roth's terms, "unlived" (in fact, unlivable), only recalled as story or deferred as reality. While Shylock thrives on a system that offers an alternative to Venetian discourse, Othello follows the conventions until the woman he "amplifies" challenges the invention by her insistence on an "increase" that keeps pace with the progression of time and that thereby challenges the stasis of Othello's narcissism (2.1.191). In his fear of change, Othello resembles the Bassanio of the casket scene, threatened by his very success. Bassanio feels to be himself a "wild of nothing" (3.2.182), outdone by the imagined "substance" of Portia's hypothetical speech. Her lips—the portals through which her anticipated and unpredictable voice might emerge—send him into a tailspin just as Desdemona's oppositional words overturn the mold Othello created in Act 1. In *Merchant*, Portia immediately converts herself to Bassanio and proceeds to act (through to the end of the play) as if his interests and values were identical to hers. In Act 1, Desdemona "consecrate[s]" (1.3.255) herself to Othello but, as early as Act 2, she commands an individual notion of love as an ongoing progress, one that countermands the "process" (1.3.143) of Othello's speaking. For Othello, "process" is a story, almost a legal document, which (by definition) must remain static. When he calls her "monumental" (5.2.5) in the end, he returns Desdemona to the stillness of her initial reflection of him. In Acts 4 and 5, having cast her as the Medusa Bassanio avoided, Othello accuses her twice of having "turned [his] heart to stone" (4.1.175, 5.2.67), rendering her in both instances the agent of a calcification that, in his desire for permanence, he actually wants.

If Shylock and Othello position themselves at opposite ends of the lyric spectrum, using the same amplification out of nothing for diametrically different purposes, Shylock and Brabanzio figure at opposite ends of the foundling plot: Shylock's rage at Jessica largely over her rejection of the ideas he propagates, and Brabanzio's over Desdemona's "treason of the blood" (1.1.167). In *Merchant of Venice*, the various adoptions (of Bassanio by Antonio and then by Portia of them both) serve to strengthen the patriarchal structures of comedy. Only Jessica at the end feels the emptiness of that system when, rebelling against Lorenzo's lyric evocation of music, she begins to sound like the father whose "manners" she earlier mocked:

> In such a night
> Did young Lorenzo swear he loved her well,
> Stealing her soul with many vows of faith,
> And ne'er a true one. (5.1.16–19)

In her belated insistence on truth, she challenges the assertions of Petrarchan foreplay (which, until Act 4, Desdemona so enjoys) and voices her fear of the Petrarchan afterlife (which, in Act 5, when faced with her failure to enact the "mend[ing]" [4.3.104] she hopes for, Desdemona reinstates). The Jessica of Act 5 feels as if she's floating in the wind, tied neither to Lorenzo nor to her father. Her reaction is to reject anything to do with the process of courtship: "I am never merry when I hear sweet music" (5.1.68). In his rage at Jessica's rebellion, Shylock projectively disowns her: "I would my daughter were dead at my foot and the jewels in her ear" (3.1.74–75). It's as if the Act 5 Jessica heard Shylock's words and finds herself stranded in the world she chose, trapped by her self-imposed familial estrangement. In contrast, Desdemona remains at the end confident of having left her father—and all that he stood for—behind.

When Brabanzio learns of Desdemona's rebellion, he retrospectively annuls her—"I had rather to adopt a child than get it" (1.3.189)—his rejection of Desdemona's body and its past connection to him as firm as Shylock's compulsion to preside over his daughter's future death, the jewels pinned to her corpse. But in the subjunctive tense Brabanzio calls into being, he (Hamlet-like) unconditionally wipes Desdemona from the table of his memory, his "had rather to" evoking the future of a past he has already annihilated. Not only is she nonexistent in the present for him, but he also wishes for her never to have been born: "Who would be a father?" (1.1.165). Contrastingly, Shylock erases neither past life nor past love. In fact, it is Jessica's apparent indifference to Leah that sets Shylock into such a rage—"I would not have given [Leah's ring] for a wilderness of monkeys" (3.1.101–2)—even as he equates both wife and daughter to the material wellsprings of his wealth. Shylock links the objects of his amplification to real bodies and sees them as corporeal beneficiaries of the imaginative "means" by which he lives. For Brabanzio, Desdemona's body is expendable, a "thing" that provokes him to scorn the psychic reality of her being.

Shylock's jewels connect him to morphology; Brabanzio's remove him from the very biological life he has hitherto led. Desdemona is superfluous, a meaningless bauble:

> For your sake, jewel,
> I am glad at soul I have no other child. (1.3.194–95)

Disowning Desdemona by proclaiming her the source of his anathema to all children, Brabanzio hands her to Othello in an oxymoronic circle of exchange that renders his daughter immaterial: "I here do give thee that with all my heart / Which, but thou hast already, with all my heart / I would keep from thee" (1.3.192–93). His heart remains cloistered as Desdemona is jettisoned from him. Denying Desdemona's bodily life, Brabanzio gives Othello both what he claims Othello already has and then, alluding to a time prior to his retrospective annulment, the one thing that (in the before-before) he would never forfeit. The presently consecrated Desdemona of the "here" is different from the previously kept Desdemona of the "then." Giving with "all his heart" now what he earlier would have withheld totally yields nothing. As a "jewel," Desdemona's meaning derives only from its proximity to him. He tosses her to a "sooty bosom" (1.2.71) just as Jessica gave Leah's ring for a monkey: "Take her since you have stolen what I have (with my 'rather') already disowned."[5] While Shylock's imaginative kindling redefines familial connections, situating their origins in the ground of a psychological kinship whose "means" he creates, Brabanzio's initial insistence on blood causes him to call Desdemona's marriage a "spite of nature" (1.3.97). Rejecting her, he does away with women's bodies altogether. In the revisionism of his "rather to," Desdemona becomes what Theseus says all daughters are in *A Midsummer Night's Dream*: a figure whom the father creates and whom he can disfigure at will.[6] There are no mothers for him. Brabanzio's waffling back and forth between total possession and complete excision is an example of what Harry Berger Jr. calls "the sexual and proprietary insecurity of husbands and fathers in a culture that promotes the distrust of wives and women."[7]

It is Desdemona who comes to believe in the power of female creative life. Her reaction toward the end of the play remains constant. Defending her renunciation of everything connected to her before-Othello life, she argues:

> If haply you my father do suspect
> An instrument of this your calling back,
> Lay not your blame on me. If you have lost him,
> Why, I have lost him too. (4.2.45–48)

Paralleling, in its foreclosure, Brabanzio's giving what he no longer has, Desdemona's pledge similarly relinquishes what she has already forsaken. But she phrases her expulsion by her father in terms that place Othello and her as the agents of their own estrangement: they created their life together. Identifying the deprivation as an act she wills (rather than, as it actually was, Brabanzio's disowning of her), she retains her autonomy and emerges the source of her own independence. In that respect, she matches Othello, letting her patrimony slip through her fingers just as Othello seems to have sprung from nowhere as a man without biological history. If, in Act 5, Jessica feels herself robbed of her "soul" (5.1.18) and Shylock feels himself bereft of his "means" (4.1.372), Desdemona claims that, together with Othello, she is the originator of her own unhinging. The foundling plot's exposures are reversed. With their marriage, Othello and Desdemona abandon Brabanzio. There are no backward glances with regard to her father, only looks ahead, even as, still later, in Act 4, she bolsters a fidelity to Othello extending from a maternal support that brings another past (one that remains independent of Brabanzio and one not mentioned at all in the early acts) into the present. It is this belief in female grounding that distinguishes her from the dislocated Jessica and that gives her a base from which to measure her filial independence.

In this chapter, I trace Othello's lyric collision course as it evolves and then declines out of his patriarchal sense of entitlement and as it contrasts to what Shylock calls "the deed of kind" (1.3.81); Shylock creates both rams and ewes in an autogenerativity that fills an emptiness with the vitality of a self-satisfying continuity—a creation out of nothingness that he portrays as a parallel to biblical multiplication. Shylock's "peel[ing] certain wands"

"God Me Such Uses Send" 163

(1.3.79) simultaneously creates a hole and then saturates it with something that grows on its own, his interjection merely a spur to a generation that multiplies independently and that therefore continues to change. Othello begins over and over again in an "imminent deadly breach" (1.3.135), which he repairs first with himself and then with the Desdemona he projects as a mirror of his invention.[8] She is part of the same abyss, offering an inarticulate echo of his storied pain: the only response he wants to his fabulation. In his account, Desdemona's lack of specific words is the oral equivalent of her specular absence of individuated body. Thus, while Shylock propagates a new breed, directed toward a fluid future, Othello makes of Desdemona a self that reflects backward always to the same thing—a vitreous replica. When she moves out of that model, she becomes intolerable and the mirror leaves him with nothing stable, a shattered image, rendered capricious as a liquid: "She was false as water" (5.2.143). In *Fugitive Pieces* and *The Winter's Tale*, as well as in Desdemona's song, fluidity is a source of a permeability that nurtures. For Othello, as for Austerlitz, it represents an instability that threatens. Having determined her being within his own constellation, he does not know how to deal with her voice. Shylock's "peeled me" (1.3.79) at once opens and closes a gap, emphasizing the fulsomeness of the creative self with a growth that multiplies. Othello's "breaches" gradually change their dimensions, narrowing in hyperbole from the "antres vast" (1.3.139) of his Act 1 wooing sequence to the tiny "corner in the thing [he] love[s]" (3.3.276). But always there remains the emptiness he fills with the "thing" he invents. Desdemona is he, to be "use[d]" (3.3.276) in order to shore up his own self-same identity.

Desdemona recovers her origins in an Irigarayan return opposite to Othello's and it is this return that I will describe later, partly by tracing her opening to a physically anchored source of language. In the next section, I trace the difference between Othello and Desdemona in terms of an Irigarayan concept of time. Desdemona envisions a mutual engenderment that sustains her and that also reconceptualizes the middle period of the foundling plot. What she remembers in the boudoir scene is a community of women who replace the revisionist history of Brabanzio's annulment and who yield instead a support independent of bloodlines. She recovers an adoptive interlude based on a reciprocation of feeling, one that includes a reaffirmed natural world and the very fluidity Othello distrusts. For the audience, Desdemona chronologically stretches the boudoir scene we witness in Act 4—with its worldly talk about "court[ing] and couch[ing]"—backward to another scene where, internalizing Barbary's world, she emerges strengthened by it.[9] As she makes present that past and becomes Barbary by adopting her plight, she is, in turn, adopted (like her mother's maid was) not only by the other women who chorus Barbary's song but also by the pastoralized nature that evokes the foundling plot's middle period. The rocks and streams of the lyric respectively cradle and echo Barbary's tears and provide in their comfort a holding space that, through the vehicle of Desdemona's mind, transfers itself from an earlier Venice to a belated Cyprus. Countering Othello's reliance on Petrarchan ruptures (necessary to lyric amplification as illustrated by Sonnet 95, the dynamics of which mirror those of the play), Desdemona insists on presence and thereby puts into practice the Irigarayan "anastrophe" I outline next. With Desdemona, Shakespeare recasts the lyric to make it the verbal foundational source for a feminist restructuring of the foundling plot.

READING OTHELLO AND DESDEMONA IN IRIGARAYAN TIME

Enacting her prescriptive that "discourse has a sex"[10] by sexualizing her own discourse, Irigaray maintains that the female "remains unformed as subject of the autonomous word. . . . [Her] coming or the subjective anastrophe (rather than the catastrophe) . . . has not yet taken place."[11] I will use Irigaray's characterization of linguistic subjectivity (the female opening into language through "anastrophe"/the male impulse toward closure or "catastrophe") to describe the trajectories that set Desdemona and Othello on a verbal collision course in Shakespeare's Venetian tragedy. The oppositions Irigaray proposes in *To Speak Is Never Neutral* are, however, complicated by what I think is a deliberate terminological slippage that renders her analysis even more pertinent to an understanding of the gender dynamics of *Othello*.

As she defines the still-unrealized potential of female subjectivity, Irigaray points to two very different and not parallel discursive practices derived from the ancient Greeks. "Anastrophe" is a *rhetorical* tactic, governing a *grammatical* inversion that almost always involves a *temporal reversal*.[12] In her parenthetical allusion to the equally ancient and presumably male "catastrophe," Irigaray refers to a course leading relentlessly forward to an inevitable *finality*—the denouement—of a dramatic form. By definition, "anastrophe" includes a movement around, or a retrieval of beginnings; "catastrophe" specifies a point of no return, or a precipitation toward endings, the "negative gradient" Sebald insists is the inevitable inclination of fiction. The parenthetical insertion of "catastrophe" is itself a rhetorical flourish. (The French even adds inverted commas around, and a question mark after, catastrophe to indicate that the female "coming" remains open, whereas the male direction seems a bit like Groucho Marx's "Hello, I must be going.") On the run from the start, the male schemata results in the inevitable climax of its own preordination; the female temporal recuperations involve the sustaining power of a language system redefined to include the morphological.[13]

Irigaray front-ends the anastrophic female linguistic approach as a way of avoiding what in her recent work she calls the "growing entropy of our sociocultural organizations" (*Between East and West*, 135)—the going nowhere new—that marks the male "form-giving" (*To Speak Is Never Neutral*, 3) enterprise as inexorably dead-ended. Dramatic tragedy contains an already determined conclusion recognized at the "catastrophic" and decisive moment. Contrastingly, "anastrophe" creates transpositions and is therefore open to an unexpected, and always still possible, emergence, one based on a recovered—or rediscovered—origination. Irigaray's terms—"anastrophe" emphasizing transformational rhetorical forms, "catastrophe" stressing fixed dramatic forms—involve determinations that are grounded in the space-time continuum governing Irigaray's linguistic theory. In that regard, we can follow Desdemona's return as she awakens in the boudoir scene of Act 4, to an origin that supports and frees her. In contrast, we can observe Othello's decline in the same act as he loses the prerogative of male narrative control he so confidently asserts in Act 1 when he constructs Desdemona in his own image, and (we learn belatedly in Act 3) when he initiated the before-play Petrarchan wooing sequence that renders Desdemona his mirror. Desdemona's anastrophe involves a return that approximates the middle section of the foundling plot through the supportive community she recovers in her mind. That sustenance enables her to offer Othello the continual engenderment that realigns the rigid bloodline connections so important to the convention. She is bolstered enough by the reawakened memories of the boudoir scene to extend to Othello, even at his worst, a sustaining love, all the more remarkable considering his Brabanzio-like disowning of her.

In this present section, I define the Irigarayan male and female linguistic paradigms and how we might read *Othello* through them. In the next section, I will compare the Petrarchan speaking dynamics at their confident height, recalled by Othello in 1.3.29–170 and by Desdemona in 3.3.67–70 (identified so well by Harry Berger Jr. as the play's prehistory)[14] to those of Sonnet 95 in order to show how the beloved of the sonnet (like Desdemona)—in disallowing action—participates in the creative process and—in enacting desire—calls a halt to it.[15] In the Petrarchan sequences of the play, Othello and Desdemona collude in creating an imagined realm free of biological origins, one tied neither to the beginning nor to the conclusion of the conventional foundling plot. In such a Rothian "unlived" territory, deferral means everything. When, in Act 4, Desdemona finds her voice and releases herself from the cultural imperatives of the Petrarchan ethos to which Othello subscribes, she recalibrates the gender structure of the play and opens to a differently based middle section of the foundling plot, one premised on the fluidity of emotional commitment rather than (as the Petrarchan system insists) on the rigidity of bodily denial. Desdemona's retrieval in the boudoir scene of a story from her distant past is as important to her characterization as is her refutation of Brabanzio's hold on her at the beginning. Pulling back from the world of fathers, she breaks the mold that first Brabanzio and then Othello prefabricate for her. Desdemona's anastrophic emergence in Act 4 approaches the not-yet-created language that determines a curious link between a future still unformed and a past still untapped. In terms of the linguistic structure, the two characters move in opposite directions. Othello's downward slide results in the "hysterical collapse,"[16] "the catastrophe" of Act 4; Desdemona's return facilitates the successful consolidation of her speaking powers at the end of that same act, when she hypothetically "unfolds" the Irigarayan "third language," one that involves "a different way of speaking, a *dialogical* way"[17] that, with the "mend[ing]" she plans, might repair the rupture between her and Othello. With her "exacting cultural effort" (*Why Different*, 10) she produces an early modern example of the new discourse Irigaray theorizes.

Tracing those divergences, I will treat the Irigarayan time scheme as indivisible from the linguistic framework. Intrinsic to each is a spatial dimension: "Living beings, insofar as they are alive, are a becoming . . . [and] no becoming is morphologically undifferentiated" (*To Speak Is Never Neutral*, 3–4). Since the word in both French and English describes bodily and grammatical structure, Irigaray's emphasis on morphology attaches physical and verbal form to the temporality of "becoming." For Irigaray "the story [of that 'becoming']" in turn controls the linear thrust of male "projections and generations" and the reversals of female "loops and repetitions," the gendered language formulae that define Othello and Desdemona respectively.

As I will indicate by focusing on Othello's creation of Desdemona in the stories he tells of their courtship in Act 1, Othello's temporality is subject to what Irigaray identifies as a physical rupture that leaves the male in a vacuum: "He must live out the pain and experience the impossibility of being cut off from and in *space* (being born, leaving the mother)" (*An Ethics of Sexual Difference*, 64). In Irigaray's terms, to be *in space* means to be depth deprived and totally without bodily grounding. That emptiness is what Othello longs to fill with his images. Because he fails to recognize that something solid exists behind "the linearity of the utterance" (*To Speak Is Never Neutral*, 203) and refuses to acknowledge that there must be a "back side" (*To Speak Is Never Neutral*, 203) to the projection, Othello wallows in a nostalgia that evolves into an anticipation. He insists on rendering the past and the future identical to the moment of his telling. Filling in the physical void with the verbal forms he creates to counter the (Irigarayan) "exile he lives out between the *never more* and *the not yet*" (*An Ethics of Sexual Difference*, 64), he depends for his linguistic presence on the maternal absence that fuels the story he tells the court, "th' imminent deadly breach" (1.3.135) "even from [his] boyish days" (1.3.131). Temporality exists for him as the empty space between memory and desire, the vacuum he sublimates with language. In fact, Othello's desire, as I will show, is for desire, his "content"—a word that resonates throughout his expressions of love (2.2.181, 189, 194) and war (3.3.350–62)—located in the parallels he draws between Petrarchan and adventure stories. For Othello, the suspension is all. He orphans himself as he becomes the inventor of his life.

Desdemona facilitates the anastrophic recovery of a maternal matrix that she opens in Act 4. In that regard, she solidifies her identity in a way opposite to Othello's. He rigidifies his self in terms of a created reality, situating Desdemona as a mirror of his invented self. After she realizes her earlier mistakes, Desdemona recovers (in Act 4) a sense of self based on a morphological linguistic structure, one that ties the body and its reality to language at its most concrete. While Desdemona builds spatial and temporal bridges, Othello burns them, leaving himself (in the terms of Arthur Little Jr.) "an outsider, looking in from the outborders, literally . . . from [the] outpost" of Cyprus.[18] For Othello, suspension—the spatial exile—is all. For Desdemona, the interweaving of past experience into the fabric of her present situation establishes her being in the origin that secures her linguistic destiny even as she consciously changes the story. Whereas Othello seeks to remain in space, constructing a middle interlude that leaves him with neither biological past nor generational future, Desdemona commemorates the mutually offered comfort and containment of the remembered boudoir scene as she carries it into the fourth act and as she prepares once more to encounter Othello in the wedding sheets that, contrary to her confident expectations, become her winding sheet in Act 5.

Desdemona's memories render the psychological interior of the room in Cyprus a pastoral enclave where Barbary's song, imaging nature as a harmonious womb, evokes a woman-to-woman nurturing (found earlier in Venice) that extends far beyond the biological mother. These adoptions—woman-by-woman—sustain Desdemona to the end, as she transfers to Othello the support she witnessed in the past, a recollection that accrues, in the present, as the stepping-stone for the new direction she takes in Act 4. The space she recovers aligns her with the heroines of Shakespeare's comedies. If the turning point of the play for Othello resides in the Act 3 temptation scene, the turning point for Desdemona lies in the Act 4 boudoir scene, where she deliberately changes her tactic. There, we see a Desdemona who no longer assumes the role Othello assigned to her in the wooing sequence, a game that she very much enjoyed and, from her very entrance in Act 1 (through to her change of heart in Act 4), is eager to perpetuate. Her early reply, "I saw Othello's visage in his mind" (1.3.251), is a Petrarchan foreshortening that illustrates her complicity in the process of Othello's self-creation that the audience witnesses in Act 1 and that Desdemona recalls in Act 3. What she sees in the "visage" of Othello's mind is the portrait, as we learn, Othello has earlier painted of her. According to that logic, Othello's mind contains Desdemona, who is—following the Petrarchan ethos—he. In the visual hall of mirrors she describes, the passage to Othello's mind parallels the linguistic exchange that defines her in terms determined by him.

As I will suggest, Desdemona transforms herself from the woman who, in Act 1, exhibits what Irigaray calls the "mimetic tendencies" that condition her to behave "like the other" (*To Speak Is Never Neutral*, 4; "my heart's subdued / Even to the very quality of my lord," 1.3.249–50) to a woman who discovers a language (the Irigarayan "third" one) that constructs her subjectivity.[19] In Act 1, Desdemona's heart beats to the rhythm of Othello's terms. But through her "anastrophe" in Act 4, she recovers a narrative origin based on an actual memory, something that she pulls out of her history and carries into the present with the willow song that will "not go from [her] mind" (4.3.29). Occupying her being (as earlier Othello had), Desdemona's reconstruction overtakes her initial mental interiorizing of Othello and evokes a long-ago Venice where (like little Mamillius teasing Hermione's women about matters sexual in *The Winter's Tale*) she overheard her mother's maid singing. The refrain of the song lives on even in Emilia when it dawns on her in Act 5 that her present synchronizes with the betrayals Barbary's lyric describes. Emilia already knows the answer to the question she asks, "What did thy song bode, lady?" (5.2.253). Her "willow, willow, willow" (5.3.255) turns the room in Cyprus into an *echo chamber* that refers back to the primal site of Venice. Barbary haunts the deathbed scene, the devastating revelations of her lyric's "court[ing] and couch[ing]" (4.3.54) anticipating the final exposure in the "tragic loading of this bed" (5.2.373).

Othello's indictment of Desdemona at the end, "she was false as water" (5.2.143), contrasts to the faithful streams of Barbary's song and defines his "catastrophic" moment as the ultimate shattering of the linguistic empire he constructed at the beginning of the play. In the simile, Othello equates Desdemona with the shifting signifier he himself devised, finding to his horror that his "constructions in language merely objectified his own hollow self."[20] His solidified mirror melts into the instability of a shape-changing liquid as Othello loses himself in the narcissistic maze of his own significatory amplification.

CUTTING "EDGES": WOOING IN VENICE AND IN SONNET 95

The form Othello can no longer find in Act 5 manifests itself in the story he tells the Venetian court in Act 1, where the narrative of his courtship (1.3.129–170) does exactly what Brabanzio means when he says, "I had rather to adopt a child than get it" (1.3.189). With that "rather," Brabanzio abandons the biological progeny and her history in favor of a daughter whom he can shape to his will and through whom he can fulfill his patriarchal design. The Othello of the Venetian tribunal "adopts" Desdemona in order to create her as his image. Othello's fluency early in the play depends on the "breach" that sets him off on a series of military and romantic exploits, the déjà vu of the adventures he recounts to the Venetians as he describes the renewable energy resources of his fabulations and the nostalgia for the before-marriage linguistic creativity, the déjà woo he rehearses in the history of his courtship and that Desdemona alludes to during the Act 3 exchange that reveals (in Harry Berger's terms) "a history that turns everything in the play upside down . . . [the extended period Desdemona recalls when she] reminds Othello that 'Cassio . . . came a-wooing with you' (3.3.70–71)."[21] Berger cites the belated disclosure to corroborate his hypothesis that the play keeps realigning triangulated relationships until it turns out that the "trouble the trio [Othello, Desdemona, Cassio] makes for themselves facilitates and exceeds the trouble Iago makes for them" ("Acts of Silence, Acts of Speech: How to Do Things with Othello and Desdemona," 13). Berger analyzes the prehistory scene before he turns to Othello's speech to the court partly because it refers to a time chronologically before the tribunal "defense" and partly because his primary interest is in demonstrating how active Desdemona is in the courtship and then how the triangulated relationship established with that beginning plays itself out in the end. In my analysis of the crucial scene in Act 3, I compare Desdemona's description of the triad as it evolves (in the interval between the prehistory and her belated allusion to it) and then her disappointment when, in the reversal of roles, she woos Othello on behalf of Cassio, thereby setting everything off balance. Once Desdemona takes over the wooing, the whole Petrarchan empire unravels. As I describe the shift in Othello's mind in Act 3 when tropes originally evoked to defer action are superseded by ones that record concrete "use" (Othello's word in 3.3.58 and a crucial one in Sonnet 95), I will compare the play's dynamics to those in the sonnet where a present situation threatens to unhinge a past comprised purely of the imaginative suggestiveness endemic to the Petrarchan lyric.

Considering Othello's version of his courtship, I argue that the Othello who invents in Act 1 extends the Othello recalled in Desdemona's prehistory: someone who creates her as the accessory to his own self-creation. Desdemona's early responses explicitly spawn "fictional amplification" just as her Act 3 rebellion is based on a replay of the foreplay she wishes to sustain. According to Othello's Act 1 account, she fully accepts the pilgrimage Othello dilates bit by bit. In her Act 3 memory, she implicitly gets to the heart of Petrarchan productivity, describing the conditions inspiring the necessary absence that produces poetic presence, just as in Act 1 Othello springs full blown as the orphan of a series of ruptures when he re-creates himself for each adventure. In both her recollection and Othello's Act 1 description, Desdemona is the source of his continuing production, demanding the "parcels" (1.3.154) that, like individual sonnets in a larger series, comprise a productive and continual sequence of what he wants her most to want: his words.

Othello's Rothian "amplification" in Act 1 depends on his repeatedly carving the linguistically productive spaces between "antres vast" (1.3.140) and "hills whose heads touch heaven" (1.3.141). He wants ever and always the old order. The passage repeats the journey from disastrous chances and "hair-breadth scapes i' th' imminent deadly breach" (1.3.135) over and over even as the "parcels" delivered to Desdemona stretch it still further. The "dilat[ion]" (1.3.154) in the continual repetition is both a spatial widening and a temporal postponement, a deferral much like the Petrarchan poetic sequence, which places desire over possession and emptiness over fullness. The more Othello tells, the more he refines the self he wants Desdemona to want. As he describes it, her wish to have "such a man" reflects his success at creating "such a man" (1.3.164): the mirror of the mirror that presupposes, as its origin, a Desdemona who becomes, through the narrative she demands, the reflection of his desire for self.

Othello creates her in his image even as he carves a self that corroborates his abilities as artist (like the one who portrayed Portia in the casket scene). If, in the Act 1 courtly tribunal, he invents the words of her reaction to him, then he remains within the process of his own encircling fabrications. But if he actually quotes her, then we see from the outset that Desdemona desires Othello's verbal self-fabrication, someone who excites her imagination in the same way as a Petrarchan poet might. Since Desdemona is not actually present at the moment of his simultaneous self-defense and self-creation, we have no way of knowing whether what she is alleged to have said is true. What we can infer, however, is that, for her, the extended "parcels" of Othello's "pilgrimage" parallel a sonnet sequence that similarly builds from poem to poem as one end yields to another beginning. It is as if she draws out, from the original breaches, the self who meets the expectations she generates by her demand for more. She is part of the game in Othello's Act 1 creation as she became part of the game, the continuing process, alluded to in Desdemona's Act 3 memory. In both scenes—the one Othello rehearses in Act 1, the one Desdemona remembers in Act 3—Desdemona prolongs the absence Othello fills with differing versions of the same self. As he keeps repeating the story (first to Brabanzio, then to Desdemona, and finally to the court), Othello defers any involvement with the future, the temporal space of the telling so satisfying a present that it needs no further enactment. Patricia Parker's point about the link between delation and dilation, meaning "not just amplifying or opening but reporting, delaying and accusing," has a particular resonance to the Petrarchan context here.[22] While Othello represents himself to the court, he reveals that each telling was—and then in the present is—an expansion out of nothingness, a history without a body.

Like love poems, Othello's war stories depend on challenges, the narrative edge of wrenching debarkations. The more he tells of the "passages," the more each passage becomes the substance of his text. In fact, the speech is framed by two identical phrases: first Brabanzio's questioning of the "battles, sieges, fortunes / That I have passed," and then Othello's summation: "She loved me for the dangers that I have passed." The prospect widens the circle from Brabanzio to Desdemona, to the court, framing the hole he fills with an evaporating substance, the emphasis always on the success that doesn't satisfy, the gap that spurs yet another narrative into being. In Othello's rehearsal for the court, he "ran it through," producing a relay race of words where he evolves (out of every ending) multiplying but identical selves, like the speaker in a sonnet series who keeps creating the same "I" out of his compounding losses as he folds one end into another beginning. The signifying redemptions at the end allow enough space for the new poem to coalesce. The collapsing border between physical passing and verbal passages extends the link between adventure and love stories. Othello's "process" leads to a present where one story simply replaces another. The tale is all, leaving no room for any enhancement beyond the present:

> Her father loved me, oft invited me,
> Still questioned me the story of my life
> From year to year, the battles sieges, fortunes
> That I have passed.
> I ran it through, even from my boyish days
> To th' very moment that he bade me tell it,
> Wherein I spoke of most disastrous chances,
> Of moving accidents by flood and field,
> Of hair-breadth scapes i' th' imminent deadly breach,
> Of being taken by the insolent foe
> And sold to slavery, of my redemption thence,
> And portance in my traveller's history,
> Wherein of antres vast and deserts idle,
> Rough quarries, rocks, and hills whose heads touch heaven
> It was my hint to speak. Such was my process . . . —
>   Which I observing,
> Took once a pliant hour, and found good means
> To draw from her a prayer of earnest heart
> That I would all my pilgrimage dilate,
> Whereof by parcels she had something heard,
> But not intentively. . . .
> She loved me for the dangers I had passed,
> And I loved her that she did pity them. (1.3.128–39, 149–54, 166–67)

When Othello claims that Desdemona loves him for "the dangers [he] had passed," he phrases her reaction so that it remains unclear whether it was the dangers or the passing she loved. If it was the dangers, then her love involves an understanding of the importance of the breach; if it was the "pass[ing]," then the pluralized dangers present always a newly re-formed self who, having slid from opening to opening, emerges ever always the same. The passing is safely contained in the past, so that the present might become "the very moment that [Brabanzio] bade me tell it" (1.3.137). Othello's exactitude in the "very" translates into a permanence; every passage is, and must be, always identical to the self he invents in the retelling. With its multiple meanings and within the circle between Brabanzio's "battles sieges, fortunes" and Desdemona's "dangers," the word "pass" includes narration, transcendence, and issue, Othello's life so conflated with the telling that his "success" (yet another result of passing) is measured in the circle between the demands of the father and the feelings of the daughter, echoed yet again in the command performance for the court. "Passing" circles round to "dangers" and each passage seems to prod another danger into being. Rather than changing from one state to another, Othello's "passing" becomes a way of remaining the same, just as the speaker in a sonnet sequence re-creates the identical self in the interspace between the end of one poem and the beginning of another. No sooner does Othello complete one "parcel," than he constructs the next one.

In Othello's story, the human landscape reflects the natural landscape, as Desdemona "devours [his] discourse," consuming his words the way "cannibals each other eat."[23] Othello feeds her hunger only to whet her appetite once more for the self who tells even as what he tells becomes the substance that evaporates through the telling. Like Cleopatra's aura that makes hungry where most she satisfies, Othello's fabulations perpetuate the desire he fosters. Othello loves Desdemona, as he says, because she loves the inventions, the "dangers" as they present themselves, the "passing," as he forms and re-forms the same self thorough the narrow birth canal of the always-about-to-become-what-already-was. In that regard, Jay Halio writes, Othello is an "absolutist."[24] He is fully himself only when he can return from the well of nothingness to the amplification that he devises. He can imagine no other self but the one who speaks the narrative, his tale replicating an already preconceived self. Finally, when Desdemona is alleged to have said that "[she wishes] heaven had made her such a man" (1.3.162), Othello (perhaps unwittingly) suggests that she acknowledges her immersion in Othello's story, not only of the self he weaves *for* her but also of the self that he molds *of* her. In the first instance, Desdemona seems to be saying that Othello's "parcels" deliver linguistic fabulations, and so she wishes that a "Heaven"-made—a fleshly rather than a storied—man might substitute for the verbally created one he so "intentively" erected: a physically activated present for the legendarily re-created past. In the second, she acknowledges that, because she has devoured the parcels, she might now, amalgamating all the pieces, similarly occupy the fully incorporated self that Othello has produced for her in his projections. But, more importantly, in requesting that "if [he] had a friend that loved [her] / [he] should but teach him how to tell [his] story" (1.3.165–66), she has already opened herself to the lieutenancy principle that governs the wooing triad to which she alludes in Act 3 when she tries to reconstruct, yet again, the "process" she so happily recollects. Using that initial "hint" as an intimation that Desdemona is hoping for a continual discourse, Othello tells the court that he spoke (1.3.163), redirecting the subject matter but retaining the manner: his war stories and his love stories merge in their methodology even if the dyad evolves into a triad, since all those involved will become versions of the self-created Othello.

The linguistic breakdown of the preplay consolidation that ends in the "catastrophic" Act 5 already begins in Act 2 where Othello seems to be denied nothing. In fact, Othello's verbal fault line is established, as Harry Berger so tellingly suggests ("Acts of Silence, Acts of Speech: How to Do Things with Othello and Desdemona," 3–35) before Iago systematically provokes him in Act 3. Its principal observer (albeit unwitting cause) is Desdemona herself. Othello's animus against Desdemona emerges not after the temptation scene but through the exchanges of 2.1.180–210 and 3.3.35–93. In the first scene, he reacts to Desdemona's contradiction of his assertion that they have attained in Cyprus the perfect climax of, and the total limit to, marital happiness by simply silencing her and thus ending the dispute (2.1.193). In the second round of verbal sparring, where Desdemona refuses to be contained by him, and when she no longer fits the image he projects, Othello's response resembles the meanderings of Lear's sputtering invective against his daughters' cruelty (*King Lear*, "I will do such things," 2.2.246). Pleading with Othello on behalf of Cassio, Desdemona observes in him the same incoherence we find in Lear: "I wonder in my soul / What you would ask me that I should deny / Or stand so mamm'ring on" (3.3.68–70). Lear's failure to define is caused by what he perceives to be his unyielding daughters. But Othello's similar verbal breakdown is charted by a woman whose kindness would "deny" him nothing (3.3.70) and who wants him to engage with her in the playful banter she expects of a partner well versed in Petrarchan foreplay and masculine war talk.[25] That Desdemona observes Othello's loss of a verbal agility she earlier enjoyed is evidenced by the passage to which Berger refers when he argues that Othello and Desdemona have a prehistory:

> I wonder in my soul
> What you would ask me that I should deny,
> Or stand so mamm'ring on? What, Michael Cassio,
> That came a-wooing with you, and so many a time
> When I have spoke of you dispraisingly
> Hath ta'en your part. (3.3.68–73)

If, in the Act 1 wooing sequence, Desdemona becomes Othello's mirror, here in Desdemona's recapitulation, there is, additionally, a vocal echo—Cassio—who stood in as poet (in the "many a time") to substantiate three versions of Othello: the one who "a-wooing" came, the Desdemona who is his image, and, finally, the Cassio whose lieutenancy, in Julia Gestner's terms, presumes that "each officer is replaceable by a subordinate who can, if necessary, assume the command which devolves on him."[26]

When she insists that Cassio took Othello's part, Desdemona defines him not so much as the man who (George Lyman Kittredge argues) praised Othello over her objections[27] but as the man who, in response to her rejection of Othello's suit, rephrased Othello's words to her. In taking Othello's part, Cassio not only defended Othello but also became him, producing still more words for Desdemona to dispraise and therefore providing other opportunities for Desdemona to play the same role in the prehistory as she will in Act 1: she compels Othello's words by subtracting them, causing the void that rendered both men, Othello and his lieutenant, fluent again. In "disprais[ing]," Desdemona devours Othello's discourse just as she did in Act 1. But her recollection here also suggests that the "teach[ing]" (1.3.166) she so ardently requested in Act 1 is successful. It reinforces the male coterie, Othello issuing and reissuing the Petrarchan praise that creates Desdemona in his image and that renders Cassio another poet who, like him, repeats the sequence that postpones, rather than urges, consummation. In the prehistory, the whole cycle continued *because* Desdemona "disses" Othello's praise, canceling the preceding poem and hence compelling Cassio or Othello to go another round. Since Cassio is merely a stand-in for Othello, Desdemona becomes, even in Cassio's poem, a mirror of Othello, thus adding merely another version of Othello's triplicate selves. In the preplay situation, Othello, Cassio, and Desdemona are the same.

When Desdemona recalls that she spoke of Othello "dispraisingly," she exploits the adverb in the same way as the speaker of 95 uses the verb—to subtract and so erase an offered paean. Apart from the fact that 95 presents a litany of conventional Petrarchan conceits ("roses," "names," "beauty") that appear in *Othello*, it demonstrates how Desdemona's dispraising tongue in the prehistory becomes identical to her devouring ear in Othello's Act 1 speech: both provide the blank space that makes room for more words. The sonnet's couplet rests on the assumption that the cutting edge of denial (like the dangers Othello confronts in the breaches he describes to the court) is the necessary void that occasions more speech. The speaker in 95 argues that (1) like Desdemona, the "dear heart" enjoys the protracted game of poetic praise a sonnet series yields, just as, in *The Merchant of Venice*, Portia urges Bassanio to "draw out in length" (3.2.22) the time before he elects the caskets; and (2) actual physicality or "use" interferes with the necessary propulsion for poetic renewal. Habitual application is the opposite of continual invention.

Because it presumes an arrangement that generates poetic production—and because it introduces a parallel change in the compact of speaker (Othello), and the "dear heart" (Desdemona) who also reflects (in his initial stages) the poet—Sonnet 95 presents an *anticipated* version of what Desdemona (in referring to Othello's "mamm'ring") despairs is a *consequence* of "use" (imagined or real) that Sonnet 95 claims might end the cycle. Signified by the expected absence of the cutting "edge" of the last line, the sonnet's threatened conclusion has already happened in Othello and it is Desdemona herself who identifies the loss even as Othello, in twice proclaiming (3.3.76 and 3.3.84) he would deny Desdemona nothing, ends the game before it can even start, a finality confirmed by Desdemona, who agrees (in 3.3.28 and 55) that she likewise would never say "no."

The important link between 95 and *Othello* lies in the sonnet's insistence on the across the board denial, eradicated by both Othello and Desdemona in Act 3 but very much a part of the preplay sparring that promotes the Petrarchan situation, the sonnet's cut paralleling the "breach" Othello needs to keep creating the Desdemona he wants. As in *Othello*, the "blots" the speaker identifies are based not on proof but on "report." The sonnet resides in the hypothetical interspace between Othello's initial suspicions and his ultimate conclusion, its couplet threatening to call an end to the Petrarchan talk that Desdemona—like the poem's "dear heart"—regenerated in the past and which she senses she can no longer inspire.

The ill user who, in 95, is the "dear heart's" alleged partner parallels the other users Othello imagines in 3.3.277 when he asserts that Desdemona's lasciviousness is damaging to him ("I am abused," 3.3.372) and, finally, the other men he protects from betrayal in Act 5 when he imagines Desdemona's multiple infidelities. But his behavior in this scene already acknowledges that "use" itself (later becoming the punitive "ab-use") is what frightens him, a locution Desdemona also will similarly enlist when she declares she "abhors" (4.2.164) the word ("whore," 4.2.91) Othello calls her. Desdemona challenges presumptuous (and she believes unwarranted) "nam[ing]." Othello punishes presumed (and he concludes substantiated) actions. The thousand acts of shame Othello imagines Desdemona committed with Cassio are versions of the identical antipoetic acts the sonnet declaims:

> How sweet and lovely dost thou dost make the shame
> Which like a canker in the fragrant rose
> Doth spot the beauty of thy budding name:
> O in what sweets dost thou thy sins enclose!
> That tongue that tells the story of thy days,
> Making lascivious comments on thy sport,
> Cannot dispraise; but in a kind of praise,
> Naming thy name, blesses an ill report.
> O what a mansion have those vices got,

> Which for their habitation chose out thee,
> Where beauty's veil doth cover every blot,
> And all things turns to fair, that eyes can see!
> Take heed, dear heart, of this large privilege,
> The hardest knife ill used doth lose his edge.[28]

As Desdemona does in *Othello*, the speaker in 95 recalls an earlier sequence between the beloved and himself, where the speaker praised and the "dear heart" denied. Then he overlays the praise with a second sequence where the speaker, incorporating into his own words the ill report of the "dear heart's" vices, proceeds nonetheless to "cover" every blot. Thus he returns to the "dear heart" the "mansion" of poetic containment. In the couplet, he delimits the duration of the recovery, threatening the "dear heart" with the imminent eviction from the poem the three quatrains of the sonnet postpone.

As Cassio "covers" for Othello in the prehistory, so the speaker's veil erases "every blot," making it "turn to fair," and thereby returning to the empty space that makes room for more words. The "turn[ing]" of the sonnet renders "fair" identical to whiteness, the blank that reflects the speaker to himself. The speaker's "covering" thus replaces the blot with the image the speaker reprojects, forming (once again) the mirror of innocence that restores the speaker to himself. In the play, Desdemona switches places, losing her silent cutting edge, to take her vocal part, and becomes Cassio *to* Othello as (earlier) Cassio had rewooed her *for* Othello. She thereby takes one "turn" too many, emerging as poet to Othello's audience. When the sonnet speaker threatens to retract the sonnet's "privilege" and habit of "turn[ing]" dispraise into praise, he may (like Othello) be saying that not only ill use but simply "use" precipitates an end to the new beginnings the "dear heart" (in the poem) and Desdemona (in the play) enjoy, just as, in Stanley Cavell's view, Othello is "rendered impotent and murderous by aroused, or by having aroused . . . sexuality . . . [and] is horrified by human sexuality, in himself and in others."[29]

The sonnet therefore actually presumes a foursome: speaker, ill reporter, the complicit "dear heart," and the hypothetical ill user whose action detracts from the "dear heart" who hears the poem, and therefore from the "I" who speaks the poem, causing the speaker to move from his initial praise into the "turn" that covers (but doesn't quite erase in his mind or that of his audience, the "dear heart," who has just heard his accusations) the alleged blots. Incorporating into his words those of the "ill reporter" and into his imagination the ill doer's deeds, he becomes a double speaker, recalling his past praise and producing his present cover even as he congratulates himself on his effort to hide the blots with the "beautiful veil" he attributes to the "dear heart." Like the scarf in Bassanio's speech about the casket he rejects, the veil becomes anamorphic. If the speaker lifts it (or the "dear heart" shifts it), it might, once more, expose the blot. When he expands himself the speaker turns the beloved's habitual denials (what Desdemona calls her earlier dispraise) into the ill reporter's usage, just as when Desdemona changes the situation, speaking on behalf of Cassio, she similarly displaces the source of the dispraise, turning it over to Othello, who doubles himself, silently including in his reaction Desdemona's alleged ill use, firmly planted in his mind by the ill report of his own suspicions. In the sonnet, the speaker expands into two selves, his old self and (as he thickens his voice) that of the rival poet, the "ill reporter" whose presence he both resents and incorporates. In the play, Othello doubles in opposition to Desdemona: Desdemona remembers the past, contrasting it to the present, while Othello dismembers the past, refusing to take part in the present. In both sonnet and play, there are too many active Petrarchs and two few passive Lauras.

Two was company; four is a crowd. But there's also a slight difference in the crowds. In the play, the doubling is complicated as Desdemona deals with her preplay memory and her current suit on behalf of Cassio and as Othello, now the audience, expands the players in his mind to imagine that they conspire to undo his earlier control. In the sonnet, the doubling is dissipated; the ill reporter and the ill user separate from the "dear heart." When she becomes the "speaker," Desdemona confirms what Othello takes to be her "ill use"; she no longer reflects Othello. For Othello, she becomes a rival speaker, solidifying Othello's suspicion that Cassio (who in the preplay sequences merely was another version of Othello) has become an "ill user." Desdemona emerges an independent suitor, the lieutenant, as she describes herself (in 3.3.45–50) for Cassio, using all her "grace or power to move [Othello]" (3.3. 46). For Othello, she attempts, therefore, to render all three of them in her image, forcing Othello to become (as she was earlier) the wooed object to her poet. Pleading for him, Desdemona renders Cassio likewise dependent on her. In claiming to be Cassio's lieutenant *now*, she is actually doing what Cassio did *then*: turning him into her just as (when he stepped in for Othello), he re-created Othello's creation of Desdemona. The likenesses spiral differently now.

If the speaker in 95 projects the possible conclusion of a static Petrarchan situation, it is Desdemona who observes an end that has already occurred: she is the one who notes that Othello has retracted her edge and that, therefore, she has lost her earlier power to inspire. Along with her admission that she would now deny Othello nothing, her word "mamm'ring" acknowledges that the game is over, Othello having forfeited what the speaker in 95 threatens to curtail: the sharpness that keeps the sonnet sequence moving from breach to breach. The "dear heart" loses his edge as the speaker includes other voices. Desdemona forfeits hers when she comes nearer to Othello, her approximation aligning her with Cassio in a scenario Othello imagines corroborates both ill report and ill use. Othello's refusal to answer Desdemona's plea to "call [Cassio] back" (3.3.50–55) indicates that he cannot "re-call" or return anything to the preplay situation Desdemona attempts to remember. Contrastingly, the speaker in Sonnet 95 facilitates recollection, giving the "dear heart" another chance. In Act 3, Othello refutes its possibility partly because Desdemona's physical closeness and verbal aggression fill the empty space occupied by Othello and his dominating selves. There is no room for anything else, past or future, the present occupied by someone who denies the breach that encouraged re-creation. Since Cassio has been incorporated by Desdemona, Othello cannot "call back" what is already too much there.

Othello's "mamm'ring" in Act 3 is caused by Desdemona's proximity in the present (a yielding she ratifies in her very solicitousness). But it reveals something else about Desdemona that is equally difficult for Othello to admit. Desdemona grants Othello all too easily the mammary access he lost in infancy as well as the desired breast he sought to reclaim in the wooing stage that before marriage became the source of his linguistic prowess. Having gotten what he wanted, he cannot be the imploring self he was before. Desdemona's word, "mamm'ring," to describe Othello's verbal inadequacy underlines the obverse relationship between Othello's earlier determination to father her through his creative powers and her desire to mother him through the generative body she calls into being. Because she duly notes Othello's verbal inadequacy now, as opposed to his obvious vocabulary then, "when he came a-wooing" (3.3.69), Desdemona reflects an understanding that her willingness to yield rather than to mirror is the cause of Othello's lack of articulation. In that regard, she performs an Irigarayan analysis *avant la lettre*.

"In French," Irigaray writes, "*mamam* means, at least phonetically, that which is kept but which cannot be represented, expressed, mastered, that which suspends consumption but favors respiration, that which covers the whole with a vast blackness expressed by the *m* and potentially matches all colors thanks to the *a*. The name is one of the most perfect words possible."[30] In Irigaray's definition, blackness is a covering that confounds the articulate self by being unrepresentable and then "favors respiration" by feeding, concluding with a conciliatory meaning of blackness—"potentially matching all colors." The redundancy in "blackness" and "all colors" suggests that, in its very accessibility (suspension followed quickly by consumption), there is an excess in *mamam*, emphasized by its twice repeated sound, just as the sonnet presents the remembered speaker and the present one and Desdemona in Act 3 recalls her dispraising earlier self and her excessively expressive self now. *Mamam*'s blackness is both a temporary suspension and (in being "all colors") an immediate granting, erasing all empty spaces, a doubling that (in blunting the edges) clogs the arteries that circulate the poem. In its protraction of the same sounds, "mamm'ring" obscures the sharp articulation associated with Petrarchan vocabulary. Describing her present solicitude for Othello, Desdemona speaks in maternal terms: "I should entreat you to wear your gloves, / or feed on nourishing dishes, or keep you warm" (3.3.76–77). In its excess, Desdemona's swaddling nourishment is smothering, reducing Othello to the "mamm'ring" of infantile linguistics.

When the speaker in 95 covers every blot and attributes to the "dear heart" the ability to "turn all things fair," he suggests that the poetic dependence on opposites vanishes in the face of the continuity of Irigarayan extensions. The breach is all. Othello similarly laments the loss of his name "that was as fresh / As Dian's visage [and is now] begrimed and black / As mine own face" (3.3.391–94) when he positions blackness as the destroyer of the blank space he calls Dian's visage. In the sonnet and the play, "blot" and "begrimed" respectively mar the purity of the fair and the fresh, muddying the mirrors concomitant to Petrarchan praise. The "names" Othello and the sonnet speaker wish to retain are associated with *absence*, the whiteness and newness of the not-yet-touched. The prehistory depends on mismatch—the blackness of void, the fairness of inaccessibility. The sonnet, likewise, depends on emptiness and unattainability, the speaker always needing the blank space generating the poetic narcissism that writes the "dear heart" as the "fair" copy of him. When she laments Othello's "mamm'ring," Desdemona mourns the lost pleasures of the game they earlier played even as she recognizes that their present situation—in fact, her very presentness—may be what's blocking him.

If Desdemona is Cassio's lieutenant here and now in the Cyprus of Act 3, she can't be what he was, then and there, in the Venice of their prehistory: the cause of poetic materialization. In taking Cassio's part, she comes too close to Othello, proffering rather than refusing. In her "turn," she emerges the Irigarayan *mamam*, blackness and all colors, allowing no space for the "edge" of articulation. The situation in Act 3 already evidences what the speaker in 95 attempts to forestall. Like the "dear heart's" one indiscretion too often in the future after the sonnet, Desdemona's one turn too many in the present of Act 3 deprives her (as it soon might the young man) of the capacity to inspire more words. In the three quatrains of 95, the speaker's double role, recalling his earlier naïve self and presenting his now-covering self, makes possible a return to an earlier "fairness." In *Othello*, Desdemona's double role (solidified by her defense of Cassio) hardens Othello (also doubled by ill reports that cause him to visualize ill use) and forces her to surrender what the "dear heart" may soon forfeit: the pleasure of the Petrarchan game.

Othello's reaction to his inadequacy in Act 3 is to refuse to confront it. Feeling hemmed in, Othello's response is to leave the scene (as the speaker in Sonnet 95 threatens to stop the poetic sequence), disengaging himself from Desdemona's sight and her words. Alone, he recognizes the connection between her stability as image and his own sense of linguistic control: "But I do love thee, and when I love thee not / Chaos is come again" (3.3.91–92).

Similarly, Hamlet pledges, and then two lines later disavows himself, to Ophelia, "I did love you once" (3.1.115) . . . "I loved you not" (3.1.117), annulling her (as Brabanzio does Desdemona) and erasing everything secure in her past. In a chiasmic locution, Othello anticipates a time when he won't love Desdemona and projects chaos as the disintegration of his articulation, a confusion already evident to Desdemona. Like Hamlet's retrospective denial, the blur of Othello's projective "not loving" dissolves the past. When Othello "love[s Desdemona] not," he alleges that she undoes the world he created in his own image. Othello's temporal trajectory depends on Desdemona's remaining in the future what he wanted her to be in the past: the mirror through which he experienced his wholeness. It's all or nothing with him.

Hamlet's retrospect and Othello's prospect denote the same erasure of the "I" who comes into being by inventing (Hamlet in the letters Ophelia calls "remembrances" [3.1.93], Othello in the wooing Desdemona recalls) the woman. Later in the play, as she moves totally out of his representational agency, Othello, like Brabanzio, erases Desdemona once again, his "wouldst thou hadst ne'er been born" (4.2.70), a repetition of Brabanzio's "I had rather to adopt a child than get it" (1.3.189). To avoid the possibility of her wavering from the specular place he created for her, the Othello of the early acts seems always to be pushing Desdemona out of sight. In 1.2.206, he hastens, "I have but an hour"; in 3.3.84–85, he begs her to "grant me this: / To leave me but a little to myself." Deferring the future by removing both the sight and sound of her, he at first anticipates and then repeats the Act 2 moment where he silenced Desdemona's tongue by occupying her mouth at the source. Locked in the embrace of their first Cyprus kiss (2.1.96), he can neither hear nor see her. Absent as maternal self, Desdemona remains present (as the "dear heart" does in 95) as the imagined other aligned to his invented self.[31] Alone once more, the Othello of Act 3 seeks to remain the poetic inventor of Act 1, countering the Desdemona who already begins to challenge him in Act 2.

COLLIDING TRAJECTORIES: OTHELLO'S ABSOLUTE, DESDEMONA'S RELATIVE

In the Venice of Act 1, Othello's evocation of the past pressed an anticipatory chain of "not yets" into being; in Cyprus the "wonder" (2.1.181) of the present suggests that this victory will "never again" be duplicated. Nothing can equal the past of the present. In fact, the opening moment of his speech repeats the pattern of the wooing sequence he describes to the court:

> If after every tempest come some calms,
> May the winds blow till they have wakened death,

> And let the laboring barque climb hills of seas
> Olympus-high, and duck again as low
> As hell's from heaven. If it were now to die
> 'Twere now to be most happy, for I fear
> My soul has her content so absolute
> That not another comfort like to this
> Succeeds in unknown fate. (2.1.182–89)

Once more Othello winds circles that create the empty spaces out of which he escapes: to the very moment. Even now he cannot admit to anything more but always only to a fabled danger. Here, his labor yields the self that emerges from the enormous void produced by the waves that make room for his invented self, the initial hills of the seas eventuating into the reflective "calm" that gives him back what he wants. At this point, he can still transfer water to glass, the absolute solid that returns him to himself. The chasm he invents grows from hell to heaven, the difference yielding the mirror of a reflective sea. The present cannot admit to the winds of change: "not another comfort like to this." For him, "such calms" disallow even the succession of the waves. Othello's play on success as gratification avoids the possibility of success as sequence. Othello's solidity here runs counter (as I will suggest in the next chapter) to Florizel's definition of a fluid succession in *The Winter's Tale*. Othello is at the "very moment" where he was in Act 1. In Othello's time scheme the future cannot exist because the only reality is the one that facilitates a return to the balm of his self-perpetuating calm:

> It gives me wonder great as my content
> To see you here before me. (2.1.180–81)

Othello's thrice-repeated "content" (2.1.180–81, 2.1.188, 2.1.193) becomes the measure of the happiness by which he secures the fullness of his being as Desdemona fleshes out his projection of himself. The "process" of Act 1 is repeated in Act 2. His appellation of Desdemona as his "fair warrior" (2.1.178) reproduces her once more as pristine copy of his invented self; extending the blank space on which he wrote himself in Act 1, the "fairness" here resembles the "fair copy" in Sonnet 95 even as it anticipates the blank space of "freshness" that is "begrimed" in 3.3.393. Othello's "now to die" bears an inverse relationship to the dangers of "th' imminent deadly breach" of 1.3.35, but comes out of the same matrix, from birth to death, from hell to heaven. Between lies "the content" he makes of the Desdemona he sees before him. In that regard, her facing him blocks anything proclaiming a future. She gives him back to himself. Succession signifies loss, a secession from the moment of power, measured by the end of metaphor: "not another comfort" can resemble this. Since he creates a Desdemona who "pities" him, she must remain totally what he wants her to be: a copy of his self.

When Desdemona contradicts him and opens to an expansion of love, she envisions both the exact duplication of *even*—an assurance that shall always be equal to theirs now—and the relative equivalent of *as*—a parallel that accommodates the progression of time with a concomitant expansion of space:

> The heavens forbid
> But that our loves and comforts should increase
> Even as our days do grow. (2.1.190–92)

Desdemona's vision is both exact and unregulated, a mutuality achieved in the doubling of "our." With the permeability of her materiality, simile folds into metonymy.[32] "Even as" allows for the increase she envisions. Attempting to inhibit that amplification, and asserting the divine authority of his control, Othello relegates Desdemona's rebuttal to the decidedly diminutive realm of feminine "sweet powers." In the equation of happiness with restraint, his "content" puts a lid on Desdemona's increase:

> Amen to that, sweet powers!
> I cannot speak enough of this content.
> It stops me here, it is too much of joy,
> And this (*they kiss*), and this the greatest discords be
> That e'er our hearts shall make. (2.1.192–96)

Joy is excessive ("it is too much") and not enough ("it stops me here") to allow him easy access through the formula of his expressiveness. It anticipates the Irigarayan *mamam*, smotheringly physical and verbally stifling. Their quarrel must be trivialized and reduced to the duration of two silencing kisses (the "this" and "this") that consequently allow him to preserve the language patterns that create Desdemona as his double. But his unease here reveals something deeper, what Irigaray calls the schizophrenic "fear of the excessive . . . mother tongue" that poses "the threat of meaning's collapse, disintegration or decomposition" (*To Speak Is Never Neutral*, 186). Desdemona's "too much" makes Othello feel too little. To stop her with a kiss is to still her tongue with his, to nullify her verbal powers by annihilating them at their source.

Yet the very "French" kiss that brings the argument to a close exposes him to the source of the boundary-crossing Irigarayan "*mucous* of the carnal . . . primary in its opening" (*An Ethics of Sexual Difference*, 162) that leaves everything at the brink of "some tactile unfinished in-finite" (*To Speak Is Never Neutral*, 240). The commanding injunction of Othello's "amen" simply cannot contain Desdemona's corporeality. Othello finds himself nevertheless stymied by the female body's two sets of lips (the mouth lips and the genital lips), the same complex that so frightened Bassanio and that (as I demonstrate in the chapter on *The Winter's Tale*) throws Leontes on the destructive course that pits him against Hermione.[33] Since, in Irigaray's analogy, merely touching one set of lips subjects him to the other/mother, Othello seesaws between two poles: the gigantism of "the mother's power to give birth, nourish, inhabit, center" (*Sexes and Genealogies*, 14) and the equally threatening specter of the woman as creator of a different language system.

When he demonizes Desdemona in the later acts, Othello fluctuates between the earlier self-promoting aggrandizement that renders him all controlling father ("I'd whistle her off and let her down the wind / to prey at fortune," 3.3.266–67) and the belated self-pitying reduction that depicts him as abandoned child: "I am abused" (3.3.272). In Act 3, his two-pronged refutation of Desdemona at first undoes temporality. Still attempting to control Desdemona's expansion, he parallels Brabanzio's retrospective annihilation of her as he invents an alternative past and future that nonetheless retains her as the object he creates:

> I had rather be a toad
> And live upon the vapour of a dungeon
> Than keep a corner in the thing I love
> For others' uses. (3.3.274–77)

After undoing time, as earlier Brabanzio did, with the subjunctive "had rather," Othello secondarily relegates Desdemona to a space too small to penetrate. Wedged into the imagined closure of "a corner," Desdemona is reduced to a nonentity contained as the "thing [he] love[s]," the same "thing" he projected in Act 1 as the object through which he identifies himself. If she is cornered here, he can remain the reflective source of her being: Desdemona is a miniscule he. Admitting his own lack of articulation, Othello now exists in the "vapor" of verbal insufficiency. Like the "dear heart" in "Sonnet 95," already hypothetically subject to other's "uses," Desdemona no longer reflects the self he wants to be. But in Act 4, even the stopgap of the subjunctive "rather be" ceases to work.

Calling Desdemona "a cistern for foul toads / to knot and gender in" (4.2.62–63), Othello overturns his earlier connection between the discursively primal genital and facial lips to convert the womb into a devouring, rather than projecting, mouth: "a sewer into which anal and urethral waste is poured" (*Sexes and Genealogies*, 16). If what overwhelms him in Act 2 is the undecidability of the half-open lips and if what satisfies him temporarily in Act 3 is the rigid containment of Desdemona's body, in Act 4 he renders her an absolute wasteland, eliminating the upper lips and their linguistic capacity entirely. She is all genital opening. Thus, when he names her "that cunning whore of Venice" (4.2.91), Othello describes Desdemona's falseness of mind in terms of the bodily part that signifies her nothingness. As Daniel Vitkus writes, "Her purportedly absent hymen—and the resulting hole, the hymenless orifice—becomes the central imaginary object of Othello's bloody thoughts. . . . Desdemona's sexual condition becomes Othello's world."[34] She is the "cunting" whore of Venice, simultaneously overrun by monsters and marked by her absence both from normative representation and discursive subjectivity. All vaginal nothingness, she can neither be the inspirational source of his representation nor the dispraiser who produces more words; castrating her verbally, he assures himself that she loses the "edge" associated with her upper lips: no tongue to articulate, no teeth to bite.

AB-HORING THE WORD, OR DESDEMONA'S RE-TURN

Desdemona's question of Iago, "am I that name" (4.2.121), contests the label that Othello assigns her. In parroting him, she asserts her own verbal dexterity. Speaking as if she were the young man of Sonnet 95 whose "name" has been vilified, she excludes herself from the very vocabulary that shames her:

> I cannot say "whore":
> It does abhor me now I speak the word.
> To do the act that might the addition earn
> Not the world's mass of vanity could make me. (4.2.165–68)

When she mouths the word apotropaically, Desdemona turns her back to it, in the "ab-hor." But in the last phrase, she declares a twofold future, annulling the methodology of Othello's original representation and subsequent disfiguration. Her "mass of vanity" indicts the very hall of mirrors through which Othello "fathered" her, dispelling the multiple versions of Othello's voluminous narcissism and defining a different genealogy for the origins of her own speech. She cannot be "made" in the sense of created by any sort of reflective verbal economy and she will not "do" the act of multiplying lovers that would justify the name.

Affirming her female bodily presence, as she has in her Acts 2 and 3 encounters with Othello, Desdemona works out of a double set of memories: one sexual, the other maternal. In the sexual memory, Desdemona thrice asserts what her love involves, each time evoking the constancy of the Irigarayan linguistic space she originally opened. First, with Iago, she calls Othello (as she will at the end) both cruel and out of character: "Unkindness may do much, / And his unkindness may defeat my life, / But never taint my love" (4.2.162–64). In the futurity of her phrasing, Desdemona remains faithful to her initial feeling. Functioning as a self-inspired entity, "[her] love" can be neither removed nor diminished; it exists as a guarantor of her renewed ambition.

In the second confirmation, "my love" acts out its intentionality and becomes the source of something Desdemona brings to Othello through the resourcefulness of her renewed affirmation. Reframing the negative into a positive by using "[her] love," she accepts his changed disposition:

> My love doth so approve him
> That even his stubbornness, his checks, his frowns—
> Prithee unpin me—have grace and favour in them. (4.3.17–19)

Her insistence this time positions "[her] love" as a stay against Othello's fall from his former self. In Desdemona's "approval," the personification of "my love" accomplishes the revolution around Desdemona that preserves Desdemona's integrity. If Othello renders Desdemona the all-devouring mouth, Desdemona refuses to eat back her love. The reproof of Othello's "checks" requires a corresponding new approach, her "approval." At the acoustic center of their different trajectories is the critical "proof" that resonates as a verbal marker throughout the play—Othello's "ocular proof" (3.3.365) and her behavioral "ap-proval." For Othello, "ocular proof" is the static specular object. For Desdemona, "ap-proval" involves an addition, a response to Othello's *reproach* with a corresponding *rapprochement* that assumes her linguistic subjectivity. The process through which Desdemona renders her inner thoughts apparent becomes the condition through which she confirms Othello's separateness.

In the last of the defense mechanisms, Desdemona turns to an offensive strategy when she characterizes love as an ongoing restorative she can wield:

> Good night, good night. God me such uses send
> Not to pick bad from bad, but by bad mend! (4.3.103–4)

Like Celia at the end of the first act of *As You Like It* ("Now go we in content / To liberty and not banishment," 1.3.132–33) and Juliet at the end of the balcony scene ("Good night, good night. Parting is such sweet sorrow / That I shall say good night till it be morrow," 2.2.229–30), Desdemona concludes the act with a couplet that pronounces her determination.[35] But unlike Celia and Juliet, whose practices involve fabulations, Desdemona operates through mechanical "use," weaving her language into the actual materiality of the experiential. Building from the base reality of her present situation, she recognizes the need for a new construction. Her definition of "use" as both a material and a verbal habit involves an acknowledgment that her methodology in the "picking" parallels Othello's in the "breaching" of his earlier fabulation. Like Othello's moving from "danger to danger," Desdemona's "pick[ing] bad from bad" encouraged the breach, just as her dispraise allowed him to move from praise of her to praise of the self he created for her to mirror. In its triple meaning of choosing, piercing, and separating, Desdemona's now rejected "pick[ing]" produced the cutting edge that, like the one in Sonnet 95, brought the Petrarchan sequence into being. Here, she attempts to build bridges of return that enable a crossing over *to* the other rather than a folding over *into* the other. With an ambiguous referent to the object of "mending" (Will she repair herself or Othello?), Desdemona accepts the need for change and the responsibility for carrying it out. Like the speaker in Sonnet 95, Othello separates physical "use" from verbal dexterity. But Desdemona phrases "use" as a link between her bodily and linguistic capacity.

If her practice at the end of the boudoir scene depends on reparation, her preparation begins with the deconstruction of "unpin[ning]" (4.3.19, 33) early on, a command she twice gives to Emilia, as if, in taking off her gown and all the accoutrements made for "these men" (4.3.58), she assumes an elemental self and a return to the female discursive matrix. Unadorned, she releases the paralyzing hold of the male narrative economy and awakens her other—the maternal—set of memories. In Barbary's song, she reverses the notion that the idealized woman is made in the image of the ideal man: "If I court more women, you'll couch with more men" (4.3.55). By taking over the man's voice, the lyric identifies male pluralized courting as the precondition for female multiple couching.[36] This line, where women ventriloquize men, challenges the handkerchief description, where Othello repeats the sibyl's words against Desdemona. In Othello's story, female slippages are responsible for male unfaithfulness.[37] But in Barbary's song, male incontinence causes female looseness.[38] Courting and couching in Barbary's song are opposed to the Petrarchan idea of courting "tout simple." They presume "use."

Desdemona's connection between primal memory and subsequent expectation spurs the willow song into being:

> My mother had a maid called Barbary.
> She was in love, and he she loved proved mad
> And did forsake her. (4.3.25–27)

Because Barbary and her song will "not go from [her] mind" (4.3.29), Desdemona is simultaneously shadowed and sustained by the memory she recovers. It's as if the song itself—and all the strength it contains (of women supporting each other, of the commiseration of rocks and streams with human frailty)—is an enlarged person who refuses to abandon her even as, by her containment, she clings to it. In the brilliant 2008 London Donmar Theatre production directed by Michael Grandage, Kelly Reilly voiced the lyrics so that they sounded as if they came from afar. Unpinned and unadorned, covered only in a shift, Reilly's Desdemona was transformed into the girl she might have been long ago in Venice. That chronological physical reversion attests to the psychological freedom from male dominion Desdemona experiences. She brings back the past to carry it over into the future. Activating Barbary's memory, Desdemona's locution recovers a coherence lost in

Othello's condemnation of her. Through the mediation of her "mind," the community of women advances into the present to form an internal protection just as Desdemona extends back to Barbary the perspective and homage of her current understanding, one that she could never have had in the past. Inwardly strengthened, Desdemona opens herself to Barbary's commemoration:

> The fresh streams ran by her and murmured her moans,
> Sing willow, willow, willow:
> Her salt tears fell from her and softened the stones. (4.3.41–44)

In Barbary's song, the streams "ran *by*" her as she positions herself in conjunction with them and sing *with* her, carrying her sadness as if it were their own. The metonymic closeness of the natural world renders the murmuring stream an echoing song, just as the salt tears soften that world and create an accommodating vessel.

Through the pressure of her tears, Barbary carves the stones into an extrauterine holding space, characterized by their changing shape and systematic enclosure. The welcoming home she sculpts with her watery tears and the sympathetic chorus she enlists in the watery streams offer the protection of the womb and the protraction of an originary comfort. The tears keep flowing just as the streams keep running, the linguistic continuity suggesting a perpetual movement that contrasts to Othello's early quest for narrative solidity. Resisting the immobility of Venetian discursive practice, Desdemona chooses a liquid mutability. The softened stones respond to the tears that forge a sustaining base. As it converts the downward flow of Barbary's tears into the lateral rush of the streams, the lyric replaces the cold accusations of Barbary's lover with a confirming mutuality. Finally, when it inverts all signs, the very blurring of the teary eyes emphasizes the tactile over the specular just as the liplike doubling of the lids renders them one of multiple female openings.[39]

The running streams similarly resist containment. Their "murmuring" empathetically repeats and so soothes Barbary's pain. The boundaries between earth and shore, solid and liquid, overflow. That effusion of diffusion survives into the last act as Desdemona speaks her own valediction and claims ownership of the deed: "Nobody. I myself. Farewell / Commend me to my kind lord" (5.2.133–34).[40] In the first line, she countermands the simulacrum of Othello's verbal mirroring and identifies the murderer as someone who, annulling the body, refuses to acknowledge the materiality of the flesh. Thus, she calls Othello "nobody" and proclaims her abandonment: "I myself." In the world of no-bodies, she is ultimately alone and responsible for her own fate. But in the "commend," she defines a measure of success, having restored Othello, by the creativity of her linguistic mending, to the status of her "kind lord." Co-mended, Othello is remanded to the self she remembers[41]—the man who originally created her in his image. They are now of the same *genus*: kind emerging in terms of kinship. In the end, Desdemona gives to Othello the gift of himself. Since she has failed in her endeavor to "mend" and so to restore her before-Othello self, she indulges him with his original image of her. With no body of her own, she can give Othello back "the edge" she knows he wants, the world of "th' imminent deadly breach" he filled with his expectations of her. Converting Othello's physical "use" of 3.3.177 back into a verbal usage, she returns him to the Petrarchan creativity of their prehistory. In the boudoir scene, Desdemona adds a line to Barbary's lyric, "let nobody blame him, his scorn I approve" (4.3.50) and then retracts it never to voice it again in her singing ("Nay, that's not next" [4.3.51]). But the lyric repeats her earlier "my love doth so approve him / That even his stubbornness, his checks, his frowns / . . . have grace and favour" (4.3.17–19). When, in the last scene, she returns Othello to his earlier status as the "kind lord" who produces her with the gift of his self-determination, she restores the "approval" of the misplaced lyric, enacting in her last words the world the "dear heart" of Sonnet 95 presumably also wishes to sustain.

Exchanging the commandeering forms of Venetian fathers for a story woven around a community of mothers, Desdemona accepts total responsibility for the life she has chosen to live and the death that, consequently, she is forced to die. Her perseverance is revealed in the lines that seem to me the most poignant in the play: "kill me tomorrow; let me live tonight" (5.2.87). The gradually decreasing time she begs for, "but half an hour [5.2.89] . . . but while I say one prayer" (5.2.91), has already been preempted by Othello's unyieldingness: "thou dost stone my heart" (5.2.67). Even at the last, her wish is phrased as a plea bargain, her prayer an attempt to effect the temporal reversal of "anastrophe." Having moved beyond the "catastrophic" moment, Othello can only respond within the confines of the oppositional trajectory I have been tracing.

In terms of the foundling plot, Desdemona's recovery of a community of women in the boudoir scene opens up a "memory" of the cultural life erased in her relationship with Othello even as the "murmuring" streams of her recollection transform Barbary's inarticulate "moans" into a new melodic counterpart for the old stories, substituting a constant lyrical flow for the cutting edge (of the preplay banter and of Sonnet 95) that spurs Petrarchan voice. Replacing Othello's inarticulate "mamm'ring" with the stream's empathetic "murmuring," her "turn" elaborates a generic construction that also projects a redefinition of adoption, one that joins lyric individuality to communal nurturing. But it represents only the beginning of a changed story, thwarted in the end by Othello's refusal to accept the permutations Desdemona advocated from their first encounter in Cyprus. In *The Winter's Tale*, Shakespeare continues to reimagine lyric engenderment and to reinvent the foundling plot, fleshing out fully the anticipation in early modern terms of the late modern revisions of poetic origination and mythological foundation theorized by the late modern writers whose work we have been following.

NOTES

1. Philip Roth, *Exit Ghost* (New York: Random House, 2007), 73.
2. "'The Ghosts of Strangers': Hospitality, Identity and Temporality in Caryl Phillips's *The Nature of Blood*," *Journal for Early Modern Cultural Studies* 6, 2 (Fall/Winter 2006): 39.
3. Caryl Phillips, *The European Tribe* (New York: Farrar, Straus and Giroux, 1987), 51.
4. "Othello's Occupation: Shakespeare and the Romance of Chivalry," *William Shakespeare's Othello*, edited by Harold Bloom (New York: Chelsea House, 1987), 62.
5. See, most importantly in the context of Brabanzio's jealousy of Othello, Margot Hendricks, who writes that Brabanzio holds an "incestuous desire for his daughter" and that "Othello's complete displacement of Brabanzio can occur only when . . . he takes to its ultimate punitive conclusion Brabanzio's disowning of his daughter." "'The Moor of Venice,' or the Italian of the Renaissance English Stage," *Shakespearean Tragedy and Gender*, edited by Shirley Nelson Garner and Madelon Sprengnether (Bloomington: Indiana University Press, 1996), 200.
6. Theseus warns Hermia, "Be advised, fair maid. / To you your father should be as a god: / One that compos'd your beauties, yea, and one / To whom you are but as a form in wax / By him imprinted, and within his power / To leave the figure, or disfigure it" (1.1.46–52).
7. "Artificial Couples: The Apprehensive Household in Dutch Pendants and *Othello*," *Center or Margin: Revisions of the English Renaissance in Honor of Leeds Barroll*, edited by Lena Cowen Orlin (Selinsgrove, PA: Susquehanna University Press, 2006), 142.
8. Janet Adelman writes of the "extent to which [Othello] describes not his heroic sufferings among men but his sufferings in the strange and desolate landscape of female deprivation, its vast and empty caves and rocks peopled by strangers and cannibals (1.3.140–45). Thus reunderstood, abandonment becomes the burden of his tale and helps to explain both his terrible hunger for Desdemona and the terrible speed with which he believes that she has abandoned him." *Suffocating Mothers: Fantasies of Maternal Origin in Shakespeare's Plays* (New York: Routledge, 1992), 66.
9. Discussing the different versions of *Othello*, Denise A. Whalen argues that there were two reasons for eliminating the willow song in quarto Q: (1) shortening the performance time in the difficult staging of undressing Desdemona and (2) "an inclination to suppress and restrain female agency." Whalen argues that the scene's content "fails to advance the plot." See "Unpinning Desdemona," *Shakespeare Quarterly* 58, 4 (2007): 508. In my reading, the song is central to the play.
10. *An Ethics of Sexual Difference*, trans. Carolyn Burke and Gillian C. Gill (Ithaca, NY: Cornell University Press, 1993), 133.
11. *To Speak Is Never Neutral*, trans. Gail Schwab (New York: Routledge, 2002), 3.
12. Patricia Parker's analysis of a parallel to rhetorical anastrophe, "hysteron proteron," in *Love's Labor's Lost* concentrates on "reversals of gender, class, and other forms of ordering" ("Preposterous Reversals: *Love's Labor's Lost*," *Modern Language Quarterly* 54, 4 [1993]: 446), which involve transferring existing terms rather than, what Irigaray proposes, "another discourse, one that is put together differently" (*An Ethics of Sexual Difference*, 177).
13. *Parler n'est jamais neutre* (Paris: Éditions de Minuit, 1985), 10.
14. "Acts of Silence, Acts of Speech: How to Do Things with Othello and Desdemona," *Renaissance Drama* 33 (2004): 3–35.
15. Indicating the connections between *Othello* and the sonnets, James Schieffer argues that "Shakespeare was either writing or revising at least some sonnets during the first decade of the 1600's, the same time that he was writing the major tragedies." See "*Othello* among the

Sonnets," *Othello, New Critical Essays*, edited by Phillip Kolin (New York: Routledge, 2002), 325. Schiefffer's emphasis is on thematic connections, mine on the Petrarchan plotting in the prehistory as recalled by Desdemona.

16. Ian Smith stresses the relationship between "cultural incivility and linguistic barbarity," which, he maintains, Iago exploits in designating Othello as a cultural alien. "Barbarian Errors: Performing Race in Early Modern England," *Shakespeare Quarterly* 49, 2 (1998): 168. Emily Bartels writes, "Within Venice itself, social standing is constantly up for grabs with gender proving as precarious a differentiation as culture, ethnicity or race. And if the Moor can be scripted as the alien within, that distinction proves him like, rather than unlike, Venice's women." "Othello and the Moor," *Early Modern English Drama: A Critical Companion*, edited by Garret A. Sullivan Jr., Patrick Cheney, and Andrew Hadfield (New York: Oxford University Press, 2006), 148.

17. "The Air of Those Who Love Each Other," *Why Different?* edited by Luce Irigaray, translated by Sylvère Lotringer (New York: Semiotext(e), 2000): 131.

18. *Shakespeare Jungle Fever* (Stanford: Stanford University Press, 2000), 101. In Little Jr.'s reading, Venice redefines Othello until Othello fits its actual expectations of him. Such a reading renders Othello the object of preconceived Venetian notions. Two recent critics also provide compelling arguments for casting Othello as the target of a racist, rather than the generator of a sexuate, power structure. Peter Erickson reasons that "racial issues shape the marital conflict" ("Images of White Identity in *Othello*," *Othello: New Critical Essays*, 138). Janet Adelman's thesis about Iago's Kleinian envy ("Iago's Alter Ego: Race as Projection in *Othello*," *Shakespeare Quarterly* 48, 2 [1997]: 125–44) specifically links misogyny and racism in the play by centralizing Iago as the necessary first cause of a domino effect that renders Othello the victim, as Emily Bartels writes, "by unfortunate chance" ("Making More of the Moor: Aaron, Othello and Renaissance Refashionings of Race," *Shakespeare Quarterly* 41, 4 [1990]: 454). But the view of Desdemona as the inheritor of Othello's feelings of inadequacy still supports the equation made by Patricia Parker ("Fantasies of 'Race' and 'Gender': Africa, *Othello*, and Bringing to Light," *Women, "Race," and Writing in the Early Modern Period*, edited by Margo Hendricks and Patricia Parker [New York: Routledge], 84–100) and Karen Newman ("'And Wash the Ethiop White': Femininity and the Monstrous in *Othello*," *Shakespeare Reproduced: The Text in History and Ideology*, edited by Jean Howard and Marion F. O'Connor [London: Routledge, 1987], 143–63) that Othello and Desdemona are caught together in the web of socially determined notions of monstrous difference.

In an important essay that reevaluates the either-or readings of the play, Carol Thomas Neely maintains that "analyses which ignore gender or analogize it to race cannot address the ways in which race and gender and sexuality inflect each other. Indeed, a number of recent essays, focusing on race in the play, have the effect of marginalizing or simplifying Desdemona's role or of blaming her for the tragedy." See "Women and Men in *Othello*," *Critical Essays on Shakespeare's Othello*, edited by Gerard Barthelemy (New York: G. K. Hall, 1994), 302. Instead, Neely describes how "the categories of gender, race and sexuality are inseparable, unstable, disunified, and mutually constitutive" (303). But finally, in arguing that Desdemona must simultaneously take her (Venetian) mother's and her (Moorish) mother-in-law's place, she sees the willow scene as emblematic of Desdemona's fall (309–11). See also Ania Loomba, who so forcefully reasons, "How do we understand the images of monstrous coupling and animal imagery that kick-start the play's relentless exploration of love across the boundaries, or the repetitive harping on a black-white dichotomy both by those opposed to the Othello-Desdemona marriage and by those sympathetic to it?" ("'Delicious Traffick': Racial and Religious Difference on Early Modern Stages," *Shakespeare and Race*, edited by Catherine M. S. Alexander and Stanley Wells [Cambridge: Cambridge University Press, 2000], 206). Loomba writes of her ambivalence and the conflicting difficulty of "being ghettoized into talking solely about the intersection of race and gender and upset when attention enough is not paid to that subject" (*Women, "Race," and Writing in the Early Modern Period*, edited by Margo Hendricks and Patricia Parker [London and New York: Routledge, 1994], 7).

Among the very strong arguments for the importance of Iago is that of Patricia Parker, who writes that his "monstrous presence . . . chart[s] the complexly and asymmetrically interrelated issues of race and gender in this play in a context that also summons the role of dilation as both engrossing narrative and bringing to 'light.'" His presence also "complicates the heterosexual erotics of the play with all its insistent homoerotic imagery, climaxing in the parody-marriage of Iago and Othello in Act III and adding to the already multiple senses of 'informing' that of the 'monstrous' shaping or giving form that comes of this displaced insemination and conception." See "Fantasies of 'Race' and 'Gender,'" *Women, "Race," and Writing in the Early Modern Period*, 98–99.

Perhaps the strongest case for early modern racism is made by Patrick C. Hogan, who maintains that Othello suffers from what Derek Walcott calls "racial despair . . . a variant of spiritual despair." It results from a sense that "one's skin is too black for anyone to accept—to forget or to 'forgive'—that one's skin blots out one's soul." See *"Othello*, Racism and Despair," *College Language Association Journal* 41, 4 (1998): 433. All these readings (mine included), however, are halted by Dympna Callaghan's admonition: "There are indeed, no authentic 'others'—raced or gendered of any kind, only their representations. But if Othello was a white man so was Desdemona." See *Shakespeare without Women: Representing Gender and Race on the Renaissance Stage* (London and New York: Routledge, 2000), 76.

19. Michael Neill argues that Desdemona doesn't change in the course of the play. Her initial view of the marriage as "a complete abdication of the will, an unqualified surrender of the self to the beloved other of which Othello is incapable: 'My heart's subdu'd / Even to the very quality of my lord,' 1.3.247-8. So absolute is this surrender that at the very point of death, Desdemona can reassert herself only through an act of quiet self-denial; questioned by Emilia as to who is responsible for her death, she quite simply offers herself in Othello's place: 'Nobody—I myself—farewell' (5.2.125) to embrace this paradox is indeed to make herself 'nobody.'" See *Putting History to the Question: Power, Politics, and Society in English Renaissance Drama* (New York: Columbia University Press, 2000), 228. James Calderwood reads this steadfastness differently. In his view Desdemona's "dying claim to have killed herself is not the lie it literally appears. She *did* kill herself. Had the love she bore Othello been less unfailingly true, more prudently prepared to alter when it alteration found, she might well have lived. Absolute constancy has small survival value; it sins against its possessor. In these last words of hers the sin of love reasserts itself by issuing a true lie. For Desdemona, 'truth' is not the mercilessly just correspondence of word to fact but the merciful 'troth' of a love so deeply plighted that it bears it out beyond all bounds of property and possession, even to the edge of doom." "Appalling Property in *Othello*," *University of Toronto Quarterly* 57, 3 (1998): 370.

20. Joel Fineman, "The Sound of O in *Othello*: The Real of the Tragedy of Desire," *Critical Essays on Shakespeare's Othello*, 110.

21. "Acts of Silence, Acts of Speech: How to Do Things with Othello and Desdemona," *Renaissance Drama* 33 (2004): 10.

22. *Shakespeare from the Margins: Language, Culture, Context* (Chicago: University of Chicago Press, 1996), 230.

23. On Desdemona's devouring, Harry Berger Jr. writes that "the speech binds them together in mutual cannibalism." See "Acts of Silence, Acts of Speech: How to Do Things with Othello and Desdemona," 22.

24. "Reading *Othello* Backwards," *Othello: New Critical Essays*, 395.

25. Of this scene, Emily Bartels writes, "[The] exchange between Desdemona and Othello adds the missing link of gender to the spectacle of race." "Making More of the Moor: Aaron, Othello and Renaissance Refashionings of Race," 796.

26. "Lieutenancy, Standing In, and *Othello*," *English Literary History* 57 (1990): 796.

27. E. A. J. Honigmann refers to Kittredge's reading, which suggests that Desdemona dispraised "of course, in order to hear Cassio praise him in reply." *Othello*, edited by E. A. J. Honigmann (London: Thomas Nelson, 1999), 212.

28. *Shakespeare's Sonnets*, edited by Katherine Duncan-Jones (Walton-on-Thames, UK: Thomas Nelson, 1997), 301.

29. "Epistemology and Tragedy: A Reading of *Othello*," *William Shakespeare's Othello*, 18.

30. *Sexes and Genealogies*, trans. Gillian C. Gill (New York: Columbia University Press, 1993), 100–101.

31. On the importance of invention for Othello, see Shawn Smith's analysis of "Astrophil and Stella," 45, arguing that (as Astrophil urges, "pitty the tale of me") "in adopting romance conventions as a means of guiding his relationship with Desdemona, Othello acquires with those conventions a tradition of love obsessed with deception and adultery." "Love, Pity and Deception in *Othello*," *Papers on Language and Literature* 44, 1 (2008): 22.

32. Irigaray stresses the male "privilege granted to metaphor (a quasi-solid) over metonymy (which is more closely allied to fluids)." *This Sex Which Is Not One*, trans. Catherine Porter with Carolyn Burke (Ithaca, NY: Cornell University Press, 1985), 110.

33. "Two sets of lips that . . . cross over each other like the arms of the cross. . . . The mouth lips and the genital lips do not point in the same direction. In some way they point in the direction opposite from the one you would expect, with the 'lower' ones forming the vertical" (*An Ethics of Sexual Difference*, 18). In the next chapter, I describe this image in greater detail as it applies to *The Winter's Tale*.

34. "The 'O' in *Othello*: Tropes of Damnation and Nothingness," in *Othello: New Critical Essays*, 352.

35. Linking Desdemona to the heroines of Shakespearean comedy, Carol Thomas Neely also comments on Desdemona's final couplet as a response that "would be more active than acceptance yet more loving than retaliation." See "Women and Men in Othello," *Critical Essays on Shakespeare's Othello*, 75.

36. On the willow song as a traditional ballad, see Joel Fineman, "The Sound of *O* in *Othello*: The Real of the Tragedy of Desire," *Critical Essays on Shakespeare's Othello*, 105.

37. Susan Frye writes, "The point of this tale is not to charm but to situate the handkerchief in a narrative that parallels the suspicion and domestic violence through which Othello is now narrating his life." "Staging Women's Relations to Textiles in Shakespeare's *Othello* and *Cymbeline*," *Early Modern Visual Culture: Representation, Race and Empire in Renaissance England*, edited by Peter Erickson and Clark Hulse (Philadelphia: University of Pennsylvania Press, 2000), 223.

38. Barbary's ventriloquizing the male voice in Desdemona's song enacts what Elizabeth D. Harvey calls Irigaray's idea of "subversively employing a traditionally patriarchal definition of women." *Ventriloquized Voices: Feminist Theory and English Renaissance Texts* (New York: Routledge, 1992), 107.

39. Irigaray suggests that the eyelids are like the lips (*An Ethics of Sexual Difference*, 49).

40. Emily Bartels writes that "Desdemona sees Othello as her kind lord (5.3.133) until she takes her last breath." See "Othello and the Moor," *Early Modern English Drama: A Critical Companion*, edited by Garret A. Sullivan Jr., Patrick Cheney, and Andrew Hadfield (New York: Oxford University Press, 2006), 148.

41. Harry Berger Jr. reasons that Desdemona's alliance here could be read simultaneously as a total victimization, a reduction of herself to poor Barbary, and a preparation for her final, at least partial, retaliation. Desdemona's "saintlike forgiveness of her tormentor vibrates through her last words and solicits a different reading: he will discover too late what a jewel he has thrown away." "Impertinent Trifling: Desdemona's Handkerchief," *Shakespeare Quarterly* 47, 3 (1996): 240.

Chapter Seven

"I Am Heir to My Affection"

Revising Family and Love in The Winter's Tale

At the beginning of *Othello*, the lyric is completed by a "you"—created out of the "breach" spurring desire—that mirrors the "I," a replication that renders the "other" the "self." Othello initially introduces the court to a Desdemona who wishes that she might find in the flesh and reflect in her body "such a man" (1.3.164) as the one Othello created in his words. In the same way, before he chooses the caskets in *Merchant of Venice*, Bassanio generates a Portia as the woman whose oxymoronic "happy torment" (3.2.37) brings him to the poetic self-sufficiency he enjoys. Similarly, in *The Winter's Tale*, we learn very early on that Leontes wooed Hermione through the vacancy of the "three crabbed months" (1.2.102) figured by her contrariness until she proclaimed herself "yours forever" (1.2.104); with that turnaround, she declared that her being would henceforth be found through his, just as Desdemona reveals a similar identification, assuring the Duke that "My heart's subdued / Even to the very quality of my lord" (1.3.250–51).

In each of the plays, the women seem to enjoy the Petrarchan exchanges. Desdemona wistfully alludes to the numerous occasions when Othello came "a-wooing" (3.3.72) with Cassio; Portia wishes to "peise" (3.2.22) the time before Bassanio chooses the caskets, and, like Desdemona on behalf of Cassio, Hermione partakes of the persuasion game with Polixenes—similarly upping it to three players—as she cajoles him to stay beyond his initial opposition (a parallel to her earlier waywardness) and also when she engages in a linguistic duel to see which of the kings is the "verier" (1.2.66). In all three plays, wooing emerges as a contest where the best speaker wins. Paulina and Leontes refer to earlier rounds of Petrarchan gaming twice in Act 5 (5.3.36 and 5.3.107) but, chiefly, when Paulina insists that Leontes remain faithful to his written encomium to the queen's everlasting (temporally retrospective and projective) supremacy: "'She had not been / Nor was not to be equalled'" (5.1.100–101). Reminding him of his creation of her in verse that "flowed with her beauty" (5.1.101), Paulina declares Hermione the static reflection of Leontes's power to bring her into being, contrasting the queen's imagistic constancy to the king's creative generativity. The "flow" in this case refers not to an Irigarayan fluidity spilling over from Hermione to Leontes but to a stylistic fluency reflecting backward to the king's linguistic mastery. Paulina's allusions here to the preplay "three crabbed months" (1.2.102) of Leontes's before-marriage wooing are reminiscent of Desdemona's reference in Act 3 of *Othello* to a similar triad with Cassio. They suggest that perhaps Paulina played a similar advocacy role then (as she will later orchestrate the reunion at the end of Act 5). All this talk even before the statue scene prepares for the restoration of everything—verbal authority and familial legacy—from which Leontes has been separated for sixteen years.

But in the long pastoral scene of *The Winter's Tale*, Shakespeare's lyric inventiveness adds something different to our concept of engendering. In the remarkable exchanges of Florizel and Perdita, he recasts both the foundling and Petrarchan plots. And he does so despite the fact that, in the other acts of *The Winter's Tale* and in the conclusion, the biological mandate weighs heavily on the minds of the protagonists, just as it does in *Merchant of Venice* and in *Othello*. In *Merchant*, Bassanio and Graziano wager for the first son. Shylock is labeled the product of a "wolfish father and an unhallowed dam." Othello (in his rage) echoes Brabantio's condemnation, wishing Desdemona had "n'er been born" (4.2.69–70). Leontes obsesses over Mamillius's likeness to him and dismisses Perdita as "another's issue" (2.3.192). Thus, each of the three plays presents an inverse connection between the essentialism of the foundling plot and its emphasis on the bloodline mandate and the lyric convention with its imaginative creation, an order set off-kilter at the thought that the woman might be the source of both a linguistic and genetic power of her own. Bassanio becomes frightened of Portia's lips when he picks the right casket. Othello is verbally infantile when Desdemona speaks for Cassio. Leontes is infuriated when Hermione succeeds in persuading Polixenes to stay.

The inverted linkage between the foundling and Petrarchan plots in *The Winter's Tale* can be illustrated by the difference between Leontes's view in the first act of "affection" as an outside force that separates him totally from himself ("affection thy intention stabs the centre," 1.2.137) and Florizel's use of "affection" as an internal feeling that replaces his patrilineal inheritance in 4.4.468–69. For Leontes, "affection" splits him from both the biological connection and the lyric creativity that defines his equanimity and it does so by introducing a third player into Leontes's ring. His question about Mamillius's duplication—as piece of his flesh—spurs his unease about Hermione's reflection as product of the words he invented for her in the "three crabbed months" (1.2.102) of his wooing. By contrast, for Florizel, "affection" is both the source of his revisionist notion of heritage and the inspiration for his poetics. As I argue later in this chapter, Florizel undoes the order of inherited chronology and the origin of lyric identity as he allows his feeling to govern dynasty and language.

Leontes's decentralization happens quickly when he moves from a fixation on Mamillius as a product of male autogeneration to a belief that he is subject to female ascendancy:

> Most dear'st, my collop! Can thy dam—May't be?—
> Affection, thy intention stabs the centre:
> Thou dost make things possible things not so held,
> Communicat'st with dreams—how can this be?—
> With what's unreal thou coactive art,
> And fellow'st nothing. Then 'tis very credent
> Thou may'st co-join with something; and thou dost—
> And that beyond commission; and I find it,
> And that to the infection of my brains
> And hard'ning of my brows. (1.2.139–48)

"Affection," as Leontes uses it is a state of mind that controls the body. But whose affection stabs him? Clearly, it is Hermione's and his condemnation is strengthened by his belief that her presumed feeling for Polixenes, first rendered palpable to him when she speaks on his behalf, is what causes his disease. Hermione is in the central position. One of the earlier meanings of affection is that of illness and Leontes ends by claiming that his brain is "infected," that the outward force he perceives as originating in Hermione, now internalized by her stab, has calcified him. His brow is "harden'd." Medusa-Hermione has turned him to stone, an echo of what Bassanio fears when he rejects the Medusa-Portia who might turn him into her. Leontes's view of Hermione's transgression calls into play Othello's view of Cassio's exceeding *his* lieutenancy when Desdemona "woos" him with *her* lieutenancy. In overstepping her bounds as his emissary to Polixenes, indeed by turning the Petrarchan dyad into a triad, Hermione (like the beloved in Sonnet 95) moves into the arena of "ill use" that Othello called "abuse" (3.3.272). Leontes is infected by a fourfold expansion of Hermione's original single mission, as he mounts in his indictment from a verbal to a physical conspiracy—involving a partnership in the "co's" ("comunicat'st . . . co-active . . . co-join . . . commission") that quickly solidifies in his mind into a pernicious campaign designed to destabilize him. Hermione's imagined feeling and agency—"affection"—moves through act, to linkage, to a partnership that results, finally, in Leontes's distraction. To catch the disease is to be turned into a woman.

Since it is Hermione who is the source of Leontes's unease, her alliance with the decentering forces sequentially results in the undoing of his ontology. As his rage mounts into tautology, the indicted forces cause his world first to collapse ("fellow'st nothing"). The fellowship insidiously eats away at the pristine quality of Leontes's self-created identity. Worming its way from inside the hollow it implodes, the conspiracy produces (in the co-joining) the substance that "infect[s his] brains." The thinking that creates the beloved out of absence can, from that same nothingness, also produce the sickness that pollutes. The very circularity makes his disease evident: he has "found" it. Hermione's excess—her moving out of place—topples Leontes's mind, since her co-activity implies a doubling based on the debilitation of Leontes's subjectivity, just as Portia's portrait stole the painter's eyes. All those "co's"—always with an imagined rival partner—leave Leontes co-opted, deprived of both biological mandate and verbal initiative, in the way that Othello and the speaker in Sonnet 95 feel their loss of creativity as the beloved object becomes the controlling subject. Leontes can no longer quite believe in Mamillius as his child or in Hermione as his mirror. Hermione has taken over and overtaken him. Even before he has the "proof" of Polixenes's hasty departure, Leontes rushes to his conclusion. When Shylock speaks on his own, Antonio feels cut to the quick and immediately responds by calling him the "devil [who] cite[s] scripture" (1.3.94). Likewise, Leontes turns Hermione into the Medusan source of his calcification.

Part of Leontes's fear of Hermione's power stems from something the audience comes to understand later in the play, something that brings up a congenital uncertainty that trumps the linguistic agency governing his world. In *Othello*, we learn of a preplay wooing sequence in Act 3, just as Paulina reminds Leontes (and the audience) of one in Act 5. If there is a poetic history in both plays—alluding to an earlier male verbal authority—so is there a genealogical one—referring to an earlier social inferiority that both heroes feel. In *The Winter's Tale* third act, we garner a piece of information that renders Hermione even more like Desdemona and Leontes as much an outsider to her kingdom as Othello was in Venice. During the trial, Hermione reveals to the court that she is the daughter of the emperor of Russia (3.2.119–23). That knowledge throws the dynastic mandate of the foundling plot off-kilter even as it pushes hard on Leontes's position in the Petrarchan plot. Hermione's status is not just a figment of poetic exaltation that renders her "[un]equall'd" (5.1.100). It is an element of real political power. Leontes and Polixenes have much smaller demesnes. So for the duration of those "three crabbed months" to which Leontes alludes, he was trying to woo a daughter as powerful in his eyes as Desdemona was in Othello's. Merely the king of Sicily, Leontes is not an emperor. No wonder he is uneasy about Hermione's vocal power. His fear takes him back to the beginning when he felt subject to the inherited position of her dynastic superiority. Like Othel-

Io's lieutenant, the "twinned lamb" (1.2.67) might replace him as partner to someone whose legacy is vaster than both of theirs. As the dispenser of an affection that threatens Leontes's hold on the world, Hermione returns him to his premarriage uncertainty.

In Act 4, Florizel frees himself from the anxiety of heritage even as he forfeits the linguistic authority that governed Leontes's feeling of power. Disowning his biological inheritance and proclaiming his love for Perdita as the origin of his being, Florizel redefines "affection" and names himself the child produced by feeling:

> From my succession wipe me father! I
> Am heir to my affection. (4.4.468–69)

His defiance is part of a remarkable lyric interchange, one where Florizel and Perdita re-create themselves, each overcoming an initial unease about the source of generation and ending in a "pair[ing]" (4.4.153) that changes everything. Florizel's redefinition turns everything around, reversing the order that reigns in Act 1 and is regained in Act 5, challenging both the dynastic mandate of the foundling, and the narcissistic self-reflection of the Petrarchan, plot.

Shakespeare's subversion of his own earlier subscription to conventional poetics can be theorized if we follow a similar change between the essentialism of Luce Irigaray's 1984 *Ethics of Sexual Difference* and her later pronouncement of a resistance to what she calls a "natural identity" (*Between East and West*, 141), a devolution in thought that parallels Shakespeare's deformations of the lyric and foundling plots in *The Winter's Tale*, where he opens himself to the radical revisionism we only see temporarily enacted in *The Merchant of Venice* and *Othello*. In the first passage below, Irigaray's original view develops a theory of language that stems from the primacy of the female body. Her revisionism (in the second passage) bypasses the fixed gender roles she delineates in her earlier writing:

> This *threshold* which has never been examined as such: the female sex. . . .
> Two sets of lips that cross over each other like the arms of the cross, the
> prototype of the crossroads *between*. The mouth lips and the genital lips do not
> point in the same direction. In some way they point in the direction opposite
> from the one you would expect, with the "lower" ones forming the vertical.[1]

> The most interesting situation is probably that of families where diverse types
> of blending [*mixité*] intersect. The resistance to belonging to a natural identity
> appears there in the horizontal axis that joins the sexes and in the vertical axis
> that links together generations.[2]

In the 1984 *Ethics of Sexual Difference*, Irigaray configures the cross, the image of male suffering and triumph in Christian experience, to symbolize *female* chronological ascendancy. She defines the importance of the woman as speaking subject and draws a line between the starting point of human life—the threshold of the vulva lips—and the initiation of feminine speech—the threshold of the mouth lips—by connecting the upper and lower parts of the woman's body: the very linkage that so terrified Othello and that caused Bassanio to feel himself "a wild of nothing" (3.2.182) in *The Merchant of Venice*.

Irigaray's feminized cross pitches the vulva phallically at the bottom of the vertical pole to render the biological place of birth the primary stem that supports the horizontal line of linguistic flowering. In that context, Leontes's indictment—"no barricado for a belly" (1.2.204)—parallels Othello's calling Desdemona "a cistern for foul toads / to knot and gender in" (4.2.62–63) and the "cunning whore of Venice" (4.2.91), both condemnations rendering mind and body identically polluted entities stemming from the same originating place. Similarly, Bassanio's fear of Portia is spurred by the connections he makes when he calls her lips "sweet bar[s]" (3.2.115) that split men in two and render them spawns of women's generating primacy. Thus, in the three plays central to this study, the image of the woman as Irigarayan linguistic and sexual generator—Portia to Bassanio, Desdemona to Othello, and Hermione to Leontes—precipitates (for each of the three men respectively) a fear of fragmentation and disintegration. Bassanio feels "unfurnished" (3.2.126); Othello, "abused" (3.3.72); and Leontes, "dissevered" (5.3.155). At the end of the three plays, each of the women—Portia in the recovered ring, Desdemona in the co-mending, and Hermione in her "preserv[ation]" (5.3.128)—returns to her respective partner a sense of male linguistic primacy associated with the recovery of a static lyric identity, one that places the man as the generator of the woman's body, as exemplified by the position of Petrarchan pursuit, recalled by Desdemona in her reference to the preplay banter she misses in Act 3, enacted by Bassanio in the sonnet duet of his complaint before he chooses the correct casket and by Leontes in his post-trial intention to "new woo my queen" (3.2.156).

When in the 1999 passage, Irigaray changes the image of the female body with a different—and double-gendered—intersection, she circumvents the essentialism of her earlier view to stress a "blending" that obviates the bloodline mandate of the foundling plot with a different and cross-gendered meeting point: the "horizontal axis that joins the sexes and the vertical axis that links the generations" (*Between East and West*, 141). The cross is still there but it is double crossed with the mutuality of what Anne Michaels calls the "rendezvous" (*The Winter Vault*, 94), superannuating "natural" identity with a reciprocal blending that supersedes the identity politics of Irigaray's earlier work. In that respect, she defines "engendering" as the continual and communal processes that Desdemona articulated in Act 4 of *Othello* when she regendered Petrarchan poetics simultaneously as she remapped the middle adoptive interlude of the foundling plot to make it a psychologically sustaining end. In the 1999 passage, Irigaray dislocates her previous script in the same way that, in the relationship of Florizel and Perdita developed in Act 4, Shakespeare abandons his more absolute use of the foundling plot as he had followed it in *A Comedy of Errors, As You Like It*, and even as late as *Pericles*. With the young lovers, Shakespeare challenges the restoration of Act 5, allowing us to read it as a reiteration of the gender hierarchies that caused so much trouble in the beginning. In Act 4, he brings to fruition a remarkable change in the lyric dynamic that he only momentarily achieved in Shylock's incorporation of female reproductive powers and Desdemona's ventriloquizing of male voice in *Merchant of Venice* and *Othello* respectively.

The double achievement in the long pastoral scene—an expansion of the realm of sexual love to include a nurturing function and also a revolution in gender expectations that bypasses masculinist creative authority with a mutually found language—favors the fourth-act discoveries over the fifth-act recoveries. Such a reading suggests that the closing "recognition scene" (so important to the happy ending of the foundling plot) returns us to the beginning of the play and to a series of subject positions that puts back in place the patriarchal imperatives causing such havoc in the early acts. In accordance with the conservative impulses of the foundling plot, the elaborate ritual of the final scene is retrogressive, reproducing all the old values.

Hermione and Leontes speak the same language at both the beginning and the end of the play and their mutual insistence on the primacy of biological inheritance adheres to a formula Shakespeare dismantles through the cultural revolution of Florizel and Perdita's achievement. The young lovers' relationship "betters" (a pivotal word in the play) that of their parents. When (as I outline in the third section of this chapter) Florizel pitches "better[ing]" (4.4.135–36) toward a future that derives from a base of present satisfaction, he removes the word from the arena of Leontes (1.2.89), Mamillius (2.1.6), and Polixenes (4.4.90), who use it to express their competitive impulses and their disappointment with things as they stand. Florizel's redeployment inspires different interpretations of, first, the foundling plot that frames the play, particularly its emphasis on bloodline supremacy; second, gender relations and their repetitive narrative patterns; third, intergenerational hierarchies and their relationship to time; and (finally) the lyric dynamic and its rigid adherence to a static self in relationship to an other created by that self. With those four shifts, he counters the linguistic symbiosis between Leontes and Hermione, echoed by Camillo, Polixenes, Paulina, and even Mamillius. All obey the patriarchal strictures of the foundling plot, a rigidity also based on the male determinations of the Petrarchan convention to which so many of the characters allude. The matter of generational identity haunts *The Winter's Tale*. The questions Leontes asks of Mamillius—"Art thou my boy?" (1.2.119)—and the answers Hermione gives when she affirms her possession of Perdita—"tell me, mine own" (5.3.124)—reiterate the bloodline hierarchy so important to the foundling plot.

In accordance with an interpretation that ends in the middle of the play, I conclude with a focus on Act 4 rather than Act 5 and describe how Florizel and Perdita retilt the axis that links together the generations, as they split open the closed circle (inscribed by Hermione's "slipping," 1.2.85, Mamillius's "wantoning," 2.1.17, and Camillo's "gazing," 4.4.109) of courtly mimetic return in favor of an interim (what Florizel calls "the while," 4.4.48) that then provides access to a changing and expansive temporal realm. With the extraordinary relationship forged by the lovers in Act 4, Shakespeare devalues the central poles—(the moment of birth at the beginning, the triumph of recovery at the end) even as he expands the middle section—of the foundling plot.

Camillo refers to the plot in the first scene and Hermione does so in similar terms in her last speech. Praising Mamillius, Camillo characterizes the young prince: "They that went on crutches ere he was born desire yet their life to see him a man" (1.1.34–35). Hermione echoes this perseverance when she declares "[I] have preserved / Myself to see the issue" (5.3.126–27), the "issue" being her grown daughter. Remaining on crutches supports the wounded body until it can heal—a presupposition that, in the interval, the "real" leg will be returned to its former status and that a cure in the body politic can be equated to a cure in the body physical. The belief in an artifice that is only temporary, like the reliance on an intermediary caretaker for the child, is based on a fiction so pervasive that it works on all levels of society, finally confirming the "naturalness" of class stratification. While they insist on visual corroboration, Camillo and Hermione center their determination on a belief in the expectation of recovery cultivated by fictive contrivances even as they reject the prosthetic devices (the false leg, the adoptive interlude) that facilitate the recognition they desire. In the tenacity of their suspension, they adhere to the catapulting and concluding poles of the formulaic foundling plot: everything depends on the initial egress from the royal womb and the concluding recovery of the imperiled dynasty. Like the crutch, the temporary parents (who do all the work of raising the child) are annulled once the true heir is recovered. In terms of children, the plotline accepts only Irigaray's "vertical axis that links together the generations": biology is everything. Hermione's view of Perdita as what Carol Thomas Neely calls "an extension of her own physical being"[3] parallels Leontes's claim that his daughter is a duplicate of Polixenes just as Mamillius is a mere "collop" (1.2.137) of himself. While it may be true that Hermione's pregnant maternal body—simply seen as the occupying discharge of Polixenes—incites Leontes's jealousy, it is also true that Hermione's attitude toward the "issue" and its attendant physical and linguistic outcomes seems hardly different from that of Leontes.[4]

In *The Winter's Tale*, even the characters allude to the foundling plot, calling Perdita's recognition scene "so like an old tale" (5.2.28, 5.2.55)[5] with all the normalized "unity in the proofs" (5.1.32) necessary for a happy ending. But the fact that the *scène à faire* concomitant to the formula occurs offstage suggests that Shakespeare may be questioning his earlier use of the plot and its way of tying things together.[6] The preservation of self (5.3.128) about which Hermione boasts at the end bespeaks the same unyieldingness to Perdita as it does to her husband. Her refusal to melt—to hazard everything in the way that Florizel puts himself at risk when he accepts Perdita's loss as his own ("I am put to sea / with her whom I cannot hold on shore," 4.4.486–87)—marks her contrast to the Ovidian Ceres rather than her idealization in comparison.[7]

Interpretations that view the triumph at the end as Hermione's cite Ceres and Proserpine to define the initial loss and later restitution.[8] But a reading that questions Hermione because her language reiterates patriarchal values without changing them involves a reconceptualization of generational and sexual expectations.[9] Hermione's failure to forgive her husband once she knows of his repentance illustrates a retrograde notion of parenting, one that identifies the woman only as the vehicle for the delivery of a child who is totally a product of its male genetic inheritance. In her sixteen-year barrenness, Hermione remains totally apart from Perdita and Florizel, who see love as a form of Irigaray's "biunivocal engendering" as they gradually come to realize that sexuality includes nurturing. Why—with the assurance that Leontes grieves for what he so abruptly caused—could she not have begged him, as Ceres did Jupiter, to help her recover their missing daughter?[10] For Hermione, as for Leontes, Perdita exists only as the compound "issue," both the dénouement of her parents' story and the destiny of her father's court—outcomes that reflect a belief in the "old tale[s]" (5.2.28, 5.2.62) that are part of the generic construct Florizel and Perdita challenge in the fourth act and that Shakespeare himself undercuts when he portrays Hermione as more like Leontes than critics, in their sanctification of the queen, have hitherto acknowledged.[11] The liaison between Hermione and Leontes in terms of their initial and concluding reliance on Petrarchan invention is thus paralleled in Hermione's belief in the bloodline mandate, revealed in her speeches in Act 5 where she defends her sixteen-year absence and reclaims her child.

Chapter 7

THE ISSUE OF THE ISSUE

In her insistence on telling her own story at her first meeting with Perdita, even before her daughter has a chance to answer the questions she raises, Hermione subscribes to the concerns about "issue" voiced from the very opening of the play:

> Tell me, mine own,
> Where hast thou been preserved? where lived? How found
> Thy father's court? For thou shalt hear that I,
> Knowing by Paulina that the oracle
> Gave hope thou wast in being, have preserved
> Myself to see the issue. (5.3.123–28)

For Camillo, Mamillius's material being is marked only by his relationship to his origin; the same is true for Hermione with regard to Perdita. Her first two questions ("where hast thou been preserved? where lived?," 5.3.123–24) are eclipsed by the third one: What accounts for Perdita's presence now?[12] But the story she demands requires answers that refer to geographical territories and geopolitical mapping, as if "[finding her] father's court" were merely a matter of Perdita's securing safe passage to Sicily. For Hermione, the only relevant moments of her daughter's life have been those feeding into the most recent events—the process of transport from the place of her less interesting "preservation" to the site of her significant origin: "thy father's court." The twice-repeated word—"preserved"—parallels her daughter's survival to her own: Hermione's statically keeping herself safe at home equals Perdita's being actively kept alive by others. By emphasizing place rather than process, Hermione both reinstates the dynastic poles of the foundling plot and suggests that Perdita somehow remains unchanged from birth. "Preservation" implies an immaculate restoration. The sixteen-year interval of Perdita's absence becomes—as it is for Hermione—merely a distillation of the bloodline. The "how" in Hermione's question is only navigational. Trusting the oracle's "hope," Hermione doesn't need to ask anything about *who* saved Perdita or what her life was like in the interval between exposure and discovery; the only thing that matters is her return to the inner circle, a reiteration of patriarchal values that resembles the Belmont ring of *Merchant of Venice*. Addressing her daughter as "mine own," she cancels out Perdita's separate being and affirms the dominating "naturalness" of the royal enclosure.

Hermione's use of "issue" here circles back to Leontes's command about what Antigonus should do with newborn Perdita ("it"):

> [B]ear it
> To some remote and desert place, quite out
> Of our dominions; . . . there thou leave it,
> Without more mercy, to its own protection

And favour of the climate. As by strange fortune
It came to us, I do in justice charge thee
On thy soul's peril and thy body's torture,
That thou commend it strangely to some place
Where chance may nurse or end it. (2.3.174–82)

Hermione's questions to Perdita conflate the bodily form of the family with the shape of a terrain; just so, viewing Perdita as the "issue" (1.3.190) of a foreign body, Leontes commands that she should be carried to a country outside "our dominions." And if Hermione preserves herself in order to hear the generically determined outcome, so Leontes (sharing a belief in the same stories) allows the "strange fortune" of Perdita's arrival to be matched by the haphazard "chance" of her nursing. Perdita's alien status demands her extradition to "some remote and desert place." Both parents regard Perdita only on their own terms: the father commanding her exile because of what he believes to be her biological estrangement, and the mother applauding her return in terms of her biological closeness. At the end, Leontes labels his mistake an "ill suspicion" (5.3.149), a tautology identical to "mine own" (5.3.123), as perfunctory in its apology as Hermione's is smug in its assurance and as false a belief in the now-proven wrong story as Hermione's is in the generically right one.

Like Hermione in the last acts, Leontes at the opening thinks in terms of the closed courtly circle and confirms his belief in the real effects produced by stories: "I / Play too; but so disgraced a part, whose issue / Will hiss me to my grave" (1.2.187–89). By the time he finishes the speech about his own cuckoldry, he links all three meanings of "issue" (bodily fluids, progeny, and the outcome of a narrative) to the Fall and therefore to the fallen body represented by the hissing of the snake's forked tongue. The serpentine activity within the womb and the diseased content Leontes visualizes are corroborated by the auditory "hissing" of the gossip pronouncing him cuckold. The assonance of "issue" and "hiss" merges the serpentine devil with the wife, a connection Hermione herself makes when, in response to Polixenes's allusion to the Fall, she accuses him of aligning all women with the satanic, an expectation she doesn't contradict. Her banter about slipping ("If you first sinned with us, and that with us / You did continue fault, and that you slipped not / With any but us," 1.2.84–86)—and its implication of a slimy, snaky, sin—precipitates Leontes's conclusion that his "wife is slippery" (1.2.273).[13] As Martine Van Elk remarks, "In the spirit of rhetorical contest, Polixenes's reference to man's fall as a result of female sin does not offend Hermione. She reads the remark as a challenge and responds to the patriarchal charge with another challenge."[14]

For both Hermione and Leontes, the female body is acceptable as an entity only when it remains within the circle ("not . . . any but us") determined by the established male order. "Slipping" becomes a self-contained pastime of the court, one that returns the tail of the snake to its own mouth, just as the tale of the gossip Leontes fears repeats its male-centered origin. In containing "sin" within the confines of the court, Hermione nevertheless concurs with Leontes's view that the "slipping" of conjugal relations is a form of diminishment. When Hermione is labeled "slippery" by Leontes, she slithers out of his orbit, confirming his centrifugal fear that the "centre is not big enough to bear / A schoolboy's top" (2.1.102–3). "Slipping" (1.2.85) dissolves into "slippery" (1.2.273) and the circle dwindles to the "nothing" (1.2.294–96) of female spaces. While Hermione labels "slipping" (1.2.85) a continual occupation connected to a discursive practice of courtly sexual repartee, Leontes similarly casts the idle chitchat of gossip as part of a circumscribed and habitual routine ("Camillo and Polixenes / Laugh at me, make their pastime at my sorrow," 2.3.23–24).[15] Hermione's language—the connection she makes between Perdita's physical placement and her father's court when she calls Perdita "mine own" (5.3.123)—corroborates Leontes's sense that there are no divisions between the royal body politic and the scions of the father. Dismissing his early "ill suspicion" (5.3.149) at the end, Leontes determines that his jealous behavior can be tossed away just as Hermione assumes that her sixteen-year absence can be excused by her desire to "see the issue" (5.3.128).

In Sicily, all subscribe to the same story. When Hermione responds to Leontes in the trial by claiming that he "speak[s] a language that [she] understands not" (3.2.80), she isn't exactly saying what she means. She knows perfectly well what he's driving at because she's as good at playing Leontes's game as he is, just as Desdemona revels in Petrarchan practices in the preplay wooing sequence recalled in Act 3 of *Othello*. Teasing Polixenes with "a lady's Verily's / As potent as a lord's" (1.2.50–51), she combines women's speech with male power. Her "verily," as honesty, is echoed in her insistence that Leontes was the superior boy: the "verier wag" (1.2.66), the forerunner of the more potent man now. The mere repetition of the Latinate "verily" and "verier" presupposes that truth is connected to masculine competition. Understanding that speech itself is contentious, Hermione emerges as Leontes's advocate and reinforces the obligation that, as guest and hence inferior, Polixenes owes in the negotiations attendant to hospitality.[16] David Schalkwyk writes, "The word 'verily' is doubly not her own but instead a property which patriarchy claims for itself."[17] Still later, when Leontes maintains that she twice spoke well, he quotes her agreement to marry him—"I am yours forever" (1.2.104)—praising her willingness to be in fact what she was in his Petrarchan pursuit: a creature governed by his language.[18] Her open hand and mouth represent the easily accessible vulva—about which Leontes later complains when he declares there is "no barricado for a belly" (1.2.204). As formerly resistant daughter of the emperor of Russia, the Hermione of Leontes's memory offers her whole being to Leontes.

The "three crabbed months" (1.2.103), when Hermione's linguistic and spatial directions were allegedly contrary to those of Leontes, ended the instant that, in the "clap[ping]" (1.2.104) of her physical turnaround, she accepted his verbal and physical dominion. Leontes's obsession over palm "paddling" (1.2.115) and its double meaning of yielding (with its reminiscence of Hermione's clap) and concealing (with its suggestion that the joined hands have something hidden in between) reflects his fear that the very openness that made Hermione his may subsequently have left her available to everybody. When she "clap[s]" herself to Leontes's love, she also signs herself over to him, naming herself ("clepe" in the now obsolete sense) according to his terms and terminology.[19] As Perdita becomes Hermione's "mine own" (5.3.123) at the end of the play, so, years before the precipitating crisis, Hermione acquiesces, in his memory, to Leontes's linguistic dominance. She promised to be "[his] love" (1.2.104), pronouncing her possession by Leontes as she later will project her relationship to Perdita: they are tied together by a belief that connects genealogy and sexuality to the patriarchal manifest destiny of the foundling plot and to Petrarchan lyric mimesis. The "father's court" (5.3.125) and courting practices are the only recognizable origin.

Hermione's scene with Mamillius and her ladies indicates that, in Leontes's orbit, everyone speaks the same sexually charged language and that women act out the same dirty dreams as men. The court ladies' bid for Mamillius to be their "play-fellow" (2.1.3) is answered in terms of Petrarchan teasing (2.1.6–11), the extravagance of praise over a mistress's eyebrow that assigns the woman's body no other purpose but to house phallic desire. Mamillius's fascination with the artifice of the eyebrow inevitably evokes the hairline of the pudendum: one marks access to a woman's reflective function, the other to her sexual function. The upper parts mirror men, while the lower parts receive them. Eye and vulva are equally passive, existing only as empty vessels for men to penetrate. The brows topping the visible eye above evoke the same invitation as the unseen and concealed hollow below. All the activities circumscribed by Hermione's "not . . . any but us" (1.2.85) are summarized by Hermione's rounded belly (2.1.16), the half-moon of the ladies' painted faces reflecting backward to Polixenes's reference to the watery star (1.2.1), and completed by the quickened approach of the full term of Hermione's pregnancy. Mamillius's words about penning and makeup are part of his Petrarchan refusal to be play-fellow to the court ladies; his put-down of "wanton[ing]" (2.1.17) casts him simultaneously as pursued other for their body play and determining author with his word play. While still unbreached physically, he declares himself licensed verbally their "better" (2.1.6). Susan Snyder suggests that this scene in which Mamillius "initiates the conversational gambits . . . [is one where] he is fully at home," largely because it is a "female enclave."[20] When Leontes interrupts, "removing him from motherly care, [he] takes away his palpable physical reality" ("Mamillius," 1). But the language spoken in that enclave replicates the values of the male court. Anxious, like Hermione, to make his speaking powers "verier," Mamillius turns play-fellowing into a test of hierarchical superiority. The court idea of "wantoning" is a game of self-aggrandizement propelled by linguistic dexterity. When Mamillius says "I love you better" (2.1.6), he implies that the physical potency aroused by his poetic sophistication gives him the authority to top the court ladies. Now that he has been kissed "hard" (2.1.5), he is their superior, both in mouthing their libidinous thoughts and in mounting their nubile bodies. The "unbreached" Mamillius plays the same linguistic games as his mother.

If the court women are, like Mamillius, played by boy actors, then everyone is always open to the same kind of "wantoning." When Mamillius complains (with a swagger) that Hermione's maids "kiss [him] hard" (2.1.5), he aligns his erect member with their open mouths. As in Leontes's chambers, Hermione's realm offers no barricades. Child play in Sicily may be playing with children, may in fact be a kind of "wantonness" that reduces children to playthings—and their things to the subject of hand play as well as mouth play: the claptrap that linked hand to mouth in Hermione's initial assent to marriage. Stanley Cavell maintains that, for Leontes at least, the tableau of Hermione and Mamillius's whispering suggests "mutually seductive gestures,"[21] a repetition of her posture with Polixenes. Such gestures heighten our sense of sexual secrets traded everywhere in Sicily as, shuttled from the initially official rooms, through the supposedly private women's chambers, and then back to the open court, we peel open a series of concentric circles where each interior matches each exterior. Leontes's dreams, which should contrast with the public arena, merely confirm what he mourns—the lack of boundaries.[22]

When, in the trial, Hermione proclaims "the flatness of [her] misery" (3.2.122), she protests its banality and defines her defenselessness in precisely the terms Leontes uses: there are no differences. All spaces in Sicily are level. Adhering to the same epistemological scheme, Hermione behaves like Leontes and, in her sixteen-year absence, retreats to the "crabbed" (1.2.103) resistance of her premarriage backward-walking position, a lapse that actually reinforces the power of male linguistic prowess. Abetted by Paulina during the period of Hermione's presumed death, Leontes returns her to the Petrarchan altar. In hallowed memory, as in Leontes's before-marriage idealized anticipation, Hermione is "a perfect woman" (5.1.15), a "sainted spirit" (5.1.57). When the court gradually fills the "wide gap" (5.3.154) through the future tale telling Leontes commands at the end, the space between Hermione's exalted state as unreachable Petrarchan object will have disappeared and she will be "level," both on the same plane as him and speaking the same language once again.

Those who read her last speech in terms of Hermione's victory view the connection between Perdita and Hermione as what Janet Adelman calls a "process [of] restoring the mother-daughter bond central to the story of Proserpina and Ceres" and an acknowledgment of "a female continuity and generativity outside the sphere of male desire."[23] But I think that Hermione at the end eliminates the space of female narrativity so central to the Ovidian Ceres in favor of the script that, in the play's last line, Leontes claims will fill the "gap" and close the temporarily "dis-severed" circle.[24] In Golding's 1567 translation of Ovid's *Metamorphoses*, the demarcations remain. When Dis steals Proserpine, he tears "an open gap" (5.127)[25] between the earth and underworld to express his fury at Cyane for trying to stop him.

In Ovid, that "gap" is finally not wholly reparable. Dividing lines (heaven and hell, gods and men, and men and women) are seen as both clearly drawn and negotiable. While Leontes proposes that the "severed" (5.3.153) parts can be joined once everyone learns what happened during the interim, in Ovid the spatial barriers that separate Proserpine from her mother spread wide enough so that she passes from kingdom to kingdom. And while Paulina makes it possible for Hermione to wait—passively—until she can see the "issue" promised by Apollo, Ovid's story contains a proactive feminine community, one that helps Ceres in her quest to find Proserpine. Finally, while Paulina is complicit in separating the king and queen, her ultimate aim, as she keeps reminding Leontes, is to keep alive the memory of Hermione's "unparalleled"—Petrarchan, idealized—former status. In the end, Paulina herself succumbs to the patriarchal necessity of comedy and marries Camillo, the witty slave who "write[s] ... down" (4.4.548) exactly the script that will allow him to reconcile the kings and "re-view Sicilia" (4.4.649). Everyone in Shakespeare's Sicily wants to end at the beginning, the physical space that seems to preserve the temporal moment of the plot's initiation.

Contrastingly, the Ovidian story emphasizes noncompliance to patriarchal imperatives. The female community actively intervenes in the rescue of Proserpine just as, in Desdemona's song, Barbary's plight is shared by all the women who echo her story. Cyane's feminine waters respond to Ceres's misery and Arethusa's sympathetic rhetoric reflects her sorrow, both evoking a sense of female difference and of the difference women make. Consumed by her pity for Proserpine, Cyane melts and, while begging for the restoration of Sicily, Arethusa tells Ceres where Proserpine is. Arethusa's story, told only after Proserpine is at least partially recovered, involves a reversal of order. First, Alphey changes his state to pursue her as a man; then he models himself on her altered situation. That union is both a return to an earlier form and a desire to enter a space redefined as feminine: "of purpose for to joyne with me and have my companie" (5.784). In *The Winter's Tale*, female power is countermanded when the male community takes over. In Ovid, male priorities sometimes dissolve in connection to the Ceres myth, as when

Alphey chooses to join the woman he earlier tried to dominate. Ceres herself pursues Jove, though she admits she has lost "the crowne and comfort of [her] life" (3.2.94)—Jove's regard—as Hermione lost Leontes's love. But she acts and speaks for her daughter, bringing suit, with all the pressure of her words, and pursuing the father with what she regards as, and he later admits is, his responsibility for the child.

When Ceres begs Jove to mediate, she first speaks of the difference between mother and father, pleading with him to get involved in her daughter's recovery despite the fact that she bore her in a body that no longer interests him:

> Hir mother stoode as starke as stone, when she these newes did heare.
> And long she was like one that in another worlde had beene.
> But when hir great amazednesse by greatnesse of hir teene
> Was put aside, she gettes hir to hir Chariot by and by
> And up to heaven in all post haste immediately doth stie.
> And there beslowbred all hir face: hir haire about hir eares,
> To royall Jove in way of plaint this spightfull tale she beares:
> As well for thy bloud as for mine a suter unto thee
> I hither come. If no regard may of the mother bee
> Yet let the childe hir father move, and have not lesser care
> Of hir (I pray) bicause that I hir in my bodie bare.
> Behold our daughter whome I sought so long is found at last:
> If finding you it terme, when of recoverie meanes is past.
> Or if you finding do it call to have a knowledge where
> She is become. Hir ravishment we might consent to beare,
> So restitution might be made. And though there were to me
> No interest in hir at all, yet foreasmuche as she
> Is yours, it is unmeete she be bestowed upon a theefe. (5.632–49)

Jove's answer, that Proserpine is a "collup of mine own flesh cut as well out of thine" (5. 652), acknowledges a responsibility shared with Ceres. Unlike Leontes, who regards Mamillius as exclusively his spawn, Jove presumes that the child has two parents. Though he thinks his brother Pluto is a fine "sonne in law" (5.654), he defers to Ceres's wishes, in part because she is the mother of his child.

When she learns what happened to Proserpine, Ceres (like Hermione) turns "as starke as stone" (5. 632), but this extreme of rigidity becomes an exemplar of a determined resistance. Because her grief forces her to "put aside" her "great amazednesse," she overcomes her feelings of inadequacy. Totally indifferent to her sexuality, she becomes a suitor, imploring Jove, face besmeared with tears and hair askew, to preserve the familial sequence. That the horizontal axis of conjugal relations coincides with the vertical axis of generational continuity is assured when, after her return to her mother, Proserpine's demeanor in the underworld changes:

And now the Goddesse Proserpine indifferently doth reigne
Above and underneath the Earth, and so doth she remaine
One halfe yeare with hir mother and the resdue with hir Feere.
Immediately she altred is as well in outwarde cheere
As inwarde minde. For where hir looke might late before appeere
Sad even to Dis, hir countnance now is full of mirth and grace
Even like as Phebus having put the watrie cloudes to chace,
Doth shew himself a Conqueror with bright and shining face. (5.702–8)

Proserpine seems equally comfortable in both worlds. The happiness of her "outward cheere" reflects her inward peace, transforming her former victimization into her latter victory. She emerges as the Apollonian "Conqueror" of her earlier sadness, her "bright and shining face" lighting up the underworld. Once she is found, she "immediately altred is," as if the recovery of her mother allows her fully to enjoy the discovery of self sexuality reveals to her.

BETTERING WHAT IS DONE

In *The Winter's Tale*, such an awakening is not contingent on return. Florizel and Perdita's Petrarchan deformations preempt the formulaic recovery of the foundling plot. When we first see them, the wives of Polixenes and the shepherd are dead, the Irigarayan vertical axis of generational protection already compromised. But, governed by a love that opposes intergenerational hierarchies as well as dynastic platitudes, Florizel introduces a different concept of gender relations, declaring Perdita to be the source of his creativity as he defines his selfhood in terms that deny his biological heritage; subsequently, he fosters her and then (with yet another recircling, in lines 4.4.130–34) she generates him yet again. This volleying back and forth continues throughout the long pastoral scene as the lovers in turn supply for each other the missing familial link. Florizel gives to Perdita what Proserpine understood only *after* her mother intervened, demonstrating that it is possible to tilt the axis in order to love in several different directions at once.

Reversing the traditional Petrarchan pattern, where the man creates the woman—as Pygmalion did—out of his own desire for self, Florizel prioritizes the morphological and, with that, opens a new discursive practice. The linguistic evolution (most fully realized in the "bettering" speech of 4.4.135–46) facilitates a generational reordering when, rejecting his biological heritage and declaring openly what he had already confided privately to Perdita, Florizel directs his father to exile him from throne and country. The violence of his defiance resonates with the new language he has come to speak in the course of the scene. If Hamlet vows to "wipe away [from the table of his memory] all trivial fond records" (*Hamlet*, 1.5.98–100) of love and learning in order to "remember" his familial heritage, Florizel does the opposite. Naming his "affection" his origin, he demands that his father "from my succession wipe me" (4.4.168–69).

The renunciation is already in progress when Perdita responds to Florizel's Ovidian comparisons, complaining that his "resolution cannot hold" (4.4.36) in the face of what she rightly assumes is royal authority. Like "issue," the word "resolution" has a tripartite meaning: the climax of a story, the strength of conviction, and its opposite—the spreading thin of component parts. Florizel happily speaks of the gods lowering themselves for love, citing metamorphoses that were at best temporary. Perdita answers that, for her, change may mean something irrevocable:

> O, but sir,
> Your resolution cannot hold when 'tis
> Opposed, as it must be, by th' power of the King.
> One of these two must be necessities,
> Which then will speak that you must change this purpose,
> Or I my life. (4.4.34–39)

Perdita insists that either Florizel must forgo his "resolution"—as purpose—or she must sacrifice her life. Abandoning his earlier lightheartedness and taking her anxiety seriously now, Florizel gives a two-part answer: the first, genealogical; the second ontological. With the first, he eliminates his own past; with the second, he suggests a future that eradicates the present of Perdita's fears. Again, Irigaray provides terms that help analyze the situation. Florizel "paint[s]" . . . or "*spatialize[s] perception* to make time *simultaneous* . . . to build bridges, establish perspectives between present-past-future."[26] While Florizel uses time in these spatial terms and while the "bridges" he builds replace the interior landscape of Perdita's fear with the exterior vista of concrete visual signs, his achievement of the crucial simultaneity is different from Irigaray's sense of futurity. Reaching backward to tap a neglected origin that might make for an alternative destiny, Irigaray's "painting" changes the ordinary sequence of chronology (past-present-future) by naming a past that she redefines as the middle term and the critical switch-point. But Florizel "paints" in a slightly different way, turning the present into a past that determines the future at the very moment it comes into being. His is a process of conversion as he formulates an altogether different dispensation out of the ground he newly establishes. Florizel's "transformations" are unlike those of the mythical gods he cites since, in declaring that "[his] desires / Run not before [his] honour" (4.4.33–34), he grounds his "petition" in Perdita's chastity.

In the first answer, Florizel forfeits his origin in order to position himself in spatial and temporal proximity to Perdita, canceling his relation to his father and rendering his future wholly otherwise:

> Thou dearest Perdita,
> With these forced thoughts, I prithee, darken not
> The mirth o' th' feast. Or I'll be thine, my fair,
> Or not my father's. For I cannot be
> Mine own, nor anything to any, if
> I be not thine. To this I am most constant,
> Though destiny say no. (4.4.40–46)

Perdita's phrasing involves an "either-or" resulting in her death; Florizel's "or . . . or" (4.4.42–43) sets a reversal into motion, one that gives Perdita the authority of coming first. In this case, "or" means "earlier," as Florizel unequivocally claims that his beginning in Perdita now exists retroactively prior to his relationship to his father. In that respect, he is looking for a new identity, one that begins concurrently with his speaking to her. When he pronounces Perdita's primacy, Florizel turns the present into a stepping-stone toward a future event and thereby alters what Perdita believes is an unchangeable destiny. While, in response to his absolute self, Othello demands an unchangeable Desdemona, Florizel assumes that his relationship with Perdita initiates a new beginning, an origin that is grounded in the fluid connection he establishes with her and that results in a future that grows with expansive love.

Next, Florizel addresses Perdita's terror that his "resolution" would result in her death. Swearing she would "swoon / to show myself a glass" (4.4.14–15), she sounds very like the Proserpine Roberto Calasso identifies through the connection between "Kore" and Narcissus:

> When the earth split open and Hades's chariot appeared, drawn by four horses abreast, Kore was looking at a narcissus. She was looking at the act of looking. She was about to pick it. And, at that very moment, she was herself plucked away by the invisible toward the invisible. Kore doesn't just mean "girl," but "pupil" too. And the pupil, as Socrates says to Alcibiades, "is the finest part of the eye," not just because it is "the part which sees" but because it is the place where another person looking will find "the image of himself looking." And if, as Socrates claims, the Delphic maxim: "Know thyself" can be understood only if translated as "Look at thyself," then the pupil becomes the sole means of self-knowledge. . . . What sets [the narcissus] apart from the violets, the crocuses, and the hyacinths that made the meadow near Henna so colorful? Narcissus is also the name of a young man who lost himself looking at himself. Kore, the pupil, was thus on a threshold. She was on the brink of meeting a gaze in which she would have seen herself. She was stretching out her hand to pluck that gaze. But Hades burst upon the scene. And Kore was plucked away by Hades. For a moment, Kore's eye had to turn away from the narcissus and meet Hades's eye. The pupil of the Pupil was met by another pupil, in which it saw itself. And that pupil belonged to the world of the invisible.[27]

Perdita's hypothetical "showing" in the "glass" (4.4.14)—its arm gesture an upward equivalent of the stretching downward of Kore's hand in the Calasso passage—similarly anticipates Narcissus's loss of being. Her fear of the reflective image illustrates what she already claims to know: like Narcissus, she will lose herself looking at herself. In that "looking," she risks mirroring Florizel and so becoming, as Proserpine did for Pluto, his possession.

But Florizel's overarching insistence in the second phase of his argument ("be merry," 4.4.46) is followed by two directions that delineate how she might find herself again: "strangle thoughts" (4.4.47) and "lift up" (4.4.49). If, in Calasso's description, Hades's violence forces Proserpine to "meet" herself in his eye down below, Florizel's eye contact reverses the directional order as he raises Perdita to his level, urging her to "lift up [her] countenance" (4.4.49) so that her inward expectations will match their earthly priorities:

> Be merry, gentle,
> Strangle such thoughts as these with anything
> That you behold the while. Your guests are coming.
> Lift up your countenance as it were the day
> Of celebration of that nuptial which
> We two have sworn shall come. (4.4.46–51)

"Spatializing" Perdita's perception, he uses an exterior expanse to block an internal fear and a temporal threshold to launch a forward-flowing chronology; the newly established past of their present postulates the Irigarayan "bridge" to their future. This remarkable redeployment unravels the circle of the courtly mind-set and directs Perdita's sight lines toward a wholly other vision. When he urges her to "strangle such thoughts," Florizel frees her from the subjugation of her own fears and refers to the present moment as a point of origination that wipes out Perdita's suspicions of transformation. Dubbed vague "suches," her indeterminate thoughts parallel his undefined "the while." But the concreteness of his "anything" in the solid world outside replaces the now whittled-to-abstraction nameless demons in her head. Thus, when Perdita faces Florizel to see herself in him, he has already directed her gaze to something that is already in motion, an "anything" that becomes the future "everything" of the world they will together build. Urging her to abandon what she cannot visually identify, he insists on the concrete vista that she sees in—and beyond—him. Calasso's Dis introduces Proserpine to the "world of the invisible" as she finds her repressed self in his eye. Enabling Perdita to recognize her desire in him, Florizel contrastingly insists on the palpable event.

Compressing the present and the future into the same psychological moment, Florizel's double use of "com[e]" (4.4.47, 51) produces the crucial Irigarayan simultaneity. As part of the "spatialization of perception," he synchronizes what Perdita sees and what she might then expect. The about-to-arrive guests form the manifest landscape bordering him and the nuptials emerge (in the second coming) as the soon-to-be-seen next event in the scenario he hypothesizes. Florizel moves through the approaching spectacle in real time (with the arriving guests) toward virtual spaces in projected time (with the anticipated nuptials). Replacing Perdita's "strangled" thoughts, the future ceremonies he plants in her mind are coterminous with the now-near guests at the festival. Through the liminal arena of his physical positioning and the temporal agenda of their already sworn allegiance, Florizel unwinds the confining noose of culturally defined thinking that so frightened Perdita. Unlike the retrogressive "frisking" (1.2.67) of Polixenes's memory, the obsessive enclosures of Hermione's "slipping" (1.2.85), or the competitive circling of Mamillius's "wanton[ing]" (2.1.18) in their contexts, Florizel's "whil[ing]" (4.4.47) here cuts through Perdita's terror, providing an interim of time that anticipates better things to come. In contrast to the courtly "frisking," "slipping," and "wantoning"—movements that go nowhere new—Florizel's "the while" (4.4.47) fosters a break from the self-reflexivity of Perdita's thoughts, a shift that favors a discovery of an alternative life rather than a recovery of a circle that only repeats a preordained expectation. Similarly, in its recognition of Perdita's visual capacity, Florizel's emphasis on what Perdita herself "beholds" contrasts with the male-dominated sight lines of patriarchal thinking.

Mamillius ignores the agency of female sight when—in penning the court ladies' eyebrows (2.1.11)—he reduces the eyes to empty vessels shaped (and held still) by the penetrating powers of his descriptive mastery. Camillo likewise speaks of stagnation when he feasts on Perdita, swallowing her whole: "I should leave grazing, were I of your flock, / And only live by gazing" (4.4.109–10). Leontes revives that same sense of male directional dominion even in the last scene when—dazzled by Hermione—he exclaims, "The fixture of her eye has motion in't / As we are mocked with art" (5.3.66–67). Eliminating Hermione's visual control with a logical contradiction (fixture has motion) that confirms his desire to hold her within the range of his space, Leontes refers back to his own concept of representation and calls art (in the "mocking") a mirror of *his* life even as he reasserts his authority with the prerogative of the royal "we." In the same way that Bassanio saw the portrait Portia's eyes "riding in the balls of mine," Leontes dismisses Hermione's power by reducing it to a simile that figures female sight as a product of what he presumes is the skill of the male artist. In contrast, Florizel lifts Perdita's gaze from the mirror of reflection to vistas of temporal and spatial expansion. In his command, "behold," he points beyond himself and recasts time ("the while") to open up an arena that is preeminently Perdita's and not his: "your guests are coming" (4.4.48).

With her reference to Proserpine in the flower speech (4.4.117–19), Perdita progresses (as Florizel does) beyond the static toward the fullness of growth she offers with the crowns and beds of lilies. For a brief moment, they change places and he reacts as if he were her earlier self, suddenly frightened that, in strewing him "o'er and o'er" (4.4.128), she blankets him with flowers that symbolize both death and royalty and that, with them, she might restore the biological origin and mortal destiny he had previously renounced. Her covering feels smothering and he panics: "What, like a corpse?" (4.4.129). Perdita's answer reveals that she is willing to be for him what he is for her:

> No, like a bank, for love to lie and play on,
> Not like a corpse—or if, not to be buried,
> But quick, and in mine arms. Come, take your flowers:
> Methinks I play as I have seen them do
> In Whitsun pastorals. Sure this robe of mine
> Does change my disposition. (4.4.130–35)

When she insists that the flowers go underneath him, Perdita supplies a soft pillow for sexual exchange as well as the firm ground for her love. Equaling Florizel's two "comings" with her double use of "play," she first places herself on the same level as him. The "bank" props her up so that they might enjoy their bodily awakening from a threshold of mutual arousal. Subsequently, her "play" as performer casts her as the source of Florizel's quickening. Perdita's allusion to the Whitsun feast, with its connection to the Holy Ghost, promises him maternal inspiration from the "bank" of her always replenishing resources. Her "o'er and o'er" (4.4.128) refers both to a psychological constancy that makes it safe for them to go on loving and to a physical enveloping that identifies him as her progeny. If Florizel begins by naming himself the child of Perdita and ends by pairing them as romantic partners, here Perdita moves chiasmically, opening with sexual play and concluding with maternal nurturance.

In her second hypothesis—"or if"—Perdita suggests that her "strew[ing]" allows Florizel to die metaphorically to his earlier self and then to be reborn within the circle of her arms, just as Florizel's "or . . . or" equates his present with Perdita as a renunciation of his biological origin. The acoustic repetition of her "o'er" and "o'er" becomes, with the alternative of her "or if," an equivalent of Florizel's earlier "or . . . or" as, through the inclination of her disposition, she emerges fully what he earlier named her: the origin of his life. Matching her floral with a verbal garland, she retreats from the sexual bank to the maternal ground and parallels Florizel's earlier beginnings with a reordering of her own. When she says, "sure this robe of mine / Does change my disposition" (4.4.133–34), she emphasizes the relationship between her spatial location (as encircler and hence protector of Florizel) and her temporal relocation as source of the self she fashions (within the folds of the robe) for him: her "dis-position" is a "re-position."

Like Proserpine's changed "countenance" (fixed by her return to Ceres), Perdita's changed "disposition" affirms that she "altred is as well in outwarde cheere / As inwarde minde" (5.708). In trading places with Florizel, she becomes Dis to his Proserpine: mother, father, and lover all at once. But if Proserpine needs Ceres, Perdita does without Hermione. No longer merely "pranking" her up, her robe and—with it—her "changed disposition" indicate that she has both inwardly and outwardly raised her "countenance" (4.4.49) to meet Florizel's love for her. That the prince understands this new intention is evident from the forward thrust of his "still betters":

> What you do
> Still betters what is done. When you speak, sweet,
> I'd have you do it ever: when you sing,
> I'd have you buy and sell so, so give alms,
> Pray so; and, for the ord'ring your affairs,
> To sing them too. When you do dance, I wish you
> A wave o' th' sea, that you might ever do
> Nothing but that, move still, still so,
> And own no other function. Each your doing,
> So singular in each particular,
> Crowns what you are doing in the present deeds,
> That all your acts are queens. (4.4.135–46)

At the end of the play, Leontes demands that each "part" fill in the "wide gap of time" so that the court can repair what was "dissever'd" (5.3.154–55) and return to an earlier social ordering. Polixenes generalizes this desire by arguing that art does not add to nature, but simply mends it and thereby builds on an all-inclusive and already prevailing biological system.[28] Instead of such retrograde visions, Florizel insists on a progression launched by Perdita's new disposition. The forward motion of his "still betters" surpasses the royal quest for cultural permanence (in the "stillness" of courtly rigidity) to prompt a continuity that provides a future of subtle permutation: "still" as more and more. Florizel's opening "still" anticipates his double use of the word in the climactic "move still, still so" (4.4.140). His "still betters" heralds an ever-increasing addition, not just "now as formerly" but "from now on"; the present of "what you do" constitutes a new world order. When he later alludes to the "wave o' th' sea," he refers in his wish to an expectation that no return or reiteration will ever be the same. Everything is fluid as Florizel deliberately spells out the minutiae of a differentiation he idealizes. With the tripling of "each . . . singular . . . particular," he maintains a linguistic separation, cataloguing every action, just as he immediately renders the present deed the past of the redetermined future.

Earlier he asked Perdita to "behold" (4.4.47) what was in front of her; here he reverses positions and, watching her, declares that what she does signifies her originality. In describing this speech, both Maurice Hunt and Martine Van Elk emphasize Florizel's praise of Perdita as an encomium that locates her royalty in physical embodiment rather than linguistic dexterity. Hunt writes, "Her deeds become physical words."[29] Citing Hunt, Van Elk argues that Perdita's "words become physical rather than verbal" ("Our Praises," 445). Both regard the speech as evidence (in Van Elk's terms) "of a crucial link between nobility and birth." But when Van Elk argues that Florizel's "praise of endless repetitions of speech, song and dance deprives Perdita's voice of its power to signify," she ignores Florizel's lack of specificity.[30] Combined with his idealization of her, the vagueness of his "so" identifies his self-acknowledged inadequacy even to catalogue, or precisely define, Perdita's language and act. Perdita leads and he follows. Her motions govern both his emotions and his language. Florizel's nostalgia is never for a fixed or a biological past but for an ongoing process defined by the dilatable motion. In his speech about "behold[ing] the while" (4.4.48), Florizel decentered the present to make it the past of the future, offering himself as a shield from the predetermination Perdita feared. He here (4.4.35–46) presses forward yet again in his wishes when, in calling Perdita a "wave o' th' sea," he evokes a constantly changing cycle. In this speech, the present immediately creates its own past, one that becomes the origin of the next act, the form-giving source of continuity. "Still" in this context carries with it the expectation of a return that is secure in its accessibility and yet—like the wave—mutable in its shifting boundaries. If the wave always moves, it frees him from the engulfment that frightened him with the lilies, even as it affords (in Irigaray's words) permeability and reproduction: "It speaks 'fluid' . . . is continuous, compressible, dilatable, viscous, conductible, diffusible . . . [I]t exert[s] pressure through the walls of a solid. . . . [I]t is already diffuse 'in itself,' which disconcerts any attempt at static identification."[31] Like the permeating tears in *Fugitive Pieces* and *Othello*, Florizel's Irigarayan waves soften and remake the world. Portraying openness and change as the determining factors and resisting any kind of "static identification," the diffusion Florizel praises (in 4.4.35–46) liberates both of them from the linguistic and genealogical confinement that governs the world of their parents.

The constancy in the prospect of "ever" that evolves into the eternity of "always" and the detail in the precision of "so" that indicates the exactitude of temporal locality seem at first like a monumentalizing of the present—the static praise of the Petrarchan eternalizing conceit. But the pairing is qualitatively different; it renders the present ("what you do") an improvement over the past ("what is done"). While Petrarchan praise freezes a single instance of perfection, Florizel already anticipates the natural passing of the moment into the future, including change in his prophecy. Moreover, rather than following the example of the Petrarchan poet who tries to "realize himself in relation to a dynamic other, constructed and energized by the self's own language,"[32] Florizel neither invents Perdita's body nor speaks in her person. He merely takes note of a sequence of actions that bears witness to her physical and speech acts. She leads and he follows. In fact, his catalogue insists on his secondary role as recorder; the word "so" testifies to the necessary precision of her actions and the effacement of his role as scribe.[33] Exacting and vague, his "so" is dependent on the uniqueness of *her* actions, his transcription returning to the verbal and behavioral model she sets. Valueless on its own, his "so" is contingent exclusively on criteria determined by her. As Seamus Heaney writes about using the tiny word to begin his translation of *Beowulf,* "The idiom 'so' operates as an expression which obliterates all previous discourse and narrative and at the same time functions as an exclamation calling for immediate attention."[34] Similarly, Florizel's "so" signals a rejection of the static determinations of courtly language and a new linguistic turn. But while Heaney's "so" annihilates the past, Florizel's "so"—despite its terminological innovations—also includes a satisfaction that renders "what you do" a present that acts as a launching ground for a process of continual regeneration.

There are four sets of pairings in the speech that anchor it in relation to the pivotal "so." The first is in relationship to the "ever" in the catalogue that begins with "speak" and ends with "sing." In that sequence, each "so" represents a multiplication, moving upward from speaking and then forward to the musicality of singing, at once converting the "dailiness" of Perdita's life into a sacramental ritual, and mixing the piety of Perdita's praying with the domesticity of "ord'ring your affairs." The differentiated auditory volumes suggest an increased visual size: all time and space are filled by an infinitely expanding sequence with Perdita at center stage. While Othello insists that Desdemona remain always "his fair warrior" and while he denies succession in his "absolute content" (2.1.87), Florizel includes an expectation of a change that exponentially increases. By anticipating the continual "crowning" of her acts, he also indicates an understanding that act rather than birth determine status and that mood or circumstance, rather than rigidity or inflexibility, will govern his relationship to her. Moreover, in the sequence from speaking to dancing, he connects her verbal grace to her corporeal adroitness. In the royalty of her queenly acts, she is the inventor of a whole new way of being, one that intertwines discourse and act. With the self-canceling oxymoron, "move still," he temporarily annuls the praise only to extend it with the "still so." Doubling "still" (but prefacing it with "move"), he emphasizes both the motion and constancy of her repetitions, as the waves keep returning to the shore of a self that is open to receiving him. Because the word "move" almost seems literally to push the word "still," he suggests a retreat that allows Perdita to recover her sense of self and prepares her for the return that replenishes him. In that sense, rather than signifying immobility, the second phrase, "still so," collapses and cancels the interior double "still." The governing idea is "move . . . so" and the expectation emerges as an always forward momentum that aligns itself with the pattern initiated by Perdita. The language is hers in the "so" Florizel cannot quite transcribe, just as the propulsion is hers in the "move" he cannot quite contain.

Moreover, in liquefying, rather than solidifying, her capacity, he alludes not only to the child she might produce in the mythological connection between the sea and the female womb as source of generativity, but also to the indeterminacy of her recurrent presence. His "so" is thus not only inadequate to the moment but also unable to prescribe her future motility. The statue scene of Act 5 presents a moving picture in a previously orchestrated design. This speech shatters the frame by pointing to Florizel's inability to delineate Perdita's uniqueness ("so singular") and Perdita's perfectly executed acts ("each particular"). She is exact. He is vague. Thus, in the third sense of "so," Florizel produces yet another oxymoron. The "so singular" indicates an enormous and seemingly immeasurable originality immediately undercut by the multiplying numbers of "each particular." The expansion-contraction parallels the motion of the sea where departure and return expose, and then cover over, the elemental core.

Finally, when he joins with Perdita in the dance, he uses the fourth "so" as a simile, indicating that their union involves a joint communion, a future design that transcends the "particular" of each physical action and yet remains—like the turtle doves—"constant" in its psychological impact, promising a continuum that includes sexual difference: the singularity of "each particular." With this "so," Florizel answers Perdita's reprimand that his "praises are too large" by naturalizing the extravagance of his previous elaboration: "so turtles pair / That never mean to part" (4.4.153–54). The exemplum marks the narrative climax of his heightened feelings in the ritual of the dance invitation and offers verifiable evidence of his glorification in the yearly returns of the pairing birds. With the mediation of "mean" as a signifier that in itself calls attention to the process of signifying, he also turns the comparison into an intention that ensures the reality of its own suppositions. Based on the fluidity and growth assumed temporarily in Shylock's initial reconception of breeding and Desdemona's belated but unavailing remembrance of a watery "murmuring," Florizel successfully bypasses the cutting edge of Petrarchan creativity to produce an alternative source—a liquid permeability—for the lyric.

The whole phrase simplifies his project in the redundancy of defining turtle doves, known for their lifelong mating habits, with a description that repeats what their name implicitly identifies. But the auditory play produced by "mean to part"—and its sounding knell of impending separation—is preempted by the "never," just as the repetition of "particular" in "part" and the "ever" in "never" echo the opening and his "have [her] do it ever" (4.4.137). Florizel's positives shift the balance, creating a progression that includes both change and return. Feeding her actions into his metaphor, he replaces a "so-so" commonplace about love with an already lived fact, and thereby returns—like the faithful turtles—to his beginning "ever so." What is feared (the parting at the end of the line) is offset by the pairing at the opening. The paring down of partition is avoided in the pairing together of faithfulness, the image alluding again to the limitless capacity of the sea.[35] Perdita's answer, "I'll swear for 'em" (4.4.155), confirms the practicality of the metaphor: "Yes, that's what turtle doves do." In her assent, she also promises, "I yield to you as my words will be corroborated by my deeds." Earlier her deeds gave birth to his words; here her words initiate his deeds in the dance. Premised on a mutual re-creation of subjectivity, the transformation of Petrarchan protocols in the poetic dialogue between Perdita and Florizel changes the dynamic of the foundling plot as well.

The assurance of Florizel's commitment is evidenced in the command that links visual dominion to linguistic certainty: "Mark our contract" (4.4.404). Like Shylock's command to Antonio—"mark what Jacob did"— Florizel demands that his father take note of his redefinition of all prescribed linguistic structures. Calling attention to their betrothal as bodily union and as sworn covenant, his "contraction" unites them in a partnership whose legitimacy is documented by their loyalty. Directed at Perdita, his question— "Why look you so upon me?" (4.4.450)—suggests that he will not budge from the love that guarantees his resolution: "What I was, I am" (4.4.452). The last phrase picks up where he left off before Polixenes's unveiling and determines the past of his beginning with Perdita as the present that shapes their future. If Perdita's actions signify what he wishes to retain in his "ever so," here, in alleviating Perdita's doubts with yet another "so," he reiterates what he announced in "marking" his beginning with her: they are bound to each other.

When he turns to Perdita and asks her once again to "lift up thy looks" (4.4.480), he echoes his earlier request to "lift up [her] countenance" (4.4.49) in order to match her faith to his faithfulness. But this time he more specifically ties her facial expression ("looks") to the act of "beholding" as his vow to become a child of love matches her earlier reflection of him:

> Lift up thy looks:
> From my succession wipe me, father! I
> Am heir to my affection. (4.4.467–69)

Referring to his now absent father, he annuls the old vertical line of his regal genealogy and pronounces himself the child of Perdita. In hypothetically addressing his biological parent, he replaces the genetics of his physical past with the psychology of his future "becoming." But in terms of the foundling plot, he actually affirms the supremacy of the artificial, using "affection," an influence he created, to replace his dynastic "succession" as the presumed source of his being. If, earlier, Leontes denounced "affection" (1.2.138) because feeling decenters his world, here Florizel declares himself the child of love. In his intransigence, he defies the unified story signified by the harmony and resolution—the all-inclusiveness—of Polixenes's "art itself is nature" (4.4.97), a philosophy that governs Camillo's allegory of the crutch as well as Leontes's and Hermione's cancellation of Perdita's adoptive parents. Declaring a "succession" that erases nature, Florizel explodes everything connected with the old genealogies: "Let nature crush the sides o' th' earth together / And mar the seeds within!" (4.4.479–80). In this speech, Florizel plays Brabanzio to his father, inverting the elder Venetian's rejection of Desdemona—"I had rather to adopt a child than get it" (*Othello*, 1.3.189)—by naming Perdita his parent and echoing Lear's condemnation of Goneril and Regan, "crack nature's moulds all germens spill at once" (*King Lear*, 3.2.8). Opting for the pattern Perdita already carved out and the enveloping family they have—in the art of their love—invented as their spatial and temporal future, he is "put to sea / with her whom here [he] cannot hold on shore" (4.4.487–88).

Since Florizel already has—and "most opportune to [their] need" (4.4.489)—a boat at the ready, he literally means that he plans to escape Bohemia with Perdita, but psychologically he pledges that, as Ceres underwent long wanderings for Proserpine, he is willing to share her loss and join her in abandonment because he cannot keep Perdita "in being"—hold to his promise to preserve her—on shore. In that sense his vow to let "nature mar the seeds within" carries with it Ceres's punishment of withholding the harvest. If he cannot have a child with Perdita, then the royal line of Bohemia—like that of Sicily—will remain barren, bereft of a future sovereign. When he declares himself "heir to my affection," he disregards the old idea of the family and identifies Perdita as the woman who gives birth to a man no longer held thrall to biological "succession."

For Mamillius, "bettering" (2.1.7) involves mastering Petrarchan poetics within the closed circle of the courtly linguistic domain; for Leontes, it entails the "better purpose" (1.2.88) of Hermione's surrender to his Petrarchan persuasion; and, for Polixenes, it prods a return to an originative and compelling order ("nature is made better by no mean / But nature makes that mean," 4.4.89–90). Used as a verb rather than an adverb or adjective, Florizel's "bettering" (4.4.136) moves in a totally other direction. It does not suggest the competitiveness of Polixenes's "mending" (4.4.96) as means, Mamillius's "love" (2.1.6) as potency, or Leontes's "purpose" (1.2.88) as reflection of an already-existing standard. Instead, it postulates a poetic connected to morphology, avoiding what will in Act 5 become the marble distillations of Pygmalion's statues, and evolving a "stillness" that projects forward to encompass change within its promise of constancy. For the self-satisfied closed gap Leontes envisions in Act 5, Florizel's Act 4 openness augurs a fundamental rupture from the returns everyone seems to be celebrating in the last scene.[36]

Does Florizel's silence in the last scene[37] similarly represent Shakespeare's wish "to tamper with the irrevocability of closure"[38] and to find an alternative to the dynastic mandates of the foundling formula? Such a reading acknowledges that the sexual and generational axes can be tilted otherwise and that one story—no matter how ingrained—cannot forever sustain a monopoly on our interpretive theories. Letting go of fixed cultural models allows us to see that, in the remarkable fourth act of *The Winter's Tale*, Shakespeare "betters" the foundling plot, challenging the primacy of inherited, essentially patriarchal, bloodlines. With the alternative promise, embodied by Perdita and Florizel, of an Irigarayan "biunivocal" and "reciprocal" engendering, he changes the formula that structures the play even as he regenders the "old tales" that script us. With the "o'er and o'er" (4.4.128) of her nurturing, Perdita promises a proactive continuity of protection just as— with his earlier "or . . . or" (4.4.43, 44)—Florizel pledges a retroactive love based on the transformational premise and mutual security of their becoming, *anew and again*. And with the fluidity of their lyric exchanges, Florizel and Perdita also cancel the Petrarchan distillations of Othello's absolute possessiveness and Bassanio's fear of Portia's linguistic origination to redefine the gender hierarchies of poetic realization even as, declaring their freedom from biological inheritance, they reject the essentialist mandates of the foundling plot. In Act 5, Shakespeare returns to all the old values—the Petrarchan reflections of Leontes's "new-woo[ing]" and the biological imperatives of Hermione's "mine own"—that steadfastly reiterate the traditional formulae, with the return to Sicily representing a parallel to the Belmont triumph in *The Merchant of Venice*. In the innovative fourth act of *The Winter's Tale*, Shakespeare projects forward, as Phillips, Jensen, Michaels, and Sebald read backward, to suggest an openness that might make a different cultural model possible.

NOTES

1. *An Ethics of Sexual Difference*, translated by Carolyn Burke and Gillian C. Gill (Ithaca, NY: Cornell University Press, 1993), 18.
2. *Between East and West: From Singularity to Community*, translated by Stephen Pluháček (New York: Columbia University Press, 2002), 111.
3. "*The Winter's Tale*: The Triumph of Speech," *The Winter's Tale: Critical Essays*, edited by Maurice Hunt (New York: Garland, 1995), 255.

4. See Janet Adelman's account of the problem of the maternal body in *Suffocating Mothers: Fantasies of Maternal Origin in Shakespeare's Plays* (New York/London: Routledge, 1992), particularly her thesis that "Leontes's psychosis illustrates in its purest form the trauma of tragic masculinity at the point of origin. Hermione's pregnant body in effect returns him to this point of origin" (226).

5. A spurt of recent criticism features the importance of stories, particularly with reference to the gendering of tales as the province of women. Writing of Mamillius's interrupted whispering, Marion Wells argues that "the tale of winter, according to Mamillius's playful introductory remarks, concerns churchyards, sprites and goblins; it is, in other words, a tale about fear and death, safely contained within the intimate safety of the mother-child dyad in which he tells his tale. With Leontes's violent irruption into this space, fear and death become real presences." Refer to "Mistress Taleporter and the Triumph of Time: Slander and Old Wives' Tales in *The Winter's Tale*," *Shakespeare Survey* 58 (2005): 253. Wells concludes that "only at the end, can the mutual exchange of 'tales'—between mother and daughter— . . . perhaps repair the earlier tale . . . [that] transformed its listeners into actors in its 'sad tale of winter'" (259). Similarly, Mary Ellen Lamb emphasizes the womanliness of the tales in *The Winter's Tale*: "What's found is not only Perdita, not only Hermione, not only the Mother but the bond with women inseparable from the winter's tale of childhood." See "Engendering the Narrative Act: Old Wives' Tales in *The Winter's Tale*, *Macbeth* and *The Tempest*," *Criticism* 60, 4 (1998): 536.

Catherine Belsey takes the fairy tale even further to conclude that Hermione's "resurrection can be seen as part of the generic undecidability of fairy tales. . . . Indeed, the distance between imagination and truth can invest old wives' tales with a unique kind of sadness for their hearers." For Belsey, Hermione is no different from Sleeping Beauty. "The Exiled Princess in a Sad Tale for Winter," *In the Footsteps of William Shakespeare*, edited by Christa Jansohn (Münster, Germany: LIT, 2005), 175. Emphasizing the feminine aspect of tales, these interpretations treat Hermione's story as the main one. Within such a context, it is Hermione, not Perdita, who holds the key to recognition. But I argue that the foundling plot is principally patriarchal (especially in *The Winter's Tale*, where it is Leontes's dynasty that is restored); the "issue" is his.

6. Maintaining that, in the four last plays, Shakespeare presents "alternative images of foster parents as actively benevolent," Marianne Novy suggests, as do I, that Shakespeare alters the conventions of the traditional plot. *Reading Adoption, Family and Difference in Fiction and Drama* (Ann Arbor: University of Michigan Press, 2005), 59.

7. Maurice Hunt ("'Bearing Hence': Shakespeare's *The Winter's Tale*," *Studies in English Literature* 44, 2 [2004]: 333) maintains that *The Winter's Tale* is "preeminently a play of Ovidian metamorphoses. The myth of Proserpina and her annual return from the underworld . . . is pervasive in the play as a way of understanding the 'rebirth' of the members of Leontes's family" (339). My foregrounding of the fourth act discoveries in opposition to the last act recoveries counters the view of Lynn Enterline that Hermione's speech at the end represents a shift in the play's emphasis from the Orphic story of Pygmalion to "a crucially different return to Ovidian narrative to pose the question of 'the other's' desire." See "'You Speak a Language That I Understand Not': The Rhetoric of Animation in *The Winter's Tale*," *Shakespeare Quarterly* 48, 1 (1997): 142. Enterline concludes, "Turning to a daughter who has already coded herself as Proserpina at the moment of dropping her flowers, Hermione models herself on Ceres as a mother unable to forget her lost, though still living, daughter" (143). On the importance of the Ceres myth, refer also to A. D. Nuttall, "*The Winter's Tale*: Ovid Transformed," *Shakespeare's Ovid, The Metamorphoses in the Plays and Poems*, edited by A. B. Taylor (Cambridge: Cambridge University Press, 2000), 135–49. Jonathan Bate (*Shakespeare and Ovid* [Oxford: Oxford University Press, 1993], 233) argues that the myth of Proserpine is secondary to that of Pygmalion: "What takes centre-stage . . . is a myth that turns back Ovid's normal pattern, a metamorphosis that is driven by art not nature and that takes the form of depetrification rather than the usual petrification."

8. Referring to the Stephen Sandy's version of Ovid, Carol Thomas Neely calls attention to Ceres's reaction to her daughter's rape and postulates that Shakespeare may have had both Ceres and Pygmalion in mind: "Having learned that Proserpina was stolen by Pluto, 'Stone-like

stood Ceres at this heavey newes; / And staring, long continued in this muse' (510–11). (Perhaps this story, as well as that of Pygmalion, suggested the statue scene to Shakespeare.)" *Broken Nuptials* (New Haven, CT: Yale University Press, 1985), 199.

9. Peter Erickson makes a case for at least a partial change: "The dramatic action [of the play] consists partly in the fashioning of a benign patriarchy—in the transition from a brutal, crude, tyrannical version to a benevolent one capable of including and valuing women." See "Patriarchal Structures in *The Winter's Tale*," *PMLA* 97, 5 (1982): 819. James A. Knapp ("Visual and Ethical Truth in *The Winter's Tale*," *Shakespeare Quarterly* 55, 3 [2004]: 254) argues for a more comprehensive change in Leontes: "When the final scene reenacts the ethical situation of the opening scene, offering the same character another impossible image [the supposed adultery in the first act, the living statue in the last] and a second chance to respond, only then does Leontes allow his response to proceed from the other." Similarly, Graham Holderness writes, "The play subverts the priorities of a patriarchal polity by problematizing masculine authority and endorsing feminine power." Refer to "*The Winter's Tale*: Country into Court," *Shakespeare Out of Court: Dramatizations of Court Society*, edited by Graham Holderness, Nick Potter, and John Turner (New York: St. Martin's, 1990), 235.

10. Michael Bristol asks a different question entirely: "Why does Hermione agree to take Leontes back and why on earth should she want him?" See "In Search of the Bear: Spatiotemporal Form and the Heterogeneity of Economies in *The Winter's Tale*," *Shakespeare Quarterly* 42, 2 (1991): 166. In linking Hermione to the forms of "reproductive time," he writes that her story has been "systematically and violently excluded from the spatiotemporal organization of this play" (167). Such a reading—including the view that reproductive time means "not only growth, change, and development but also the intersubjective or dialogic fullness of time symbolized so powerfully in the gestation of the child in the mother's body" (167)—endorses precisely the sort of idealization of Hermione's silence that I question here. By overemphasizing the *short-lived* moments of pregnancy and birth, Bristol adheres to the poles of the foundling formula and thereby annuls the *long process* of rearing the child in the middle interlude.

11. Among those who question Hermione are Howard Felperin, who argues that we can never be sure of her initial innocence because we have no "ocular proof" either of her duplicity or her veracity. In that context, language is always "mediated action, action estranged by the linguistic medium in which it has existence. . . . This world of reference . . . in *The Winter's Tale* finally has no objective reality or ontological stability, but recedes into an infinite play of signs and deferral of affirmed or authoritative meaning." See "'Tongue-Tied Our Queen?': The Deconstruction of Presence in *The Winter's Tale*," *Shakespeare and the Question of Theory*, edited by Patricia Parker and Geoffrey Hartman (New York: Methuen, 1985), 16.

If Felperin equivocates about Hermione's virtue because language itself is indeterminate, other critics (who also challenge the unreserved idealization of Hermione) move away from linguistic arguments toward a contrasting corporeal filter. However, those critics also tend to feel that Hermione is somehow exonerated with Leontes at the end and that the redeeming factor is precisely the maternal instinct that I contend she represses. Leonard Barkan maintains that "Hermione's choice—if we can call it that—to freeze herself in time and space for sixteen years is as extreme in the way of a solution as was Leontes's jealousy in the way of a problem." Refer to "'Living Sculptures': Ovid, Michelangelo, and *The Winter's Tale*," *English Literary History* 48 (1981): 659. Finally, however, Barkan agrees with most critics that "with the discovery of Perdita . . . a softening begins to take place."

In the same vein, Theresa Krier writes convincingly that "it is all too easy to use the play's nostalgia for the maternal to screen the aggression of the mothers Hermione and Paulina, and to focus on blaming Leontes as the central critical issue of the play. There is not only victimization in the trial scene but also aggression, in Hermione's choice to let Leontes believe her dead. Her aggression is visible in the ghost of Hermione, in Antigonus's dream, and then in the bear who rends and eats Antigonus. Hermione's aggression is carried throughout by her surrogate Paulina." Avoiding the usual images of Hermione as victim, pure and simple, Krier nevertheless characterizes her retaliatory impulses as directed only toward Leontes, claiming that her separation from her child is instead a longer version of the distancing that, in Winnicott's view, is fundamental to human development. "Hermione's is the most literal and the most tested parturition [of the premodern works in her study]." *Birth Passages: Maternity and Nostalgia,*

Antiquity to Shakespeare (Ithaca, NY: Cornell University Press, 2001), 246. Like Barkan, Krier also excuses Hermione, reasoning that, in her maternal instinct, she "gathers her forces of aggression in order to create an enclave of air for her daughter and herself" (*Birth Passages*, 248).

I argue that Barkan's softening and Krier's "enclave" come too little and too late and that Hermione's "freezing" can be defined as passive-aggressive behavior, not just toward Leontes but also toward her child. Abbe Blum connects Hermione to Leontes (and female procreative activity to male creative artistry) when she writes that "to stir life from stone and to make stone of life positively and negatively represent the desire to create." See "'Strike All That Look upon Them with Mar[ble]': Monumentalizing Women in Shakespeare's Plays," *The Renaissance Englishwoman in Print: Counterbalancing the Canon*, eds. Anne M. Haselkorn and Betty S. Travitsky (Amherst: University of Massachusetts Press, 1990), 112. Blum reads the statue scene as a "redrawing of gendered cultural boundaries" (112), whereas I see it as a reiteration of patriarchal social hierarchies.

12. Calling Hermione the "play's most capable rhetorician," Adam McKeon reasons that "when, at last, she speaks again, it is not to answer questions but to ask them, not to solve mysteries, but to heighten them, not to persuade but to pray." See "The Rhetoric of Tragedy of *The Winter's Tale*," *Upstart Crow* 20 (2004): 121, 129. I think Hermione is trying to persuade Perdita here that she is (and was during her sixteen-year absence), indeed, a good mother.

13. About the relationship between "slippery" and "slip," Joel Davis ("Paulina's Paint and the Dialectic of Masculine Desire in the *Metamorphoses*, *Pandosto*, and *The Winter's Tale*," *Papers on Language and Literature* 39, 2 [2003]: 132) maintains that Hermione's "diction suffers from the linguistic slippage between the sexual and courtly senses by which she flatters Polixenes." Graham Holderness makes a similar point (*"The Winter's Tale*: Country into Court," 205).

14. "'Our Praises Are Our Wages': Courtly Exchange, Social Mobility, and Female Speech in *The Winter's Tale*," *Philological Quarterly* 79, 4 (2000): 438.

15. See Martine Van Elk's ("'Our Praises Are Our Wages,'" 437–38) analysis of courtly repartee, especially for her emphasis on Hermione's need (as "queen by marriage rather than by birth," 438) to take part in the game precisely because of her position as outsider. "*The Winter's Tale* makes the duality of the position of the queen by marriage crucial to the crisis that unfolds. The importance of rhetorical performance to the court permits Hermione to contribute with remarkable freedom to the conversation of the two kings" (438). But if what Hermione says in the trial about her father having been the emperor of Russia is true, Hermione's birth is higher than that of Leontes.

16. On gift giving, see "Patriarchal Structures in *The Winter's Tale*," 819.

17. "'A Lady's "Verily" Is as Potent as a Lord's': Women, Word and Witchcraft in *The Winter's Tale*," *English Literary Renaissance* 22 (1992): 250. Schalkwyk concludes, "Among Jacobean plays, *The Winter's Tale* is remarkable for the extent to which both truth and power are invested in women. . . . The play stops far short of maintaining such power in the bodies and words of women" (267).

18. Lynn Enterline writes about the Petrarchan poet's image of himself, that "male triumph requires female absence or resistance." See "'You Speak a Language That I Understand Not': The Rhetoric of Animation in *The Winter's Tale*," 23. A. E. B. Coldiron also cites the Petrarchan tropes in the play. "'Tis Rigor and Not Law': Trials of Women as Trials of Patriarchy in *The Winter's Tale*," *Renaissance Papers* (2004): 36.

19. Patricia Parker elaborates on multiple meanings of "bear" as carrying and giving birth to a child and as the brutalizing treatment of those "borne by women" epitomized by the literal bear at the beginning of Act 3. "Sound Government, Polymorphic Bears, *The Winter's Tale* and Other Metamorphoses of Eye and Ear," *The Wordsworthian Enlightenment: Romantic Poetry and the Ecology of Reading*, edited by Helen Regueiro, Frances Ferguson, and Geoffrey H. Hartman (Baltimore: Johns Hopkins University Press, 2005), 172–90. Writing about a play where so much seems to depend on ocular proof, Parker demonstrates how much Shakespeare also gave his audience oracular evidence to corroborate what it sees and to highlight what can't

be seen. Following her attention to the multiplicities of verbal innuendo, I suggest that, when Hermione names herself as his, she becomes the child of his naming, the Petrarchan "issue" of his invention.

20. "Mamillius and Gender Polarization in *The Winter's Tale*," *Shakespeare Quarterly* 50, 1 (1999): 1. Marion Wells ("Mistress Taleporter and the Triumph of Time: Slander and Old Wives' Tales in *The Winter's Tale*") similarly writes, "The scene seems to explore the origins of the male subject in an exclusively female environment in which physical nurture and tales are indivisibly linked" (251).

21. *Disowning Knowledge in Six Plays of Shakespeare* (Cambridge: Cambridge University Press, 1987), 194. Graham Holderness ("*The Winter's Tale*: Country into Court," 201) suggests about this scene that "the substance of the play involves a very adult consciousness of sexual courtly behavior. The women invite [Mamillius] with sublimated licentiousness into the sexual games of courtly love."

22. Susan Bruce ("Mamillius and Leontes: Their Final Exchange," *ANQ* 16, 3 [2003]: 9–12) argues contrastingly about Mamillius's exchange with Leontes that it renders him a less passive figure. Helen Hackett refers to Mamillius as "still at his mother's knee, living like most small children in an intimate circle of nurturing women," in "Gracious Be the Issue: Maternity and Narrative in Shakespeare's Late Plays," *Shakespeare's Late Plays: New Readings*, edited by Jennifer Richards and James Knowles (Edinburgh: Edinburgh University Press, 1999), 36.

23. *Suffocating Mothers: Fantasies of Maternal Origin in Shakespeare's Plays* (New York: Routledge, 1992), 124.

24. In the program notes to the 1976 Royal Shakespeare Company production, directed by John Barton with Trevor Nunn, the myth is described in terms that render Ceres more of a parallel to Hermione than she is in the Golding Ovid:

> Persephone (also called Proserpina), the beautiful daughter of the corn-goddess Demeter, was gathering flowers in the meadow when she was suddenly carried off by Pluto and held captive in the underworld to be his queen. Demeter went into mourning and withdrew to Eleusis swearing to leave the earth barren of corn until her daughter was restored to her. Zeus intervened, ruling that Pluto should keep Persephone with him in the underworld for only one third of the year, at other times she should return to her mother. In her joy at recovering her daughter, Demeter made the corn shoot from the barren earth and flowers bloom in plenty.
>
> This Greek story which represents the seasonal cycles of the year had equivalents throughout Europe, particularly in the North where the "corn dollies" and the "corn maidens" are still made each harvest time as the last reincarnations of Demeter and Persephone who also seem to live again in Hermione and Perdita.

The "explanation" of the Ceres connection leaves almost everything to the fathers—Zeus and Pluto—while Ceres just seems to withdraw into barrenness. Is Hermione the "corn dolly"—the little statue who comes to life when she finds her "corn-maiden" daughter? The view of Hermione as "corn dolly" renders her a bit like Disney's Sleeping Beauty, totally the innocent victim of a wounding enemy.

25. *Ovid's Metamorphoses, the Arthur Golding Translation of 1567*, edited by John Fredrick Nims (Philadelphia: Paul Dry, 2000), 127. Future references are cited by book and line numbers in the text.

26. *Sexes and Genealogies*, translated by Gillian C. Gill (New York: Columbia University Press, 1993), 155.

27. *The Marriage of Cadmus and Harmony*, translated by Tim Parks (New York: Knopf, 1993), 209.

28. Of the sense of male triumph in Leontes's command, Lori Humphrey Newcomb writes, "And so Leontes ends the play with a sharp twist against the women who have unsettled the monument, a comment pointing out that their agency, too, is nothing but spectacle." See "'If That Which Is Lost Be Not Found': Monumental Bodies, Spectacular Bodies in *The Winter's Tale*," *Ovid and the Renaissance Body*, edited by Goran V. Stanivukovic (Toronto: University of Toronto Press, 2001), 256. Newcomb speaks of the split in the play between "impulses that I

call monumentalizing and spectacular, impulses that evince very different conceptions of the body." She uses those distinctions to describe the fault lines between Leontes and Hermione: "On one hand, the play is marked by a strong tendency to monumentalize: to shape and fix texts, to demand singular control of the art object, to memorialize the body in an exact duplicate, to contain women in immobility. On the other hand, it also dares to be spectacular—to leave texts behind to embrace collaboration and proliferation, to celebrate the changefulness of the human body, even the female body" (240). When I argue that the play could end in Act 4, I mean that it is Florizel who insists on the proliferation Newcomb so astutely chronicles.

29. *Shakespeare's Romance of the Word* (Lewisburg, PA, and London: Bucknell University Press, 1990), 100; Van Elk, "'Our Praises Are Our Wages,'" 445.

30. "'Our Praises Are Our Wages,'" 445. Contrastingly, A. E. B. Coldiron writes, "In Florizel's alternative judgment, a woman's speech, variety, agency and motion are valued." See "'Tis Rigor and Not Law': Trials of Women as Trials of Patriarchy in *The Winter's Tale*," 60.

31. *This Sex Which Is Not One*, translated by Catherine Porter with Carolyn Burke (Ithaca, NY: Cornell University Press, 1985), 111.

32. Thomas Greene, "The Poetics of Discovery: A Reading of Donne's 'Elegy 19,'" *Yale Journal of Criticism* 2 (1989): 133.

33. Maurice Hunt speaks to one aspect of the word when he writes, "The repeated so's in Florizel's speech of praise stand for dramatic gestures representing the inexpressible" (*Shakespeare's Romance*, 101). But Hunt uses "so" only in the sense of inexactitude primarily because he views the whole pastoral scene as a Sidneyan "speaking picture." Hunt does not emphasize that the "so" represents Florizel's imprecise vocabulary—not Perdita's. Thus, he regards this scene as a preview of the statue scene with Florizel as the spectator of Perdita's performance. In contrast, I see Florizel's "so" as an inadequate attempt to depict Perdita's redefinition of courtly values.

34. "Introduction," *Beowulf* (New York: Norton, 2000), xxvii.

35. Stanley Cavell also speaks about the significance of "parting" and its various emanations in *Disowning Knowledge in Six Shakespeare Plays*, 206–13.

36. Marion Wells writes that the last scene "returns the mother to the centre of the family circle from which she was abruptly taken when [Mamillus's] tale was interrupted" ("Mistress Taleporter and the Triumph of Time: Slander and Old Wives' Tales in *The Winter's Tale*," 257). Martine Van Elk ("'Our Praises Are Our Wages,'" 451–52) insists that—despite the performative nature of the orchestrated final scene—the "behavior of women is a crucial means to gauge the social order and that a reconfiguration of courtly femininity serves to anchor social hierarchies and harness elite identity."

37. Of Florizel's silence in this scene, Abbe Blum asks, "One would want to know where Florizel is. Is he as superfluous as the king of France in *Lear* or part of the silent glue of the scene?" See "'Strike All That Look upon Them with Mar[ble]': Monumentalizing Women in Shakespeare's Plays," 110.

38. Edward Said, "Thoughts on Late Style," *London Review of Books* 26, 15 (2004): 3.

Afterword

The Myths Redeployed

Transferring the dynastic signification of "blood" as a determinant of kinship to its sexual meaning as the seat of passion, the Countess of Roussillon in *All's Well That Ends Well* revises the foundling and Petrarchan plots and anticipates the revisionary agendas of the video works I describe in this chapter:

> Even so it was with me when I was young.
> If ever we are nature's, these are ours: this thorn
> Doth to our rose of youth rightly belong.
> Our blood to us, this to our blood is born;
> It is the show and seal of nature's truth,
> Where love's strong passion is impressed in youth.
> By our remembrances of days forgone,
> Such were our faults—or then we thought them none.
> ....
> I say I am your mother,
> And put you in the catalogue of those
> That were enwombed mine. 'Tis often seen
> Adoption strives with nature, and choice breeds
> A native slip to us from foreign seeds.
> You ne'er oppress'd me with a mother's groan,
> Yet I express to you a mother's care. (1.3.112–18, 127–32)

Remembering her own youth as she observes Helena, and then speaking directly to her as a child she "adopts" and deems a suitable consort for her son, the Countess of Roussillon annuls the passive feminine object of the Petrarchan complex and the biological imperatives of the foundling plot. The blood that defines "nature's truth" is not that of inherited dynasty but that of an aroused sexuality that she categorizes in terms of "nature's [gendered] truth," using "our" to refer to all women. Thus she feminizes passion even as she places Helena in the same familial "catalogue" as those children hers by biology alone. When she learns of Helena's love for her son, the Countess relives her own earlier pain (in the thorn) and projected pleasure (in the rose) of love. Unlike Cleopatra's "lover's pinch, / which hurts and is desired" (5.2.286–87), reminiscent of experienced passion, the "thorn" here derives from the agony of a coveted but still-unrealized sexuality. Beginning with "even so," implying the exactitude of an understood sisterly identity spurred into being by the commonality of gender, the Countess moves forward in the next speech to the motherhood of emotional, rather than physical, bonding when she insists that her adoption renders Helena equal to those "enwombed mine," a connection prioritizing the foreign seed over the native slip in an assurance that, in the pursuit of love, women share the "truth" (rather than the fantasized abstraction) of lived experience. Unlike Polixenes, who uses a similar metaphor of grafting in *The Winter's Tale* to claim the overarching superiority of nature, the Countess insists that the communion of shared feeling trumps a common genetic thread.

Moving from a chronologically backward position, she first refers to her youth, then aligns her "adoption" of Helena with her biological motherhood, and, finally, from the unity of shared experience, assumes (in her "care") responsibility for Helena's future success. In the first instance, like the speaker in Sonnet 3 who tells the young man that looking into her son's eyes restores the mother to the "lovely April of her prime," the Countess returns to her own premarriage youth. Then she reverts to her mature generativity when, in reference to what she calls her "adoption," she confers on Helena the identical status as those she carried in her body. Assuming a "mother's care," she advances to the present and anticipates the future, her protection of Helena's interest contemporaneous to her eagerness now to bring to the surface and then to fruition Helena's still-inchoate desire. When she shares in the memory of retrospect and assumes in the pledge of prospect, the burden of Helena's troubles, the Countess's "care" emerges as an acknowledgment of an ongoing concern.

The interior rhymes between the speeches suggest that desire in all its permutations—from the initial stages, with the entrance of the first psychological "impress[ion]," through dynastic achievement and the "groans" of physical "oppress[ion]," to the extrafamilial adoption in the "express[ion]" of a "mother's care"—opens to a circle of engenderment that revises the two central plots of this study. In the Countess's confidence, the Petrarchan quest can be converted from imagined idealization to complete realization, just as her faith in adoption, in supererogating the bloodline connection, proclaims the grafted seed of art a competitor (in the early modern meaning of "strive") with the biological reproduction of a "native slip," interchangeable with it. The chosen child adheres to the adoptive mother's being and the mediated breeding (of thoughtful representation) equals the expulsion (as bodily release) of maternal birthing. The force of the thrice-repeated "press" in the verbal "catalogue" carves the Countess's empathy for Helena into a form of physical kinship that (in its turn) mutualizes the understood "strong passion" with which the Countess begins. In the repeated sense of urgency of the three "presses," the Countess parallels the Irigarayan conviction that "the horizontal axis that joins the sexes is more important than the vertical axis that links together the generations" (*Between East and West*, 141). Asserting that the affinities of gender inscribe a unity of kind, she asserts a communal motherhood, like the one that sustains Desdemona in the boudoir scene, and that similarly determines the challenge to fixed cultural expectations Mieke Bal and Mona Hatoum depict in their videos.

COUNTERING THE MYTHOLOGY

Moving forward in time, I turn here to two nonfiction models that, in echoing the maternal solicitude the Countess of Roussillon demonstrates, perform the revisionism Irigaray propounds, documenting in cinematic terms the difficulties of the diaspora I briefly chronicled in the preface but enacting the mythical revisions that *Austerlitz, Fugitive Pieces, Ark Baby,* and *The Nature of Blood* theorize and that enable us to experience the new readings I propose for *The Merchant of Venice, Othello,* and *The Winter's Tale*. They thereby connect the three stages of the foundling plot to political and social realities and, from there, back to a reconfiguration of what familial and love relationships might mean. The first model includes the videos (*Nothing Is Missing* and *Lost in Space*) of Mieke Bal, filmed in 2005, as scholarly records of the effect of twenty-first-century political upheaval on families. Bal's work illustrates how the foundling plot can mutate naturally into viable alternative life stories; the second is yet another video work—that of Mona Hatoum, *Measures of Distance* (1988), exemplifying a mix of visual art and written narrative that, in bridging the division of war-impelled diaspora, also collapses the generational gap to recast the Ceres-Proserpine story. Bal's *Nothing Is Missing* emphasizes a total upheaval of expectations in the generic expectations of all three stages of the foundling myth: the opening rupture is voluntary, the middle interlude is fraught with difficulties not experienced in the safe havens of the usually pastoralized setting, and the concluding return is impossible. In *Measures of Distance*, the necessity of generational separation also encourages a feminine defiance of the patriarchal strictures of Petrarchan determinism. In both instances, the maternal instinct, like that of the Countess of Roussillon, changes the story that otherwise might have set a predetermined script. Defining the mother-daughter bond as a sisterly sustenance that fosters creative as well as procreative energies, Hatoum situates nurturing in terms that encourage the sexual union denied by the Petrarchan *impossibilia* of a male-generated poetic and Bal locates nurturing as a presence in absence that defies the foundling plot's insistence on physical proximity.

The return in Hatoum's video is "measured" (limited in inverse proportion to the "distance"—both emotional and physical—from the homeland). The separation in time and place expands from the initial site of what begins as a mother-daughter reunion. The set of the film, a shower room in Lebanon, has two soundtracks: that of a conversation recorded separately but experienced concomitantly with the visual images and that of an English translation of a series of letters superimposed on the screen written by the mother to the daughter (living in London), who is the filmmaker. The dual recordings—one in Arabic, the other in English—are, in turn, compounded because the voice of the translated letter reader is the filmmaker herself. Ventriloquizing her mother's words, she adopts her feelings as her own, an aural "measure" that closes both the elapsed time between the written rendition and the physical space between the writer and reader. Such an attenuation in the textual material evokes the ambiguity of the visual doubling—the daughter might be the mother, the mother the daughter—that forms the landscape of the film. Like the Countess of Roussillon's "even so," Hatoum's conflation enacts a reconciliation that bridges physical and temporal distance with psychological affinity.

If the Ceres-Proserpine story begins with a fall—the precipitous yanking downward of the Kore—the images in Hatoum's film emerge as ladders of retrieval with the horizontal thrust of the written words that appear in Arabic on the screen remaining (like a barbed wire fence) impenetrable and the verticals of the bodily images inclining upward, towering above the limitations of the situation. Hatoum's sculptural works often threaten established ideas about domesticity—at best trivializing it, and at worst marking it as dangerous. They play off her nomadic position. In another work, *Homebound*, the return so essential to the foundling plot (and achieved psychologically by the genre bending in *Measures of Distance*) is seen as a trap and an unreachable destination, a mere "emblem" of memory. As Edward Said writes, "An abiding locale is no longer possible in the world of Mona Hatoum."[1] For Hatoum, as for Bal, the whole idea of home as a physical and psychological haven is challenged. Both *Measures of Distance* and *Nothing Is Missing* speak to the spatial dimension of the foundling plot, as they recast the originative homeland and the diaspora site into places that subvert the expected sanctuary of the middle interlude and the presumably happy return of the normative ending. The two locales of the theme, the temporary setting of the adoption, the permanent ground of the restoration, are situated in an unease totally opposite to the image of Chase's orphan with which we began. Home, as a destination, is "bound" with the same dangers as the diaspora: no place is safe. In this nomadic situation, the sites of the originary debarkation and of the middle interlude present an anxiety altogether different from those of the mythological models. Even when they are contested, however, the thematic concerns of both the foundling and the Petrarchan plots hover in the background as presumed cultural expectations that render the revisions all the more remarkable.

Hatoum's work is decidedly female. The mother and the daughter conspire toward their liberation against the physically absent (deliberately excluded but psychologically present) father. The video work self-consciously establishes (via the record of a superimposed and separately recorded soundtrack) a feminine space that "measures" spatial distance by closing the psychological gap so that mother and daughter together create a primal scene. They thereby transcend the physical separation incurred by patriarchal priorities that are equated with war-enforced separation. Established in the rhythm, Hatoum's "measures" are countermeasures, forming a union that crosses the divide of familial and governmental violence. The mother's body fuses with her daughter's as her words in the letters inextricably bind them. At the conclusion of the video, even the letters themselves are stopped because the means of communication has been cut off. The film ends in blackout. The local post office is destroyed by a car bomb. The waters of the shower scene dry up, preserved only in a memory kept flowing by the film imagery.

That imagery is virtually sculpted by Hatoum to create both a unifying effect and the visual and oral depth of a composite. As Hatoum explains, "The shots in the shower were all shot on slide film. The slides were then projected and filmed on video with the fading from one image to the other done at this stage. The conversation was . . . recorded separately from the shower scene and the translation of the letters was done in my own English."[2] The process of the film is thus layered, the unity of the distinct parts—stills, slide projection, recorded conversation—simultaneously compounded by the time travel of the letters, which move even further backward to chronicle the history of the family diaspora and forward into the scattering of the family's three daughters away, in their moves, from the family home. The measures accumulate seamlessly even as the countermeasure of the spatial and temporal distance forms the discursive subject of fragmentation. The medium itself operates as a faucet, promising (in the rerun) a visual return and threatening (in the blackout) the always present reality of blockage, a closure that banishes the very audience initially beckoned into the intimate scenario. In a gallery, the film automatically reruns. The viewer cannot turn the dials. Thus control remains in the hands of the filmmaker and the audience is left without recourse and unable—as with a book whose pages can be opened at will—to reconnect to the story on its own. Power is firmly situated in the *auteur*-controlled machine.

The automata rule so that the blackout is a miniature version of the war-caused closure and reminds us always of the omnipresent separation anxiety that is the unspoken threat throughout. Where Hatoum's "measures" establish a rhythm that overcomes, and then reinforces, the identity crisis of separation, Bal's discourses *accept* the distance, opening up in this new space a way to recalibrate the essentialist emphasis of the foundling plot. Both works similarly reconstruct the Petrarchan formula: Bal's because the mother (whose words form the title of the work) relinquishes to her daughter-in-law the power to remake her son in the image of returned love, and Hatoum's because, in its celebration of female sexuality, it disrupts the patrilineal control of the lyric.

THE UNCHARTED COUNTRY OF MOTHERHOOD: MIEKE BAL'S *NOTHING IS MISSING*

As part of the *mise-en-scène* in *Nothing Is Missing*, Bal situates four televisions in "a gallery" of a hypothetical living room with four videos running simultaneously so that the comfortably seated viewers can hear all at once while watching each subtitled screen in sequence. Immediately, the constructed setting and the actual subject offer a contrast: the cozy (and contrived) "home" where the viewer sits against the real (and unmediated) situation of an uninhabitable terrain on the screen. If Hatoum's videos are designed to make the audience uncomfortable, Bal's installation insists on the contrast between the audience in its presupposed intimacy and the on-screen isolation of the mothers remaining in their inhospitable "homelands." The "talking heads" are linked in that they are all mothers who were left behind when their grown children escaped their non-Western countries (Serbia, Tunisia, Iran, and Turkey) to make a better life in Western Europe. Each responds to questions about her feelings of isolation, raising issues related to the mythologies that influence audience and speaker alike. The interlocutors are the very children (or their spouses or grandchildren) who came back to conduct the interviews. The videos run simultaneously in languages most Westerners cannot understand. To the listening ear, they unsettle the cozy physical situation of a living room and function as a Greek chorus might, filling the atmosphere with a wail of deadening hopelessness in an unknown tongue. To the observing eye, however, the subtitles countermand the impact of the funereal sounds to offer specific examples of coping mechanisms. "The form of the films," Bal writes, "is a restrained version of a migratory

Aesthetic." For Bal, "that term indicates an harmonious blend of the small cultural aspects of everyday life played against the large cultural divide. Indirectly, the installation constitutes a monument to those mothers who were left behind bereft of those they most cherished."[3]

In Shakespeare's *Pericles*, Marina is monumentalized by her father, who praises her in regal terms, comparing her to statues on kings' graves that "smil[e] extremity out of act" (5.1.130).[4] Pericles's statues are signatures of acceptance, demonstrating an endurance that outfaces whatever adversity their subjects might have encountered. In *Twelfth Night*, Viola speaks of her restraint in love as a similar figure of stoicism, casting her lovelorn self, in the little allegory she tells Orsino, as "patience on a monument" (2.4.113). Both instances of Shakespearean self-abnegation promulgate a brave front in the face of losses that feel like death, the physical paralysis resulting from the psychological stasis that looms as irremediable. Persistence in both instances is not so much a matter of choice but of culturally determined confinement in the realm that demands silent endurance. The triumphant denial of self is registered as a refusal of expectation, an anorexia of emotional attachment willed by the mind over the body's instinct to hold, and to hold on to, the desired object.

Nothing Is Missing. Cinema Suitcase, edited by Mieke Bal, Zen Marie, and Gary Ward. Multiple screen video installation, 35 minutes, looped, 2006–ongoing. (Courtesy of Mieke Bal; photograph by Astrid Weyenberg)

In contrast, Bal reconceptualizes patience, categorizing it as a consequence of a life force each of the women propels on her own. Because of war, revolution, familial violence, or famine, each encouraged her children to leave. The very deprivation that Pericles and Viola cite emerges in the videos as a superflux of nurture. While both Shakespearean characters refer to a fundamental inability to offset the calamity of difficult psychological circumstances, these mothers choose to become the voluntary architects of their own destiny, accepting their losses freely. As chiasmic versions of the sometimes unavailing mother in the foundling plot, they neither abandon their children at the beginning nor wish for their return as a hypothetical happy ending. But the interviews give them what Viola and Pericles deem impossible—an opportunity to fill the void of absence with a language that registers the pain. Bal's women speak their own lives, writing themselves into a scenario that challenges the mythological models coinciding with their lives. The figure of the *statuas moving*, at the heart of the performative fiction in the happy ending of so many foundling dramas, here is naturalized in the "performance" of a lived necessity. The ultimate act of mothering in the video installation is to let the child go. The Shakespearean monument suffers silently and inwardly, impassively "smiling" at unalterable grief; the monuments Bal cites release their private emotions even as they voluntarily relinquish their outward ties.

While the sound of the voices conveys a sense of elegiac mourning, the substance of the translated subtitles demonstrates an active desire on the part of the mothers to defy the loss they suffer. As Bal suggests, "No drama but resignation, for the sake of a better future for their loved ones" ("Commentary on *Nothing Is Missing*"). Nadine Gordimer describes a similar sense of continual engenderment in *Get a Life*: "Parents are responsible for bringing into the world their progeniture whether deliberately or carelessly and theirs is an unwritten covenant that the life of the child and by descent the child's child is to be valued above that of the original progenitors."[5] In its strict formulation, the foundling plot violates the unwritten covenant Gordimer cites. At the beginning, the child's life is secondary to that of the parent. The infant is defined as a possession gone missing: the child is lost to the parent. Released from the difficulties of raising that child, the parent at the end of the plot is doubly freed: first, from the guilt of the initial exposure and, second, from the risk of a ruptured dynasty. In those respects, the typical plot presents a victory all around. The child gains its inheritance. The parent regains its imperial destiny. Contrastingly, Bal's installation begins with a sacrificed parent—a mother left behind by the child who seeks the better life of the diaspora. Like the narrator in *Get a Life*, these mothers acknowledge that "begetting" devalues the parent's life even as they remold themselves to provide ongoing support to the children they love. "Getting" in this case means "giving," letting the child go in the way that Prospero sets Ariel free in *The Tempest*.

The presupposed return of the child in the formula promises not only to preserve a bloodline but also to afford the parent a protected old age: the unspoken outcome of the return in the myth is that the now-grown child can nurture the parent during the period of his or her decline, the way Marina pledges in *Pericles*. Contrastingly, in Bal's videos, the mothers create a future that is altogether otherwise, partly because they *chose* their isolation, allowing themselves to be exposed to the elements of aging alone while their children attempted to better themselves abroad. Left to fend for themselves in the circumstances their children escape, their declaration that "nothing is missing" turns the absence they experience into a dislocation that is desired. They have fulfilled their mission.

In three of the four cases, the children cannot come home again because to do so would force them to endure the very hardship that caused them to leave. In the fourth instance, the children return to their native land of Turkey because (what Bal calls) the "itinerary to [their] past" looms more importantly than the success they have already charted in Western Europe. The diaspora provided the opportunity to so improve their lives that they had a choice. For the interlocutors, the important questions involve the key stations of the foundling formula—the moment of birth or the moment of separation. The children adhere to the stages of the formula: "How did you feel when your child came into the world?" asks the Turkish granddaughter of the aged Ümmühan. "How did you feel when your daughter left for Holland?" For the mothers, those moments dissolve in the long-term reality of a separation that they neither expect nor wish to be repaired. The interlocutors pull the emotion out, revitalizing their mothers verbally and following an instinct opposite to Marina's desire to move inward, back to the body of her mother. In the videos, the linguistic expression, rather than the physical bond, is reopened.

The Turkish granddaughter, who initially remained behind while the rest of her family fled, begged her (at first hesitant) grandmother to sing the lament she remembers hearing. She has to ask several times for the lyrics, which, reluctantly, are then rehearsed: "Oh mountains . . . gone is my lamb . . . I only wear black." Like those in Desdemona's "willow song" ("The poor soul sat sighing by a sycamore tree / . . . The fresh streams ran by her and murmur'd her moans," 4.3.40–44), the lyrics turn the landscape into the sympathetic holding space that becomes the vessel for the mother's tears. In Desdemona's song, the motion of the waters carries Barbary's lament, their murmuring an echo of her complaint. In the video, the singer mirrors the mountains, stony in her resolve. But, because they are invoked, the mountains also absorb the mother's grief, rendering the natural surroundings a mirror of the mother's mirror of them, a *mise-en-abyme* of sympathetic

Nothing Is Missing. Cinema Suitcase, edited by Mieke Bal, Zen Marie, and Gary Ward. Multiple screen video installation, 35 minutes, looped, 2006–ongoing. (Courtesy of Mieke Bal; photograph by Mieke Bal)

nature. The mountains witness and reflect the mother's isolation. Like the mountains, the Ümmühan survives the loss and looms above the circumstances confining her. The comparisons humanize the mountains even as they naturalize the mother, almost as if she is adopted by the nature of her homeland, sustained by the constant presence of the landscape into which she merges despite the fact that the cultural and political conditions promulgate her helplessness.

For much of the time, the immobility of the faces in the video casts all the mothers, like the mountains of the lyric, as seemingly unmoved by the events they narrate. Through prodding, however, the interlocutors compel a release that becomes an expression of the child's value *and* a sign that in some ways the mothers, like the mountains, have withstood the pain and have lived beyond it. Moreover, they have been transformed by the reality they themselves shaped. In *The Winter's Tale*, Hermione's sixteen-year burial—until her lost child is found—mocks (imitates) death. Ceres's revenge and Hermione's retreat (presumably underground somewhere) negate life to create the winter's tale that signifies the absence the goddess and Shakespeare's heroine mourn. Here the mothers go on living to render their engenderment continual and, like the mountains, visible and clear. While the interlocutors are curious about the moment of birth, these mothers speak to a lifetime of nurturing, a giving over with no expectation of getting back. In these stories, as Bal writes, "the mothers left behind tend to a life that continues to struggle to survive and that, injured by colonization as it has been, possesses its own beauty in traditions from which Western Europeans can learn a great deal" ("Commentary on *Nothing Is Missing*").

The mothers describe the loss in terms that simultaneously express the void and that identify the value of the child they sacrifice. Gordana Jelenic of Serbia refers to the daughter who went to live in Spain as "someone who made her life more beautiful . . . with her life is more interesting. I miss her mostly as the content of my life." The play in English on the absent joy (contentment) and the now-unfilled space (content) contrasts the current state of emptiness defined by the child's absence to the earlier sense of plenitude enjoyed in the child's presence. The title of the installation, *Nothing Is Missing*, derives from the Tunisian mother who assures her daughter-in-law that, despite the fact that she was deprived of the customary parental "say" in the marriage choice, she is satisfied. But the words also suggest that—in Elizabethan terms—she lacks the "no-thing" that defines her femininity. Thus the title is paradoxical; what is missing is her own womanhood while what is there—her daughter-in-law who is now everything in her son's life—takes her place. Yielding the role of engenderment that was originally hers, she achieves the monumental grace Bal ascribes to her and that the Countess of Roussillon bequeaths in her adoption to Helena.

But the void that defines the maternal situation is also measured in Bal's other film about the children who migrated and who experience the problems of being "heimatloss"—without a homeland or mother tongue—in the countries to which they have emigrated, as displaced persons whose very cultural relocation caused them to feel "lost in space." Like the left-behind mothers, they are fragmented without a certain future and without ties to their past. *Nothing Is Missing* allows the mothers to speak and to replace the emptiness with the words through which they create a whole new reality in a language that bypasses the poles of the myth. The interrogation provides a vehicle, as Bal puts it, of a self-expression that creates its own formula. The mothers who stay behind—and let go—achieve their monumental endurance through their ties to the very hostile landscape where they must remain in isolation. Unbound, the children understand their loss and are defined by it.

Lost in Space, Bal's film about the children who left, is about permanent homelessness. Because of their having to speak in translation, the diaspora children have forfeited the expression—the vernacular—the mothers retain. Without the certainty of cultural acceptance and without a proper adoption into the new society, there is nobody to pick up the fragmentary pieces of the migratory self. Unlike Austerlitz, whose linguistic loss is self-reflexive, a form of unease he can at least make understood to the sympathetic narrator, these children lack an audience who will share their cause or to whom, in Austerlitz's terms, they can "relate." In mythology, language is not an issue. Either the infant is taught to speak by the adoptive parents or the acculturation occurs quickly. But in *Lost in Space*, the guest workers, asylum seekers, or homeless people are branded by accented speech so that they can never be "at home" in their current physical habitat. Uprooted linguistically by their inability to say what they are missing in a language that would accommodate their loss, they are deprived of mother, mother country, and mother tongue, isolated emotionally, physically, and linguistically. One of the interviewed Arab migrants describes his dislocation under the increased surveillance measurements since 9/11 on the part of Westerners who treat all foreigners as suspect. He complains that "their security increases my insecurity." Like their mothers who are unable to leave, the migrant children are unable to find a threshold from which to launch their new lives. Locked in isolation, asylum seekers cannot plant roots they trust. Bal's title for this film, *Lost in Space*, suggests a freefall in the diaspora, the terror of being without foothold in the very place that the migrant expected to make his own. Because remaining at home and relocating elsewhere are both unsustainable, these refugees are lost where, mythologically, they might have found themselves. And, as I argued in the "Introduction," particularly with the deteriorating economic situation in Western countries, they remain aliens and alienated.

Bal's work here "privileges the voices" of the migrants who feel themselves as exiles in the societies they enter and of the mothers left behind in untenable situations. Playing the harsh reality against the dreamscape of cultural norms, Bal opens up the dark corners of Western life and the uninhabitable "homelands" of non-Western cultures to redefine the mythologies that predetermine both locales in our minds. When the adopted country emerges inhospitable and the left-behind terrain is uninhabitable, the fixed stations of the myth—the supportive middle ground of adoption, the recovered security in the expected reunion at the end—fall apart and we have to rethink an entire cultural apparatus. With the phrase "nothing is missing," the mother gives to her child the chance to make a new life. Accepting her son's absence as a condition of a redefined completion, she merges herself with the body of her daughter-in-law and insists that her wholeness derives from her son's happiness. When the migrating child in *Lost in Space* confesses an estrangement in the land where he expected to find comfort, he similarly alters the expected mythical scenario, challenging the protectiveness of the middle interlude. Unable to return home and uneasy in the new terrain, he leads us to understand what the mythologies deny: the loss is irreparable. Homelessness as psychological state and physical reality may be a permanent condition. Bal's unobtrusive self—"I leave the room once the camera has been set"—allows the migratory Aesthetic to find a voice. Only this time it signals a protest in the absence of the mythological comfort of the middle period.

While Kwame Appiah links culture talk to race talk in discursive practice, Bal unhinges both, finding a new way of looking at loss against the mythologies that form a backdrop of expectation her installations override. Bal's work is political in that it paves the way for what Rosi Braidotti calls "the ethical transformation all the way to a new universal that will no longer be colonized by the same."[6] Like Braidotti, Bal poses as a necessity a new look at foundational stories, one that demands a retrospective realignment of our mythically determined presumptions. Her work unravels the culture she challenges, loosening the fixed forms so embedded that we cannot tell the difference anymore between what part of us is DNA of a genetically determined destiny and what part of is GNA, what I call a generically naturalized art: we are no longer certain about where our bodies leave off and our acculturation begins. Renegotiating all the stages of the foundling plot, Bal renders the initial ruptures as a survival strategy for the child, the diaspora a questionable sanctuary, and the end a structural impossibility. But, with that, she also demonstrates how maternal love supersedes mythological expectation. *Measures of Distance* moves in a different direction, displaying a female bodily pleasure that transcends the separation anxiety of the foundling plot by establishing a form of identity that undoes Petrarchan determinism.

BRIDGING THE GENERATIONS: MONA HATOUM'S *MEASURES OF DISTANCE*

In *Nothing Is Missing*, the camera remains fixed on the mothers' faces, emphasizing, in Bal's words, the "monumental" triumph of speech against an immutable fate; Hatoum's primary focus fluctuates between the female breast and female face—ambiguously mother's or daughter's—suggesting the continuity of a mutual nurturing and the connectivity of a sympathetic verbal exchange. The uncertain demarcation between mother and daughter is heightened by the question of the medium itself: Was the camera set on automatic exposure before the filming or was the daughter standing behind the camera? Does the daughter merge with her mother as narrative subject or is she—separate from her mother—consciously staging the fusion? Unlike in the Ceres-Proserpine story, where there is a period of nutritional withholding in defiance of Pluto's treachery, here the sustaining image is preserved as an enjoyment of the sexuality that in the Ovidian story separates mother and daughter or unites them (as in the Homeric hymns) only in the violation of rape that the Greek Demeter endures in her journey to find Persephone. The narrative substance contrasts both with the male violence of war and with the male possession of the female body, and it thereby bends both the nationalistic mandate of the foundling plot and the sexual deformations of the Petrarchan poetic.

The images work, first, as a variant of the duck-rabbit optical illusion. The breasts often appear as faces so that it is difficult to distinguish between the physically/nurturing and the verbally/comforting woman. Second, the enigmatic shape is veiled behind what looks like a shower curtain of Arabic writing. Within that scenario, the script of the letters seems to form a horizontal line of barbed wire through which the vertical images of the female body are seen alternatively to triumph in the freedom of discourse and to be imprisoned by a series of concentric enclosures signified by the "curtain": inside the shower room, inside the house, inside the war zone. Since the calligraphy on the screen is the content of the letters and since the letters defy the containment they describe, there is a sense in which the narrative reading voice emerges as a musical measure that rises above the limits of physical space. On yet another level, precisely because of the indestructibility of the video projection and the always duplicable capacity of the medium itself, the body seems to escape the end run of the political situation. The setting of the film evokes the shower scene in *Psycho*, playing off the same slippage between presumed safety and looming violation that Hitchcock exploited to such effect. The image of the raised elbow, with which the film opens, suggests that the hand is personally and politically ready, both intimately to bathe the private parts and imminently to slam a hatchet at the intruder. The inside space remains in constant danger of disruption by the interloping father, by the war going on outside the house contemporaneously during the filming, and (finally, decades later) by the visual gaze of the audience also invading the privacy of the scene. The female arm emerges phallic in its determination as the dialogue clearly raises the women over the situation that binds them. In turn, the intrusion of the viewer is also part of the film that sutures the audience in and then threatens to turn on it, exactly as the subjects are made to feel their vulnerability. In that respect, the viewer's gaze is recalibrated as both mother and daughter command and direct its presence to signify a defiance of the patrilineal injunction against it and the political threat to its very existence.

The narrative plays itself out in a triadic aural-oral structure: first, the sound of the recorded shower conversation—its give and take—against the visual backdrop of the shower scene paralleling the permeating tears in *Fugitive Pieces*, the murmuring stream in *Othello*, and the ebb and flow of the waves in *The Winter's Tale* to suggest the fluidity of a primal comfort; second, the letters written by the mother; and, third, the translated English voiceover. Thus, there are the taped conversations with their musical laughter, the words written across the screen, and, finally, the retrospective record

Mona Hatoum, *Measures of Distance* (1988). Color video with sound / A Western Video Production, Vancouver © Mona Hatoum. (Courtesy of White Cube)

of the read-aloud letters. The triple play is actualized by the Arabic script running across the screen (the translation of the letters into the language of the diaspora) and the filmmaker's repetition, in the voiceover, of the mother's initial words. That doubling (both in the ventriloquism—daughter mouthing mother's words—and in the actuality—mother writing the words the daughter reads) emphasizes the union that has taken place, each feeling as the other. Still, a more important fusion is achieved in the mother's understanding of the daughter and in the daughter's recording of the mother's advice. The giving of the letters is thus returned in their preservation. They come later as recollections of the filming itself and of the life before and after, skipping in chronology simultaneously as they carefully shape the discourse to suggest a distance that—despite all measures—is incalculable and inversely commensurate to the closeness achieved as Hatoum bridges the gap of time and space through the precision of her medium.

Finally, the substance of the letters becomes collaborative. The mother emerges artistic model and mental support but her engendering moves toward a recognition of the daughter's independence even as she equates bodily pleasure with creative enterprise. The mother's openness about her sexuality also licenses the daughter's artistic expression. Liberating the body frees the art. The mother encourages the work and the daughter actualizes the mother's vision when she records and repeats her mother's words. The collaboration is part of the composition: visually in terms of the mother's sustained physical presence, verbally in terms of her consistent narrative voice, and substantively in terms of her understanding of the daughter's artistic drive. If the tone of the Mieke Bal installations is elegiac, that of Hatoum's work is comic, not only in the laughter of the recorded voices, forming the back and forth of playful teasing, but also in the triumph of female conspiracy. The blackout indicates the disruption of the lines of communication as a result of the war but it also extends to the audience so that it is made to feel the same void, as if the opening hatchet is itself the source (for the audience) of the concluding cut. The end is already known (to the filmmaker) at the beginning. In deliberately preserving the blackout as part of the film's content, the filmmaker renders the silence, like Hermione's entombment or Ceres's barrenness, itself an act of revenge, as if to say to the viewer, "When we are stopped, you too are blank." There is no end, merely a void that threatens recollection, converting the liveliness of the shower flow and its watery life into a visual and oral wasteland. If the disturbance ends, so does the exhilaration.

The temporal feeling of the video is fourfold: first is the actual scene of the color slides subsequently shot on video; second is the recording made later in recollection of the shower scene; third is the retrospective voice of the letters referring back to the initial photo shoot even as their content refers backward still further to the historical events occurring before the shower scene and describing the family's initial diaspora from Palestine; and fourth, it moves chronologically forward to the subsequent separation of the mother from her daughters as they left Lebanon to make their lives elsewhere. Thus the video sculpts time as well as space as it dilates and distills, compressing familial history within the context of larger political events. The final product was part of a London Arts Council exhibit (*How to Improve the World: 60 Years of Arts Council Art*) held at the Hayward Gallery during the summer of 2006 when Lebanon was again besieged. The effect is to contemporize even further the imminent repetition of the blackout at the end and to emphasize the constant possibility of an unbroken bond in the collapse of the generations, the mother nurturing the daughter's creative enterprise, the creative act in turn sustaining (by memorializing) the mother. The wall card in the Hayward Gallery exhibit explains that the letters record "the traumatic social rupture in which the personal and political are intertwined." Every letter begins with the sense of absence similar to that in the Bal installation: "My dear Mona, the apple of my eyes. You will never know how much I miss you. . . . I wish this bloody war will be over soon so you and your sisters can return and we will all be together again like the good old days." Only in the last letter—where the situation becomes more urgent—is the encomium condensed: "My dear Mona, etc. etc.," the formula abbreviated because of the dramatic turn of events that results in blackout.

The narrative steadily describes the worsening political situation, moving back and forth chronologically between the family's original deportation from Palestine to Lebanon, to the photo shoot in 1981, superseded by the later moments of the letters, when the mother's three daughters have left to find safe haven in Europe, and then (geographically) to the worsening state in Lebanon where, finally, the post office that enabled the correspondence to go on, is blown up by a car bomb and beyond repair, thus ending the exchange of letters that has been, throughout, so invigorating:

> Yes, things were very different for your sisters because before we ended up in Lebanon we were living on our own land in a village with all our family and friends around us always ready to lend us a hand. We felt happy and secure and it was paradise compared to where we are now. . . .
> Can you imagine us having to separate from all our loved ones, leaving everything behind and starting again from scratch? . . .
> I personally felt as if I had been stripped naked of my very soul and I'm not just talking about the land and property we left behind but with that our identity and sense of pride in who we are went out the window. . . .
> And now that you and your sisters have left Lebanon, you are again living in another exile and in a culture that is totally different to your own. So when you talk about a feeling of fragmentation and not knowing where you belong, well this has been the painful reality of all our people.

While the letters graphically describe the political situation in 1981 when the video was originally made, they also transcribe the promise of what becomes in the end simultaneously a defiance of entrapment and an artistic reordering of the patriarchal generational line. The letters also record sequential fragmentations—of family heritage, of homeland, of belonging—catalogued in the mother's initial loss of the Palestinian homeland, subsequent diaspora in Lebanon, and further disintegration in the scattering of her three daughters. Beyond the irreparable political separation is the liaison that is formed as the subject matter of the letters shifts and comes closer to the visual context. Temporally, the mother moves in her lament from the original evacuation of her own family as they were forced out of Palestine in the first diaspora to Lebanon and then to the subsequent separation from her children, leaving her exposed in a terrain that constitutes *her* diaspora and that becomes as threatening to her survival as the loss of her original homeland was. Thus she remains physically exposed. But, psychologically, she crosses the timeline as, like the Countess of Roussillon to Helena, she finds in her relationship with her daughter a bond that overcomes the political insecurity.

The sensuality of the visual scene and the sexuality of the letters bridge the gap between mother and daughter, making them seem as one woman (a verbal union corroborated by the visual enjambment so that it is difficult to tell mother from daughter, photographer from subject, body part from body part). At the same time, the narrative in the translated voiceover is consistently the mother's. Despite the separation, it is she who urges the union and who keeps trying to find a way to communicate. The original Arabic soundtrack records a conversation that is mutual and involves a laughing give and take. In translating the letters, the daughter takes what the mother gives and feeds it back to her in the superimposed English, as a sign of collaboration and as a tribute to the originator. The conversation shifts from the political to the personal:

> I enjoyed very much all those intimate conversations we had about women's things and all that. . . .
> Why don't you come back and live here and we can make all the photographs and tapes you want.
> You asked me in your last letter if you could use my pictures in your work. Go ahead and use them but don't mention a thing about it to your father. You remember how he was shocked when he caught us taking the pictures in the shower during his afternoon nap? . . . I actually enjoyed this session because I felt we were like sisters, close together with nothing to hide from each other. I enjoyed the feeling of intimacy that developed between us.

When the mother urges the daughter to come home (though she doesn't mean it because to return would mean experiencing the war all over again), she lures her with an offer of complete artistic license: "We can make all the photographs and tapes you want." The tapes drive a wedge between the mother and her husband and unite the daughter and mother against the intrusiveness of the father who attempts to block them. As the mother drifts back in her letters (obviously responding to the daughter's questions), she recalls the moment of her daughter's first menstrual cycle and her transformation from a "little devil" to a quiet young woman. That change marks not only the daughter's sexual coming of age but also the beginning of her artistic introspection, a precursor to the withdrawal that leads to the videotape's moving inside the inside, beyond the curtain, to the stage of mutual "stark nakedness" only interrupted by the father's discovery of an intimacy from which he was excluded. Unlike Pluto's snatching of Proserpine, the father's intrusion does not separate mother from daughter. As a response to the familial and global forces conspiring against it, the film moves control of "the end of the story" away from the patriarchal injunction and (in the union between mother and daughter) closes the matriarchal generational gap. Mother and daughter emerge as "sisters close together with nothing to hide from each other." In that sisterhood of remembered and anticipated sexuality, they reiterate the "even so" of the Countess of Roussillon's sense of shared female passion as they acknowledge feelings repressed in Petrarchan conventionality.

Writing of Hatoum's 2000 Tate Gallery Installation *Homebound*, Edward Said notes her "relentless catalogue of disaffected, dislocated, oddly deformed objects," maintaining that "there is . . . a sense of focusing on what is there without expressing much interest in the ambition to rescue the object from its strangeness or, more importantly, trying to forget or shake off the memory of how nice it was" ("The Art of Displacement: Mona Hatoum's Logic of Irreconcilables," 17). For Hatoum, Said argues, "The past cannot entirely be recuperated from so much power arrayed against it on the other side. It can only be restated in the form of an object without conclusion" ("The Art of Displacement: Mona Hatoum's Logic of Irreconcilables," 17). But in *Measures of Distance*, Hatoum's image of the female breast and sounds of feminine conspiracy defy the "power arrayed against [them]" to invent an inner space of memory where a momentary beauty—a continual and reciprocal engenderment—triumphs. Hatoum's reunion that ends in blackout captures a communion that outfaces even the need for the closure Hatoum herself refuses to name: blackness for the false light of return.

In *Measures of Distance*, Hatoum testifies, as Desdemona's "willow song" does, to the possibility of a vital connection, a spiritual union between mother and daughter. If physical return is neither possible nor desirable, the psychological presence of the mother—visually recorded in the video, verbally witnessed in the letters (remembering the moments of the daughter's womanhood, commemorating the pleasures of her own selfhood)—forms an alternative to the unreturnable: the irrepressible. In terms of the foundling plot, Hatoum's video work does something unique: it collapses the generations by uniting mother and daughter in the interchangeable breast and voice. Whom do we see—mother or daughter? Who speaks in the video—mother writing to daughter, or daughter reading the mother's words? The fusion obviates both separation and recovery in the typical plot, signifying, in the bodily indeterminacy, a psychological oneness. Acknowledging the impossibility or even the desirability of physical return, *Measures of Distance* testifies to, and preserves, a comfort and nurture available in the *diaspora* that the conventional foundling plot deems possible only as an end.

The persistence of the maternal instinct allies Bal's installation with Hatoum's video and both to the Countess of Roussillon's understanding that the forward thrust of Helena's adopted fate initiates a retrograde memory of her youthful passion. All three—Bal's in its defiance of the necessity of return, Hatoum's in its realignment of the generations, and the Countess's care for the "foreign slip"—play with the mythic structure to offer an alternative to the dynastic imperative. In all, the middle period of the cycle is realigned so that the mothers are psychologically present even in their physical absence.

Moreover, their acceptance of the diaspora also emphasizes a new attention to sexual generativity. Bal's mothers acknowledge that the "nothing" of Petrarchan denial is overcome in the "something" of their children's new lives and Hatoum's mother records the triumph of a feminist creativity that subverts the very repressive forces of artistic and political patriarchy it nonetheless—and unflinchingly—chronicles. When the Countess of Roussillon puts aside the aristocracy of the familial mandate, anointing Helena as a suitable consort for her son, she undoes the expectations so often connected to the Petrarchan ethos (where the man constructs the woman in the image of himself) and the foundling plot (where marriage becomes a question of genetic suitability) to render her foster child good enough to break the convention associated with newly emerging nationalistic exigencies.

Similarly shattering formulaically conditioned dictates, against a backdrop of twenty-first-century nationalisms, Bal and Hatoum create alternative constructs that liberate their subjects from mind-sets Shakespeare questioned in his early modern revisionism and that Jensen, Michaels, Phillips, and Sebald also challenge. The mothers in *Nothing Is Missing* adhere to a maternal instinct that contravenes the physical holding space of its originating function, defying the forces that would bind them (as Viola and Marina are) to an unavailing search for a comfort they can never achieve. Their love for their children persists in relinquishment, a letting go that sacrifices all hope of return. And in *Measures of Distance*, a mutually expressed bodily pleasure counters the father's impulse to control the women in his life and the social pressure that represses female desire in a Petrarchan structure based on a fabricated insistence that sexuality reigns exclusively within the confines of a male-generated demesne. Despite their nearly total reconstruction of the plots, both videos work from an understanding that the constructs they defy exist in our minds as part of the same cultural unconscious that Shakespeare challenged in *Merchant of Venice*, *Othello*, and *The Winter's Tale* when he recast the "old tales" that structured those plays by following the "law of writ" (*Hamlet*, 2.2.384) and taking "liber[ties]" (3.2.384) with it.

"The imitation of formal models in the Renaissance," Rosalie Colie maintains, "was in spite of its inbuilt conservatism a factor for literary change and imaginative experiment."[7] Colie reasons further that the dual function operated in the early modern period as a matter of "social importance" (*Resources of Kind*, 8). Similarly, when Anne Michaels argues, as she did so eloquently in London in 2009, that it is the "reader who pulls Jakob Beer out of the mud,"[8] she emphasizes the empathy that enables a collaborative acknowledgment of loss. Thus the reader meets the writer. Together, they challenge gender and plot expectations, in the same way that Caryl Phillips, Liz Jensen, W. G. Sebald, and Michaels herself do when (in the postcolonial moves Peter Hitchcock identifies) they "dissolve the very classifications that produced"[9] the forms they use, opening things up with Shakespearean "scenes individable and poems unlimited" (*Hamlet*, 2.2.381–82). Identifying what Rosi Braidotti calls "the in-between spaces, the transit areas, the . . . shifts that make up the nomadic itinerary" ("Afterword," 163), all the works in this study share the underlying premise that the connection between mythological origins and political destinies persists and that it is possible and necessary to transform the constructs—in memory and imagination—that continue to shape our lives.

NOTES

1. "The Art of Displacement: Mona Hatoum's Logic of Irreconcilables," *Mona Hatoum: The Entire World as Foreign Land* (London: Tate Gallery Publishing, 2000), 15.
2. Notes about the process sent to me in an e-mail, May 30, 2011.
3. Mieke Bal, "Commentary on *Nothing Is Missing*," Cogut Center, Brown University, April 11, 2006. In an e-mail to me, Bal notes that the tapings have expanded and that she now has recorded seventeen mothers so that the exhibition varies from showing to showing.
4. *Pericles*, edited by Suzanne Gossett, *The Arden Shakespeare*, 3rd series (London: Methuen, 2004), 382. Future references are cited in the text.
5. Nadine Gordimer, *Get a Life* (London: Penguin, 2006), 47.
6. "Afterword," *Luce Irigaray and Premodern Culture: Thresholds of History*, edited by Theresa Krier and Elizabeth D. Harvey (New York: Routledge, 2004), 165.
7. *The Resources of Kind: Genre Theory in the Renaissance*, edited by Barbara K. Lewalski (Berkeley: University of California Press, 1973), 8.
8. "Orange Prize Reading," Royal Festival Hall, London, July 6, 2009.
9. "The Genre of Postcoloniality," *New Literary History* 34, 2 (2003): 327.

Index

9/11, xxii, 9

Adelman, Janet, 149n2, 149n5, 152n15, 153n28, 155n52, 155n55, 189n8, 190n18, 207, 222n4
adoption, xix, xxii, xxiv, 6–10, 14, 24–26, 27–29, 35, 42, 53, 68, 88, 90–91, 92, 94, 109, 115, 122, 160, 167, 180, 188, 227–228, 230, 237
Adorno, Theodor, 103n6
Agamben, Giorgio, xxii
Alexander, Catherine M. S., 190n18
anamorphism, 128, 129, 177
anastrophe, 163, 164–165, 168, 188
Appiah, Kwame, xxii, 29, 239
Armstrong, Andrew, xxviin26, 25
asylum seekers, xxvi, 9–12, 237
Auden, W. H., 152n19
Auschwitz, xxiv, 17n11, 103n5, 103n6, 156n56, 148

Bahti, Timothy, xxviin14, 83n3
Baker, D. Fredrick, 17n2
Bal, Mieke, xxvi, 228, 229, 230, 232, 239, 241, 245, 246, 247n3; *Lost in Space*, 229, 237–239; *Nothing Is Missing*, 230, 232–237, 239
Barkan, Leonard, 223n11
Bartels, Emily, 190n16, 190n18, 191n25, 192n40
Barthelemy, Gerard, 190n18

Barton, John, 225n24
Bate, Jonathan, 222n7
Bauman, Zygmunt, xvii, xxiii, xxvin9, 5
Belsey, Catherine, 131, 150n11, 222n5
Benjamin, Jessica, 60, 61
Beowulf, 216
Berek, Peter, 132
Berger, Harry, Jr., 154n31, 161, 165, 168, 173, 191n23, 192n41
Bernstein, Nina, 12, 18n18–18n19, 18n21, 18n26
Bible: Esau, 112, 117, 118; Genesis 2, 82, 88, 89, 130, 142; Jacob, 111–112, 113, 114, 117, 118, 119, 124, 136–138, 141, 142, 145, 158, 171, 219; Jonah, 49, 50, 54, 61, 62; Joseph, 112, 119; Moses, 68, 79–80; Noah, 48, 54, 56, 62
blood and race, xvii–xviii, xix, xxi, xxii, xxiii–xxiv, xxv, 5, 6–12, 15, 23–44, 55, 59, 63, 92, 96, 101, 102, 109, 110, 118, 119, 123, 139, 149n4, 150n10, 150n11, 153n28, 155n55, 158, 160, 161, 163, 165, 190n16, 190n18, 191n25, 194, 196, 198, 199, 201, 202, 221, 227, 228, 235
Bloom, Harold, 189n4
Blum, Abbé, 226n37
Boose, Lynda E., 150n11
Borchardt, Danuta, 104n7
Borden, Lizzie, 5
Bostic, Heidi, 18n32

Boswell, John, 6–7, 8, 12
Braidotti, Rosi, xxvi, 15, 239, 246
Bristol, Michael, 223n10
Brontë, Charlotte, 44; *Jane Eyre*, 50, 52, 53, 62
Brose, Margaret, xviii
Brothers, Caroline, 18n25
Bruce, Susan, 225n22
Burke, Carolyn, 189n10, 192n32, 221n1, 226n31
Bush, George W., 9, 18n17

Calasso, Roberto, 211–212
Calbi, Maurizio, 157
Calder, David, xxviin17
Calderwood, James, 191n19
Callaghan, Dympna, 190n18
Cavell, Stanley, 176, 205, 226n35
Chase, William Merritt: *Young Orphan, Study of a Young Girl at her Ease*, 1, 2–6, 12, 17n5
Cheney, Patrick, 190n16, 192n40
Ciocia, Stefania, 29
Clingman, Stephen, xxviin27, 26, 29
Coffey, Donna, 103n5
Cohen, D. M., 150n11
Coldiron, A. E. B., 224n18, 226n30
Colie, Rosalie, xx, xxi, 246
Cook, Méira, 103n6
Cowen Orlin, Lena, 189n7
Coyle, Martin, 149n7, 151n13
culture and mythology, xiii, xiv, xviii, xix–xxii, xxiv, 1–16, 23, 24, 25, 26–30, 30–31, 32, 33, 36, 39, 42–43, 48, 49–50, 52, 55, 56, 57, 68, 72–73, 75, 79, 82, 87, 90–91, 92, 96, 99, 100, 101, 102, 109, 111–112, 139, 158, 162, 165, 188, 208–209, 210, 218

Dancygier, Rafaela M., xxii
Danson, Lawrence, 155n52
Darwin, Charles, 44, 58
Darwinian theory, xxiv, 53–54, 57
Davis, Joel, 224n13
Dawson, Ashley, xxviin14
de Lauretis, Teresa, 64n9
deParle, Jason, xviii
Desmet, Christy, 154n44
diaspora, 8, 9, 79, 82, 114, 229–246

Dickens, Charles, 10
Dimock, Wey Chee, xxi
Donadio, Rachel, 18n27
Donne, John, 51
Drakakis, John, 149n7
Dugger, Celia E., 17n4
Duncan Jones, E. E., 103n2
Duncan-Jones, Katherine, 191n28
Durling, Robert, xxviin12, 104n8, 150n8

Eckstein, Lars, 45n13
Eliot, T. S., 150n11
Elliott, Patrick, 45n15
Engle, Lars, 154n45
Enterline, Lynn, 155n48, 222n7, 224n18
Erickson, Peter, 152n19, 190n18, 192n37, 223n9
Eschel, Amir, 78, 83n8

fairy tales, 9, 17n8, 201, 221, 222n5, 246
Fekete, Liz, 11, 12, 18n24
Felperin, Howard, 223n11
Ferber, Michael, 146
Ferguson, Frances, 224n19
Fernie, Ewan, 149n3
fiction as theory, 13–16
Fineman, Joel, 168, 191n20, 192n36
foundling plot: adoptive interlude, xvi, xix, xxvi, 8–9, 12, 14, 15, 25, 27–28, 32, 42–43, 48, 52, 53–54, 68, 70, 72, 86, 94, 96, 100, 108, 109, 111, 114, 116, 117, 120, 132, 147, 158, 162, 165, 167, 186–188, 198, 200, 210–221, 229, 230, 232–239, 245; defined, xiii, xvii–xix, 1–4, 66, 107, 108–109, 111, 113, 117, 120–123, 160, 161–162, 234, 238, 245, 246; revised, xiv, xvii–xxii, xxvi, 1–5, 8–9, 14, 40, 42–44, 47–62, 85–102, 115–121, 163, 186, 188, 209–221, 227–228, 232–239, 245, 246
Fourteenth Amendment, xxii
Fowler, Alaistair, xx, 15
Frank, Anne, 24, 25
Freud, Sigmund, xiv, 61, 128, 154n32, 154n34
Friedlander, Saul, 44n8
Frye, Susan, 192n37
Fumerton, Patricia, 153n22

Gallagher, Lowell, 149n3, 153n25
Gallati, Barbara Dayer, 17n2
Garber, Marjorie, 154n32
Gatward, Rebecca, 130
Geary, Keith, 152n19
gender, xviii, xxiv, xxv–xxvi, 1–5, 6, 13–16, 24, 27–30, 41, 47–48, 52, 62, 69, 77, 81–82, 90, 92, 94–95, 99, 102, 109–110, 112, 118–120, 124–148, 164–168, 174–188, 197–199, 205–206, 209–221, 227–228, 239–246
genre, xx–xxi, 15, 73, 103n5, 149n4, 149n6, 150n11, 152n18, 230, 246
Giacometti, Alberto, 40, 45n15
Gill, Gillian C., 189n10, 191n30, 221n1, 225n26
Girard, René, 155n48
Globe Theatre, London, 130
Goldberg, Jonathan, xxiv, 113
Golding, Arthur, 225n25
Goldstein, Amy, 9
Gombrowicz, Witold, 104n9
Gordimer, Nadine: *Get a Life*, 234, 247n5
Gossett, Suzanne, 83n1, 247n4
Gottlieb, Amy, 12
Grandage, Michael, 186
Greene, Thomas, 2, 216, 226n32
Greenhouse, Linda, xxii
Griswold, Jerry, xxviin8
Gross, Kenneth, 149n4, 150n9, 155n51, 156n58
Gubar, Susan, 103n5

Hackett, Helen, 225n22
Hadfield, Andrew, 190n16, 192n40
Haidu, Peter, 44n8
Halio, Jay, 172
Hall, Kim, 134, 150n11
Hamburger, Michael, 83n5
Harris, Wilson, xxviin26, 44n4
Hartman, Geoffrey, xxviin30, 152n17, 223n11, 224n19
Harvey, Elizabeth, xxviin32, 192n38, 247n6
Haselkorn, Anne M., 223n11
Hatoum, Mona: *Homebound*, 230, 245; *Measures of Distance*, xxvi, 18n28, 228, 229–232, 239–245
Heaney, Seamus, 216

Hendricks, Margot, 154n43, 189n5, 190n18
Himmler, Heinrich, 44n8
Hirschfeld, Heather, 124, 138, 153n28
Hitchcock, Alfred: *Psycho*, 240
Hitchcock, Peter, xxi, 152n17, 246
Hogan, Patrick, 190n18
Holderness, Graham, 223n9, 224n13, 225n21
Holmer, Joan Ozark, 156n61
Holocaust, xvii, xxiv, xxviin9, 14, 16, 23–44, 44n2, 47, 63, 65–82, 85–103, 103n5
Honigmann, E. A. J., 191n27, 192n35
Howard, Jean, 190n18
Hulse, Clark, 192n37
Humphrey Newcomb, Lori, 225n28
Hunt, Maurice, 216, 221n3, 222n7, 226n33
Hutson, Lorna, 152n21
Hyman, Lawrence W., 152n19
Hytner, Nicholas, xxviin17

identity politics, xiv, xix, xxii, 14, 15, 29, 122, 132, 150n11, 159, 194, 196, 197, 198, 211, 227–246
immigration policy, xiv, xvii, xxii–xxiii, 6–12
Irigaray, Luce: *Between East and West*, xviii, xxviin6, 15, 19n33, 49, 165, 197, 198, 221n2, 228; biunivocal engendering and, 14–15, 47, 59, 60, 85–87, 92, 94–99, 178, 182, 209–221; *An Ethics of Sexual Difference*, 166, 182, 189n10, 189n12, 192n33, 192n39, 197, 202, 221n1; *I Love to You*, 12, 18n29, 86, 94; *Parler n'est jamais neutre*, 164, 189n13; *Sexes and Genealogies*, 178, 182, 210; *This Sex Which Is Not One*, 131, 154n39, 192n32, 216, 226n31; *To Speak Is Never Neutral*, 164, 165, 168, 182, 189n10; third language and, xxiv, 47–63, 165; *The Way of Love*, 14–15; *Why Different?*, xxiv, xxviin28, 48–49, 63n4, 165, 190n17
Iyengar, Sujata, 15

Jackson, Michael, 150n11
Jacobson, Dan, 70

Jansohn, Christa, 222n5
Japtok, Martin, 150n11
Jardine, Lisa, 149n6
Jauss, Hans Robert, xxviin14, 83n3, 83n9
Jelenic, Gordana, 237
Jenkins, Harold, xxviin15
Jensen, Liz, xviii, xxv, 44, 63, 64n8, 102, 221, 246; *Ark Baby*, xx, xxiv, xxv, 44, 47–63, 63n1; *The Rapture*, 63n3
Julius, Anthony, 150n11

Kahn, Coppélia, 152n19, 155n52
Kaplan, M. Lindsay, 153n28–154n29, 155n55
Katz, David D., 150n11, 142
Kellogg, Stuart, 152n20
Kennedy, William J., 154n33
Kimmelman, Michael, xxvin1
kindertransport, 65, 76, 79
Kittredge, George Lyman, 174, 191n27
Kleinberg, Seymour, 152n20, 153n27
Knapp, James A., 223n9
Knowles, James, 225n22
Kolin, Phillip, 189n15
Krier, Theresa, xxviin32, 223n11, 247n6

Lamb, Mary Ellen, 222n5
Lane, Carolyn K., 17n2
Lang, Berel, 5, 74
Langer, Lawrence, 29
Lanzmann, Claude, 5, 17n7
Ledente, Bénédicte, 44n4, 45n13
Legouis, Pierre, 103n2
Le Page, Robert, 4
Levi, Primo, xxiv, 148
Lewalski, Barbara K., xxviin12, 104n11
Liebman, Stuart, xxvin7
Lifton, Robert J., xxviin10, 44n2
Little, Arthur, Jr., 167, 190n18
Lomperis, Linda, xxvin4
London Arts Council, 242
Loomba, Ania, 190n18
Lotringer, Sylvère, xxviin28, 63n4, 190n17
Lowell, Robert, 51
Lubow, Arthur, 68
Lucking, David, 152n18, 154n31
Lyotard, Jean-Francois, 27, 77

MacCary, Thomas W., 152n19

Mackey, Robert, 18n23
Marchiettello, Howard, 155n52
Margoliouth, H. H., 103n2
Marie, Zen, 233, 235
Markussen, Eric, 44n2
Marlowe, Christopher, 150n11
Maroni, Ernesto, 12, 18n27
Martin, Alison, xxviin31, 18n29, 64n6, 103n3
Marvell, Andrew, xxi, 103n2
Marx, Groucho, 164
McKeon, Adam, 224n12
Metzger, Mary Jannell, 149n7, 155n55
Michaels, Anne, 246; *Fugitive Pieces*, xx, xxiii, xxiv, 14, 15, 38, 85–103, 103n5, 162, 216, 229, 240; *The Winter Vault*, 13, 85, 87, 98, 100, 198
Miller, Jonathan, 146
Morrison, Toni, 8
Munch, Edward, 70

Napolitano, Janet, 10
nationalism, xiv, xvii–xix, xxii–xxiii, 5, 6–12, 17n15, 29, 30, 53, 63, 101, 102, 158–159, 187, 219, 229–247
Neely, Carol Thomas, 15, 190n18, 192n35, 200, 222n8
Neill, Michael, 191n19
Nelson Garner, Shirley, 189n5
Newman, Karen, 149n6, 150n11, 190n18
Newton, Isaac, 78, 79
Nims, John Fredrick, 153n26, 225n25
Novy, Marianne: *Adoption: Family and Difference in Fiction*, xix, 222n6; *Love's Argument: Gender Relations in Shakespeare*, 152n16
Nunn, Trevor, 146, 225n24
Nuttall, A. D., 222n7

Obama, Barack, 10
O'Connor, Marion F., 190n18
Olivier, Laurence, 146
Ondaatje, Michael, 103n5
Orphan Annie, xiii, xviii, 25
orphans, xiii–xiv, xvii–xviii, xix, 1–12, 17n4, 18n23, 25, 27, 35, 37, 67, 68, 76, 95, 98, 120
Ovid: Apollo-Daphne, xix, 110, 125, 127, 130, 144, 207, 209; Arethusa and

Cyane, 207; Ceres-Proserpine, 28, 30, 31, 58, 201, 207, 208–209, 215, 220, 222n7–222n8, 225n24, 229, 230, 236, 239, 241; Medea, 112, 113, 119, 122–124, 126, 137, 139; Medusa, 40, 110, 125, 127–130, 135, 139, 141–143, 144, 145, 147, 158, 160, 195–196; Narcissus, 27, 145, 168, 211–212; Procne/Philomela, 122; Pygmalion, 27, 39, 72, 209, 220, 222n7–222n8
Oz, Amos, xiii, xix

Pareles, John, 150n11
Parker, Patricia, xxviin30, 116, 152n17, 153n24, 154n43, 170, 189n12, 190n18, 223n11
Parks, Tim, 154n35, 225n27
Parten, Anne, 154n41, 156n61
Peat, Wilbur D., 17n5
Penuel, Suzanne, 153n23
Pequigney, Joseph, 150n11, 152n19, 155n53
Petrarca, Francesco, 7; *Rime sparse*, xix, 12, 110, 125; *Rime sparse* 128, xviii, 7, 9, 17n12; *Rime sparse* 197, 127, 145; *Rime sparse* 265, 95, 104n8, 144
Petrarchan plot: defined, xiii–xiv, xvii–xviii, xix–xxii, 1–14, 69, 70, 95, 107, 109, 110–111, 113, 124–148, 157–162, 166–180, 193, 198, 199, 213, 216, 227; revised, xiv, xix, xxii, xxiii, xxiv, xxv–xxvi, 8, 14, 27, 39–44, 48, 53, 59, 59–62, 81–82, 85–86, 94–95, 98–99, 102, 125, 148, 163, 167, 177, 181–182, 184–188, 194, 209–221, 227–228, 239–244
Phillips, Caryl, 246; "Blood", 25, 44n3, 40; "Extravagant Strangers", xxiii, xxvin9, 5, 26, 44n1, 48, 63n2; *The Nature of Blood*, xxiv, xxviin26, 15–16, 17n14, 18n30, 23–44, 63, 91, 102, 103n4, 158, 221
photographs: as DNA future, 97; Sebald on use of, 66–67, 97
Pianiani, Gaia, xxviin27
Picker, John, 154n45
Pinter, Harold, 102; *No Man's Land*, 107, 111, 118, 120, 145, 148n1
Pisano, Ronald G., 17n2, 17n5

Pluháček, Stephen, xxvin6, 18n32, 19n33, 221n2
politics and art, xiv, xvii, xviii, xxii–xxiii, 5
Porter, Catherine, 154n39, 192n32, 226n31
postcolonial theory, xxi, 246
Potter, Nick, 223n9
Preston, Julia, 10
Priest, Diana, 9

Ragussis, Michael, 146, 150n11
Readings, Bill, 83n11
Regueiro, Helen, 224n19
Reilly, Kelly, 186
"restavek" system, 18n23
Richards, Jennifer, 225n22
Rose, Mark, 159
Roth, Philip, 165, 170; *Exit Ghost*, 157, 189n1
Royal National Theatre, xxviin17
Royal Shakespeare Company, 225n24
Ryan, Judith, 83n6

Said, Edward, 12, 226n38, 230, 245
Sandy, Stephen, 222n8
Satz, Martha, xxvin8, 64n8
Savage, Charles, 18n17
Save the Children, 11, 17n4
Schalkwyk, David, 204, 224n17
Schaum, Melita, xxii
Schieffer, James, 189n15
Schleiner, Winfried, 150n11
Schwab, Gail, 189n11
Schwartz, Lyn Sharon, 83n2
Schwartz, Murray M., 152n19
Schwartz, Regina M., 156n57
Sebald, W. G., 246; *After Nature*, 68, 83n5; *Austerlitz*, xxiv, xxv, 15, 36, 63, 65–82, 85, 87–88, 89, 90, 94, 95, 97–98, 101–102, 120, 162, 221, 227, 229, 237
Segert, Alexander, political posters of, xvii–xviii
Shakespeare, William, 73, 150n11, 193, 219, 222n8; *All's Well That Ends Well*, xxvi, 227–228, 230, 237; *As You Like It*, 148, 185, 198; *The Comedy of Errors*, 47, 59, 198; *Hamlet*, xx, xxiv, xxviin15, xxviin17, 63, 65, 66, 73, 82, 85, 86, 87, 92, 96, 116, 146, 161,

179–180, 209, 246; *King Lear*, 144, 154n32, 173, 219; *The Merchant of Venice*, xvii, xviii, xx, xxiii, xxiv, 7–8, 12, 15, 23, 24, 26, 29, 38, 47, 55, 102, 107–148, 157, 157–158, 174, 193, 194, 198, 202, 219, 221, 229, 246; *A Midsummer Night's Dream*, 4, 98, 130, 161; *Much Ado about Nothing*, 113; *Othello*, xviii, xx, xxiii, xxiv, xxv, 7–8, 15, 23, 24, 26, 27, 29, 30, 33–34, 38, 39, 40, 41–42, 86, 100, 102, 157–189, 194, 195–196, 197, 198, 204, 211, 216, 221, 229; *Pericles*, 63, 65, 86, 198, 233, 235, 246; *Romeo and Juliet*, xxi, 126, 185; Sonnet 3, 228; Sonnet 95, xxv, 163, 168–180, 185; *The Tempest*, 47, 55, 234; *Twelfth Night*, 233–234, 246; *The Winter's Tale*, xviii, xx, xxiv, xxv, 7–8, 12, 15, 31–33, 86–87, 100, 102, 130, 155n48, 162, 168, 181, 182, 188, 193–221, 227, 229, 236, 240, 246
Shapiro, James, 150n11
Shapiro, Michael, 156n56
Shell, Marc, 154n45, 155n52
Siebers, Tobin, 129
Silverblatt, Michael, 83n7
Sinfield, Alan, 112
Smith, Ian, 190n16
Smith, Shawn, 192n31
Snyder, Susan, 205
Sontag, Susan, 104n9
Spiller, Elizabeth, 149n4, 150n10
Sprengnether, Madelon, 189n5
Stanbury, Sarah, xxvin4
standpoint theory, xix
Stanivukovic, Goran V., 225n28
Stevens, Paul, 111, 148
Stevens, Wallace: "So-And-So Reclining on her Couch", 1–5
Stewart, Stanley, 155n47

Stoos, Toni, 45n15
Strachey, James, 154n34
Sullivan, Garret A., Jr., 190n16, 192n40

Taylor, A. B., 222n7
Tennenhouse, Leonard, 152n19
Travitsky, Betty S., 223n11
Turner, John, 223n9

UNICEF, 17n4
United Nations Convention on the Rights of the Child, 11

Van den Abeele, G., 44n7
Van Elk, Martine, 203, 216, 224n15, 226n29, 226n37
Vickers, Nancy, xviii
Vitkus, Daniel, 183

Wachtel, Eleanor, 83n2
Walcott, Derek, 190n18
Ward, Gary, 233, 236
Weber, Bruce, 17n2
Weinbaum, Alys Eve, 15
Wells, Marion, 222n5, 225n20, 226n36
Wells, Stanley, 190n18
Wertheim, Albert, 154n31
Whalen, Denise A., 189n9
Whistler, James McNeill, 2
Wilson, Scott, 154n30
Winnicott, D. W., 60; *Playing and Reality*, 61, 63n5, 91, 223n11
Wittgenstein, Ludwig, 70
Wyatt, Thomas, 144

Yaffee, Martin, 150n11
Young, James, 103n5

Zwerdling, Daniel, 10

About the Author

Barbara L. Estrin is professor emerita of English at Stonehill College, as well as the author of *The Raven and the Lark: Lost Children in Literature of the English Renaissance* (1985), *Laura: Uncovering Gender and Genre in the Wyatt, Donne and Marvell* (1995), and *The American Love Lyric after Auschwitz and Hiroshima* (2002). She has also written numerous articles about early modern and contemporary topics.